The Chinook Indians

The Chinook Indians

Traders of the Lower Columbia River

By Robert H. Ruby
and John A. Brown

Foreword by the Reverend Stephen A. Meriwether
Introduction by Deward E. Walker, Jr.

UNIVERSITY OF OKLAHOMA PRESS
NORMAN AND LONDON

By Robert H. Ruby and John A. Brown

Half-Sun on the Columbia: A Biography of Chief Moses (Norman, 1965)
The Spokane Indians: Children of the Sun (Norman, 1970)
The Cayuse Indians: Imperial Tribesmen of Old Oregon (Norman, 1972)
The Chinook Indians: Traders of the Lower Columbia River (Norman, 1976)
Indians of the Pacific Northwest: A History (Norman, 1981)
A Guide to the Indian Tribes of the Pacific Northwest (Norman, 1986)

Library of Congress Cataloging in Publication Data

Ruby, Robert H.
    The Chinook Indians.

    (The Civilization of the American Indian series)
    Bibliography
    Includes index.
    1. Chinook Indians. I. Brown, John Arthur, joint author. II. Title. III. Series.
E99.C57R82   970'.004'97   75–40148
ISBN: 0–8061–1325–1
ISBN: 0–8061–2107–6 (pbk.)

The Chinook Indians: Traders of the Lower Columbia River is Volume 138 in *The Civilization of the American Indian Series*.

3   4   5   6   7   8   9   10   11   12

Dedicated to
Mary Louise
and to
Marguerite and Will

Foreword

By the Reverend Stephen A. Meriwether

As a small boy going to school in Ilwaco, a fishing village nestled between the forest and the waters of the Columbia River, I was startled to learn that I was unique among my classmates—I was extinct! Before that moody winter's day I had blithely presumed that extinction was a murky fate reserved for dinosaurs and the comical dodo bird. Alas, my fate was sealed as firmly as the long-gone passenger pigeon. This unusual status began innocuously enough with an assignment to write a short paper about my ancestors. While classmates rushed to the encyclopedia to look up the histories and cultures of Finland, Norway, and Sweden, I could find very little information about the Chinooks, just scattered mention in several slim volumes. Most of my information had to come from my grandmother and other relatives: stories about Chinook life, of fishing along the banks of the Columbia, of winters on the sheltered waters of Willapa Bay, of gathering oysters and cranberries, stories about the arrival of European traders, of Meriwether Lewis and William Clark, of the building of Astoria, and of the arrival of French trappers who left the service of Hudson's Bay to settle and marry.

On the day that our inexpert and scrawled reports were due, I was perplexed by my instructor's reaction. As anyone could have told me, there were no Chinooks left; they had all died in the plagues that broke out along the Columbia after the arrival of ships and overland trapping expeditions. That day I knew that someone had to write a history of the Chinooks; someone was needed to pull together the facts and paint a picture of life along the Columbia before, during, and after the advent of Euro-Americans.

In high school and college, when I was working as a secretary with the Chinook Tribal Council, the need for a Chinook history became more apparent since even the government, through the agencies of the Bureau of Indian Affairs, was of a mind that we no longer existed. It was not as though nothing had been written about the Chinooks, but the body of information was scanty, scattered, and often inaccurate. There were references to the Chinooks in the diaries of the Lewis and Clark Expedition, and there were disparate accounts in the journals of numerous sea captains. Passing missionaries gave attention to the Chinooks, and the arrival of the Hudson's Bay Company created a mountain of bureaucratic ledger entries on Chinook commerce. Washington Irving even tried his hand at history in *Astoria*, but that turned into a romantic's view of life along the Columbia. There was indeed information of varying quality available for the intrepid hunter, but what was needed was a synthesis and perspective.

When I first met Dr. Ruby and John Brown, I was amazed that anyone was interested in the history of the Chinooks. After all, the mouth of the Columbia had never become the great commercial metropolis that John Jacob Astor had envisioned. I was more surprised yet to learn that these men wanted to write a book that would pull together the far-flung pieces of the Chinook story. They wanted to learn about the Chinooks, not as a historic curiosity but as a continuing reality, a people aware of their past and continuing to live and struggle in the present.

When it was first published, "The Chinook Book," as this volume instantly became known, was an immediate best seller—that is, if you acknowledge the reaction of the people about whom, and I believe for whom, the account was written. Members of the tribe felt that a copy of this book was a must-have in every home. Anyone who has ever driven along the twisting banks of the lower Columbia River or through the lustrous forests crowding the waters of Willapa Bay cannot help but wonder what life must have been like before settlers arrived from other lands. As the state of Washington nears its one hundredth birthday, some citizens must ask about the history that came before, a history that has its roots many hundreds of years ago. As environmental destruction threatens the survival of our fisheries and timber resources, people must ask what life was like when nature and man were in harmony. This book is a necessary part of the answer to these questions. For Chinooks it is a needed resource and a proud statement of survival; for those who have adopted this land, it is an introduction to their own history and culture.

Introduction to the Paperback Edition

By Deward E. Walker, Jr.

T HIS IS A BOOK of lasting value to both scholars and laymen. We owe a debt of gratitude to the University of Oklahoma Press, and especially to Robert H. Ruby and John A. Brown. The book is a benchmark of historical research on one of the most significant tribal groups of the Northwest. Their experience at the hands of Euro-Americans is well documented by Ruby and Brown, who have provided a major factual enrichment to our understanding of the ethnohistory of the Chinooks. They have also provided a research paradigm for other scholars who must study cultural contact and acculturation primarily through documentary sources. Because it is a chronicle of cultural extinction, it details the dispersion and absorption of mixed-blood descendants of the once-mighty Chinookan trading tribes. It tells of the coldly calculating divestment of the Chinookans of their rich natural environment by ever more numerous and powerful Euro-Americans who saw the many misfortunes of the Chinookans as the work of a divine providence. This book also makes clear that the Chinookans were the first to experience what other tribes throughout the Northwest were to experience later. This is one of the rare, well-documented examples of the various processes that lead to cultural extinction among Native Americans.

Chapter 1 provides a brief introduction to anthropological information on the Chinooks. It is not exhaustive but does paint an accurate picture of the main features of traditional Chinookan cultural patterns. It correctly emphasizes the cultural focus of the Chinookans as trade and commerce. Chapter 2 provides valuable insights into the early stages of cultural contact between Chinookans and Euro-Americans in the shipwrecks, ship sightings, and occasional visits by Spaniards, English, Americans, and Russians, some before the beginning of the eighteenth century. The Chinookans were quickly affected by the exotic trade goods, intermarriage, disease, alcohol, and alien ideologies. Chapter 3 documents the principal motive for the Euro-American exploration of the Columbia River: pelts and profits. The Chinookans, traders that they were, adapted to this with zeal and helped set the stage for their own rapid absorption and virtual extinction at the hands of the sailors and others whom they welcomed so eagerly.

Chapter 4 ably presents the international conflict and competition that ensued for domination of this wealthy region lying between the Russian-dominated North and the Spanish-dominated South. Eventually, the growing intensity of trading and the increasing intimacy between the Chinookans and Euro-American sailors and traders produced an inevitable consequence, epidemic disease. This and introduction of alcohol with its inevitable consequences are also outlined in Chapters 4 and 5, where growing numbers of open conflicts and Chinookan enslavement of sailors and traders are documented. Chinookan women figured importantly in trade with Euro-Americans as it expanded to the limit of the available animal populations. Chapter 6 describes the visit of the Lewis and Clark Expedition, which found the Chinookans already exposed to Euro-Americans and quite familiar with their needs. The Lewis and Clark records are still the best scientific observations we possess for the Chinooks of this period.

Chapter 7 outlines the abortive efforts by the Russians to establish a presence on the Columbia River and the Americans' efforts to discourage them. Chapters 8 and 9 unfold largely by recounting the visits of various ships to the Columbia River. Each ship's impact on the Chinooks is detailed. American influence increased with the development of Astoria, which was to become the major trade center on the lower Columbia. It also spelled the end of Chinookan dominance of the Columbia River fur trade. This paralleled an increasing development of trading ties with the interior tribes farther up the Columbia River and its tributaries.

Chapter 10 describes the activities of George Simpson, whose observations on the Chinooks are generally reliable. They indicate that intermarriage and assimilation were proceeding rapidly among the Chinooks as conflict between them and the traders was also increasing. Chapter 11 describes yet another devastating epidemic, "intermitting fever," which further reduced their numbers and influence. Infant deaths were also becoming more common, and the Chinooks were unable to recover from their population losses. By 1850, Chinook strength and dominance had largely failed. An important shift in trade with Euro-Americans is noted in Chapter 11, where salmon are described as taking on increased commercial importance. This shift was to become ever more apparent as the fur trade declined.

By the middle of the nineteenth century, representatives of missionary groups and the United States Indian Affairs officers made their appearance in Chinookan affairs. Anson Dart, Oregon superintendent of Indian affairs, attempted to correct the abuses of more than fifty years of Chinookan exposure to traders and sailors, but could achieve little. Removal of the Chinooks and other tribes from direct contact with the increasing tide of American settlement was attempted. In fact, their removal to reservations east of the Cascades was seriously proposed. As these policies took form, there began the era of treaty making that was to dominate Indian affairs for the next several decades as the United States established a system of reservations throughout the region. Ultimately the Chinooks signed a treaty ceding most of their lands, but one that did not require their removal from the region. Chapter 13 provides a good summary of the many treaties negotiated by Dart and others with the various lower Columbia tribes shortly after 1850, especially at Tansey Point.

Chapter 14 is the account of Governor Stevens's beginning efforts at treaty making. Several of Stevens's erroneous assumptions about the tribes are described and documented, such as their willingness to join together on one large reservation. Such assumptions, coupled with Stevens's well-known inability to prevent depredations on the tribes by settlers, set the stage for later open warfare as the tribes resisted efforts to remove them from their homelands. Chapter 14 provides a useful introduction to the "salmon wars" that still rage on the Columbia River between Indians and non-Indians—continuing efforts by non-Indians to exclude Indians from fishing and hunting areas that they have used since prehistoric times. The book concludes with a discussion of the efforts of the scattered and largely assimilated Chinookan descendants, beginning about 1900, to gain compensation for all they lost. These efforts culminated in the 1950's with the Indian Claims Commission.

Preface

WHEN WE BEGAN writing the books that subsequently appeared in THE CIVILIZATION OF THE AMERICAN INDIAN SERIES, we prided ourselves that we knew better than to succumb to the common misconception that all early American Indians were alike. Yet we confess that in pursuing our researches we discovered considerably more diversity among Columbia River peoples than we had expected. Their differences were, in fact, as varied as their homelands along their mighty stream, which, gathering waters from lofty western mountains, flowed exotically yet turbulently through arid lands and majestically past verdant shores to the misty sea.

On the lower river lived Chinookan-speaking groups. Bearing certain characteristics of their upriver brothers, they also bore those of peoples of the Northwest Coast. The designation Chinook Indians has been applied to natives from the Dalles, the separation point between interior and coastal peoples and environments, downriver to the Pacific Ocean. The name of one group at the mouth of the Columbia, the Chinooks, is that which has been applied through common usage to all Chinookan groups. In this manuscript we use the designation Chinooks when referring to the one group bearing that name and sometimes to all Chinookan peoples as well. We are primarily concerned with four Chinookan groups which because of certain characteristics are grouped together and termed Lower Chinooks—Chinooks (the ones sometimes referred to as "Chinooks proper"), Clatsops, Wahkiakums, and Kathlamets. Of these Chinookan groups the first two, living as they did at the entrance to the broad Columbia, came first and most frequently in contact with white men touching the coast or seeking passage through their portallike lands to the Columbia hinterland. Because they lived at a breaking point of nature and commerce, they, especially the Chinooks proper, were destined to trade, as did other Northwest Coast and Columbia River peoples, with a sophistication commonly believed to have been the province of white men. Although we are concerned with all phases of their life, it is their great propensity for trade which primarily concerns us here.

It was also commonly believed that, following the appearance of Robert Gray, supposedly the first American trader to enter the Columbia River, there was no trade at its mouth until the overland arrival there of Lewis and Clark thirteen years later. Our researches have proved, contrariwise, that it was during this period a beehive of Indian-white trade activity. How Chinooks and Clatsops responded to this as well as to previous and to subsequent commercial activity is a dominant theme of our book. In many respects the story itself, especially that part of it pertaining to the (white) contact and postcontact periods, is a familiar one, with the appearance among the natives of old and familiar villains—disease and drink corroding them to within an eyelash of extinction. Yet they responded to white men, as they had also responded to red ones, in their own fashion, making their story in a sense an unfamiliar one hitherto escaping the historian's pen.

In preparing this manuscript we are indebted to many. Especially are we indebted to Hazel Mills and Nancy Pryor, Washington State Library, Olympia, who answered our many requests for information. We owe much to other Pacific Northwest librarians: Audrey Kolb, Betty J. Gibson, Arvilla Scofield, and Lila Lyons, Wenatchee Valley College; Betty Shambrook, Big Bend Community College, Moses Lake; Marie Kennedy, Irma McKenzie, Glenna Bingham, Jean Graham, and Pearl C. Munson, Moses Lake Public Library; Mildred Sherwood, Andrew F. Johnson, and Mrs. Erven Kloostra, Suzzallo Library, University of Washington, Seattle; and Earle Connette, Archives, Holland Library, Washington State University, Pullman. We are also indebted to the staff of the Oregon Historical Society, Portland, especially to Priscilla Knuth, Jack Cleaver, and Janice K. Duncan. Others to whom we owe much are Winifred Collins, Massachusetts Historical Society, Boston; and Carolyn Jakeman, Houghton Library, Harvard University, Cambridge. From the latter institution we acknowledge the assistance of Robert W. Lovett and Eleanor C. Bishop, Baker Library, Harvard University Graduate School of Business Administration. We also acknowledge the assistance of Ellen Oldham, Boston Public Library; Ruth H. Hill, Beverly Historical Society, Beverly, Massachusetts; Mary E. Brown, American Antiquarian Society, Worcester, Massachusetts; Samuel J. Hough III, John Carter Brown Library, Brown University, Providence; Gladys Bolhouse, Newport Historical Society; Archibald Hanna and Joan Hofmann, Beinecke Library, Yale University, New Haven; Harriet S. Bishop, New Haven Colony Historical Society; Jean McNiece and John Stinson, New York Public Library; Mrs. Charles A. Potter, Essex Institute, Salem, Massachusetts; Nancy G. Boles, Maryland Historical Society, Baltimore; Mrs. Jean Mills, Peabody Museum, Salem, Massachusetts; and Ruth Dixon, Pacific County Historical Society, Raymond, Washington.

Others whose assistance we acknowledge are Willard Ireland, Archives of British Columbia, Victoria; John Barr Tompkins, Irene Moran, and Estelle Rebec, Bancroft Library, Berkeley, California; Mary Isabel Fry and Noelle Jackson, Huntington Library, San Marino, California; Jay Williar, California Historical Society, San Francisco; and Allan C. DeLacy, College of Fisheries, University of Washington. We acknowledge the assistance of Jean S. Sharpless, Hawaiian Historical Society, Honolulu; Agnes C. Conrad, Public Archives, state of Hawaii, Honolulu; and A. Grove Day and Frances Jackson, University of Hawaii, Honolulu. From the Chinook Indian community we acknowledge the assistance of Stephen A. Meriwether and Anna Koontz. From governmental services we are grateful to Paul A. Kohl, Region 10, National Archives and Records Service; Guy Lovell and C. J. Higman, Bureau of Indian Affairs; David H. Bigelow, Indian Claims Commission; Roy P. Basler, Paul G. Sifton, Library of Congress; and to Edna Ruby, for researching Hawaiian archives.

We also thank Ruth Dixon, Pacific County Historical Society, Raymond, Washington, for her assistance, as we do Donald R. Espen, the Chancery, Archdiocese of Seattle; Ursula Young, Royal Ontario Museum; and Paul Stowell and Harold Laney for their assistance with photographic materials. We thank Charles Walters, Wenatchee Valley College, and Winston Wutkee, University of California, for translations of materials from the Spanish; Elisabeth A. Seeger, from the Russian; and S. Hollingsworth, from the French. We also thank the Hudson's Bay Company for permission to include a Chinook population report compiled by Chief Factor Alexander Kennedy. And certainly not least do we thank Ruth, Donna, and Wesley Rawhouser; George Smith; Wilbur Brown; Charles, Lea, David, and Blanche Hansen; and Guy Reed Ramsey.

Assistance of the foregoing has not merely lightened, but made possible the painstaking task of pulling aside the curtain veiling Chinook and Clatsop Indian history to make it available to our readers. To these who have assisted us we shall always be grateful.

Moses Lake, Washington   ROBERT H. RUBY

Wenatchee, Washington   JOHN A. BROWN

Contents

Illustrations

xxi

Maps

Contents

The Chinook Indians

1. A Cloud-Topp'd Hill

> Yet simple Nature to his hope has giv'n
> Behind the cloud-topp'd hill, an humbler
> heav'n.
>
> Alexander Pope, *Essay on Man*

WHEN ALEXANDER POPE in 1734 published his *Essay on Man,* that portion of the human race, "The poor Indian" inhabiting the shores of the American Northwest, was not long to enjoy the primoridial bliss the poet had pictured for him. With Renaissance-expanded minds, employing what Pope termed "proud Science" and thirsting for material things, Europeans were about to break the aboriginal silence of a land where hitherto, as Pope had written, no fiends had tormented nor had Christians thirsted for gold. Less than seventy years before the *Essay* was published, King Charles II had officially approved articles of incorporation of the "Governor and Company of Adventurers of England Tradeing into Hudsons Bay." Yet it would take those trading adventurers 150 years of operations across America to reach Pacific shores. Hoping to get there more quickly, one Major Robert Rogers in 1765 would petition the "Right Honourable the Lords Committee of His Majesty's Council" to cross America to the river Ourigan (Columbia)[1] to establish an "Intercourse of Traffic" with its natives. Nearly two hundred years earlier Pope's freebooting countryman, Sir Francis Drake, had sailed along western Pacific shores as had his Spanish rivals hoping to expand northerly their American conquests. To the north in 1741 Vitus Bering, in the service of the Russian czar, was credited with discovering Alaska, from where that emperor's subjects would seek to expand trade and holdings to the south. Thus, by land and sea Christian adventurers hoped to make myth and memory of what Pope had termed the Indian's "safer world."

White men, coming first by sea, would in a part of that world soon meet and traffic with Chinook and Clatsop peoples living near where the Columbia joined the Pacific Ocean. Until then, fulfilling Pope's environmental prerequisite for peaceful primordial habitation replete with "cloud-topp'd hill" flanked by "depth of woods," the Chinooks of the two peoples lived in a "humbler heav'n." A classical "cloud-topp'd hill" stood in the land of the Chinooks. Named by them Kah'eese,[2] and later Cape Disappointment after its discovery by the British explorer Captain John Meares,[3] the oft cloud-shrouded headland rose boldly some seven hundred feet above the sea on the north bank of the river and overlooked the vast Pacific and an almost five-mile opening to the south, where the river Yakaitl-Wimakl (Columbia),[4] a flood of melted snows from a quarter-million-acre land mass, met the sea in a tidal deluge of as many as a million cubic feet per second. Below the promontory, sediment from annual discharges of the river formed treacherous shifting shoals extending across the river mouth and up to three miles outside a southerly line to the opposite shore to Point Adams, called by the natives Klaat-sop, the name of the people (Clatsop) who lived there. Over this treacherous barrier in stormy weather the ocean broke with great fury as incoming waves met outrushing spent ones, flinging spray high—sometimes two hundred feet over the rocks at the cape. The obstruction, known as the "bar," would be the bane of white mariners unfamiliar with the shifts, depth, and shape of its channels moreso than it would be to Chinooks and Clatsops, who for ages had learned to live with it and respect it as its breakers reminded them of its presence even when fogs or gale-driven mists blotted it from their sight.

When white men broke the aboriginal isolation of the lower Columbia, there were four groups of a larger family bearing the designation Chinookan peoples who lived in villages mostly at stream mouths along the Columbia and up its southern tributary, the Willamette River, to present-day Oregon City and inland some 220 miles to the head of the Dalles. There the Columbia boiled and tumbled through a restricted channel over an ancient uplift where merged coastal and interior environments.[5] Chinookan peoples drifted down the Columbia to wedge between Salish peoples at the mouth of that river, pressing Tillamooks as far south as Tillamook Head (Oregon), and on the north above Willapa Bay pressing Chehalis peoples, from whose language the name T'sinu'k (Tsinūk) or Chinook was derived. Coastal Salish drift to the Pacific west coast had been down the Fraser River to its mouth,* spilling

---

* Another Interior Salish expansion was down the Columbia River drainage area as far as the Dalles, where these people at one time became neighbors of Upper Chinookan peoples.

out along the lower end of Vancouver Island, Puget Sound, and the coasts of Washington and upper Oregon.[6]

The ribbon of Chinookan peoples from the Dalles to the mouth of the Columbia was interrupted by pockets of natives bearing other family designations—the Cowlitz, a Salish people on the north bank from just east of Oak Point (Washington) to the Cowlitz River,[7] and the Klatskanies, an Athabaskan people across the Columbia from the Salish at a point about fifty miles from its mouth, west of the beginning of Cowlitz territory.[8] Athabaskan drift was from north to south in the Columbia Plateau east of the Cascade Mountains. Klatskanies and other Athabaskans north of the Columbia River, the Kwalhioquas (Willopahs, Wheelappas), came west probably through Cascade Mountain passes and not down the Columbia.*[9]

The designation *Lower Chinooks* is applied by anthropologists to two classifications of groups, one linguistic, the other cultural.† Linguistically there were among Chinookan peoples two major dialects—Upper and Lower Chinook.‡ Two minor dialect variations were spoken by Lower Chinooks, dividing them into "Chinooks proper" (a term used by ethnologists to distinguish them from all other Chinookan people) and Clatsops.[10] (The other major dialect, Upper Chinook, had numerous variations.) On a cultural basis Chinooks, Clatsops, Wahkiakums, and Kathlamets were ethnically similar. The latter two groups spoke the Kathlamet language, a variation of the Upper Chinook dialect.

Through common usage the designation *Chinook* has been applied to all four groups. First exposed to white traders, the Chinooks proper dominated commerce at the mouth of the Columbia River and prospered. Because of their dominance in the eyes of white men, the latter came to refer to Clatsops, Wahkiakums, and Kathlamets as "Chinooks"

* The Kwalhioquas occupied territory along the Willapa (Willopa or Willopah) River north of the Chinooks and Kathlamets. Anthropologist Leslie Spier presents evidence to support the thesis that the Kwalhioquas were Salish. *Tribunal Distribution in Washington,* General Series in Anthropology, No. 3, 29, 30.

† The anthropologist Verne Ray divides Lower Chinooks geographically into three groups: those from the mouth of Grays Bay to Cape Disappointment; those to the north on Shoalwater Bay; and those southerly opposite Cape Disappointment on and near Point Adams. *Lower Chinook Ethnographic Notes,* University of Washington Publications in Anthropology, Vol. VII, No. 2, 7. The nineteenth-century ethnologist George Gibbs is criticized by Spier for having classified Kathlamets with Lower Chinooks. Gibbs's classification was undoubtedly on an ethnic rather than a linguistic basis. George Gibbs, *Tribes of Western Washington and Northwestern Oregon,* Contributions to North American Ethnology, Vol. I, 182; Spier, *Tribal Distribution in Washington,* 21–22.

‡ "The Chinook language has no close affiliates," writes anthropologist Philip Drucker, "but is grouped by some linguists into a larger language entity called Penutian." *Cultures of the North Pacific Coast,* 108.

also. This has created a dual designation for these Lower Chinooks in which each has its own group name as well as the collective name *Chinook*, a duality employed in this manuscript.

Chinooks, or the Chinooks proper, occupied villages on the north shore of the Columbia from Grays Bay to Cape Disappointment and, to the north, Willapa Bay. Clatsops occupied villages on the south shore of the Columbia from west of Tongue Point (Soo-kum-its-é-ah) to Point Adams and south along the coast to Tillamook Head. Wahkiakums lived from Oak Point downriver along the Columbia to the mouth of Deep River (Alamicut), a Columbia tributary entering Grays Bay some ten miles from the mouth of the river. A large Wahkiakum village lay some two miles northwest of the present town of Cathlamet, Washington, where it moved around 1810, probably because of fire.[11] Kathlamet villages at white contact were on the Oregon side of the Columbia from a point opposite present-day Skamokawa, Washington, along the river to Tongue Point thirteen and one-half miles from the sea. About 1810 Kathlamet villagers moved north across the Columbia to settle in the Wahkiakum village.*[12]

Thus, Lower Chinooks on an ethnic basis included all Chinookan peoples from the mouth of the Columbia upriver to Cowlitz peoples on the north shore and Klatskanies on the south. Wahkiakums and Kathlamets were said to have originally belonged to Chinooks and Clatsops before splintering into their own villages.[13]

Lower Chinooks lived in a biseasonal world on the lower Columbia. From late winter until fall the Chinooks proper were at the site of present-day Ilwaco, Washington, and elsewhere on the lee side of Cape Disappointment around Bakers Bay at the mouths of streams. One of these streams was the Wallicut (Wallakhut) or James.[14] Up the Columbia two miles from the Wallicut was Chinook River, or Ellemeeks[15] or Wappaloochee. Inhabitants hugged the shore at Chinook Point (Nóse-to-ilse)[16] at the base of an eight-hundred-foot rise, Chinook Hill, later called Scarborough or Scarboro. Clatsop summer homes were on Point Adams near present-day Fort Stevens and Hammon, Oregon. Their winter homes were on the Neacoxie (Neahcoxie), a branch of the Necanicum River near present-day Seaside, Oregon.[17] Between Clatsop winter and summer homes lay the sand-ridged Clatsop Plain, which extended along the coast from a mere point at its southern extremity to a width of some five miles on the Columbia River.

In the busy warmer season sturdy Chinooks and Clatsops plied equally sturdy canoes across the broad Columbia to visit, trade, and some-

---

* In a letter to Reuben Gold Thwaites, June 17, 1904, Thomas Nelson Strong wrote that Kathlamets crossed to the north side because of pestilence. Eva Emery Dye Papers.

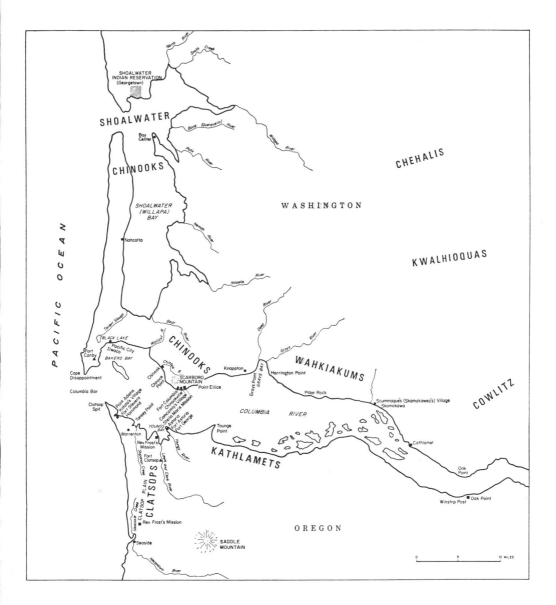

Lower Chinook Lands

7

times war with each other and with Wahkiakums, Kathlamets, and other peoples further upstream. They skimmed to their destinations aided by onshore northwesterly winds, in which they believed they were aided by their deities, hearing them, as Pope suggested, in the wind. These winds sweeping up the Columbia and Willamette valleys were called by early white men in Oregon Chinook winds since they blew from the direction of Chinook villages. Today, chinook winds are recognized as warm, dry foehn winds that melt snows as they blow down western mountainsides.[18] That they should thus blow was established in Chinook mythology when Coyote (Talapas), teacher, trickster, arbiter, hero, converter of Skokums, creator of many places and things, and killer of man-eating monsters, decreed an end to a feud between Walla Walla brothers of the Cold Wind from the interior and their counterparts from among the Chinooks. Showdown between the two wind forces had been hastened by a challenge from a surviving son of one of five Chinook brothers, all of whom had died at the hands of their Walla Walla adversaries. In revenge, the youth had killed all of the Cold Wind brothers but one, who, at Coyote's intervention, had survived to blow his icy breath.

In this warmer season nature yielded bounties of land and sea, permitting her children to survive with relative ease. The other season, winter, was a time of little freezing and occasional snow when southerly winds pelted the lower Columbia with relentless drizzles and drenching rains. Then Clatsops retreated to their winter homes south of Clatsop Plain and Chinooks to theirs on the peninsula forming the western shores of Willapa Bay and to sheltered rivers entering that body of water. In this region were village sites on the Willapa, Naselle, Nemah, Querquelin (Bone or Mouse), Palix, and North rivers, and on Smith Creek.[19] Villages at the southern end of the peninsula were occupied the year around.

Chinooks and Clatsops were part of the rich and unique coastal complex which extended from their lands north to Alaska. Their affluent, materialistic, and competitive way of life stemmed from the productivity of their economy, which resulted from their cool marine environment.[20] Although highly developed among natives of the Queen Charlotte Islands to the north and on the adjacent mainland, much of this culture diffused southerly to Lower Chinooks from Vancouver Island through coastal Salish peoples and by direct contact as well. Chinook, Clatsop, Wahkiakum, and Kathlamet cultural patterns were modified from those of the Northwest Coast by those of the Columbia Plateau in the interior to the east.

Just as the Lower Chinook year was divided, so, in a sense, was their society of freemen and slaves living out their days in autonomous villages, their most fundamental social and political unit.[21] Among extended families of freemen held together by blood ties there were no classes, as nobility or commoners, although white men, impressed by regal prerogatives of Lower Chinookan aristocracy, would bestow royal designations on certain families, especially Chinooks proper. Among freemen no two individuals were of precisely the same status.[22] Movement upward from one station to another was achieved by acquisition of wealth, such mobility increasing with increased trade of the white contact period.

Because of their wealth and hereditary preeminence, upper ranking individuals, despite smaller numbers, assumed leadership roles in the society of these peoples, but by no means was the authority of leaders, as chiefs, shamans, and warriors, absolute. Authority lay with the kin group, which could replace chiefs with those considered better qualified.[23] Under a polygamous system which prevailed especially among wealthy males, eldest sons of highest-ranking wives might gain the chieftaincy. When male contenders for leadership were lacking, women held the position, as they also held property independently of males. They engaged frequently in village council debates, sometimes vociferously, approving or disapproving decisions, as did the males, by acclamation or silence.[24]

The lot of women, however, was harder than that of men. Like most other native American women, they performed myriad tasks.[25] Until they married they were the property of their fathers or nearest relatives. Husbands purchased them[26] and put them to work so these lords could purchase other wives;[27] or they traded them, gambled them away,[28] or even killed them. On their husbands' deaths, the males' properties, rather than passing to the wives, passed to eldest sons, accoutered graves, or were destroyed. Widows were expected to observe mourning tabus and not remarry too quickly. On the deaths of their husbands, wives passed into the care of their husbands' brothers.

Lower Chinook leaders judged, settled quarrels, and supervised economic and war activities. In the last responsibility they did not defer to specialized war chiefs, as did leaders of the peoples of the Columbia Plateau and Great Plains. Of course, Chinook chiefs gained special privileges because of their aristocracy. Besides the fruits of the village's industry, they had rights to the surplus of its economy and received special remuneration such as the first measure of blubber from whales stranded on the beach and of game brought in by hunters. High-ranking persons owned as many as a dozen slaves,* such wealth a testimonial to Chinook preeminence in trade and occasional war. One anthropologist states: "There is no doubt that the Chinook not only possessed more slaves per capita than any surrounding people, but that their eminence as traders was largely responsible."[29]

Slaves lived in their masters' houses as a rule,[30] although these owners communicated with them through intermediaries. Female slaves, like free women, were truly hewers of wood and carriers of water. Their male counterparts were compelled to build and repair houses, fish, secure and preserve other foods as well, paddle their masters' canoes, and even commit murder for them.[31] They were even used as a medium of exchange and indemnification in settling various debts.[32] In sickness and in health their lot was indeed harsh.[33] In their masters' rigid dining codes, for example, they were forced to eat meals often thrown to them[34] and were denied nourishment for a day or two for failure to clean a dish. When incapacitated, as they often were by forced unhealthful eating practices, they were left to perish, often in inclement weather against which their inferior clothing offered little protection.[35] Seldom did medicine men conjure evil spirits from their sick bodies, and when they died other slaves threw their bodies to the wild animals, into the river, or into coverless pits. In some instances they were tied to their owners' sepulchers and left to starve to death[36] to serve their masters in the other world as their fellow slaves in this one were forced to mourn their masters' passing.

Within the complex Lower Chinook social code the offspring of high-ranking persons married to slaves became slaves. Orphans of freemen were occasionally enslaved. Should freemen's daughters who were married to slaves become widowed, they returned free to their families. Slaves were used as wedding gifts and as money to pay debts or a "blood price" to families of slain persons. Upon their sale, these unfortunates carried guarantees to the purchasers that should they die within a short time of purchase their price would be refunded. Only rarely did slaves purchase their freedom, and even then they were looked upon as inferior.

One anthropologist believes that perhaps no other aspect of Lower Chinook life approached so nearly the attitude of typical Northwest

* Silas B. Smith, who had a white father and a Clatsop mother, says of Northwest Coast slavery, "Almost every leading family held from one to half a dozen slaves, and some of the chiefs having even many more." See "Primitive Customs and Religious Beliefs of the Indians of the Pacific Northwest Coast," *Oregon Historical Quarterly*, II (1901), 257–58. Chinook Chief Comcomly was said to have been preceded by a vanguard of three hundred slaves. A. G. Harvey, "Chief Concomly's Skull," *Oregon Historical Quarterly*, XL (1939), 162. Verne Ray, however, states that Comcomly owned only ten or twelve slaves. *Lower Chinook Ethnographic Notes*, 51.

Coastal peoples as did their emphasis on rank, with any variance from the standards of that region "[one] in degree, not in kind."[37] Chinook social position, determined thus by heredity and wealth, was more rigid than that of peoples further down the Pacific Coast and of those up the Columbia, whom Lower Chinooks regarded as peoples inferior to themselves.

Variations in status of Northwest Coastal peoples were demonstrated graphically in the potlatch ceremony,[38] which, like so many other manifestations of their competitiveness, reached its height at about the time of the arrival of trade goods. Whereas Lower Chinooks borrowed from the North the concept of status distinctions, those distinctions were displayed less flagrantly in their potlatches than were those of northern peoples, who achieved power and influence by lavish distributions of gifts in their ceremonies. Among these Chinooks, contrariwise, the potlatch process was atypical of Northwest Coastal ceremony and more like that of the Columbia Plateau. Although overlain with ceremony and a protocol requiring invitation to commoners to attend secular potlatches, they were less formal than those of the North, amounting to little more than feasting and gift giving. Also, among Lower Chinooks the distinction between the potlatch and the winter dance, a sacred ceremony borrowed from plateau peoples, was less complete than it was among the latter.[39]

As among the Nootkas of Vancouver Island, the clan concept among Lower Chinooks was developed and symbolized by the adoption of crests, which were carved or dye-painted on properties. The use of crests owned by individuals was forbidden to others.[40] Symbolizing position, crests were passed on to family members. These Chinooks followed no precise detail in fabricating wood products, unlike their northern fellows, and they did not engage in totem pole carving.* Chinook men and women, however, carved effigies, sticks, dance rattles, and boards with figures representing the guardian spirits from which they received their power. Painted house posts, images, and figures around house doors and on canoe prows and sterns symbolized spirit protection. Chinook-carved wood and animal-horn eating utensils represented Northwest Coastal animal art forms, although plateau influences also revealed their geometrical designs on Chinook utensils. Chinook carving on utilitarian

---

* Among Haidas and Tsimshians such carving was highly developed to commemorate specific events in the history of particular families. The tradition was shared to a lesser extent by peoples along northeastern Vancouver Island, but was missing among Salish to the south of the island, where carvings and paintings represented individual privilege and served as decorations only. H. G. Barnett, "The Southern Extent of Totem Pole Carving," *Pacific Northwest Quarterly*, XXXIII, 4 (October, 1942), 379, 389.

objects from cups to canoes was less stylized than that to the north.[41]

There was but little question of the Chinooks' borrowing of the all-important guardian spirit concept from northern tribes. Although the dance, associated with the spirit concept, showed cultural affiliation with the dance of northern peoples, the spirit quest practiced by Chinooks, and showing affiliation with that of plateau peoples, enabled them to perform feats and guarantee success in fishing and other exploits. Important trappings of the Lower Chinook spirit dance, like those of the North, were diamond-shaped decorated boards, painted poles used as dance wands, and planks or roof boards against which poles were beaten. Inactivity of the novitiate during the Chinook spirit dance period was like that of the North.[42] Art forms associated with guardian spirit ceremonies probably replaced an earlier type of expression found in ribbed wood-carved effigies, a more rudimentary school of sculpture than the better-known Northwest Coast art style. These effigies in wood as well as those in stone, representing the dead, probably evinced a "ghost" style in vogue prior to that borrowed from the North.* These effigies were also found in Puget Sound and western Canadian coastal areas but survived no longer than the beginning of the nineteenth century.

Among Coast Salish peoples were fully developed secret societies, formal complex clan developments, but Chinooks appear to have had no such societies until around the time of contact with whites. Membership in those societies, which were limited to high-ranking individuals, was attained by performing tricks and withstanding pain. Initiation into such societies involved some scarification, and the novices were taught tricks.[43]

A glance at Chinook culture reveals that it was influenced by an environment of aquatic wealth from sea and river. The first offerings of the warming season were candlefish (smelt—Eulachon) swarming from sea to river.† With curved blades set with bone or wooden teeth, Chinooks, Clatsops, Wahkiakums, and Kathlamets raked in swarms of these tiny creatures, knocking them into the bottoms of their canoes.[44] In contrast to fishing for these tiny creatures, they probed the river bottom with

---

* These effigies were also found in the Puget Sound and western Canadian coastal areas, surviving no longer than 1800. William Duncan Strong, "The Occurence and Wider Implications of a 'Ghost Cult' on the Columbia River Suggested by Carvings in Wood, Bone and Stone," *American Anthropologist*, n.s., XLVII, 2 (April, 1945), 252.

† In a letter dated April 21, 1972, to the authors, Douglas G. Chapman, Dean of the College of Fisheries in the University of Washington, Seattle, writes: ". . . the fish that these early explorers called candlefish are in fact the ones we call smelt today. The Indians used them to make candles because of their high oil content and hence the name applied to them. There are other fish elsewhere in the world that are named candlefish that are a quite different species. . . ."

seventy to eighty-foot poles with detachable spears, catching giant sturgeon weighing up to six hundred pounds,[45] wearing them down, knocking them in the head with wooden mallets, and hauling them into their craft.

The finny namesake of the Lower Chinooks, the large, rich-flavored Chinook (king) salmon, entered the Columbia in March, with the peak run in late April and May.[46] As the salmon milled at the river mouth awaiting right conditions for their runs, the people made their own preparations to catch them. To insure good harvests they prayed their benevolent divinity Ecahnie (Ecannum) to guide the large fish into the river. They caught and handled the first ones with care, following tabus born from the myth-legends of a distant past just as they followed strict tabus in the disposition of whales found on beaches or game brought in from the hills.[47] A shaman offered the first salmon to the deity, closely overseeing the preparation of the fish to insure the productivity of the fishery for the season. The fish was split down the back, never cut crosswise,[48] and it was cooked before sunset of the day it was caught.[49] It was never thrown into the water or to the dogs.[50] After the villagers cooked it they feasted and danced. Ceremonials concluded, they busily harvested the fish. From summer to fall they caught the blueback (sockeye), humpback (pink), silver (coho), and dog (chum) salmon.[51]

At fisheries on the north side of the Columbia where salmon entered the river, and at mouths of tributaries,* men cast hundred-foot-long seines into the river, drawing their catches ashore and killing them with mallets. Women cut them lengthwise, throwing away hearts and backbones and keeping heads and tails, which they considered delicacies, and placed the fish in the sun or in lodges to cure. Salmon taken in later runs were considered inferior, although they were nutritious and easily dried.[52] Fish of these later runs were stored in great quantities for winter use and trade.[53]

Chinooks, Clatsops, and their upriver neighbors also caught steelhead trout in the spring and fall and collected the fish roe by sinking large pieces of cedar bark in shallow water, camouflaging them with green leaves to catch the spawn. They also ate portions of whales and sea lions,† which they did not hunt but took when these mammals were

---

* Clatsops fished off Point Adams. Clarke, S. A. *Pioneer Days of Oregon History*, II, 420. Chinooks took late salmon from fall runs in Columbia River tributaries. D. Lee and J. H. Frost, *Ten Years in Oregon*, 99. Clatsops took their fall catches south of Niekaskis (present-day Neacoxie) at the southern end of Clatsop Plain near Cape Lookout, where a stream emptied into the ocean. Nellie B. Pipes (ed.), "Journal of John H. Frost, 1840–43," *Oregon Historical Quarterly*, XXXV (1934), 71.

† Sea lions are often confused with sea otters. Sea lions are pinniped carnivores of the Otariidae family. Sea otters are fissiped carnivores of the Mustelidae family. Sea otters have

stranded ashore. They took clams and oysters, especially at Willapa Bay during their winter stays at that place.[54]

Multitudes of wildfowl in sloughs and marshes, bays and rivers of Lower Chinook country gave its people a choice of foods and feathers from species ranging from pelicans, gulls, and snipes to the more common ducks and geese.

Lower Chinook environment was also one of vegetal wealth, as the land yielded its wealth of fruits and roots. An important fruit for Chinooks, not only for its edibility but for its ceremonial role, was the salmonberry, one of which was placed in the mouth of a salmon caught and released to make its way amply nourished on its otherwise foodless journey to its parent stream.[55] Chinooks also had a choice of huckleberries, raspberries, strawberries, and salal berries, which they ate raw or sometimes boiled into a pasty soup. They gathered one of their most important fruits, cranberries, in early fall along the peninsula by Willapa Bay.* The subsoil yielded its bulbs and roots. Chinooks roasted egg-sized wappatoe roots, which grew in marshy places along the upper Columbia, from whose people they imported them. They also ate roots of lupin, fern, thistle, cattail, and skunk cabbage, varying their diet somewhat with rush roots and other vegetables.

Chinook reliance on nature was evident by the equipment they used to gather and prepare their food, clothing, and shelter. They made and

---

never been authentically recorded as living in a natural freshwater environment such as the Columbia River. Karl Kenyon, U.S. Department of the Interior Fish and Wildlife Service, to the authors, April 21, 1972. The fur trader George Simpson in the 1820's observed that when sea lions entered the Columbia, natives would kill them. Frederick Merk (ed.), *Fur Trade and Empire: George Simpson's Journal*, 102–103. Simpson was thus apparently aware of the difference between sea lions and sea otters. Ancient Kathlamet hunting techniques involved drives to capture and harpoon sea lions down toward the sea. Franz Boas, *Kathlamet Texts*, Bureau of American Ethnology *Bulletin 26*, 241–44. Another fur trader on the Columbia a decade before Simpson was Alexander Henry, who described the natives' methods of catching at Oak Point what he called sea lions (harbor seals [*phoca vitulina*]), which often journeyed up the Columbia. Henry recorded the Indians' technique of capturing these animals: "Two canoes being lashed together, they approach very softly, and throw their spears, which are fastened by a long, strong cord, with a barb so fixed in a socket that, when it strikes the animal and pierces the flesh, it is detached from the shaft of the spear, but remains fastened to the cord. This is instantly made fast between the canoes; the animal dives and swims down river, dragging the canoes with such velocity that they may be in danger of filling, and require great skill in steering. In this manner they are carried down some miles before the animal becomes exhausted with loss of blood, makes for the shore, and lies on the beach, where they dispatch and cut it up." Elliott Coues (ed.), *New Light on the Early History of the Greater Northwest*, II, 857–58.

* Native cranberry bogs began about four miles north of present-day Ilwaco, Washington, and extended northerly.

embellished wooden boxes with sea shells, enclosing them with other boxes to waterproof valuables such as fishing tackle and twine.* From nettles, wild flax, silk grass, white cedar bark, roots, and other materials received in trade from distant tribes they fabricated fishing cordage, seines, and nets.[56] They made from the heart of the arborvitae, or white cedar, neat and highly elastic bows, the backs of which were covered with elk sinew (the same material used for their strings) laid on with glue made from the sturgeon. These weapons were some two and one-half feet long and two inches wide at the center, tapering down to one-half inch at the ends. Arrows were formed of two sections, the longer one of a light wood so it could be more easily retrieved from water, where many of the arrows were shot. Other weapons were bone or wooden harpoons. From bone the Chinooks made fishhooks and spears. They used ash and cedar in manufacturing dishes, bowls, trays, and ladles. They wove tight silk grass baskets in which they boiled salmon by dropping in hot stones. For other purposes they used baskets of spruce roots and rushes. Fibers that satisfied the tailoring needs of their busy women were bear and squaw grass, tule, rush, flag, wild flax, willow, and cedar. They placed grasses over heated stones in pits to steam cook the wappatoe root. Acorns were placed with grass and dirt in pits into which the Indians would urinate from time to time. Thus marinated, and then cooked in separate cooking pits, the result, "Chinook olives," they considered a delicacy.[57]

Sometimes men wore mat robes not so much for warmth but to shed rain. For the same reason they wore wide-brimmed hats of woven bear grass or cedar bark of multicolored design. In winter they wore thigh-length robes and blankets of skin, hair, or the wool of dogs and mountain sheep. In summer women frequently wore fringed, knee-length skirts of cedar bark twisted with silk grass and knotted at the ends; in winter they wore muskrat, rabbit, and gooseskin strips twisted with feathers which faced outward.[58] The continuous moisture of their country, unlike that of the plateau and plains, prevented the use of leather, an exception being their clamons,† elkskin cuirasses purchased by Chinooks from their Clatsop neighbors across the river and from other peoples upstream. Finding their arrows often ineffective in felling elk, Clatsops trapped the large beasts in pits a dozen feet deep and overlain with boughs. Sometimes they used elk heads to decoy this animal just

---

* Although Chinooks made kerfed boxes, they obtained most of theirs through trade from Coastal Salish peoples to the north and from Nootkas.

† The skin armour was frequently spelled "clemel" or "clemons." Many traders spoke of these "mooseskin" body coverings, but they were mistaken. Clamons were made from elk skins.

as they used deer heads to lure the smaller beast. Since satisfactory footware was hard to maintain, Chinooks and Clatsops went barefoot even in occasional snow.

Chinook-Clatsop summer and winter houses were gabled wooden structures*[59] arranged in rows to form villages averaging some thirty dwellings.[60] Like most Pacific Northwest dwellings, they sat atop three-foot pits and had walls averaging some eight feet high.†[61] They varied from twenty to sixty feet long and from fourteen to twenty feet wide.[62] Some lodged three or four families; others sheltered ten to fifteen such groups. The basic framework of these dwellings was four corner timbers and two crotched endposts supporting ridgepoles and rafters. Over this framework Chinooks, Clatsops, Wahkiakums, and Kathlamets placed vertical or horizontal straight-grained cedar planks up to three feet wide and one-half foot thick. Over the rafters they placed thatched bark. To manufacture this planking they first split logs with elkhorn, stone, or wooden (crabapple) wedges[63] and then shaped the planks with adzes of the same material.[64] They split small boards with beavers' teeth.

Entering a Chinook house, a person passed through the mouth section of a large carved and painted wooden animal or other effigy to descend by a notched ladder to the pit floor. There, he saw as many fires as there were families. In these poorly ventilated, windowless structures smoke escaped through roof apertures, curing rafter-stored salmon, venison, roots, and berries. Foods and fishing boxes were stored beneath one- to three-foot-high bunks flanking the walls.

The richness of their environment would seem to have obviated Chinook-Clatsop need to trade and travel as widely as did peoples upriver and those of plateau and plains, where nature scattered her bounties and where, with the coming of the horse about the middle of the eighteenth century, these gifts became, in those lands, prizes of internecine warfare. Chinook-Clatsop affluence was stimulated no less from their acquisition of goods which, when unsatisfied from local environs, were secured elsewhere. Occasionally armed with bows and arrows, spears, and double-edged war clubs, they fought to obtain material things and to revenge insult, injury, and murder.[65] To protect themselves they wore

* The predecessor of the frame house was the earth-covered or semisubterranean type of house, distribution of which suggests that it was first built in Asia and was then brought to the unfrozen portions of Northwestern North America and down the coast and plateau to the borders of Mexico, with its subsequent replacement by the plank house in the Northwest Coast area. A. L. Kroeber, "American Culture and the Northwest Coast," *American Anthropologist*, n.s., XXV, 1 (January, 1923), 13.

† The very few houses without pits seem to have been among Upper Chinooks on the Willamette River. Hubert Howe Bancroft, *The Native Races*, Vol. I, *Wild Tribes*. Vol. I of *The Works of Hubert Howe Bancroft*, 231.

hardwood armor and cedar-bark corsets laced with tough grasses or full-length, doubled, arrow-resistant elk skins, the clamons, with holes for head and arms.[66] They found these cuirasses good items to trade, especially to northern tribes like the Haidas in the Queen Charlotte Islands. The clamons were in great demand among these northern natives, who used them more frequently than did the less sanguine Chinooks.[67]

Not always were Lower Chinooks less warlike than northern Indians. Shortly after the middle of the eighteenth century, for example, they battled the Upper Chinooks who came to their country annually for canoeloads of clams. Warriors from Qwatsamuts, a Chinook village at the mouth of the Wallicut River, and others of the principal Chinook village, located between Chinook Point and Point Ellice (No-wehtl-kai-ilse) at the eastern end of Bakers Bay, had warned these visitors that there would be war should they invade the clam beds that fall. The warning was to no avail, and the Lower Chinook chief, Komkomis, father of the famed Chinook chief Comcomly (Madsu, or Thunder), reportedly led some thousand warriors into battle against the upriver peoples, who were weakened from battles on their way downstream. In one version of the encounter the Chinooks were said to have tricked the enemy into pursuing them through waist-high sword grass, where hidden defenders suddenly sprang from concealment to slay the invaders. For years their bones would litter an eroding Columbia shoreline.[68] A few years later, about 1789, one hundred large and one hundred small Chinook canoes traveled twenty days up the Columbia past "some great Water fall" to a lake to destroy the men of a large tribe inhabiting its shores, enslaving their women and children.[69]

The major Chinook-Clatsop occupation was trade, not war. Encouraging them in this occupation was their strategic location at the mouth of the Columbia, gateway to the coast and the interior.[70] Besides items of trade, the canoes to which these people took with the same naturalness and skill that their interior brothers took to the horse kept commerce moving in these waters. One type of canoe used in traveling inland waters was the shovel-nosed canoe (probably of Chinook and Chehalis innovation), with rounded stern and prow. Constructed from a single fifteen-foot log, it was manned by one or two people working notched paddles.* It took a man sometimes three months to make a canoe of this type by burning and gouging out a cavity in a log.[71]

---

* When British explorer Captain James Cook came to the Northwest Coast, natives apparently had not evolved sails; the master of the American ship *Jefferson* was said to have introduced this innovation to the coast. Frederic W. Howay, "A Yankee Trader on the Northwest Coast, 1791–1795," *Washington Historical Quarterly*, XXI, 2 (April, 1930), 90–91.

The large canoe, called the Chinook canoe,* was obtained by trade with Nootkas of Vancouver Island, since Chinook country produced white cedar too small for such craft. One anthropologist states: "The number of these canoes on the lower river attested not to the industry of the Chinook but to their trading abilities."⁷² With carved animals or human effigies, or inlaid with bits of shells, the large canoe had a vertical bow and stern with an elongated prow to break sea or rough water, as was often experienced on the lower Columbia. The bow and stern were projections—separate boards fastened to the canoe. Made from a single log, such a canoe averaged about six feet across and some thirty-five feet long, narrowing at the ends, and carried a dozen people who, with the exception of a steersman, propelled it with five- or six-foot ashen paddles, usually pointed for smooth water or notched for river use.⁷³ Canoemen paddled from a kneeling position. Leaning against rough water, they gained equilibrium by throwing their craft to one side, leaning over the upper gunwales and thrusting their paddles deep to catch and force water under the craft.† They beached the boat stern first for quick embarkation or high and dry for an extended land stay.

The third type of canoe used by Chinooks was the cutwater,⁷⁴ which had an inch-thick piece of shaped board added to the undercut bow and sometimes another added to the stern. This craft, averaging thirty-five feet in length, was made in the North and was also obtained by Chinooks in trade with intermediary peoples along the trade routes to the north. Chinooks and their neighbors operated this craft much like they did the Chinook canoe.

Just as Chinooks proper considered their sturdy canoes to be the best transportation on earth, they and Clatsops also considered them the best conveyance to their heaven. Thus, the craft were often found at burial spots on scaffolding accoutered with items of native manufacture to subsist and comfort the deceased within them on their last long journey. As these (had they been good) traveled to their destination,

---

* The designation "Chinook canoe" is a misnomer and probably was a name used after the development of the Chinook Jargon, the trade language. This type of canoe is more accurately called the "Nootka canoe." "The Chinook canoe was a model of naval architecture, as perfect in its kind as the best clipper ship ever launched from an American shipyard." "The Lost Tribes of the Chinooks and Clatsops," *San Francisco Chronicle*, June 1, 1884. David Thompson noted in 1811 that Chinook-Clatsop canoes were made from trees drifted down the (Columbia) river, some of which were up to fifty feet in length, and from four to five feet in width. *Thompson's Narrative*, 363.

† The Chinook or Nootka canoe was used as an oceangoing craft. Captain C. E. Barrett-Lennard, who left England in 1859 for a two-year visit to Vancouver Island, reported that northern natives made voyages by sea of many hundred miles in their canoes. *Travels in British Columbia*, 40.

"The Land of the South" (Temath), their survivors, Chinooks moreso than Clatsops, pursued their mercantile rounds in the North. In trading in that quarter, as along the Pacific to the south, they seldom took their large canoes along the ocean but followed inland coastal routes. They most frequently journeyed up the Chinook River, portaging to Bear River and on to Willapa Bay, a distance of some four or five miles. They also traveled to that bay via present-day Ilwaco, up a beaver-dammed, spring-fed swamp near Bakers Bay, from which they portaged to Black Lake and down Talilt (Tarlett) Slough, a distance of six miles or roughly two miles further than the other route.[75] Continuing northerly, they portaged to Grays Harbor,[76] following a forested coastal shoreline trail, hugging ocean cliffs, and rafting rivers along the way.[77] When traveling to Puget Sound, they broke from Willapa Bay, canoed up the Willapa River, and portaged to the Chehalis River or went via Grays Harbor up the Chehalis to the Black River, portaging from (another) Black Lake to Budd Inlet on lower Puget Sound. Wahkiakums and Kathlamets went to Willapa Bay by one of two portages used by Chinooks or by trail from the head of Deep River (about one mile west of Grays River) to the Naselle, four miles away, and from this stream they pushed on to the south fork of the Willapa.[78]

Chinooks purchased their canoes from peoples between them and the Nootkan source of the craft, although they are said to have occasionally gone to the source for them.* Coastal Salish, besides trading in the north, traded with interior Salish, principally via the Fraser River and also through Cascade Mountain passes east of Puget Sound. Important middlemen in the canoe trade were Makahs at Cape Flattery (at the northwest tip of the Olympic Peninsula) who obtained their craft from Nootkas in exchange for whale oil, blubber, or dried halibut. In their homeland, Makahs traded canoes to Chinooks, but more often they journeyed south to trade them at Point Grenville along the Pacific Ocean in Quinault territory—the western shores of the Olympic Peninsula, a point roughly halfway between Lower Chinook and Makah lands. Like Nootkas, Makahs also traded whale oil, blubber, and dried halibut to Chinooks. Sometimes Chinooks traded for canoes and other commodities with Quinaults and their neighbors, the Quillayutes, who likewise had secured them from Makahs and Nootkas.[79] These Chinooks most likely paddled their canoes homeward along the coast instead of following interior land routes.

---

* Most authorities agree that Chinook excursions to trade with Nootkas on northern Vancouver Island were irregular; however, one author states that "the original Chinook Indians . . . for centuries had been the leading traders at Nootka, before the white men came. . . ." Tom MacInnes, *Chinook Days*, 29.

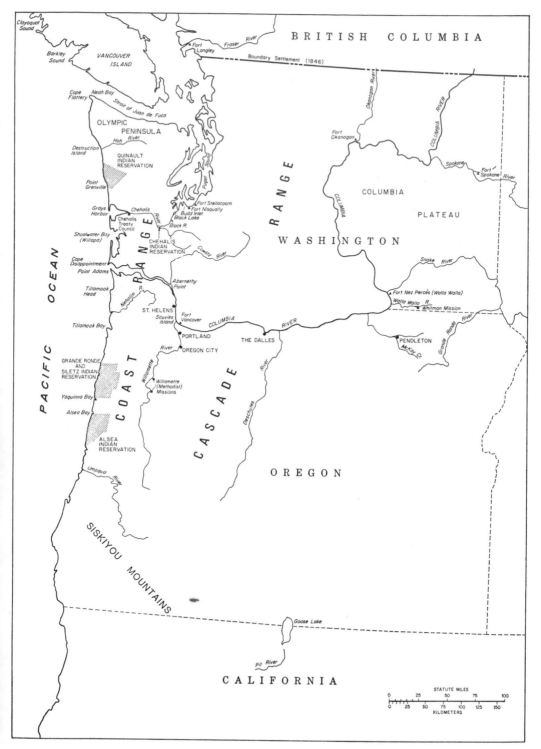

Pacific Northwest Coast

Goods which Chinooks traded north were by no mea[...]
own lands and hands, for many came from other people[...]
sought them out to trade at the Columbia mouth. Som[...]
and Clatsops brought home goods from journeys up[...]
miles to the lower end of the Cascades of the Columbia, where the [...]
broke a line of Cascade Mountains. But it was further upstream at the
Dalles in late summer and early fall that tribes from as far as Canada
to the north, California to the south, and the Great Plains to the east
gathered in the homeland of Upper Chinookan Wishrams and Wascos
to trade, wager, and frolic in the largest native mart in the Pacific
Northwest.

At the Dalles, Chinooks, Clatsops, Wahkiakums, and Kathlamets
traded goods obtained from the north Pacific as well as marine products
of their own country and wappatoe harvested by their Columbia River
neighbors. At the busy portage market they purchased goods collected
from half a continent away. From Chinookan peoples of the Dalles they
secured the great product of that place—salmon pounded fine and
packed in ninety-pound pieces in two-foot-high rush and salmon-skin
baskets protected by cord-laced fish skins.[80] Since the product remained
edible up to two seasons, Lower Chinooks found that it supplemented
their own winter's supply of dried salmon, especially since they appear
not to have understood, or at least practiced, the technique of salmon
packing. They also obtained at the Dalles, for their own use and for
trade, grasses and other fibers of superior quality, pipes, and European-
manufactured battle axes from beyond the Rocky Mountains.[81] From
intermontane areas and California they purchased tobacco, which they
smoked in long-stemmed pipes. From mountain tribes they purchased
animal skins, buffalo meat, and sheep horn from which, after steaming
and boiling it and carving it into geometric designs, they made eating
utensils and bows.[82]

The variety of Chinook-Clatsop trade items was impressive. Two,
however, stand out uniquely—one animate, the other inanimate. The
one—slaves—was perhaps the foremost commodity of Chinook commerce. They kept some slaves but sold most of them for canoes to
peoples of the North, where, far from their homelands, the slaves were
less likely to escape and, in Pope's words, would no more "their native
land behold." Chinooks and Clatsops took as slaves mostly women and
children, for males were harder to take and keep. They purchased some
of their human property from Kalapuya, Modoc, and Klamath Indians
of Oregon and Shastas of California who had gotten them from tribes
near the Umpqua River of southern Oregon and the Siskiyou Mountains or from the Oregon-California borderlands.[83] They also purchased

.aves from their Tillamook neighbors, who raided for them in the south, and sometimes from up the Columbia, where the slave trade was perhaps heavier than at any other place in the Pacific Northwest. At that place lower Columbia peoples bought and resold slaves from such tribes as Snakes of eastern Oregon, Achomawis and Atsugewis of the Pit River in northern California, Upland Takelmas of the upper Rogue River, and Shastas of northern California. The advent of the horse in the Pacific Northwest about the middle of the eighteenth century enabled fast-striking raiders to capture their human prizes with more ease, thus enlarging the market supply.[84]

The other major item of Chinook trade, *Dentalium indianorum* and *Dentalium pretiosum*,[85] was the principal medium of exchange on the Northwest Coast. These sea shells, referred to as dentalia or *hiqua* (a word thought to refer originally to a string of dentalia of specific size and length but now commonly used interchangeably with the word "dentalia"), were principally a Nootkan trade item especially since they were found in waters off Vancouver Island. Lower Chinooks called them *ta-cópe-ta-cópe*. Dentalia were found as well off other islands to the north and the mainland north to Alaska. Standard value of dentalia at the contact period was forty shells to a fathom (six feet) or the length to which a man could stretch his arms. A fathom of smaller shells was sometimes worth but half a fathom of forty, and, conversely, longer shells were considered superior and of increased value. Dentalia, milk white, extremely hard, and half an inch long in some varieties, were tapered at one end and curved slightly to resemble an extended horn of plenty. Natives often raked them from the ocean floor, but more often gathered them by dropping pieces of deer flesh or fish, to which the dentalia clung, near the ocean bottom.[86] Processed, the shells were readied for sale to natives who proudly wore them sometimes hundreds of miles from their source. Chinooks and Clatsops also valued them highly not only as adornment for the living and the dead, but also to pay shamans for services rendered.

The great distance between these people and the source of their prized import was short compared with the distance from which they would later obtain other goods half an earth away in Europe. Their coming exposure to products carried by white men in "white-winged canoes," though indirect at first, would eventually result in direct mercantile confrontations. In these as in other such encounters, the aboriginals held their own in the cultural ledger. And although Chinooks and Clatsops would eventually succumb to products and skills of "proud science," they would prove to its purveyors that their own skills and science were hardly those of the "untutored minds" of "poor Indians," as Pope had suggested they were. And they would also prove to their white trader counterparts that they could match their own skills with the whites' as they clung to goods as various as slaves and shells until in a no longer "safer World" they would relinquish them. Then, like white men, they would have no need of such things.

2. Those Who Drift Ashore

> Gold is not an object of more eager desire
> in Europe, than iron in this part of America.
>
> Jean de La Pérouse

It would have surprised advocates of Europe's vaunted civilization to think that reaching western America before them were perhaps men of Cathay, of whose culture a cycle's worth, in the words of one of Pope's successors, hardly matched a half-century of theirs. From his map, some students of one Hwui Shan have conjectured that in the fifth century after Christ this Buddhist monk, sailing from China to a distant land, Fusang, reportedly touched Alaska, the mouth of the Columbia River, and a point near present-day San Francisco.[1] Hwui Shan's descriptions fit those of the Northwest Pacific Coast culture complex, for some were naked, and some used copper (Alaskan natives were believed to have fabricated copper objects)[2] but no iron.[3] They lived in wooden houses and used large horn utensils. Their women nursed their young over their shoulders. These characteristics, at least at a later time, are descriptive of peoples of the lower Columbia River and other areas of the Pacific Northwest Coast.*[4]

Unlike people of Cathay, Northwest Coastal natives left few if any written records to throw light on the journey of Hwui Shan, nor does their oral folklore illuminate the journey, whose details have been lost in the misty millenium before Europeans appeared off their coasts. Na-

---

* "The Pacific Northwest is commonly regarded as a conventional area defined by treaties. It can be located between the forty-second parallel north lattitude on the south, fifty-four degrees forty minutes on the north, the water's edge on the west, and the Rocky Mountain divide on the east." Richard W. Van Alstyne, "International Rivalries in Pacific Northwest," *Oregon Historical Quarterly*, XLVI, 3 (September, 1945), 185.

tive tradition does tell of non-Europeans wrecked off western Pacific shores, but American natives perhaps would not have known from where they came. Possibly it was from China, but more likely it was from Kamchatka, Okhotsk,[5] or the Japanese Islands that they were carried on westerly currents across the Pacific rim to American shores. In rare cases, from three to four hundred years ago some of these travelers were thought to have returned to their homes in the Orient. About 1639 Japanese officials ordered all junks to be built with open sterns and square rudders to render them unfit for ocean travel, thus helping to insure the isolation of the islands.[6] Once at sea, the junks' rudders sometimes washed away, and as late as the nineteenth century such craft were known to drift to America.

An English traveler later in the Pacific Northwest would write that Japanese probably left at the mouth of the Columbia River the small, long-haired dog of North American natives. Whether they did or not, dogs, especially bitches, appear prominently in Chinook mythology. That traveler would also suggest that Chinook Indians learned from the same Japanese the art of weaving mats and dog-hair blankets, a more materialistic use of man's best friend than having him keep his master company, as suggested by Pope in his "Essay." The weaving of dog hair would die out among Chinooks at European contact, but it would prevail among the Salish of Puget Sound until the easy purchase of Hudson's Bay Company blankets would eliminate the need for such weaving.[7]

There are those who believe that domestic cats among the Chinooks descended from the cats of Spanish ships wrecked a few miles south of the Columbia River.[8] European traders in this area in the early nineteenth century wrote of such animals there, in some instances referring to those brought north from California about that time.

Had these animals truly been washed from early ships near the Columbia, they, with their masters and their cargoes, became flotsam and jetsam tokens of Spanish failure to discover in the North American Pacific the gold-rich islands and the fabled Strait of Anian through the American land mass. The Columbia River estuary had long been associated with the Strait of Anian, on which some believed lay the mythical kingdom of Quivira.[9] The Spaniard Martin de Aguilar, sailing north from Monterey in command of the *Tres Reyes* to survey the Pacific Coast to facilitate Spanish navigation in those waters and counter Drake's voyage there in 1579, found himself in January, 1603, in what he reckoned to be north latitude 43°, where he discovered the mouth of a "very copious and soundable river."[10] Two centuries later cartographers would place their "River of the West" at north latitude 42°51′, drawing it with what could be interpreted as a tide extending some distance upstream.[11] One cartographer drew a map including a river which he called "Aguilar's River" at north latitude 45°—the approximate location of the Columbia.* Aguilar was known to have erred as many as three degrees in his reckonings, giving credence to the fact that he may have discovered the mouth of the Columbia River, although it is possible that he discovered the mouth of the Umpqua River just south of north latitude 44°. A Spanish crewman with Aguilar expressed failure to enter the broad stream quite simply: ". . . the current would not permit it."[12] Thus, Aguilar may have forfeited a closer search for the treasures of Quivira and the passage of Anian and, more practically, possible confrontation with Chinook and Clatsop Indians. For nearly two hundred years thereafter other sailors would apparently fail to find the river and the peoples of its shores.†

Between 1769 and 1776, with the establishment in Alta California of Spanish missions and presidios at a time when silver mines in Mexico (Baja California) were idled and the Spanish Empire was liberalizing its colonial policies, Spanish ships sailed into the north Pacific. Tradition persisted four generations later among Chinooks, Clatsops, and their neighbors of confrontations with Spanish sailors from lost ships. Quillayutes and Makahs also told of Spanish galleons along their shores and of the "Drifting White People" from these ships living among them.[13] Although there are numerous versions of these traditions, their persistence and similarity tend to give them some credibility. One of them concerned a fight between a presumed pirate ship and two merchantmen, whose smoking guns attempted to hold off the briny brigands before being sent to the bottom.[14] It is possible that pirates prowling the Pacific preyed on ships carrying supplies from the Philippine Islands[15]

---

* Hubert Howe Bancroft collected Pacific Northwest Coast maps made by Europeans in the eighteenth century. One map he overlooked when preparing his *History of the Northwest Coast*, Vol. I (Vol. XXVII of *The Works of Hubert Howe Bancroft*), was that of cartographer Thomas Jefferys, published in John Green, *Remarks in Support of the New Chart of North and South America*. The map in Green's book shows a river referred to by many cartographers as the Rio de Martin Aguilar and situated on the map near the location of the Columbia River with what appears to be tidewater extending upriver. Many maps of the era show the Strait of Juan de Fuca connected with Aguilar's River by an extension to the south of what was later called Puget Sound. Some maps of the period show the "River of the West" connecting with the Great Lakes and labeled the (mythical) Strait of Anian.

† It is believed that the source of the Columbia River was not discovered by white men until 1807, with the journeys of North West Company trader David Thompson to that region.

or on ships out of San Blas (in present-day Mexico) carrying supplies for missions in Alta California.*

According to one version of the above story, of thirty crewmen stranded off the Oregon coast near the Columbia, four went overland north, where they might have been picked up by a vessel, and their fellows remaining behind buried a proverbial treasure ashore.[16] Other accounts have it that after the crew buried the treasure they separated. Rogue River Indians killed those returning south, and Clatsops killed two in a fight.[17] Another native account has it that the ship's crew landed at Point Adams, where twenty armed men buried some chests.[18] Another dates the wreck at about 1700, when twenty-five to thirty men landed near the Nehalem River (some forty miles below the Columbia mouth), where they built a house and lived for some time with native women. Irritated by their talking, the natives killed them.[19] Some have suggested that the castaways were Japanese, since Tillamook descendants have more yellowish complexions and more oblique, elongated eyes than their neighbors.[20]

Still another story has a ship, sometime near the mid-1700's,[21] washing ashore near the Columbia River to give its natives their first confrontation with the men they would call "Tlohon-nipts" ("Those Who Drift Ashore").[22] The anthropologist Franz Boas, fearing Lower Chinooks to be on the verge of extinction, searched through the summers of 1890 and 1891 for some of their number who might tell him about their people. He found living among the Chehalis on Willapa Bay only two people who spoke Chinook. One of them, Charles Cultee, "a veritable storehouse of information," supplied Boas details for his *Chinook Texts* (1894), which included the following account of the arrival of the first white men:

> ... an old woman ... wailed for ... [her dead son] a whole year. ... Now one day she went to Seaside [near Clatsop]. ... She saw something. She thought it was a whale ... [with] two spruce trees standing upright on it. She reached the thing that lay there ... [with] its outer side ... covered with copper. Ropes were tied to those spruce trees and it was full of iron.

---

* Lost Spanish ships along the coasts of California and Mexico were not likely to have drifted to the Northwest Coast, since prevailing winds and currents were southerly along the coast. However, those Spanish ships which sailed from Acapulco on a southerly route for the Philippines returned on a circle route past Japan because of winds and currents which swept them to the western Pacific Coast, where they usually tried to approach the continent at about Cape Mendocino in Alta California. There, they would turn south two hundred miles at sea from the cape. It is possible that those ships wrecked off the Pacific Coast may have been ones lost while returning on the circle route.

Then a bear came out of it . . . but his face was that of a human being. Then she went home . . . and cried. [The villagers thinking] somebody struck her . . . made themselves ready. . . . Now she said all the time, "Oh, my son is dead, and the thing about which we heard in tales is on shore." . . . [The villagers] said, "What is it?" . . . "There are two bears on it, or maybe they are people." Then the people ran. They reached the thing that lay there. Now the [strange] people . . . held two copper kettles in their hands [and] took their hands to their mouths and gave the people their kettles . . . The men pointed inland and asked for water. . . . One man . . . found brass buttons in strings half a fathom long. . . . [They] set fire to the ship. . . . It burnt just like fat. Then the Clatsops gathered the iron, the copper, and the brass. . . . The two persons were taken to the chief of the Clatsop. . . . Now the Quenaiult, the Chehalis, the Cascades, the Cowlitz, and the Klickatat learned about it and they all went to Clatsop. . . . Strips of copper two fingers wide and going around the arm were exchanged for one slave each. . . . A nail was sold for a good curried deerskin. Several nails were given for long dentalia. The people bought this and the Clatsops became rich. Then iron and brass were seen for the first time. Now they kept these two persons. . . .[23]

The account has come down with variations on this text. According to one version, as many as four strange, pale, bearded men found cast ashore were parching maize and making signs of wanting water.[24] Nor do the versions agree as to the number of survivors. One says that of three crewmen one died and two were enslaved after the natives burned the ship.[25] In enslaving the two men the Clatsops would have been in character, for they and the Chinooks never missed opportunities to secure this most important of all trade goods. The two were taken to separate Clatsop villages, where their masters put one of them, an armorer, to work fabricating their metallic things into useful tools.

The story of the newcomers did not end there. Native tradition says that since no ships on which they might have returned home had come to the mouth of the Columbia, they started inland hoping to find white men (since natives of that interior region possessed European goods). A native reportedly killed one of them. One bore the name Kanopee.*

---

* The Spanish are thought to have searched the Pacific Northwest for gold. An *arrastra*, once believed to have been of Spanish origin and predating any known historic visit by other than natives to central Washington State, is described in an article in the *Wenatchee Daily World*, March 13, 1966. The Spanish origin of the instrument has since been disproven. A native village near Cape Disappointment was once called Kanopee. When traders later visited the river, bringing coins with square holes, the coins were called "Kanopee money." J. Neilson Barry, "Spaniards in Early Oregon," *Washington Historical Quarterly*, XXIII, 1 (January, 1932), 26. For an explanation of the Spanish derivation of the word *Kanopee*, see *Morning Oregonian*, December 11, 1899.

Many years later (in 1811) an aged blind man living at the Cascades, giving his name as Soto, would claim that his father was Kanopee, who had come to the area when a Spanish galleon wrecked near the mouth of the Columbia River. According to his version of that story, four men, including his father, had escaped to the Cascades (or to the Dalles?).[26] There they had married native women and settled down. Silas Smith, son of a Clatsop woman, would claim to have met on the lower Columbia a sixty-year-old woman who said she was the daughter of Kanopee.[27] Accounts of early-day whites coming to the Chinook and Clatsops are as confused as are those of early-day shipwrecks. Soto is confused at times with another, Jack Ramsay, a freckled, red-haired Clatsop, probably the son of a Clatsop woman and an English crewman (Old Ramsay) escaped from a ship. One account has it that in a violent storm in December, 1760, at Nehalem a ship wrecked from which one man survived, a red-bearded Scotchman,[28] possibly Jack's father. Another account has it that a shipwreck in 1745 was the source of this red-bearded white man.[29] Old Ramsay (Jack's father) was said to have died about the contact period in a smallpox epidemic, and one of his alleged daughters was supposed to have married the son of a fur trader.[30] George Ramsay, a Columbia River pilot in later years, may have been the son of Old Ramsay. The red-haired youth, Jack, would be noted by many whites in the area moreso than "blood" offspring of early white mariners. The latter did not always inherit such striking characteristics from their fathers.[31] Red-haired Clatsops and Chinooks, descending from interracial marriages at the beginning of white trade, only further confused the identity of "bloods" and the accounts about those from whom they sprang.[32]

There are legends of other ships bringing strange-looking people to the Columbia River area long before the close of the eighteenth century. Inscription-bearing rocks uncovered in 1865 were thought to have some relevance to accounts of treasures buried by strangers near the Columbia mouth.[33] One legacy of shipwrecks more evident than gold was beeswax, great quantities of which were spilled along the coast. Many blocks of wax were trademarked,[34] and several, found in the Nehalem area, bore the date 1679.[35] Familiar with legends of his mother's Clatsop people, Smith told of a wrecked ship, probably Spanish, which spilled ashore a large cargo of the tallowlike substance near Nehalem. The ship's crew, he related, became obnoxious to native women, paying for their indiscretions with their lives.[36] One story surviving generations of telling has it that Japanese crewmen of a beeswax ship were drowned along the coast.[37] Tillamook Indians told of a similar ship wrecked off their coasts, possibly the one leaving La Paz, Baja

29

California, on June 16, 1769, with supplies for a Roman Catholic mission at San Diego, Alta California, but never heard of again.[38]

Clatsop Beach near Point Adams became the graveyard of still another off-course ship of Spain—of her Oriental fleet,* carrying beeswax and bric-a-brac—but not much more is known of her.[39] Like bones from ancient burials, wax washed up on Clatsop Beach until the twentieth century. The discovery of tons of it at different beach spots has raised speculation whether a single ship could have carried so large a cargo. Yet no matter how many carriers there had been or what had happened to them and their crews, proof that these foreign craft had indeed wrecked on the Oregon coast remains in records written in wax on the Oregon sands.

Since the wax resembled ozocerite, a wax of mineral origin, white men took samples of it to various universities and the Smithsonian Institution to discover that it was most likely beeswax.† Giving further credibility to this conclusion was the fact that the substance would have been an important part of the paraphernalia of Spanish priests in the Orient

* In his *Pioneer Days of Oregon History*, I, 169, S. A. Clarke writes that one vessel wrecked off the coast may have been under Chinese sail. The ship has also been said to have been Japanese. William S. Lewis and Naojiro Murakami, (eds.), *Ranald MacDonald: The Narrative of His Early Life on the Columbia under the Hudson's Bay Company's Regime; of His Experiences in the Pacific Whale Fishery; and of His Great Adventure to Japan; with a Sketch of His Later Life on the Western Frontier, 1824–1894*, 122n. This being the case, these wrecked seamen, as Orientals, could not have been confused with wrecked crews of bearded men, since Orientals, for the most part, were beardless. In his *Tribes of Western Washington and Northwestern Oregon*, 238, Gibbs states: "The vessel [carrying wax] was probably a Japanese junk, several of which have from time to time been cast away on the coast. It is noticeable that many of the Tilamuk [Tillamooks immediately south of the Clatsops] differ in personal appearance from their neighbors to this day, so as easily to be recognized by those acquainted with the peculiarity. Their complexion is yellower than ordinary, and their eyes more oblique and elongated." Some sources locate the wrecking of the beeswax ship at Point Adams (Clatsop Beach). Hubert Howe Bancroft, *History of the Northwest Coast*, Vol. II. Vol. XXVIII of *The Works of Hubert Howe Bancroft*, 532n.; James G. Swan, *The Northwest Coast; or, Three Years' Residence in Washington Territory*, 206; *Report of the Superintendent of the Coast Survey Showing the Progress of the Survey during the Year 1858*, Senate Exec. Doc. No. 14, 35 Cong., 2 sess., 1859, 387. One writer reports traditions of a Spanish ship laden with beeswax on a trip from China wrecking off the northern shore of the mouth of the Columbia River. E. W. Wright (ed.), *Lewis & Dryden's Marine History of the Pacific Northwest*, 2. That a portion of the wax had been shipped in the form of candles is seen in the story of a native woman who said she found long tapers with "rope" (the wick) still intact. S. J. Cotton, *Stories of Nehalem*, 47, 50. Wax tapers have been found with tiny passages through them which may have been left by rotted wicks.

† Fairly recent microscopic studies have found pollen and bee stingers in the material, thus confirming it to be wax. Carbon-14 studies date its origin to fewer than three hundred years ago. "The Oregon Beeswax Mystery," *Shell News*, XXIX, 12 (1961), 20–21.

and the New World. But instead of complementing religious services and comforting the faithful, it came to rest on the beaches of Oregon, whose natives had no idea what it was. The mercantilist Chinooks and Clatsops no doubt tried to trade it to other natives, who would have found no use for it either. They would later try to sell it to whites, but most of them, too, would have little use for it. The natives would have more success selling salvaged goods such as Oriental pottery (from such sources as wrecked Japanese junks) to white men who had more use for it.

If beeswax and pottery were of little utilitarian value to Chinooks and Clatsops, there were to them more practical things from breached ships. According to Clatsop stories, they took iron, brass, copper,[40] nails, and coins with square holes in them from the ships. Clatsops were represented as having become rich and powerful by trading beachcombed treasures. Because of their oceanside location, they would for years enjoy the privilege of claiming what the ocean yielded—an advantage Chinooks living on the ocean side of the peninsula would also share— moreso than would their fellows along the river inside the bar.

The deceptiveness of the Columbia River estuary, because of often heavy mists and its shoreline appearance, helped prevent ships at sea from detecting there a river mouth. And when one was detected, the vastness of the bar discouraged entry. Returning southerly to San Blas from travels as far north as latitude 58°, where he had gone to check reports of Russians, as had Juan Perez the year before, the Spanish explorer Bruno de Hezeta (Heceta), at about 6:00 P.M. of August 17, 1775, in the flagship *Santiago*, discovered at about north latitude 46°16′ the entrance to a river. He made the following entry in his journal under that date:

This afternoon I discovered a great bay which was given the name "Asuncion," the outlines of which are on the sketch which is going to be inserted in this diary, its latitude and amplitude subject to the most exact demarcation which the theory and practice of that career permits.

The latitudes of the most prominent capes of said bay, especially that to the North, are calculated by the observations of this day.

Being already past six of the afternoon and the Frigate situated almost between the two capes, and in a sounding of 24 fathoms, the swirl and turbulence of the current was so great that even with force of sail it was laborious keeping off the cape to the North, the current having an inclination to the North or East depending on the flux of the tide.

These currents and the roughness of the water lead me to believe it may be the mouth of some great river or pass to some other sea.

If the latitude in which the Bay is situated were not defined by the observations of the day I would believe without difficulty that this was the pass discovered by Juan de Fuca in the year 1692, which charts locate between 48° and 47° latitude but which I am without doubt will not be found there, having reconnoitered the area in the center of these latitudes the 14th day of July and examining several times these surroundings.

The great difference in the location of this Bay and the pass discovered by Juan de Fuca is lessened as is the doubt that they are the same inasmuch as I have observed there is equal variance or better in the latitudes of capes and ports of this coast and in all cases the assigned latitude is greater than their true location.

The not entering and exploring in the port came as a result of having consulted the opinions of the second Captain, Don Juan Perez, and Pilot Don Manuel Revilla who insisted that we ought not execute same since dropping the anchor we might not have people with which to retrieve it because of the toil involved. For these reasons and for having to look into the matter of anchorage, it was necessary to put out the launch manned by fourteen individuals of the crew at least and without these I could not commit myself, and noting at the same time it was late I resolved to tack to the outside and finding myself at some three or four leagues distance anchored. Experienced this night strong currents to the S.W. which negated my intent to explore in this bay the morning of the day following.

Which also makes me think that on the ebb a great quantity of water flowed out of the Bay.

The two capes cited on the map as San Roque and Frondoso run at an angle of 10° of the third quadrant, both are craggy, of colored earth with little elevation.[41]

Hezeta's resolve to put out to sea and return to Mexico put off again what might have been for the Chinooks and Clatsops a direct confrontation with Europeans.[42] Such a meeting might have proven unfriendly because of events of the previous month, when natives north of the Columbia (which the Spanish would call La Entrada de Hezeta) had brought skins to trade the Spanish.[43] In the *Santiago*, anchored in a shallow bay under Point Grenville at north latitude 47°20', Hezeta on July 14 made intent and extent of the act of possessing the land for Spain. At the same time, second in command Juan Francisco de Bodega y Quadra, anchored in the schooner *Sonora*, sent a crew ashore for fresh water from the Quinault River. The men were killed by natives. As the Indians attempted to surround the *Sonora*, her guns were fired into a canoe, killing six of the attackers. Stories of such encounters, carried to both whites and natives along the coast, would create a legacy of suspicion, clouding meetings of the two races with mutual fear for years to come.

Before attacking the crew from the *Sonora*, the natives had appeared

"eager to trade, especially for articles of iron."[44] Chinooks and Clatsops were aware of iron long before this time, perhaps even before their experiences with wrecked ships, having obtained the metal through channels of trade.* Nails, spikes, and iron from casks had washed up on wrecks and pieces of driftwood along the western Pacific for a long time.[45] As early as the sixteenth century a coastal California native had a knife made from a spike found in driftwood.[46] Far to the north driftwood floating westerly from the Orient washed up on beaches of the Aleutian Islands and the Alaskan mainland. In the first half of the eighteenth century travelers to those places from Russia[47] reported finding metal knives and iron-pointed weapons which natives had fabricated from iron washed ashore.† In their colony established on Kodiak Island, the Russians, who had developed a reputation for cruelty, in lieu of oxen were requiring the natives to pull plows.[48] Had these plows been of iron, their work would indeed have been burdensome. When British fur traders came to the lower Columbia, they found its natives with Russian coins which might have worked their way, through trade, down to that place.[49]

From Alaska iron may well have been traded southerly to tribes which traded it or fabricated it into weapons for hunting and killing.‡

* The Washington State University Department of Anthropology excavated, beginning in 1970, the first of six frame houses at Point Alava on the Washington coast. Many wooden and woven articles used by Ozette peoples, a branch of the Makahs, were found well preserved. Dr. Richard Daugherty, Professor of Anthropology in the university, wrote to the authors on April 17, 1972: "We now have six hafted tools with badly rusted iron blades from the first of six buried houses we are excavating at Ozette. These objects are definitely pre-contact in time . . . they date from somewhere between 500 and 300 years ago."

† In 1741 the *Saint Peter* and the *Saint Paul*, commanded by Vitus Bering and Alexei Chirikov, sailed from Kamchatka. Chirikov sighted the American coast on July 15, 1741, at about north latitude 57°, but loss of his small boats forced him to return to his home port. In the meantime, Bering sighted the coast on July 16 but was forced to winter on Bering Island, where he and many of his crew died. The survivors returned with sea otter furs, and within a decade Siberian traders, the *promyshleniki*, were voyaging yearly to the Aleutian Islands, collecting many furs.

It was Georg Wilhelm Steller (Stoeller), a German naturalist with Bering and Chirikov, who reported finding Alaskan natives in 1741 with arrows fashioned by iron tools and a whetstone on which copper instruments had been sharpened. William Coxe, *Account of the Russian Discoveries between Asia and America, to Which are Added, the Conquest of Siberia, and the History of the Transactions and Commerce between Russia and China*, 31, 33. In 1763 Aleuts stripped all the iron from a captured Russian ship. Two years later natives used lances made from the iron to attack other Russians. T. A. Rickard, "Drift Iron, a Fortuitous Factor in Primitive Culture," *The Geographical Review*, XXIV, 4 (October, 1934), 542–43.

‡ Chinooks also treasured copper. Pieces of it, probably coming through trade from Alaska, were found in their burials before 1800. Mildred Colbert, *Kutkos Chinook Tyee*,

As effective as these tools were, they could not match another Russian import in their swiftness to kill. Some time around 1750 disease spread from "far to the north," where it had been borne by a wrecked ship reported to have previously acquired the contagion in a Chinese port. The plague moved rapidly to the south, trapping susceptible natives in its death swath and wiping out nearly three-quarters of a village at the mouth of the Columbia River near present-day Ilwaco. To prevent its further ravages, Chinook survivors put their lodges, clothing, and other effects to the torch, a practice which some of them would continue until the late nineteenth century.[50] The once proud and powerful villagers, the scourge of natives in all quarters, now stood scourged themselves and in fear that the Great Spirit would return to vent the rest of his wrath on them.

This would not be the last Lower Chinook exposure to imported disease. Striking them as it had natives as far east as the Missouri River, where it had been introduced by white traders, the smallpox moved up that river to reach the Columbia sometime about 1782–83, or nearly a quarter of a century before white men would follow its lethal path to the Pacific.[51] As natives succumbed to its ravages, the British blamed it on American traders, the Americans blamed it on the French, and the French in turn, on the Spanish.[52]

In 1774 the Spanish explorer Juan Perez, visiting Nootka Sound on Vancouver Island,* with whose natives the Chinooks, as noted above, had established trade, found the people of Nootka with a few iron articles such as arrow tips and knives,[53] of which they could not get enough.[54] The year after Perez' visit, Nootka natives expressed their iron hunger by putting their hands to the rudder irons of a Spanish ship.[55] They appeared to have cared little for beads and trinkets,[56] developing a liking for such ornaments later, apparently after their wish for iron had been satisfied.

Spanish coins dated 1777 and 1779, found in a burial near Willapa Bay, may have come to that place through half a dozen trade channels,[57] as may have Spanish crucifixes found among Chinooks in the early nineteenth century.[58] The British explorer Captain James Cook, reaching Nootka Sound in 1778, was surprised to see natives with iron and imported beads. It was believed that the iron had come overland to the

---

224. One source of native copper was raw copper found on the Copper River in Alaska. From it, natives in that north country made knives, swords, whistles, rattles, and ornamental breastplates. Frederic W. Howay, "William Sturgis: The Northwest Fur Trade," *British Columbia Historical Quarterly*, VIII, 1 (January, 1944).

* The Spanish named the sound San Lorenzo Bay. The English then called it King George Sound. It was American fur traders who later named it Nootka Sound.

Pacific.*[59] A decade later the Britisher John Meares found among the Nootka natives forged tools for hollowing out trees.[60]

Iron fragments, believed to have been protohistoric (ca. 1750), were found in cremation pits at the confluence of the Deschutes and Columbia rivers near the Dalles.[61] At the confluence of the Willamette and Columbia rivers Upper Chinooks of Sauvies Island before 1792 had an iron dagger believed to have come from an easterly direction.[62] By 1785 Nootka natives cared less for iron products such as knives, chisels, swords, and the like,[63] than they did for beads and muskets. Yet in 1792 American traders in Grays (Bulfinch's) Harbor on the Washington coast gave blankets and iron for furs.[64] By 1793 Chinooks and Clatsops, like their northern neighbors, cared less for iron to the extent that it was difficult for ships' crews to sell it.[65] The adeptness of these two peoples for trade had gained them enough iron from other tribes to satisfy their needs. Moreover, relying on goods of their own manufacture and not being engaged in making large canoes, for which iron tools were advantageous, the Chinooks had less need for that material.

In trading iron, beads, muskets, and other goods, white men were finding skins of the sea otter to be a valuable trade item for the Chinese market. When pieced together, the skins enrobed wealthy mandarins, whose ladies wore them as capes, belts, and sashes draped with pearls. The Chinese used pieces of otter fur in trimming caps and mittens and for bordering exquisite gowns for their wealthy.

A fully grown sea otter, powerful and mobile with its slightly webbed feet and flat tail and reaching up to five feet in length and one and one-half in width, provided a skin stretching out considerably larger than

---

* Samuel Hearne of the Hudson's Bay Company, exploring from 1768 to 1772 overland from the American east coast and searching for the Strait of Anian, in 1771 found Arctic Eskimos with small bits of iron and beads of a type not sold by his company. He surmised that natives on the Coppermine River (in the north central Mackenzie District of the Northwest Territories of Canada) had contacts with Danish sailors on Davis Strait, located between southwest Greenland and East Baffin Island and connecting Baffin Island with the Atlantic. Gordon Speck, *Samuel Hearne and the Northwest Passage*, 210. Alexander Mackenzie of the North West Company, traveling north in 1789 on the Canadian river bearing his name, found at first only ornaments and wooden, horn, and bone utensils among the natives, but further toward the Arctic Ocean he found iron objects, indicating that they had come from the north. Further downstream he obtained iron knives from Arctic natives who had gotten them some ten years earlier from whites. T. H. McDonald (ed.), *Exploring the Northwest Territory*, 16–18. In 1793 near the headwaters of the Parsnip River in Canada Mackenzie found natives who had not seen whites but who had white-produced iron weapon points which they had obtained from people eleven days to the west. The latter in turn had gotten the points from others still further west on the coast, where the weapons were brought by whites. Walter Sheppe (ed.), *First Man West: Alexander Mackenzie's Journal of His Voyage to the Pacific Coast of Canada in 1793*, 118.

the live animal itself. These prime beasts, with their pups and old ones, lived in communities from Alta California shores north to those of Grays Harbor and Point Grenville and further north to coastal islands and mainlands of Canada and Alaska.*

Perhaps no single commodity brought the Chinooks and Clatsops more into early contact with white men and their goods (albeit often indirectly) than did this furry Pacific mammal, although these people seldom hunted it. Had the coast near their homelands better supported the sea otter, the Chinook people might have been hunters. Apparently their country lacked the conditions needed to support sizable colonies of these animals, since there was no protection from heavy storms and no adequate kelp-bed feeding grounds along the rocks which otter depended upon to supply the large quantities of shellfish needed to fill their stomachs. Occasionally natives at the mouth of the Columbia hunted the sea otter with spears and two-pointed gigs, the same weapon used in taking river otter and beaver. Not noted for their otter-hunting prowess, Chinooks especially were content to leave much of that activity to others, applying their skill and energy instead to trade with northern coastal tribes and to securing items those peoples in turn had gotten from ships. Like Chinese mandarins, Chinook royalty often garbed itself in rich furs of the sea otter, but more practically it used them as items of the slave trade. To help balance trade in the fur market, Chinooks levied on their suppliers tribute in the form of hunting, fishing, trapping, and clam digging privileges in Chinook territory.[66]

Since the early eighteenth century the Spanish had known of sea otter bands off the California coast, and by trading various items to California natives they had encouraged the Indians to procure the animals' fur, which was especially rich and brown in that region. But California natives were less interested in fur hunting than were their brothers in northern climes. The Spanish, too, seldom hunted the otter, a task they considered too arduous. Thus, those animals were not vigorously pursued there until the beginning of the nineteenth century, when Russians and natives would come south from Alaska to hunt them. The Spaniards' Russian rivals, having discovered sea otter on the Kamchatka coast at the end of the seventeenth century, were well aware of the value of their skins.† Well should they have prized the skins of those northern regions,

---

*Skins from otters (*Enhydra lutris lutris*) in the north are superior to those skins of otters off the California coast (*Enhydra lutris nereis*).

† Primitive Ainu peoples of Japan hunted sea otters on Hokkaido a century before this. Later, the Ainus migrated to the Kurile Islands to hunt with bows, arrows, and clubs. Russians, invading those islands in 1711 before their American explorations, collided with the Ainus some time around 1765. T. A. Rickard, "The Sea-Otter in History," *British Columbia Historical Quarterly*, XI, 1 (January, 1947), 19.

for every inch of a full-grown animal's jet black three-quarter-inch fur, shimmering silver-tinged when rippled, was as useful as it was beautiful. In fact, the French explorer Jean de La Pérouse found it too beautiful for words. "The sea-otter," he wrote, "is an amphibious animal, better known for the beauty of its skin, than by any accurate description."[67]

Bering's discoveries for Russia served to enhance that nation's interest in Alaska. Two years after his discoveries the *promyshleniki* (mountain men and many former criminals) began voyaging to the new land in crude ships to strip the valuable beasts from the rocky shorelines. When cornered, the furry prey darted swiftly about, attempting to escape the hunters' blows, their powerful flipper-like limbs carrying them rapidly across their rookeries but not fast enough to escape capture.*[68] Initially uninterested in fur trade, the Russian government would later authorize mercantile ventures in Alaska.

Captain Cook stumbled on the furry treasure in a corner of the vast Pacific when after his third journey to the Northwest Coast some skins he had purchased for a pittance sold for $120 apiece in China. Many accounts of his exploits excited Britains and Americans in the possibilities of the trade in pelts, which, exuberated Cook, were "softer and finer than that of any other we know of."[69] The year following publication of his narrative, his fellow countryman James Hanna arrived in Nootka Sound to trade in earnest.[70] His skins averaged $37 apiece in China, but along with one James Strange he sold others there at more than double that figure.[71] During the next decade the British were out on the coast in numbers, and during this time Nootka Sound, along with other spots on Vancouver Island such as Clayoquot Sound, became a trade center. The *Harmon*, fitted out by Britishers in China, was dispatched by other British merchants in China and India.

Another Britisher lured to the Northwest Coast by furs for the China trade was Charles W. Barkley, whose countrymen, becoming more expansive in their quest for pelts, began searches south of Nootka, bringing them closer to the mouth of the Columbia River and its people. Sailing the *Imperial Eagle*, Barkley is credited with the 1787 discovery of the Strait of Juan de Fuca, which separates Vancouver Island from the mainland, the Olympic Peninsula to the south in present-day Washing-

---

* The sea otter often floats on its back with its forepaws folded on its breast. The fore and hind limbs differ; the former are very short and thick, with naked, black, granulated palms and toes closely connected in arched claws. The hind legs are longer and flipperlike, and the toes are webbed by hair-covered membrances. On smooth ground the otter moves rapidly, but on rocks it is slow. Its tail is flat, about a foot or less in length, and stiff, serving as a rudder in the water. The adult measures from four to five feet from nose to tip of tail, weighing up to eighty pounds. Its head is short and blunt, and its neck is thick. It has short white whiskers.

ton. He sent a landing party ashore at north latitude 47°43' on the Washington coast near a small river.*[72] Quinault Indians invited the party to trade and then killed them (a Quinault chief would later accuse neighboring Quillayutes of the deed),[73] hacking their flesh to pieces and distributing it to various peoples of the country. Offered the grisly trade items, the Chinooks refused them,[74] accepting instead only clothing and, in curiosity, arms and some of the victims' hair.[75]

In the following year, 1788, Meares, unlicensed in order to escape paying a fee to the British East India Company to trade in Chinese waters,† sailed under British and Portuguese colors with a map prepared by Spaniards that showed Hezeta's (the Columbia) river. In searching the Northwest Coast for that stream Meares was possibly the first white trader to deal directly with Chinooks—of the Willapa Bay area—when on Saturday, July 5, he entered that long arm of the sea which he named Shoalwater Bay, the name white men would call it as well as the name Willapa.[76] Then a canoe approached carrying a man and boy holding up two otter skins. Since they refused to board the ship, "trifling articles"[77] tied to a cord were lowered to them over the side. The lad instantly seized the articles and delivered them to the man, who quickly tied the two skins to the cord for the crew to recover. Soon, observed Meares, "their curiosity . . . entirely transferred to the ship, and their eyes ran over every part of it with a most rapid transition, while their actions expressed such extreme admiration and astonishment, as gave us every reason to conclude that this was the first time they had ever been gratified with the sight of such an object."[78] Meares had no way of knowing this for sure, as the two had not understood the language of Nootka Sound in which he addressed them. Yet he noted that the way they held up the skins and the manner in which they later conducted themselves proved that they had some notion of trade, indicating to him that natives who had contacted whites had communicated to their fellows word of the fur-seeking white men.

Meares sailed out of the bay and southerly along the coast looking for the river located by Hezeta, concluding that "there is no such river as that of Saint Roc exists, as laid down in the Spanish charts."[79] He

* The river Ohahlat (the Hoh?) was first named Destruction River, but later that name was transferred to the island just south of the river mouth. The Spanish had named the island Isla de Delores.

† The British trade in China was controlled by the East India Company, which was given exclusive rights to trade in the Orient. In effect, oriental ports were closed to British ships not licensed by the company. This forced some British ships to sail under foreign flags. Another British company with a charter giving them exclusive rights to trade in the Pacific was the South Sea Company. With such monopolies Britons shut out some of their countrymen wishing to trade. Rickard, "Sea-Otter in History," 30.

did not miss the high promontory guarding the river entrance, naming it Cape Disappointment, a fitting designation, for it not only symbolized his own disappointment at not finding the river, but that of others who would find that the treachery of the bar had robbed them entry to the stream. Some white men would forfeit their lives in attempting to negotiate the bar.[80]

But the cape, frowning down on those oblivious to the bar and river at its base, or on those failing to breach this barrier to enter the vast Columbia interior, would eventually yield to the seekers. These restless ones, ever expanding their searches for lands and treasure and driven by mercantile and national pressures, would soon open the door. Once inside, they would find Chinook and Clatsop natives at either side of the entrance. Until then, the mighty Columbia River would pour three more floods to the sea; the white men would seek and the natives would wait.

3. White Sails on the Oregon

> This River in my opinion, wou'd be a fine
> place for to sett up a *Factory*. The Indians
> are very numerous, and appear'd very civil
> (not even offering to steal).
>
> John Boit's "Journal of a Voyage
> Round the Globe"

THE SHORES OF Bakers Bay, silent in winter, now pulsed with the spring excitement of Chinook and Clatsop natives returned from winter villages. Their return, like that of leaves to trees once winter-gaunt among the evergreens flanking the bay and splashing their verdure up the Columbia River, or like salmon returning to that stream, was their measure of time in the rhythmical clock of nature. As the sun climbed in the heavens shortly before noon of May 11, 1792, in the white man's measure of time, the natives looked up to see a vessel riding in across the bar.* Aboard the 212-ton two-decker ship *Columbia Rediviva*, so intent was the American Captain Robert Gray in guiding his ship behind a boat sent ahead to seek a channel to enter the river that he perhaps took little note of the panoramic river and woodland before him, sight of which was nature's reward to those who passed her severe test at the bar. At best, to Gray such things would have been extraneous to his world of pelts and profits, for he was a fur trader.

At sight of the sails the natives interrupted the sounds of their occupations with sounds of alarm. There was much talk now of flight to the hills to hide from the invader. To those unfamiliar with such craft it loomed like a floating island or an "overgrown monster come to devour them."[1] It even alarmed those who were aware of such things, for along a

---

* It is reported that one crewman on the *Columbia*, sent ahead to sound the Columbia River, went ashore, became lost, was captured by natives, and lived on the Willamette River with a native woman until he escaped south two years later. *Weekly Oregonian*, March 17, 1893.

native grapevine strung from Tlingit villages on the north to those of Tillamooks to the south word would have passed of the big canoes and their barking guns that bit, sometimes mortally, other natives along the coast. Earlier that year, before sailing to the Columbia River from Vancouver Island near Adventure Cove, where he had wintered, Captain Gray had ordered the destruction of a native village containing nearly two hundred houses of priceless carved images. Of this mercantile-inspired iconoclasm John Boit, fifth mate of the *Columbia*, wrote: "This fine Village, the work of ages, was in a short time totally destroyed."[2] Sailing down the coast on the *Columbia* toward the river that would bear the name of that ship, Gray's disposition improved but little. On May 7 he had apprehensively put his ship into a harbor he named "Bulfinch's" but which would one day bear his own name. Boit described what happened next: "Vast many canoes came off, full of Indians. They appear'd to be a savage sett and was well arm'd, every man having his Quiver and Bow slung over his shoulder."[3]

That same day, from canoes alongside the ship, natives had sold many furs to Gray.* The following day they had come off again trading more furs for "blankets,"[4] possibly coarse cloth, as Gray was known to have carried no blankets. Years later an old chief, Kaukauan, at Chehalis Point informed George Gibbs that he had seen Captain Gray, possibly at this time, and from him had purchased axes and knives, the first he had seen, as well as a musket and some cartridges from which Gray had cut the balls. Ignorant of the use of the firearm, the chief and his men assumed that it was for making a big noise, firing it until their powder was gone and then smashing it to pieces.[5]

That night (May 8) "hooting" sounds from excited natives drifted over the harbor to the *Columbia*, sending her nervous crew to its guns. When several canoes passed the ship in the moonlight, fire from the crew's muskets blazed over the heads of the natives in their craft, and then fire from her mounted guns into a canoe splintered it and sent some of its occupants to a watery grave. As such incidents did not long deter the natives' routine, resident and visiting red men paddled out to the ship the next day to peddle their furs. Chinooks believed to have been at Grays Harbor brought an unpleasant report to the Columbia River of events at that place. Some of them were on shore as gray moved toward an anchorage in Bakers Bay.[6]

Putting it mildly, Gray had not endeared himself to his red customers. From Boston on October 1, 1787, under special papers of the Conti-

* Gray had learned from a previous trip to the Northwest Coast that it was impossible to pawn anything off on natives after they declined purchasing from his cargo of trade items, consisting of Jew's harps, snuff bottles, and rat traps.

nental Congress,[7] he had sailed to the Northwest Coast on the ninety-ton sloop *Lady Washington* in company with Captain John Kendrick in *Columbia Rediviva*.* Before sailing from the coast to China on July 30, 1789, Kendrick had ordered him to take command of the *Columbia*[8] to carry their fur harvest to that Oriental market.† Intrigued by troubles between the British and the Spanish at Nootka, Kendrick had remained on the coast in the *Lady Washington*. American promoters of the enterprise, caught up in their country's post–Revolutionary War expansion and freed of the restrictions of the British East India Company monopoly in the China trade, had for the venture great hopes which outdistanced their knowledge of it, for the ships had sailed from Boston poorly supplied for the trade.[9] The promoters hoped to make the Northwest Coast a vertex of sorts in a triangular trade from Boston to China and return.‡ This vertex would provide furs, the major in-

* One Simon Metcalfe is thought to have been the first American to have undertaken to sail to the Northwest Coast in search of furs. Little is known of his journey. If he had sponsors, they are now unknown. Frederic W. Howay, "Indian Attacks upon Maritime Traders of the North-West Coast, 1785–1805," *The Canadian Historical Review*, VI, 4 (December, 1925), 298.

† Gray arrived back in Boston on August 9, 1790. The *Columbia* was the first American vessel to circumnavigate the earth. The reception Gray received was a federal salute of thirteen guns and huzzas from citizens assembled at various wharves on the waterfront. He was given a reception by Governor Hancock. This was a much greater attention paid him than that on his return from the Northwest Coast to Boston (via China) a second time after making a discovery far more important to the United States.

‡ Possibilities of the China trade were evident when an American, Samuel Shaw in the *Empress of China*, reached Whampoa, anchorage for Canton on August 28, 1784. Howard Corning, "Augustine Heard and the China Trade in the 1830's," *Essex Institute Historical Collections*, LXXX (1944), 270. Next to enter Canton was the *Grand Turk*, owned by Elias Hasket Derby, who returned to Salem, Massachusetts in 1787. Henry Lee, "The Magee Family and the Origins of the China Trade," *Proceedings of the Massachusetts Historical Society*, LXXXI (1969), 105, 106. Before 1787 Britain, France, and Holland had dominated western commerce to the Far East. Of fifteen American vessels visiting China between 1788 and 1791, all had gone there directly except Gray. Items carried were sparse amounts of specie, beef, flour, iron, wine, butter, candles, and ginseng. Chinese goods shipped to New England were tea, satins, sinshaws, sarsenets, lustrings, crapes, levantines (Asian cotton), pongees, and nankeens. Umbrellas with whalebone or bamboo sticks were also shipped, as were fans, tortoiseshell and ivory combs, marble dog figurines, paper hangings, glass paintings (including those of President Washington, other American notables, and scenery), artificial flowers, bamboo writing desks and washstands, rattan chair bottoms, hinges, candlesticks, dice, snuffboxes, mugs, tea trays, shawls, men's and boys' straw hats, women's satin shoes, silk shoestrings, shawls, asafetida, camphor, and, of course, chinaware. Homeward bound cargoes also included pepper (first imported in 1797) from Sumatra; silks purchased in India; coffee from Arabia; spice from Batavia; gumcopal, a resinous substance from tropical trees used in making varnishes, lacquers, and linoleum, from Zanzibar; and European products. D. Hamilton Hurd (ed.), *History of Essex County, Massachusetts, with*

gredient in exchange for Chinese goods, since American production otherwise could only partially supply the needs of the Oriental market.[10]

International rivalries on the Northwest Coast had caused officials to caution Gray and Kendrick to avoid the Spanish, who were then seeking American favor in their dispute with Britain over claims to the region. Tensions from this conflict, actually as old as English swashbuckling sailors and Spanish conquistadores, and intensified by renewed Euro-American maritime activity on the coast, were felt in London and Madrid as well as in Nootka Sound, the trader-explorer "capital" of the Northwest Coast. But scarcely had Gray and Kendrick reached this region than they realized their conflict would be as much with its natives as with Europeans. In August, 1788, Gray, in the *Lady Washington*, had dropped anchor in (possibly) Tillamook Bay, where, after some trading, a native killed his black servant. The crew, ashore, scurried back to the ship, which sailed out of "Murderer's Harbor" with a changing tide and on to Nootka. Reaching China after his July, 1789, departure from the Northwest Coast, he had sold 1,050 furs from both ships for $21,404.71 or about $21.00 apiece—not a particularly good price. Returning home with teakwood, his was the first ship to fly the American flag around the globe.*

Now, after all these events had taken him from one end of the earth to the other, Gray was on the Columbia River to begin another mercantile venture, which he hoped would bring more profits in the China market than before, and especially more than to his British rivals, whom he and his promoters feared would glut that Oriental trade center unless they got there first.[11] Very possibly he hoped, too, that in the virgin Columbia River Valley he might experience better relations with natives than he had with those north along the coast, where he had fallen from their favor just as his goods had fallen from their market. When first on the coast, he had once purchased two hundred sea otter pelts for a chisel apiece, but recently he had seldom purchased a skin for less than six to ten of the tools. A skin now cost him roughly a "blanket"; four skins, a pistol; and six, a musket.[12] Generally, the price now paid for skins was about four times that paid at the beginning of the maritime trade. Long skilled in barter before dealing with whites, natives easily detected the white men's wish to acquire skins to satisfy the hungry

Biographical Sketches of Many of Its Pioneer and Prominent Men, I, 67; "Invoice of the Ship *Resource* [1803]," manuscript, Baker Library, Harvard University; "Account book of the ship Eliza, 1805, on voyage from New York to Canton," William Bell Papers, Constable-Pierrepont Papers.

* After subtracting the expenses of the first voyage of the *Columbia*, its owners discovered its journey to have been a financial failure. Samuel Eliot Morison, *The Maritime History of Massachusetts, 1783–1860*, 66.

Chinese market. By contrast, their own demand for iron and other products carried in the ships had declined on the coast. Had the whites been dealing with less affluent peoples, it might have been a different story. Understanding the workings of the marketplace as well as any white economist or trader, the natives had raised their prices to help create what white men believed was an unfavorable balance of trade.

As tensions at the marketplace had sometimes been resolved with muskets, Gray's promoters had urged both friendship and firmness in dealing with natives. One of these promoters, Joseph Barrell, had written Gray on September 25, 1790: "It is of importance, and we therefore enjoin it, upon you, that the most, friendly intercourse be observed in all your traffick with the Natives and no unjust, advantage taken of them in trade, but endeavour by your honourable conduct, to impress them with a respect for Americans."[13] On the Northwest Coast, far from his promoters, Gray had interpreted the injunction quite liberally, having learned on a crude coast instead of in a cultured countinghouse how to do business which often called for a show of arms. Consequently, on the Columbia he was now extremely observant of the presence or absence of such arms among his hoped-for native clientele. Boit was certain that natives of Grays Harbor had never before seen guns, but possibly some of them had in contacts with Vancouver Island natives, who used firearms for hunting.[14] One influential Nootka chief, Maquinna, had garnered a considerable arsenal, and his braves had all but abandoned their traditional weapons. Head chief of Clayoquot Sound Wickananish (Wincomish) had guns for his four hundred men and ammunition to fire in them.*[15] Muskets which had brought six or seven otter skins at the island were now going for one or two;† but without assurance of obtaining ammunition, natives would trade no skins at all.[16] Makahs at Cape Flattery undoubtedly understood the use of guns, seeking them in trade from British explorer Captain George Vancouver on the coast in 1792.[17] As noted above, some natives at Grays Harbor, including the Chehalis who often came there, had possibly never seen guns before. Neither had the natives of Puget Sound. A quarter of a century later the Chehalis, who traded with Chinooks and Clatsops, would be well supplied with firearms, while for many years natives of

* Natives of Clayoquot Sound on Vancouver Island were sufficiently sophisticated in the use of the new firearms to induce a turncoat on Gray's crew in 1791 to wet the priming apparatus of the crew's guns. The plot was discovered. Howay, "Indian Attacks upon Maritime Traders of the North-West Coast," 294.

† In 1806 only the best muskets would sell to the natives. Brass blunderbusses sold well. Pistols did not sell. One merchant noted that "Powder in 25 lbs Kegs will ever be saleable." William Sturgis to John Dorr, October (n.d.), 1806, in Ebenezer Dorr, "Collection of letters ship documents and receipts, 1795–1820," manuscript, Archives of British Columbia.

the sound would have but few. As late as 1808 in their homeland, Quinaults, apparently without firearms, would hurl spears and stones at Russians armed with muskets.[18]

Prevalence of guns on upper Vancouver Island indicated that white traders had visited that area at an earlier time; paucity of guns in the south indicated that northern natives followed a strategy of withholding arms in trade to other peoples to achieve and maintain superiority over them. This strategy certainly was not new among American Indians. Once armed, the Blackfeet of the plains, for example, tried to prevent their neighbors from obtaining guns.[19] Having traded for few if any guns and ammunition, Chinooks would have found them of little immediate value, especially one without the other. Their inability to match the weapons of the *Columbia* may have increased their fear of the ship.

Once inside the bar, that ship moved upstream past natives lining the shore, with some following the strange craft. Twenty canoes filled with apparently benign natives paddled out to her as she moved to anchor at 1:00 P.M. one-half mile from the north shore, some three-quarters of a mile southeast of the village of Chinook chief Polack.[20] From canoes the next day, May 12,* natives watched the strangers fill casks with water, the same fresh water Gray had noted at north latitude 46°10′ en route to Nootka in late April, causing him at that time to suppose it to be the discharge of a river. At that time he had waited nine days for favorable conditions to cross the bar. As long as this wait was, it would not match that of some ships, which would stand off six to eight weeks awaiting favorable conditions for an entrance.† Wishing to wait no longer, Gray had pushed north. On April 29, in the vicinity of the Strait of Juan de Fuca, he had informed Vancouver of his discovery. Ironically, Vancouver had failed to detect the deceptive opening[21] to the

---

* Gray's and Boit's logs vary one day in the events described. Frederic W. Howay, *Voyages of the "Columbia" to the Northwest Coast, 1787–1790 and 1790 and 1793*, 397n. Dates of Gray's logs are used here.

† Many vessels waited to enter the river or to put out to sea over the bar. Many of those trying to enter gave up their wait and sailed off. But once inside, in order to escape the fury of the ocean, ships had to wait for ideal conditions to get out again. In 1847 the *Cadboro* waited inside the bar from November 17 to January 18 because of bad weather. Neil M. Howison, *Report of Lieut. Neil M. Howison, United States Navy, to the Commander of the Pacific Squadron; Being the Result of an Examination in the Year 1846 of the Coast, Harbors, Rivers, Soil, Productions, Climate, and Population of the Territory of Oregon, House Exec. Doc., Miscellaneous* No. 29, 30 Cong., 1 sess., 1848, 14. The *Beaver* was delayed thirty-five days in 1812 before being permitted by river and weather conditions to cross the bar. The *Columbia* (not Gray's vessel) in 1843 waited forty days; the *Isaac Todd* in 1814, forty-one days; the *William and Anne* in 1825, forty-two days; the *Nereide* and the *Llama* in 1837, fifty days. J. Neilson Barry, "Who Discovered the Columbia River?" *Oregon Historical Quarterly*, XXXIX (1938), 154 and n.

Columbia, which he had been commissioned to seek as entrance to a possible Northwest Passage.

Appearing friendly enough, the Chinooks evinced an axiom of Indian-white contact in the Pacific Northwest, if not in America at large—that the hostility of its people was in direct proportion to their frequency of contact with white men. Whether or not Gray and his men believed this proposition, Boit did make a simple observation: "The Indians are very numerous, and appear'd very civil (not even offering to steal)."[22] As traders, not scientists, Boit and his fellows were primarily interested in the natives' attitudes and behavior as they affected the trade. Land-based traders, living among the Chinooks and Clatsops at a later time, would have more time to describe and evaluate them than did sea traders, who made but fleeting contacts with them.

The appearance of these lower Columbia peoples, however, did not startle traders as it would other men who had no previous contact with Northwest Coastal peoples to cushion the shock of confrontation. Resembling other coastal natives, Chinooks and Clatsops would have warranted scant descriptions from these early merchants. Influenced perhaps by a lengthy absence from home, Boit .thought the Chinook daughters pretty and only slightly less in "a state of Nature" than the fine-looking, straight-limbed males, since the women wore "a leaf Apron ... [which] some of our gentlemen, that examin'd them [perhaps out of nonscientific curiosity] pretty close, and *near*, both *within* and *without*" reported them "not a leaf but a nice wove mat in resemblance!!"[23]

A description of Chinooks and Clatsops more complete than Boit's would have revealed the adults to be thick-set, averaging some five feet, five inches in height, with skin light to olive inclined to coppery. Their faces were broad; their eyes were small and slanted; and their noses were broad, flat at the tops and fleshy at the tips, with large nostrils and the septums perforated, as were their ears, for wearing ornaments such as dentalia, beads, and copper. Their mouths were wide and their lips thick. Their teeth were often irregular and dirty, and among the elderly they were often worn to the gums. Their legs were bowed,* a seeming contradiction to Boit's observation, leading some to speculate that they were the limbs of slaves.[24] Their thick ankles were said to have been caused by too much sitting and squatting, and those of women were usually swollen from tight bindings. The men plucked their beards. Chinook-Clatsop hair was coarse black, worn full length and smeared

---

* Silas B. Smith maintained that his mother's Clatsop people and the Chinooks were straight-limbed, and that the misshapen ones were slaves. "Primitive Customs and Religious Beliefs of the Indians of the Pacific Northwest Coast," *Oregon Historical Quarterly*, II (1901), 257–58.

with odoriferous fish oil, with which they also covered their bodies. They washed themselves, but they denied such lavation to their clothing, perhaps to protect it from deterioration. They tattooed their bodies, usually with pulverized charcoal dots pricked into their arms, legs, and cheeks.

To a stranger the most striking physical characteristic of these people was their flattened heads. The custom of flattening the heads of infants, said to have originated at the mouth of the Columbia,[25] extended northerly, where a flattened head was less esteemed than it was among the peoples of the lower Columbia.[26] Varying somewhat from village to village, the practice also extended southerly to the Tillamooks and easterly along the Columbia to Upper Chinookan peoples at the Dalles. Beyond there the practice was less common. A less severe type of head flattening was occasionally found among Cayuses[27] of eastern Oregon. Contrary to their name, the Flathead Indians on the western slopes of the Rocky Mountains did not flatten their heads.[28]

Chinooks and Clatsops considered a flattened head a "badge of aristocracy,"[29] a distinction denied slaves and their offspring. In fact, on raids these people did not enslave those with flattened heads. Awaiting the birth of her child, a mother was subject to a gamut of tabus dictating what she should or should not do, just as she had been subject to similar tabus in her menstrual cycles. Shortly after the birth of the child[30] the mother placed her infant on its back on a cradleboard (*tumchasas*) matching the child's height—wide at the head end, narrow at the foot. The board was padded with grass, skin, and fur,[31] and the upper end was sometimes scooped out to accommodate the child's head. To this board the mother fastened a narrow piece of skin along each side, with loopholes at short distances through which she laced cord ties over the child's body to confine it so that it and the board became one like a chrysalis in a cocoon. A trader among these people would observe that ". . . their Infants have their heads pressed more flatt I think than the Nootka people do theirs, and this in side view gives the head a most distorted appearance resembling an human face carved out of a Flatt piece of plank. . . ."[32]

This appearance was produced by two types of boards to achieve a straight line from the tip of the nose to the top of the head. One type consisted of a wooden extension lashed to the cradleboard by fibres through holes at its end. Tied at the ends and along the sides,[33] this extension served as a hinged flap to apply pressure against the child's head.[34] Pressure was kept constant by tightening the side ties from time to time. The other type of flattening device was an unhinged strip of padded board or bark (sometimes a band of animal skin was substituted) placed across the forehead and tied down at the sides.[35] Occasionally the mother placed a brace over the neck to keep the infant's chin from pressing its chest.[36] The average time the child was in this confinement was about one year.* Most observers noted that it was not removed from its board until the head flattening process was complete.†

A Chinook or Clatsop mother suspended her cradled baby from beams in her house, rocking it and breast feeding it by loosening the board and turning cradleboard and baby on the side without removing it.[37] When traveling, she placed branches around the top of the board to keep bushes from hitting the child's face. Of the flattening process one white man observed: ". . . multitudes of them die in this cruel process. A few survived. . . ."[38] It is more likely that the deaths were from some disease. In some dim past, in perfecting the technique, a mother, by applying too much pressure, may have unwittingly killed her offspring, but she and her sisters persisted until they perfected the process, for a well-flattened head seemed to have meant more to them than it did to their men. To the south, Siuslaw Indians in the mid-nineteenth century attempted to introduce the fashion among their people. Their ineptness in the process brought death to all of their chil-

---

* Accounts of the length of time an infant spent in a cradleboard vary greatly. From a few weeks to a year, wrote a mid-nineteenth-century ethnologist, Charles De Wolf Brownell. It is unlikely that a few weeks of head confinement would produce sufficient permanent moulding. *The Indian Races of North and South America,* 475. A surgeon with Captain Edward Belcher on the British ship *Sulphur,* Richard Brinsely Hinds, when that ship was at the mouth of the Columbia in 1839, states in his "Journal" (Kenneth L. Holmes Collection, Oregon Historical Society) that confinement lasted from five to ten months. The artist Paul Kane states that it was from eight to twelve months. *Wanderings of an Artist Among the Indians of North America, from Canada to Vancouver's Island and Oregon through the Hudson's Bay Company's Territory and Back Again, by Paul Kane,* 123. Two writers state the time was nearly a year. John Dunn, *History of the Oregon Territory, and British North-American Fur Trade, with an Account of the Habits and Customs of the Principal Native Tribes on the Northern Continent,* 129, and Abbé EM. Domenech, *Seven Years' Residence in the Great Deserts of North America,* II, 294. Gibbs says one year. *Tribes of Western Washington and Northwestern Oregon,* 211. A year or more says Zechariah Atwell Mudge in *Sketches of Mission Life among the Indians of Oregon,* 81. Eighteen months, says George Simpson. Frederick Merk (ed.), *Fur Trade and Empire: George Simpson's Journal,* 96. One writer says three years. Marguerite Eyer Wilbur (ed.), *Duflot de Mofras' Travels on the Pacific Coast,* II, 181. Another who tends to agree with the last estimate is A. N. Armstrong, who says the child was kept on the board until it was old enough to walk. *Oregon: Comprising a Brief History and Full Description of the Territories of Oregon and Washington,* 105.

† Zechariah Mudge, the clergyman, stated that the child was kept on the board from twelve to eighteen hours daily. *Sketches of Mission Life among the Indians of Oregon,* 80. Two sources say that the bandages were removed for cleansing. Bancroft, *Native Races,* Vol. I, *Wild Tribes,* 227; "Samoan and Chinook Head-Flattening," *Frank Leslie's Popular Monthly,* II, 4 (October, 1876), 448.

dren so treated, and when the malpractice continued, Siuslaw men killed three or four mothers.[39] When properly carried out, the process was neither painful nor damaging. Interested in cranial studies, white men would be intrigued by the effects of the practice on intelligence and personality. By contrast, early traders apparently took the practice for granted, learning from experience that Chinook and Clatsop intelligence had suffered none from it and that although their heads were flat, they were good at trading. Among the first to find this out were Captain Gray and his crew.

The two parties traded apparently without benefit of mutually intelligible language, for the natives appeared to have understood none of the jargon used in the North, where trade between the races limped along on a few words. Through sign language the crew could easily have expressed its need for food, which the natives satisfied by trading it roots and salmon, two of the latter going for a nail. Some sea otter skins the natives brought went for cloth and copper. For a sheet of the latter they gave four otter; beaver skins went for two spikes each, and land furs for one spike each. For Gray these prices were at a better exchange rate than he had found in the North, perhaps because he now had the advantage of the element of surprise among a people still hungry for goods. Aboard the *Columbia*, besides copper, cloth, and nails, Gray had a variety of articles to gladden the heart of an unspoiled aborigine—steel bars, spikes, thimbles, and buttons.

The hearts of the crewmen would have been gladdened had they been permitted to trade a little on their own, but in July, 1791, by written agreement with the ship's owners, they had been restricted from trading with natives for private gain. They had also been forbidden to give presents to officers and were encouraged to inform on their fellows for irregularities. A more favorable provision in the agreement had permitted them, on reaching Canton, China, to have three months' wages and the privilege of shipping home free any item purchased there.[40]

Word of the ship's arrival, spreading rapidly upriver from village to village, brought natives to the principal habitation, which white men named Chinook Village. To the ship they brought skins, including that of the land otter. Although valuable, it was less so than that of the marine otter, whose fur was softer, denser, longer, and darker. With a native gallery watching on May 14, the *Columbia*'s anchor was hoisted and she moved upstream. After sailing some twelve to fifteen miles, she grounded at 4:00 P.M. on a sandy bottom near present-day Harrington Point, the easterly entrance to Grays Bay.[41] Despite rainy weather the natives came alongside to trade that day and the next as word of the *Columbia*'s presence spread upriver, bringing people of that region down

49

to see and to trade. On the second day Gray dropped downriver seven or eight miles to better anchorage off Point Gray (near present-day Frankfort, Washington). In the afternoon he and a clerk, John Hoskins, went ashore, but natives kept their distance from them. On the sixteenth Gray twice dropped the *Columbia* downstream, anchoring for two days on the upper or lee side of Point Ellice, from which many natives canoed out to the ship. The next day, despite squally weather, many canoes came off to trade as crewmen painted, calked the pinnace, and applied tar to the ship's side. On the eighteenth Gray weighed anchor and made for the sea, but unfavorable winds prevented him from crossing the bar. However, choppy waves did not deter the Chinooks from paddling out to trade. Anchored off Chinook Point* on the nineteenth, Gray gave the name of his ship to the river, calling it "Columbia's."† He also named the north entrance to the river Cape Hancock, and the south entrance, Point Adams.[42] One source states that the American flag was raised, and coins were planted under a large pine tree, although no information extant confirms this contention.‡ Early on the twentieth,

---

* The military Fort Columbia was located in this area.

† In 1845 John Quincy Adams, in a letter to John Hay of the New York Historical Society, wrote in part concerning the name "United States of America": "Before the close of the Revolutionary War, the name of 'Columbia' was assumed by general consent, as significant of the whole Union, and has been familiarized to every mind by two popular and patriotic songs. . . . The same name was given in 1787 to the vessel commanded by Gray, by which the great river of the West was discovered, and received from him the same name, because it was the name of the ship, and because the ship was so named to represent the nation. The same name was also given by the Act of Congress which organized the District, ordained by the Constitution to be governed by the exclusive jurisdiction of the whole Union. . . ." *Proceedings of the Massachusetts Historical Society*, II (1835–55), 315n. Long before the Revolutionary War, Americans thought the country should be named after its discoverer, Christopher Columbus. The word *Columbia* was first used by Phillis Wheatley, a black slave, in a poem honoring George Washington. Other poems were written using the word. The name first appeared in law in 1784, when King's College in New York City became Columbia College.

‡ John Fiske, "Oration," in *Transactions of the Twentieth Annual Reunion of the Oregon Pioneer Association for 1892*, 81. Another author states that on May 19 the American flag was raised and coins were planted under a tree, "thus taking possession in the name of the United States." Edward G. Porter, "The Ship Columbia and the Discovery of Oregon," *The New England Magazine*, VI, 4 (June, 1892), 486. But the authors do not document their statement. It has been claimed that Boit also recorded in his log that Gray on May 17 took possession of the land. However, writes Howay, the additional "words 'and take possession' were inserted at a later time and are in a quite different ink." *Voyages of the "Columbia" to the Northwest Coast*, 398n. Years after Gray's entry into the Columbia, his widow, Martha, hoped to become heiress to land on the Columbia, which she maintained her husband had purchased from natives. The logs and journals extant do not substantiate her claim. The claim (submitted in a bill to the thirty-second Congress) was not for her relief only, but for heirs of John Kendrick as well. Howay, *Voyages of the "Columbia" to the*

natives came out to trade once more before the *Columbia* put to sea. At 1:00 P.M. the anchor was weighed, and she got under sail. By late afternoon she had cleared the bar.*[43]

No one knows how the Chinooks and other river peoples evaluated their meeting with Gray. Boit may have expressed the opinion of his fellow shipmates of that meeting when he wrote that it

> wou'd be a fine place for to set up a *Factory*. . . . During our short stay we collected 150 Otter, 300 Beaver, and twice the Number of other land furs. The river abounds with excellent *Salmon*, and most other River fish, and the Woods with plenty of Moose [elk] and Deer, the skins of which was brought us in great plenty, and the Banks produces a ground Nut [wappatoe], which is an excellent substitute for either bread or Potatoes. We found plenty of Oak, Ash, and Walnut trees, and clear ground in plenty, which with little labour might be made fit to raise such seeds as is necessary for the sustenance of inhabitants, and in short a factory set up here, another at Hancock's River, in the Queen Charlotte Isles, wou'd engross the whole trade of the NW. Coast (with the help of a few small coasting vessells).[44]

Before pushing on to Cape Flattery, Gray traded off the coast at north latitude 47°55'. Leaving the natives to wonder how soon their river would again be breached, he sailed in October to Canton to sell the season's take of furs†[45] for ninety thousand dollars.[46] This time he

Northwest Coast, 398n. See also Joseph Barrell, "Miscellany," manuscript, Oregon Historical Society. Martha Gray's petition (January 17, 1846), which states that her husband was the one "who first unfurled the flag of our country upon the 'great river of the west,' and who was the first to bear this flag in triumph round the world," appears in Edmond S. Meany, "The Widow of Captain Robert Gray," *Washington Historical Quarterly*, XX, 3 (July, 1929), 192–95. On October 3, 1866, sixteen heirs of Kendrick authorized a John Jolliffe to petition Congress in their behalf for relief or compensation for the captain's services and expenditures in the discovery of the Columbia River and its adjacent territory. "Kendrick, John, ca. 1740–1794," manuscript, Beinecke Library, Yale University.

* The United States Coast Survey would report in 1858 that there was probably one channel in the mouth of the river when Gray was there. That channel, surmised the team of the coast survey, was north of Sand Island, then connected to Point Adams. *Report of the Superintendent of the Coast Survey Showing the Progress of the Survey during the Year 1858, Senate Exec. Doc.* No. 14, 35 Cong., 2 sess., 391. A clerk of the British ship *Chatham*, which entered the river in 1792 after Gray, states that the *Chatham's* commander, W. R. Broughton, had a map of the river mouth prepared by Gray showing two channels. J. Neilson Barry, "Columbia River Exploration, 1792," *Oregon Historical Quarterly*, XXXIII (1932), 36.

† Robert Haswell on the voyage wrote in June, several months before sailing for Canton, that Gray had by then collected nearly seven hundred sea otter skins and nearly fifteen thousand skins of various other fur-bearing species. Robert Haswell, "A voyage on Discoveries in the Ship Columbia Rediviva," copy of manuscript, Archives of British Columbia, entries June 16 and 17, 1792.

carried homeward to Boston a diverse cargo of teas, nankeens (cloth),*
sugar, and porcelain.

The success of his journey would have considerable consequence for
both white Americans on the east coast and Indian ones on the west, for
it placed the former in the triangular trade route which their ships followed not only from Boston but also from Salem, Providence, Philadelphia, and New York to the Northwest Coast, China, and return. In
a later struggle with Britain over ownership of the Oregon country,
Americans would claim that Gray had won "The River of the West" for
the United States.† Yet his return would create no excitement in his
homeland, whose *Independent Chronicle* of Boston, Thursday, August
1, 1793, would tersely report that "Last Friday [July 26] arrived in
this port, the ship *Columbia*, Capt. Gray, from *China*, which she left
the 9th February." It would seem that Gray's second journey had created a lesser stir on the east coast than it had on the west.[47]

Americans of that east coast knew scarcely more of Gray's clientele
of the west than the latter knew of them. The two were not only a continent but also a cultural world apart, a condition Gray's journeys would
do little to breach. The bow and arrow he returned from the Northwest
Coast would more deeply confirm the opinion of "civilized" eastern
white men that its natives were savage.‡[48] Only slowly would easterners
learn about inhabitants of the misty Northwest Coast.

In the meantime, Chinooks and Clatsops would be introduced to the
"King George Men" (Englishmen) counterpart of the "Boston Men"
(Americans), for once the Columbia door had been unlocked, it would
not take long for others to enter.§ The next ship to enter to seek trade

---

* Nankeen is a cloth named for Nanking, China. It is firm-textured cotton of great dura-
bility which is made in various grades and bale sizes. Nankeens are naturally brown, but
westerners preferred those dyed blue and yellow and bleached white. Other cloths besides
silk were muslin and flannel.

† The maritime fur trade passed rapidly from the British to the Americans beginning
in 1792, and it remained with the latter for twenty years. Many of Britain's reasons for
withdrawing from the trade on the Northwest Coast were results of restrictions on her
traders in China by British monopolies and of her involvement in international problems.
The Northwest Coast "fur trade between Boston, the Pacific Coast, and China, was an
important stage in American expansion." "Book Reviews," *Washington Historical Quarterly*, XI, 4 (October, 1920), 303.

‡ Andrew D. Ash, Jr., of the Massachusetts Historical Society, to which organization
Gray gave the Northwest Coast native weapons, in a letter to the authors on February 8,
1972, writes that the society is not now in possession of the bow and arrow.

§ Another ship, the *Margaret*, is reported to have sailed from Hawaii on July 19, 1792,
for the Columbia River in search of furs. "On her return she reported but little success."
Frederic W. Howay, "The Ship Margaret: Her History and Historian," *Thirty-Eight An-*

with the natives was the *Jenny*, Captain James Baker, a seventy-eight-ton, three-masted schooner and former slaver from Bristol, England. Her visit to the river in October, 1792, was her second. She had been there previously that year,[49] but little is known about that visit, leading to a British contention that she had beaten the *Columbia* into the river of its name.[50] Chinooks, however, maintained that it was Gray who had first entered the stream.[51]

Captain Baker's experiences on the coast were somewhat like those of Gray. Reaching there in 1791 and finding natives troublesome at Murderer's Harbor, he had sailed on without stopping to trade. In 1791/92 he had wintered in the Sandwich (Hawaiian) Islands before sailing for the coast early in the season, crossing over the Columbia bar sometime between April and August before sailing north.[52] It was on October 2 that he left Nootka on his second and better known visit to the Columbia. His crew must have taken but few furs from natives on this journey, because when they departed the coast the *Jenny* carried a mere 350 sea otter skins, the sparse cargo due partly to a poor assortment of items she had brought to trade. Her crew occupied most of its time hunting wildfowl in marshes along the Wallicut* and Chinook rivers and in making observations of the bar.[53] Before leaving the river, the *Jenny* was joined by the 135-ton brig and armed tender H.M.S. *Chatham*, Lieutenant William Robert Broughton, under orders to explore the Columbia River and take possession of its tributary lands should a claim to discovery and exploration be supported. After talking with Gray in April, Vancouver, in the sloop of war H.M.S. *Discovery*, accompanied by Broughton in the *Chatham* to the Northwest Coast, had sailed on to Nootka to learn that Gray had indeed entered a large river.†[54] Vancouver and Broughton had sailed south to see for themselves.

It was now 5:30 P.M. on October 20. The *Chatham* was inside the breakers. Not wishing to risk the 340-ton *Discovery* to the treachery of those shoals, Vancouver backed off with the tide and left the area. The next day, having in hand Gray's sketch showing two channels in the Columbia, Broughton sailed his craft up the north channel into Bakers

---

nual *Report of the Hawaiian Historical Society*, 35. A record of her visit to the Columbia River, if indeed she reached there, is nonexistent.

* Later the Wallicut River was given the name "James River," probably for Captain James Baker. Barry, "Columbia River Exploration, 1792," 35.

† Vancouver was on the coast looking after British claims to trade and his country's interests in Nootka Sound. For details of Britain's conflict with the Spanish, leading to the so-called Nootka Sound Controversy, see Joseph Ingraham, "Journal of a voyage in the Hope, 1790–1792," photocopy of original manuscript in the Library of Congress, Archives of British Columbia, Vol. IV.

Bay to discover the *Jenny* and to name that body of water for her captain. He anchored at about the same spot that Gray had but did not find the water deep and fresh as Gray had because the river was not then in flood stage. It was this factor that produced considerable argument by the British that Gray had not been in the river at all, but in a bay. That the tide extended upriver (where Gray had sailed), in fact, as far as the Cascades[55] would have given added weight to their argument.[56]

The *Jenny* moved upriver a short distance in wind and rain to be met by only three canoes of Indians coming off to trade salmon. On national, rather than mercantile, business, the *Chatham* was not in the market for furs, but its crew, like others, did not reject the proffered salmon, of which it purchased three. The natives indicated that they would return to the ship.[57] The next day, October 22, Broughton and a clerk, Edward Bell, went ashore at the "Chinooke" Village, which they found deserted. Broughton observed that its houses appeared more comfortable than those of Nootka and had a greater inclination to their roofs. He found the village to be quite uncomfortable, for, wrote Bell, when they (Broughton and some of his men) "got up to it, they were surrounded with Swarms of Fleas, that soon settled in quantities on their Cloathes, and they were all obliged to run into the water to rid themselves of their unpleasant companions . . . a circumstance commonly observed before by us, at deserted Villages [whose inhabitants were driven from them] . . . by the swarms of Vermin occasioned by their own extreme filth and nastiness."[58] Broughton and Bell moved from the flea-infested village in launch and cutter to the south bank of the Columbia, where on a high sandbank they observed many raised canoes containing the bodies of what they assumed to have been chiefs. That evening they ascended a stream which Broughton named Youngs River for a George Young of the Royal Navy, camping there for the night apparently without seeing native Clatsops who, like many Chinooks, were in winter quarters. The two returned down Youngs River, crossing the Columbia to the *Chatham*. Broughton maneuvered that ship upriver no further than some two miles because of the shallowness of the water and anchored off present-day Knappton, Washington, north of Point Ellice. A large canoe-load of twenty-five natives (the second canoe seen in the river) came alongside and sold salmon to the crew for copper. Broughton thought the native merchants "seem'd to know the value of . . . [otter skins brought for sale] very well."[59]

The red merchants did not know the precise mission of their guests. In years to come, mercantile Chinooks and Clatsops would believe that strangers had come to their river only to trade. Although all of these visitors to follow would do some trading, they would have different missions to fulfill just as did those aboard the *Chatham*. The natives discovered that regardless of their missions, white men had similar possessive ideas regarding private property; when one of two or three natives permitted aboard the *Chatham* was detected with an iron stanchion concealed under his garment, Bell struck him several blows to the back.[60]

On the following day, October 24, Broughton and Bell, with launch and cutter and a week's provisions, set out to explore upriver, leaving the *Chatham* at anchor with one Thomas Manby in command.* The two pushed twenty-five miles upstream, spending the first night on Grays Point. In Broughton's absence, Manby ordered the crew to replenish the ship's wood and water and to guard against possible attack. He maneuvered the ship closer to shore to purchase a Chinook version of a jolly boat for shuttling from ship to shore. A native party, possibly Chinook, although Manby would not have distinguished them from their neighbors, took up residence under a tree on shore near the vessel to which "the men supplied us with fish and the good natured females, came daily on board, to get themselves adorned with Beads and Buttons" to embellish their coarse black hair, shoulder coverings, and small skin or twisted-grass skirts. The men and boys were naked. Manby noted that in true aboriginal style the men hunted and their women prepared foods which, in his opinion, were only half-cooked. Of the hunting abilities of the men Manby noted: "[They] never move with out their Quivers, filled with Arrows, all of which are stained with various Colors, and pointed with the flint made exceeding sharp, they seldom miss a mark at twenty yards, and will often kill a bird at forty."[61] He noted, too, that they smoked "a strong smelling herb" in long wooden pipes from which each family member inhaled big draughts before passing the pipes on to the others.[62]

Meanwhile, Broughton and his party spent October 25 near present-day Skamokawa at a point some twenty-five miles upstream from Cape Disappointment.† The next day they got under way, and in the afternoon they were joined by natives in two canoes who sold them bows and arrows. After these departed, four other canoes holding a dozen men

---

* Entries were made in the log of the *Chatham* by its master, Thomas Manby, during Broughton's absence up the Columbia in a small craft. There is a discrepancy in the date of one day in his entries. T. C. Elliott (ed.), "The Log of the H.M.S. 'Chatham,' " *Oregon Historical Quarterly*, XVIII (1927), 238n. Manby was writing to amuse his friends, and he was more interested in human relations than in mere chronology. Frederic W. Howay and T. C. Elliott (eds.), "Vancouver's Brig Chatham in the Columbia," *Oregon Historical Quarterly*, XLIII (1942), 319.

† Broughton believed the Columbia River to be a large bay (into which emptied numerous rivers), with the mouth of the river at present-day Skamokawa, Washington.

clad in deer and otter skins purloined a drinking pot, perhaps under one of these garments. Natives followed the launch and cutter, setting up a "dismal howl," which was answered by their fellows ashore. About dark, reaching a large village on the north shore near present-day Abernethy Point in Cowlitz County, Washington (which Chinooks and Clatsops had often visited as they had other villages along the route of Broughton and Bell), they were "importuned" by a native to remain with them for the night. Instead they pushed on upstream after giving the man some presents. After making every effort to show natives crowding around that they did not wish to spend the night with them, the party pushed off to make camp. Shortly, two or three canoes approached their camp. Unnerved by the persistence of the natives' hospitality, which he thought would soon cool, Broughton crossed his men to the south Columbia shore. The natives followed. Broughton ordered them away, but they crossed a nearby stream where they stayed all night, excepting a "Friendly Old Chief" whom Broughton admitted to his camp.[63] This old man, seen shortly after the *Chatham* entered the river, proved to be half-Spanish, which might explain his willingness to talk to those with whom he had some racial association.[64] The following day, October 27, the launch and cutter moved deeper into country of the natives, who collected about the strangers watching them make calculations on the river and assay geographical features, many of which they named, as had their hosts' ancestors long before.[65] The natives told the party that others living upstream owned many sea otter skins which they may have thought the party wished to buy.

The evening of the next day (October 28), Broughton and party came to a place he named Point Warrior (near present-day St. Helens, Oregon)[66] to find themselves surrounded by twenty-three canoes carrying from three to a dozen natives each.* Now deep in strange country, hemmed in by hills, the crew must have been apprehensive of those about them all war-garbed and combat-ready with bows and arrows, copper swords,† and iron battle-axes.[67] All shipside guns were readied.

* In his diary Bell states that each canoe held ten to twelve natives, nearly two hundred in all, paddling around the launch and cutter. Barry, "Columbia River Exploration, 1792," 143.

† Although they had had no previously recorded contact with whites, the natives had other metal items, such as brass ornaments in their ears. Thomas Manby, "Manby's Journal of H.M.S. Discovery 1791 & 2," manuscript, Beinecke Library, Yale University. Bell noted that the curious iron weapons were fitted with wooden handles. He had not seen this type of weapon before on the coast. As the exploring party progressed upriver, they saw more of the same type of weapons. Natives indicated to Bell that they had received them by barter from inland. Barry, "Columbia River Exploration, 1792," 144. For illustrations of copper war clubs and swords, see Roy Franklin Jones, *Wappato Indians of the Lower Columbia River Valley*, 115–16.

Muskets and pistols were loaded with ball; the swivel was primed and a match kept burning. To show the ship's preparedness, a crewman fired into the water, sending terrified natives scurrying below the gunwales of their canoes.[68] Friendly-looking natives, following the party upstream, discouraged their menacing brothers from further threats of force. Responding to their admonishers, these threw off their war garments to trade their weapons for buttons and beads—quite a concession in the interest of peace and trade, for they were proud of their cuirasses, believing them to be good protection from weapons. The noise of the guns frightened them, as did the effectiveness of these weapons, which brought down many birds. When Broughton, at their request, fired through a cuirass "twice doubled," they were "still more alarmed."[69] By coincidence, a similar demonstration back at the *Chatham*, when six muskets were fired to protect two men sent ashore to cut wood, may have similarly terrified the Chinooks.[70]

On October 29 the party was still further upstream, and the canoes that had pressed it the previous night collected again. Broughton estimated that his men were joined by 150 men, women, and children in twenty-five canoes.*[71] Landing on the beach with his men, Broughton drew a line, as was his custom, warning the natives not to cross it. The "Friendly Old Chief" and two other headmen with him were exempted from this ultimatum. One chief with enough authority to demand part of the catch of each hunter and fisherman supplied the party with fish and agreed to lead it still further upstream. On October 30 Broughton took possession of the country at Point Vancouver (east of present-day Vancouver, Washington).† With but little food left, and believing the source of the river to be not far distant, he decided to return to the *Chatham*.

At the uppermost point of their journey,‡ the copper-hued hosts offered the pale-faced travelers a goose, cranberries, and oil in a farewell gesture as the latter prepared to return downriver. As they passed downstream they improved their larder with salmon and sturgeon purchased along the way. They reached the *Chatham* on November 2. The next day Broughton prepared to sail downriver, but strong southerly

* Bell states that they were joined by 250 natives in thirty to forty canoes. There were men, women, and children. Barry, "Columbia River Explorations, 1792," 144.

† The upriver point which Broughton reached was Lawton Creek on the Washington side of the river, two and one-half miles east of present-day Cottonwood Point and four miles east of Washougal. J. Neilson Barry, "Broughton, up Columbia River, 1792," *Oregon Historical Quarterly*, XXXII (1931), 301n.

‡ Broughton was eighty-four miles from present-day Skamokawa, which he believed to be·the mouth of the Columbia. Oregon State engineers put the upriver point which he reached at 119.3 miles from the mouth of the river, reckoned at Cape Disappointment.

winds kept the *Chatham* from reaching its previous berth. With a shifting wind to the north, the ship moved on November 6 into Bakers Bay, where Broughton and his crew found the *Jenny*. Captain Baker came aboard the *Chatham* to dine on fare better than was formerly on the craft, for natives had provided her with salmon, sturgeon, "herrings," "sardines," roots, and berries. The crew added its bit to the food supply by furnishing wild fowl it had hunted. Food traffic of Chinooks to the ship afforded Broughton opportunity to describe the carriers: "[They] differed in nothing very materially from those we had visited during the summer, but in the decoration of their persons; in this respect, they surpassed all the other tribes with paints of different colours, feathers, and other ornaments."[72]

Both captains awaited improving weather to cross the bar outbound, but not until four days later would the river's swells subside sufficiently to allow them to escape. On November 11 the *Chatham* slipped out to sea behind the *Jenny* and sailed for California to join Captain Vancouver.[73]

Of the three ships visiting the Columbia River this year of 1792, only one, the *Jenny*, would return; but others would soon follow now that the Columbia bar had been breached. The international economic and political repercussions of such crossings would be felt not only in Europe and in the rising American republic but also among Chinooks, Clatsops, and their neighbors. For when the sails of the *Chatham* dipped out of sight in the broad Pacific to end another chapter in the story of the white man's contact with the red man in the New World, these peoples in the Columbia River corner of that world, whether they knew it or not, would be changed forever.

4. Clamor and Clamons

> . . . but the best trade is the Leather War
> Dresses, articles to be disposed of, on other
> parts of the Coast, to great advantage. . . .
> Captain Charles Bishop, "Commercial
> *Journal* of Ship Ruby's voyage"

ARMED WITH BOWS and arrows, natives of Bakers Bay paddled out on August 11, 1793, to a vessel at anchor inside the bar under the cape.[1] She was the Spanish transport *Mexicana*, Captain Don Juan Martinez y Zayas. Her crew asked information of the natives regarding the whereabout of their countryman-explorer Don Francisco de Eliza, who had been ordered by Bodega y Quadra, commander of Spanish naval surveying expeditions out of San Blas, to explore, among other places along the Northwest Coast, La Entrada de Hezeta.[2] Eliza's mission was to search the river to its source for the fabled Northwest Passage.* His preparations for that task had taken into account natives of this region, for he was supplied with beads and trinkets to secure their much needed

* Instructions in part to Eliza and Martinez y Zayas were: "One of the most interesting points on the coast is the Rio Columbia in 46°12′ of latitude. This demands a long and minute examination. After the brigantine has anchored inside in the most convenient place, the sloop will go on, with appropriate instructions, as far as the circumstances may allow, towing the longboat of the brigantine. When she anchors she will dispatch the longboat in the best ship possible to stem and cut the currents, manned by a chosen crew, and provided with all the food she can carry and with arms and ammunition to continue the survey. It would be advisable for two pilots to go in her carrying two compasses for taking bearings. They should follow the river until they reach its source, but taking note of the state of their provisions in order to calculate the proper note of the state of their provisions in order to calculate the proper time to return so as to reach the sloop and receive food and continue their survey in case this has not been concluded with the first reserve of food. The making of the chart can be done by estimated bearings and distances in view of the fact that the current will not permit distances traveled to be measured by the log." Henry R. Wagner, *The Cartography of the Northwest Coast of America to the Year 1800*, I, 237.

good will if Spain were to succeed in a planned settlement at the ou[...]
of the passage, the mouth of the Columbia River. Like the waters s[...]
ing at that place, Spain was caught up in a Northwest Coast swirl[...]
nations that were rapidly moving toward a showdown. Dreaming[...]
former glories, Spain hoped that by pursuing the fur trade of the re[...]
she might discourage other powers from engaging in it and at the sa[...]
time maintain her rights on the coast south of the Strait of Juan [...]
Fuca, where the previous year at Neah Bay her explorers had est[...]
lished a village, Nuñez Gaona. They shortly abandoned the village. [...]
Strait of Juan de Fuca failed to lead to the fabled Anian passage acr[...]
the continent.

Chinooks and possibly other natives gathering about them to fish [...]
trade could give the crew of the *Mexicana* no word of Eliza. The n[...]
morning they followed the ship upstream in their canoes, impressing [...]
visitors as ". . . corpulent, strong people of good appearance." At no[...]
after sailing fourteen miles, the *Mexicana* grounded, at which, accord[...]
to Martinez y Zayas, "The Indians rejoiced at our misfortune and w[...]
so insolent that the more we asked them to go away so we could extr[...]
ourselves from this dangerous situation the closer they came, bendi[...]
their bows and wetting the feathers of their arrows."[3] Like other w[...]
traders, these Spaniards judged the natives' behavior by that of aggr[...]
sive northern tribes. To white men their craft were "war canoes," bo[...]
and arrows were weapons of war, and gestures were signs of hostili[...]
Making the confrontation somewhat awkward for the Spanish was th[...]
knowledge that although a week earlier six canoes of natives that h[...]
paddled out to the *Mexicana* had offered them sealskins for copper a[...]
clothing, the natives of Grays Harbor (Puerto Grek) four days lat[...]
had fled from their presence.[4]

These same Spaniards now in the river took to their own arms, whi[...]
the natives apparently thought would only make a big noise "until th[...]
saw the ravages made in one of their canoes."[5] At this, they withdre[...]
Martinez y Zayas awaited a rising tide to back his vessel off and po[...]
dered the wisdom of further upstream exploration. This, of necessit[...]
would have been by launch, leaving a mere dozen men with the *Me[...]
cana*, "where the Indians, arrogant on account of their arms and the[...]
number, could attempt some treachery."[6] Martinez y Zayas made h[...]
decision and turned his ship downstream on the tide to anchor und[...]
the cape. Despite the Spaniard's offer of presents, the natives kept the[...]
distance from the ship. The next morning, with her sailing, the Spaniar[...]
abandoned not only the river but also, virtually, their nation's endeav[...]
on the Northwest Coast.[7] Like Hezeta before him, Martinez y Zay[...]
had failed at the river. This year, 1793, and the following would ma[...]

the decline of Spain's sovereignty in the region where, as previously noted, her claims had been challenged by Britain.* The confrontation of the two powers had led to the "Nootka Sound controversy," smoldering since the Nootka Convention of 1790, when representatives of both nations had failed to reach agreement over each other's claims. Now the two governments were terminating the controversy with agreements whereby both could navigate the Pacific, fish Arctic waters, and trade with coastal Indians, but neither was to found colonies north of Spain's northernmost settlement at Nootka.[8]

As the eighteenth century drew to a close, the British appeared to be the winner among claimants to that vast coastal area lying between Russian America in Alaska and Spanish America in California. But titles to unoccupied lands in the region were hard to defend, and although the British had taken much of the coastal fur harvests, that trade was beginning to fall into American hands. Two American vessels, the ship *Jefferson* of Boston, Captain Josiah Roberts, and the schooner *Resolution*, Captain Samuel Burling,[9] reached the Northwest Coast in May, 1793, trading that season from the Columbia River to as far north as the Queen Charlotte Islands and Alaska. Their captains had great hopes for the trade, although they carried goods inadequate for it. In his logbook, Bernard Magee, first officer of the *Jefferson*, wrote: "Our next attention was to prepare the little schooner [the *Resolution*] on a voyage to the southward to the Columby's River in the lat. 46°55′, where we had good information of clamons to be procured, and has been purchased by several for three chisels apiece and afterwards bartered skin for skin."[10]

Fastest-moving items in the northern market were the clamons, the protective armor so demanded by oft-warring peoples of Vancouver and the Queen Charlotte Islands and other points on the upper Northwest Coast. Chinooks had carried on a clamon trade with northern peoples for years, but now white traders saw the protective hides as a good commodity to trade to those peoples in exchange for sea otter pelts

* The Spanish had begun sailing north from their headquarters at San Blas in 1774 to check on rumors of Russian expansion into their claimed Northwest Coast territory. Instead, they came up against the British at Nootka Sound in 1788 when Don Esteban Jose Martinez seized British ships commanded by Meares, James Colnett, and Thomas Hudson. The British government made an issue of damages to her subjects' ships and crews. She was not about to permit Spain to claim and close off the north Pacific, which Spain claimed by discovery. The position of Britain, which had begun a settlement before the confrontation, was that occupation and settlement were requirements to claim the territory. In her contest with Britain, Spain was aided by France; Britain was aided by Holland, Prussia, and, she hoped, the young United States. Spain had many domestic and international troubles on her hands, causing her to decide in favor of a peaceful settlement.

for the China trade. In their journals, Cook, Boit, and others had familiarized clamons to white traders, who quickly learned of their potential in the trade.[11]

In July Captain Roberts dispatched the *Resolution* from Bucareli Bay, Alaska, to gather furs and clamons at the Columbia River, the key distribution point for the coveted article. At the Columbia Captain Burling obtained from Chinooks sixty-three sea otter skins and twenty-seven clamons at a rate of two sea otter skins and four clamons per copper sheet; for a jacket and trousers he received one sea otter skin. He discovered that iron, formerly in demand, now had little appeal to lower Columbia peoples. They let him know that they would not accept it for sea otter pelts,[12] but would trade those skins for four-foot swords if they were made of iron. For such a sword they would give one clamon; for two swords they would give a sea otter skin. If the swords were of copper they would give one sea otter skin per weapon.

Burling hurried north to meet the *Jefferson* to winter at Barkley Sound on the southwest side of Vancouver Island. During the season, Roberts traded with natives living at this white traders' winter quarters at a rate of one musket per clamon, which he intended to trade further to the north. At the same time, he exchanged powder at a rate of five pounds per fathom of dentalia for the Columbia River trade in order to secure more of its clamons, thus becoming a middleman in this commerce of native products. To the natives dentalia had lost none of their magic, maintaining commercial value as items to be traded for other highly valued commodities. Taking a particular fancy to them, Quillayutes bought them from Chinooks. Northern tribes, as did others, knew their commercial value but also knew that, unlike clamons, they offered no protection from enemy missiles. Roberts knew this, too, and with typical Yankee ingenuity he sought to manufacture clamons by substituting sealskin for elkskin. His efforts were to no avail, for the natives most likely had already attempted to use sealskin for protective armor. Making the white traders' supply of clamons all the shorter was the October 23 return of the *Resolution* after an absence of nearly a month of foul weather, which had denied her a second entrance to the Columbia River.[13]

During the winter of 1793/94, the *Jefferson*'s smith set to work making iron swords, to which the Chinooks and Clatsops had taken a fancy, although they would have preferred them of copper. The sheets of iron which white traders brought to the coast were of insufficient thickness for swords, yet to satisfy this native whim the smith melted the sheets, attempting to cast the metal into greater thickness. But again to no avail—Chinooks and Clatsops had shifted their fancy from iron to copper not only in the form of swords, but also in fifty- and sixty-pound sheets or as utensils such as tea kettles imported from Holland. As they did with other prized imports, they put the tea pots to uses for which they had never been intended, making them into items of interest, symbols of prestige, and ornaments for their houses and persons.[14] With a bent to opulence and with little understanding of the tastes and techniques of white men, they would not have used these metallic prizes as did their suppliers.

On Vancouver Island Captain Roberts had agreed to sell the *Resolution* to Chief Wickananish for fifty prime sea otter skins. Wishing to send the schooner on another try to the Columbia River before disposing of her, he dispatched her there on April 3, 1794, after bad weather delayed her departure. Aboard she carried 378 iron swords, fifty-two copper sheets, eleven trade muskets, seven pistols, eight copper-mounted cutlasses, and some 150 fathoms of dentalia. This cargo her captain, Burling, hoped to exchange for more than four hundred otter skins by season's end; he would discover, as had so many others, that in the hazardous Northwest Coastal trade hopes came cheap and fulfillment high. He successfully negotiated a Columbia entrance, garnering all the clamons he could from the natives in Bakers Bay. After sailing from the river at the end of April, the *Resolution* failed to contact the *Jefferson*. One rumor reported that she had wrecked in one of the violent storms that lashed the coast at this season. Another had it that natives to the north had captured the ship and killed her crew.[15]

Shortly thereafter, on May 11, 1794, the *Jenny* was back in the river.[16] Her captain, John William Adamson, was new to her but an old hand in the trade, having been on the coast with Meares in 1788. The ship was now licensed from the East India Company to dispose of her return cargo in China. With an outbound cargo which her owner, Sidenham Teast, had improved from that of her previous ventures, she did considerable business in the Columbia, or "Chinook" River, as Adamson called it[17] from ignorance of its true name or from an attempt to detract from Gray's exploits.[18] Adamson maintained friendly relations with Chinooks and on one occasion was visited by one of their chiefs, Taucum, who told him the *Resolution* had sailed north with all the clamons she could buy. With sea otters obtained both in direct trade and in exchange for clamons, Adamson amassed on the Northwest Coast a cargo of two thousand skins, with which he sailed to Canton. Arriving there on December 25, 1794, he exchanged the *Jenny*'s cargo for tea for the European market.

The coming of ships was now changing not only the tools and techniques (technical culture) but also the "dispositions and manners" (nontechnical culture) of these "less refined species." Chinook women, for example, increasingly mingled with ships' crews, precipitating the sale of a human commodity. Usually older women aboard their "business canoes"* transported cargoes of younger free and slave females—sisters, daughters and other relatives—to the ships like any other product. On board, this female merchandise was itself often enticed by "A trifling Present [which] now and then gratified their Desires . . ."[19] just as this merchandise enticed its own purchasers. But the chief income from the sale of themselves and their slaves went to their masters, who permitted their use by sailors in exchange for goods as cheap as fishhooks and trinkets.[20] One nonmercantile repercussion of this activity was the reputation it gave Chinook women for years for looseness and carrying on in public, a characteristic shared less by their Clatsop sisters,[21] who had less access to the ships.

The cultural background of these activities might provide at least a partial explanation of the practice. Chinook husbands, owning the bodies and wills of their women, submitted them to prostitution from which these Chinook lords took the earnings. Although they took these financial rewards from female bodies, they did not take properties made by women's hands, such as mats and baskets.† Moreover, because Chinooks did not consider cohabitation a disgrace (unlike incest), it was quite natural that the practice shifted from shore to ship. Generally, they believed the only disgraceful aspect of this cohabitation was pregnancy and the birth of children. It had been the custom of Chinook and Clatsop women to abort such pregnancies, but apparently the practice was not universal—or successful—at least among slaves; one belonging to a second Chinook chief, Shelathwell, as a consequence of a shipboard affair with a Mr. William, first officer of the *Jenny*, gave birth to a child the following winter.[22] Abortion, precipitated by the rejection by Chinook men of these "breeds," was accomplished by medication with certain plants and by more violent methods such as placing the belly over a stick or tree trunk and pressing heavily.[23] Infanticides became com-

---

* Chinook men did not own all the canoes. Women owned property which included slaves and business canoes. John Minto, "The Number and Condition of the Native Race in Oregon When First Seen by White Men," *Oregon Historical Quarterly*, I (1900), 300. Part of the women's rights was ownership of property apart from that of their men. They kept earnings from sales of their baskets and other weavings and from produce they harvested. A chief was given the fruits of village industry besides claiming rights to surplus products.

† Properties in Chinook society were not disposed of before death. Occasionally an item was willed to certain individuals. At death, various personal properties of the deceased were destroyed. The remainder went to the grave or was taken by relatives and grown sons. Wives and young children usually got nothing. Gibbs, *Tribes of Western Washington and Northwestern Oregon*, 187.

monplace among Chinooks and Clatsops. When Chinook men denied paternity of the newborn, mothers threw these offspring into the river.[24]

Obviously, the permissiveness of Chinook women and their shipside paramours was a two-way street, with neither party sharing total blame in this traffic of furs and favors, skins and sex. Writing fifty years later when the practice prevailed, a pioneer newspaperman would evaluate it as an evil resulting from the intercourse of native women "with a vicious class of men—the dregs of the white races—floated to their shores, by chance, in trading ships, or seeking here adventures more exciting than civilized countries afforded."[25] This caused Chinook women, in the words of a British representative of the Aboriginal Protection Society on the lower Columbia, to become "as accomplished courtesans as any upon the face of the whole earth: inferior to none in profligacy, disease and extravagance."[26]

Of the association of Chinook women with white traders there were certain by-products other than occasional babies. Despite the unsavory aspects of their contacts, stemming less from love than from a love of money that made them haggling hags,[27] Chinook women enhanced their statures in their own society, wherein they already had considerable influence. Chinook exposure to increased numbers and varieties of trade goods and to their purveyors increased their English vocabularies,[28] especially those of their women. They moulded strange white men's words to suit their own tongues by softening or dropping their own gutteral sounds, modifying unpronounceable English sounds as "f" and "r" into "p" and "l."[29] As many of their men slipped into the commercial background, Chinook women would soon greet incoming ships on their own and deal with the crews in all aspects of the trade. Crewmen understandably feared this gentler sex less than they did the males, from whom they always feared trouble. Association of Chinook women with white traders kept mercantile channels open to the benefit of both. Sometimes the women warned the traders of evil designs on them, a few of which their own men may have plotted in revenge for the actions of exploitive shipmasters and supercargoes. For their loyalty Chinook women, ironically, achieved no equality with white males, who saw no reason to change their dominant sex role on a trading frontier.[30] Had it not been for Chinook males, visiting ship captains would perhaps have needed few security measures such as keeping Chinook merchants at safe distances in Bakers Bay until their friendship could be ascertained and then permitting but limited numbers aboard ship at any one time.[31] By now, Chinook men had learned the dispositions of certain captains and crews, many of whom they had come to know, returning hostility or friendship in kind. At some places on the coast the true disposition of shipside natives was ascertained too late to avoid disaster for visiting ships; by the same token, natives sometimes learned too late the true disposition of the white men.

During the winter of 1794/95, the Chinooks received a visit from the *Phoenix*, a British Bengalese snow, Captain Hugh Moore. On this, her second visit to the Northwest Coast, she wintered inside the bar, the first to do so, just as the *Columbia* and the *Washington* had in 1788/89 been the first to winter at Nootka. Before then, ships wintered in the balmy Hawaiian Islands. Like the *Jenny*, the *Phoenix* was a mystery ship, for when she left the river in late winter or early spring she apparently left no record of her transactions at that place.[32]

. In the spring (May, 1795), Captain John Myers, a former British Navy man, sailed on a trading junket to the Northwest Coast in the one-hundred-ton British vessel *Jane*.* A quarter-century later he would publish a highly flavored account of his travels. As he would describe her, the *Jane* was a virtual floating hardware and department store, with a multifarious cargo of axes, brandy, iron bars, paints, clothing, chisels, hammers, copper sheets, small bells, tobacco, china beads, buckets, looking glasses, firearms, and ammunition. The cargo certainly indicated that white traders such as Myers had adjusted their merchandise to fit native tastes. A simple glance at their own tastes should have told them that these changed with time, but several outrunners of white men's culture apparently believed that Chinooks, Clatsops, and other "savages" of the Northwest Coast were immune to such change. But they were not. Of these changes Myers noted that "the disposition of the rude Indian is subject to the same fluctuation and caprice as the more cultivated natives of Europe: that experience and observation on the manners and customs of others, without addressing the rational or sensitive faculties, have given them the opportunity of judging between articles of necessity and superfluity; and that they would now prefer a Blanket, or a piece of Cloth, to the unprofitable possession of a ring or necklace."[33]

Native wants made it possible for Myers to obtain "a great number" of otter, martin, and beaver for articles which he thought trivial. Although their ignorance made it possible, as Myers tells it, to trade a small iron spear for an otter skin going for $80.00 in China, he respected these native businessmen. "The canoes," he wrote, "loaded with

* In the decade 1785–95, thirty-five British and fifteen American vessels took part in the Northwest Coast fur trade. The next decade would see sixty-eight American and nine British ships in those waters. Frederic W. Howay, "A List of Trading Vessels in the Maritime Fur Trade, 1795–1804," *Proceedings and Transactions of the Royal Society of Canada*, 3d ser. XXIV (1930), 118.

the inhabitants, bringing the produce of Sea and Land, have a tendency to excite respect for man even in a savage state, and remove any impressions that at first we may be induced to believe unfavourable, as to the dispositions and manners of our more hardy and less refined species."[34]

Communication of the arrival of ships in the river was speeded now by Chinooks firing a musket to signal the event, as happened when the 101-ton *Ruby*, Captain Charles Bishop, out of Bristol, England, crossed the bar on May 22, 1795,[35] to anchor in Bakers Bay one-quarter mile offshore. In response to musket fire at daylight, May 23, a canoe flotilla paddled from all quarters to the ship. Aboard her were nearly fifty separate trade items displayed on deck to excite the appetites of the red customers. No furs were exchanged this day; the Chinooks saw to that. Instead, they sized up the goods, bargained and haggled, were possibly given a gift as a tip, a common practice of traders to get their customers into a good mood, and then paddled ashore to end the day. The next morning, the twenty-fourth, they came off in great numbers to renew the huckster-haggle process in which they and their coastal neighbors had no peer, as attested to by French trader Étienne Marchand on the Northwest Coast in 1791. "The Modern Hebrew," wrote Marchand, "could teach the Indians nothing in the art of bargaining."[36] Knowing he would keep his ship in the bay for a week, Captain Bishop let his customers depart a second time.

On May 25, with the natives' return to the ship, jockeying between the two parties for rates of exchange was finally ended, and prices were fixed. Usually skins of prime quality, after being haggled over, were fixed at a standard price.[37] Once this price was established, equivalents were set for axes, knives, files, and so on. At this point white traders usually stiffened their trading posture, fearing the economic consequences should they relax established standards.

In her remaining eleven days on the river Chinooks brought to the *Ruby* 111 good sea otter skins and a variety of land animals until they frankly admitted they had no more. Bishop thought the rate of exchange a little higher than before, but more reasonable than he had expected.[38] In the brisk trading as many as two hundred natives came alongside the *Ruby* in canoes, and lesser numbers clambered on deck at a time. With such heavy traffic at the floating marketplace the crew dared not relax its vigilance lest some incident provoke trouble and disrupt trade altogether. As the natives seldom traveled without bows and arrows, and now "some muskets,"[39] their presence had a more ominous look than they intended. The crew, however, was generally pleased with their demeanor and happy for the large elk and three deer they brought aboard—among the first fresh food it had eaten in weeks. Unlike their energetic and aggressive northern brothers, who often traveled long distances for food and other needs, Chinooks and Clatsops, in food gathering, were fishermen primarily and hunters secondarily, satisfying their needs closer to home and tending to become, in the eyes of their visitors, "indolent and inert."[40]

At this juncture the natives offered the *Ruby* crew salmon for trade, but not until after the first catch, the natives' tabu tempering their trade. Fearing to exchange salmon before salmonberries were ripe, when strangers might cut the fish the wrong way,[41] the Chinooks withheld this delicacy from those now among them, teaching them to expect little in the way of salmon trade before June. Whatever Bishop and his men may have thought of this trade-restricting tabu, they, as did others, found it virtually impossible to dislodge their clientele from their sacred prohibition. Before departing the river on June 5 for the north, Bishop planted potatoes, peas, peach stones, radishes, mustard, cress, and celery on one of two small islands in Bakers Bay.[42] Where in Bishop's own homeland men had their own "tabus" about such plantings, the Chinooks had none, simply because they did not plant. Had they done so they would have had tabus aplenty, as they had in their other food-gathering activities. Bishop planned to return to winter in the Columbia, where his crew might be sustained by the fresh vegetables it would miss on land and sea in the north.

In those northern parts, trading in command of the American sloop *Union* of Newport, Rhode Island, John Boit successfully repelled attacks by natives of the Queen Charlotte Islands, killing a chief and forty braves,[43] but went down to defeat at the bar, where bad weather in mid-July (1795) backed him off the "murderous Harbor" and sent him north.[44] Often from atop the cape Chinooks set signal fires in bad weather to guide ships to the river mouth.* But standing off that place, mariners knew their successful entry depended more on weather signs than on those flashing from the cape.

After a successful northern summer the *Ruby* in October literally blew over the bar into the Columbia amid breakers surging from shore

---

* There are navigational aids today for vessels. The first lighthouse was established at Cape Disappointment in 1856. A fog whistle there, considered impractical since it could not be heard, was discontinued in 1881. Then the lighthouse on Point Adams was established in 1875 along with another fog whistle, which was also discontinued in 1881. There are now two lighthouses on Cape Disappointment. One is Canby Light, situated east of the high point of McKenzie's Head, and the other is North Head Light on the extreme western bluff of the cape. A jetty has been built from each lip of the river mouth. The south jetty was begun in 1885 and is the longer. It greatly reduces hazards of the bar, as does the shorter north jetty, construction of which was begun later.

to shore.[45] Bishop found that his potatoes had grown; most of his other vegetables for one reason or another had not. On Wednesday, October 21, a few natives appeared with salmon and cranberries to trade, but not until the first of November did they show up in any number and despite miserable weather, which they ascribed to their visitors for pointing fingers at the new moon.[46] At this transgression of an ancient tabu the Chinooks grasped the moon-pointing digits of their guests, crying, "Peeshac!"—their word that the whites would be punished by continuing bad weather. The deities dutifully maintained the inclemency of their weather. But they always did in winter. The fact that Chinooks this year had not hied to their protected villages but had exposed themselves to white visitors and winter gales assured them that weather demons had truly sent bad weather to punish these visitors for violating an ancient tabu.

It was well into December before Chief Taucum, followed by several subchiefs, came down to visit the captain from his Wallicut village, where with his reputed ten wives he had repaired because of poor salmon runs near his village on the Columbia River. The chief learned that Bishop had traded with little trouble, possibly because when natives purloined knives or other articles from his stores he immediately reported the thefts to the chiefs, who usually saw to it that he got the items back the next day. The chiefs must have been impressed with the captain's sternness and adherence to a single standard, for when a crew member stole an arrow from a native he had the thief tied and flogged as an object lesson for the continuance of good relations aboard. Fears that whites would steal the offspring of his slave and the *Jenny*'s first officer prompted Chief Shelathwell to keep the child off the ship.[47] His fears perhaps were groundless, for seldom did white traders return home with the products of these illegitimate unions. At the same time, Chinooks did not withhold from the crew their "well Featured" daughters who, failing abortions or infanticides, might have produced new members for the Chinook community.

Bishop believed that the Chinooks' good behavior was due to his good treatment of them on his spring visit—a wise policy, to his way of thinking, that had it not been followed might have resulted in their takeover of his ship. Not all captains enjoyed such good relations with their customers, for the Chinook chief told him they were then "at war" with three shipmasters for having fired on them, inflicting some injury. At this Bishop wrote in his journal that one had "to expect in these people all the Wiley guile ascribed to the Savage race, as a stranger or an Enemy, and a Generous hospitality in their Friendship and confidance." Yet he ordered his men to maintain their vigil.[48]

One proof that the presence of the *Ruby* in their midst had altered Chinook winter patterns was evident in December when Chief Shelathwell and another, the stocky, one-eyed Comcomly, moved their houses down the bay to be near the ship. Comcomly had ingratiated himself with Bishop to the extent that the captain permitted him to sleep in his cabin aboard ship and had made for him a jacket and trousers—not the last such rewards that chief would receive for his diplomacy. The two chiefs, perhaps because of an intratribal tiff, so common among Pacific Northwest natives, seemed to have been out of sorts with Taucum, making a point not to visit the *Ruby* when he was aboard. It seems that after one of Taucum's people had insulted Shelathwell, Taucum had chosen not to punish the wrongdoer by cutting off his head. Shelathwell's honor had thus gone unsatisfied, especially since the five arrows he had been allowed to shoot into the offender's tied-up body had not proven fatal.

The presence of the *Ruby* certainly stimulated the Chinooks to greater effort in the trade. On Sunday, December 6, Comcomly and Shelathwell left with ten armed men on a two- or three-hundred-mile expedition upriver to trade for the elkskin so much wanted by Bishop, who observed of their value in relation to other skins:

> The Sea Otter skins procured here, are of an Excellent Quality and large size, but they are not in abundance and the Natives themselves set great value on them. Beaver and two or three kind of Fox Skins, Martin and River Otter are also bought here—but the best trade is the Leather War Dresses, articles to be disposed of, on other parts of the Coast, to great advantage, we procured such a Quantity, that at the least estimation is expected will procure us near 700 Prime Sea otter Skins. These dresses are . . . a compleate defence against a Spear or an Arrow, and sufficient almost to resist a Pistol Ball.[49]

Neighboring tribes also brought clamons to sell. On December 8 one Bucquoinue, a Quinault chief, accompanied by two slaves, came down to sell two of these skins. He may have wished he had stayed home, for Bishop lashed into him as being one of the killers of the boat crew sent ashore by Charles Barkley off the Washington coast in 1787. Bishop accused natives there of butchering the crew and glutting themselves on its flesh.[50] Bucquoinue maintained that it had been neither he nor his people, but Quillayutes, who had butchered the crew. The Chinooks told Bishop that the blood of Englishmen had truly flowed among the Quillayutes, but when these natives offered grisly tokens of the deed to them they took only clothing. Unsatisfied with Bucquoinue's explanation and still shaken by the killings, Bishop threatened to clap the

Quinault chief in chains for delivery to the father of one of the murdered Englishmen. Understanding the workings of revenge well enough, for it was practiced among natives as it was among whites, Bucquoinue did not wince but "submitted to his situation with great manliness."[51] The accused happily got off the hook when one of Shelathwell's wives interceded with Bishop on the Quinault chief's behalf, stating that the chief had come to arrange a marriage-treaty with one of her daughters —an arrangement by which it was hoped a Quinault-Chinook alliance could be forged. Bishop was glad for "an opportunity of shewing these people how we would act if driven to desperate measures, I became glad of this excuse of letting him go, making him Promise, which I am pretty shure he never will perform, to come on board when Shelathwell returns, and I keept his two Leather War Dresses as his hostages, he was visibly delighted when set at liberty and hastened into the cannoe, fearful we should repent our clemency."[52]

Before spring, Bucquoinue would die not in remote Britain but right at home when the gunpowder he was drying before a fire exploded and blew him to pieces. Such accidents were becoming more commonplace among natives unused to firearms and ammunition.[53]

On December 20 Comcomly returned home from his hinterland trip with Shelathwell, whom he left at the house of one of his fathers-in-law up the Columbia. (In his journal Bishop refers to the Columbia as the Chinook River.) After leaving Shelathwell, Comcomly's canoe upset, spilling into the river two guns, two clamons, and a deer intended as a gift for the *Ruby*'s crew. From another canoe a venison of some age and "only fitt for the *Delicate* venison eaters in England"[54] was offered to Bishop, who refused it but not a clamon and several bows and arrows. The next day Shelathwell returned to the ship, seeking to repay a visit the captain had paid one of Shelathwell's houses and wives, and brought along to sell five clamons gathered on his excursion with Comcomly. After purchasing them, Bishop noticed that two had been punctured by bullets. From one of Comcomly's brothers Bishop learned the story of the riddled clamons. It seems, as Bishop narrated it, that Comcomly and Shelathwell on December 6

> took their departure on the Expidition before alluded to they where in a single cannoe paddled with 10 men, each arm'd with a muskett. Comcomally had one of his Wives and a Child, and we dressed him in his Jackett and trowsers and appurtenances of European cloathing their mode of trade is somwhat curious, and afforded us an hearty laugh has he more curiously discribed it they go up the River Chinook [Columbia] two or three hundred miles and come to strange villages, where they land and offer trade with some trifling pieces of Copper or Iron the Strangers naturally demand more,

the chief then gives the Signal and they all discharge their pieces laden with powder, into the air, these people never having heard or seen such a strange phenomena, throw of their Skins and Leather War Dresses and fly into the woods, while the others pick them up, and leave on the spott the articles first offered, they then proceed to other places in like manner and thus for the Quantity of goods we pay for one of these dresses they get sometimes twenty, but we soppose this mode cannot last long, as they will naturally be aware of a second visit of the kind.[55]

In his journal Bishop confessed that when he purchased the clamons he was unaware they had been gotten by musket diplomacy in which blood had been spilled. Yet he does not record returning them. He may not have known that the Chinooks were not above securing such prizes by foul means, especially from "inferior" peoples up the Columbia River with whom they had shared bad blood for years.

Bishop figured that these clamons, added to others perhaps purchased more peaceably, would make him a total harvest of 192, which would bring him in trade 677 prime sea otter skins in such places as the Queen Charlotte Islands. In exchange for the clamons he traded the Chinooks a variety of items to satisfy their expanding demands—ten pounds of powder, four muskets, 304 copper rods, seventy-three tea kettles, sixteen pounds of sheet copper, twenty-six sheets of sheathing copper, three quart-sized copper cups, six copper sauce pans, one pewter jug, eighteen silver-hilted swords, four common swords, sixty-two bars of iron, three hundred pounds of musket balls, four yards of cloth, eight blankets, sixteen copper buckets, seven files, three tin powder flasks, six yards of baize, two brass Guinea kettles, and thirty dozen buttons.[56]

In contrast to this variety of products from an expanding industrial revolution abroad, the Chinooks could match but a few, albeit important, products of their own manufacture. One of Shelathwell's wives brought Bishop a hat she had made. Some items traded to him were also used in the native trade. A chief, Telemmecks, at that time purchased Shelathwell's eldest daughter for twenty otter skins, twenty clamons, and a canoe, any of which Bishop could have used in the trade. He might have found embarrassing the twenty slaves offered to seal the arrangement, as traffic in that human commodity was now coming under great criticism in his own country. On one occasion Shelathwell demanded of Bishop fifty sheets of copper, twenty fathoms of cloth, and a pledge of safety for his daughter, Sitelmayoe, to accompany the captain to his ship. Like Boit, Bishop and his men found Chinook maidens, "the Fair Sex in this quarter of the Globe," not unattractive, especially when adorned with copper pieces and beads around their necks, wrists, and fingers. Yet he found their lot degrading compared with that of "ye Beauties of Albion."[57]

Trade continued into the new year 1796. On January 7 Taucum traded at the *Ruby* accompanied by a Chinook chief, Chinini, a newcomer to the ship perhaps because of a "mental indisposition" during which he had given away all his possessions—wives, house, canoes, skins, bows, and arrows; but now that his "sanity" had been restored, so had his possessions.*

Continuous exposure to each other did little to increase basic understanding between the visiting white traders and their Chinook counterparts, who the former, as did most others of their race, characterized as "saucy." An incident that in their minds confirmed this characterization occurred on Wednesday, January 13, when Comcomly, scuffling on deck with an officer, received a blow to his royal face. Considering the incident an insult, he complained to Bishop, but the captain laughed it off. This angered the chief all the more. He left the ship, masking his ruffled feelings fairly well, but that evening, in apparent anger, he fired his musket at the vessel. The next day, having considered the consequences of his act, he sent several of his wives to invite Bishop to come see him. Bishop said he could not; he was too busy. The next morning he weighed anchor and hauled further out in the bay, not wanting Comcomly, with shots from his one-man war, to rock the boat of diplomacy the captain was trying to maintain in his relations with the natives. And besides, Bishop wanted to move further out in the bay anyway. Possibly fearing retaliation, Comcomly came aboard as the *Ruby* set sail, claiming that the shot fired at the ship had been intended for ducks floating in the twilight. Of the episode Bishop wrote: "We gave this story (in our minds) the credit it deserved, nevertheless as I ever have determined to avoid as much as possible, committing any hostility amongst these savage nations, we appeared satisfied with it and a small Present was mutually exchanged—he is going tomorrow in his canoe up the River to kill Wild Geese and procure some Fresh fish for us previous to our Sailing and Shelathwell is going away to get 'Wapatoes' (wild potatoes) as his parting gift."[58]

Shelathwell returned the evening of the twenty-second with three bushels of wappatoes for Bishop and one for the ship's surgeon, who had loaned the chief a coat (which he returned) and medicines to improve his health. The next day the natives crowded around the *Ruby*.

---

* Some white men had misinterpreted potlatch gift giving as evidence of mental imbalance. Possibly Bishop may have thus misinterpreted Chinini's giving.

The women, who had endeared themselves to captain and crew, presented them farewell gifts, among which were fish and wappatoes. At three o'clock in the afternoon the *Ruby* crossed the bar into a raging sea which damaged the vessel, but not enough to prevent her from sailing to China. Bishop planned to hold his clamons on board to trade on the upper Northwest Coast on a second visit. Such journeys were becoming more common before a return to European or American home ports.

It had been a successful gathering season on the Columbia; for each fur item that had cost fifty cents Bishop hoped to receive twelve dollars on the China market, or a 2,300 percent turnover. Aboard ship he carried a good many separate pieces: 864 otter skins, forty-seven large sea otter cloaks (usually called cutsarks and consisting of three skins each), 483 sea otter tails (frequently sold separately because of their perfect furring), 169 pieces of sea-otter skins, 104 beaver skins and pieces, twenty-five silver gray fox, thirty-eight marten, twenty raccoon, one lynx, twenty river otter, four wolf, twelve black fox, fourteen deer, and 150 marmot.

As the *Ruby* passed from the Northwest Coast, so, in a sense, did the initiative of the British in the maritime fur trade of the region. By 1801 their ships would disappear from the coast for over a decade.[59] One proof that the exploits of Drake's British successors had truly shrunk the earth was that events in their homeland directly affected those in a small corner of the globe thousands of miles away. Britain's wars with France, a legacy of the eighteenth century, would continue into the nineteenth as she struggled with Napoleon who was seeking mastery of Europe. Northwest Coastal natives may not have known of such struggles, so occupied were they with their own, yet they would not escape repercussions from them. Into the vacuum created by these international developments American shippers would press their trading efforts on the Northwest Coast more firmly than ever. On the lower Columbia River portion of that coast their trading success would depend upon ladies of wood and of flesh and blood: their sturdy ships bringing them around a dangerous Cape Horn and across the broad Pacific, and Chinook women, their chief customer-merchants at the marketplace.

5. Ladies in the Trade

> Among a portion of the Indians, the management of trade is entrusted to the women. The reason given by the men was, that women could talk with white men *better* than they could, and were willing to talk *more*.
>
> William Sturgis' Address to the Mercantile Library Association of Boston

As TRADERS OF OLD England withdrew from the Northwest Coast, those of New England quickened their efforts in that quarter. Typical of instructions from Yankee owners to the captains of their ships were those of August 8, 1789, by James and Thomas Handasyd Perkins of Boston to Captain James Rowan of one of the staunch ladies of the trade, the nearly 160-ton ship *Eliza* of Boston, to "Explore the Coast from one end to the other,"[1] offering as much in trade as other vessels but not outbidding them, a "bad policy."[2] So much for the white competition; as for relations with native customer-merchants, Rowan was warned to be constantly on his guard, not suffering his officers or men "to put themselves into the power of them or to go on shore at any time unless absolutely necessary. . . ."[3]

Since American sea otter trade began on the Northwest Coast from the vicinity of the Columbia River northward, traders in areas of its heaviest concentration—from lower Vancouver Island to Alaska—had applied to the entire coast standards and procedures in the trade employed there. With native-white tensions in those quarters increasing in direct proportion to increasing trade, it was quite natural for American fur trade entrepreneurs to place all coastal peoples, including Chinooks and Clatsops, under the same blanket. Their warnings to captains to be constantly on guard when trading applied to all Indian customers alike, although the two peoples of the lower Columbia were less hostile than those to the north and immediately to the south of them.

It could be said that at the river mouth the greatest threat to traders came not from man but from nature, as many of them discovered to their sorrow. A case in point was the threat to those aboard the 159-ton brig aptly named the *Hazard*, of Boston, Captain Benjamin Swift,[4] whose chief officer and four men were drowned in 1789 attempting to sound the bar.[5] Of such sacrifices did the trade consist, but it continued apace. New Englanders may have decried such human sacrifices to material gain, but they did not withhold their sons and others from the trade. One of the *Hazard*'s owners would happily report that Captain Swift had made the largest collections of skins ever on the coast.[6]

As nineteenth-century frontiers retreated from America's east coast, voices there would cry louder than in any other place in the land for the protection of the American Indian. And a century later an ecology-minded society would decry the slaughter of the sea otter for profit.* From these tragic legacies of the trade a general indictment of it would follow. Yet viewing the trade in its historical perspective, one sees two sides of the coin of a mercantile business in which both red men and white men had a stake. The Northwest Coast–China trade, like any other merchandising, involved risking, besides lives, large amounts of capital. Sometimes Yankee enterprisers won; frequently they broke even; sometimes they lost. Charges that they dealt unjustly with their Chinook clientele have been overstressed, for the natives took good commercial care of themselves, generally setting their own prices in the marketplace. When saturated with an item, they simply switched their demands to another. And as white traders carried trophies from that marketplace to seek profits on them in the marketplace of China, Chinooks and Clatsops, as well as others, carried their own trophies of the white man's trade to native markets to seek profits for themselves.

The Chinese vertex of the "triangular trade" (New England–Northwest Coast–China and return) produced trading procedures as interesting as those of the Chinooks and Clatsops. From exchange arrangements in China emerged a complex trading pattern (long after the first East India Company had been established there).† It began at Canton

* The United States was the first country to protect the sea otter in 1911. Now they are protected by every government on whose coast the few of them survive. Edna M. Fisher, "Prices of Sea Otter Pelts," *California Fish and Game*, XXVII, 4 (October, 1941), 264. They have been transplanted along the Washington State coast since 1970.

† There were two East India Companies (the older incorporated in 1579) which amalgamated in 1600 to become the United East India Company. William C. Hunter, *The Fan Kwae' at Canton before Treaty Days, 1825–1844*, 30. East India Company vessels had exclusive rights over other British vessels to deal in China. Other British vessels had to sell their cargoes to the company or pass through its hands at a commission. Outside British vessels could not take Chinese products home to sell; they had to take specie. This gave American traders an advantage. In time, American vessels would carry British fur cargoes

in 1745 when Emperor Yung Ching ordered all foreign trade confined to the Cantonese port of Whampoa, where government-appointed representatives exacted fees and kept watch on foreigners. Various nations trading in the Celestial Empire had agency headquarters, referred to as factories and located in the same sector of the city. In a large council hall foreign agents were summoned to meet Chinese merchants, usually to learn of new regulations, and to receive latest information. Strange Chinese customs had led to the creation of Boston mercantile agencies in Canton, freeing inexperienced supercargoes from attempting business transactions. The first such agency had been established in 1786 by Major Samuel Shaw, the American consul, for those Bostonians trading in China.[7] In 1789 Thomas H. Perkins established an agency in Canton for handling his furs.[8] His firm, Perkins & Co., handled business for the many ships in which he had an interest as well as for ships of other Americans, charging a percentage of the business transacted.

In 1799 New Englander Ebenezer Dorr sent his son to Canton to establish a factory.[9] To enter Canton a ship's supercargo had to obtain a stamp or seal called a *chop* to do business with a security merchant (a guarantor) of his choice at a *hong*, technically a place of business. The number of *hong* merchants was limited by the emperor to thirteen men who paid him large sums for their appointments. They were also called upon to contribute to public works. Collectively they were called the *Co-Hong*, the official licensed merchant monopoly. During the era of the New England trader in China, one *hong* merchant, Hoqua, was best known and most trusted—to the point that the Perkins company, doing all its business through him, named one of their ships for him as white men would later name craft for Chinooks and Clatsops. Unlike the mandarin in Canton who estimated his fortune at twenty-six million dollars,[10] most *hong* merchants were poor.[11] The number of them doing business for Americans varied from time to time, but most generally five or six performed most of the services of these "foreign devils."[12]

On sailing into the port of Whampoa, ten miles from Canton, a vessel was first detained by the linguist (interpreter), who "measured" Chinook-bought furs for a *Chumsha*, a (required) tip or present as a guarantee of service. The ship's captain turned his cargo over to the *hoppo* (customs officer), who exacted his fees, giving a *chop* for Chinese craft to carry the furs to the Canton factories, where business was conducted. There, the *hong*'s comprador (Chinese broker) arranged for purchases of Chinese goods from the sale of furs.[13] Contractors for *hong* merchants arranged for deliveries on the items purchased in reasonable time; goods

to China. Marion O'Neil, "The Maritime Activities of the North West Company, 1813–1821," *Washington Historical Quarterly*, XXI, 4 (October, 1930), 244, 265–66.

contracted with non-*hong* merchants were not delivered as promptly as were those passing through regular *hong* channels.[14] One unfamiliar with Chinese trade was easily lost in this maze of technicalities of a system based on Oriental patronage and patience. Even after a western trader learned the ropes, it was a clever one who expended less than six thousand dollars to exchange his goods.[15] No such sums did they have to pay Chinooks and other coastal natives although they gave "presents" to these mercantilists,[16] whom some believed had descended from Orientals.

Irregularities which fur traders attempted in China were usually intercepted by the crafty Orientals, who forced the visitors to use wile and finesse in their China dealings. By contrast, their dealings with natives of the Northwest Coast were sometimes harsh and crude, as the region recorded a dismal catalog of injustices by ships' captains and crews against these inhabitants. With guns and powder (which Chinese had manufactured long before them) whites on the coast often assumed a domineering posture toward the natives that eventuated in conflict. Often the traders' reaction stemmed from some native action, which, although compatible with native mores, was not so with those of visiting traders, especially those from New England, whose society stressed hard work and the accumulation of private property. The whirlwind of this market-disrupting cultural conflict was sown in losses in lives and the properties of natives. Sometimes they were held aboardships for failure to keep promises whites said they had made, and sometimes they were forced at gunpoint to sell skins for prices white men wished to pay.[17] Nor could Russian cruelty to Alaskan natives excuse Americans for their own cruelties.* Yet those Yankees needed to have gone some to surpass the Russians in cruelties imposed on Aleuts and Tlingits, whom they sometimes held hostage, forcing their fellows to bring in trophies of the hunt.[18] Hunting was for these people, at best, very difficult, often tearing them from their families for long periods of time. When they killed Russians to avenge these wrongs, the latter plundered their villages and murdered their people.[19]

Maltreatment of Northwest Coastal natives, regardless of the source,

* In 1785 a group of Russian merchants formed an association to hunt otters in Alaska. They became the Russian American Company, created by Ukase in 1799 with the aid of Count Nikolai Petrovich de Rezanov, with exclusive privilege of procuring furs within Russian limits of the territory stretching north from north latitude 54°40′ for a period of twenty years. In 1799, the year before the company moved its base from Kodiak Island (from which the Russians had operated since 1783) to Norfolk Sound (Sitka), it was reported that one Russian merchant alone had 1,300 natives out hunting. Elliott C. Cowdin, "The Northwest Fur Trade," *Hunt's Merchant Magazine*, XIV (1846), 537–38; "Ship Hancock Logbook," manuscript, Houghton Library, entry June 19, 1799.

caused them, especially in northern quarters already bent toward com-
bativeness, to retaliate in kind, vowing to make white men pay for their
cruelties. Fear of this native retaliation drove American shipowners to
equip their craft with the "paraphernalia of a miniature man of war,"
with guns and swivels at the ready.* When surrounded by canoe flotillas, ships' crews responded with cannon well shotted with grape and
langrage to keep natives at respectful distances. Even when native wom-
en customer-merchants, always more welcome on board than were their
men, rushed toward trading counters, seamen in the crosstrees brandished blunderbusses to check their aggressions.

At times the trading process degenerated into something like open
warfare, which natives did not always lose. In more publicized conflicts,
Boston ships, the *Boston* in 1803 and the *Atahualpa* two years later,
would go down to defeat in northern waters with heavy loss of life.[20]
To meet native retaliation merchant crews were frequently enlarged
with riffraff whose behavior tried the patience of Chinooks and other
natives. Some of these flotsam crews were ". . . of the worse class . . .
deserters from other vessels, who were hanging about Canton, ready to
take up with any means of egress that offered"—a conglomeration of
American, English, Irish, Welsh, Swedish, and French drifters, mu-
tineers, runaways, and escapees from Botany Bay. Even innocent Hawaiians (Owhyhees or Kanakas) were hired on to give a Polynesian
flavor to the polyglot crews who did battle with the native Americans.
Of these motley mariners one trader would recall that "we were oblig'd
to take anybody that offered to make up a proper compliment."[21]

The "compliment" may have been proper; its actions were hardly
so, for nothing in its trans-Pacific journey to the Northwest Coast altered its character. One crew member called that coast a "horrid Savage
land."[22] His fellows had helped make it that way. Any formula for
improving the dispositions of its natives would have to have gone much
deeper than that suggested in a July 6, 1802, letter of James Lamb to
his sons: "You will have Mollasses & rice in plenty on the Coast to
Sweeten the tawny stomachs of those savages." The previous summer
(1801), Samuel A. Dorr wrote to Ebenezer Dorr, "the most valuable
and saleable articles here [Meare's Bay in Nootka Sound] are Molasses,

---

* The addition of more equipment on fur-trading vessels had a dual purpose. The vessels
had to defend themselves not only from natives, but also from French privateers. In 1798
the "seas were not very safe—England and France were at war." Horatio Appleton Lamb,
"Notes on Trade with the Northwest Coast, 1790–1810. Made by Horatio Appleton Lamb,
from the records of James and Thomas Lamb, Merchant Shippers of Boston, 1781–1813,"
Houghton Library, Harvard University, 35. The *Jenny*, Captain Bowers, had an encounter
with French privateers in 1801 but arrived safely in the port of Boston. *Independent
Chronicle*, June 1, 1801.

Rice and Bread, and ere long Rum may be added to the list. . . ."
Molasses was popular in the north because near Chatham Straits, "the
central rendezvous of many powerful tribes," the clamon market was
temporarily glutted. This problem of oversupply, if harming the clamon
trade of the Chinooks, chief suppliers of that commodity, would be
temporary.[23]

A most tarnished spot on the trade coin was white sea and land trader-
imported liquor, the undoing of natives who never bargained for such
an import. No one knows for sure when the Chinooks got their first taste
of liquor. A Chinook woman told a white man among her people in the
1850's that they drank some rum from a wine glass, got drunk, and were
so scared at the strange feeling that they ran into the woods and hid until
they were sober. She said that the one who gave them the intoxicant was
a *tyee*, or chief, of a man-of-war vessel with "gold dollar" things, meaning epaulets, on his shoulders. The white man believed the officer to
have been Lieutenant Broughton. Although Chinooks and surrounding
peoples would have a few more years' respite from liquor than would
their more exposed coastal fellows, there would be ample time for it to
do its pernicious work among them. Before their stomachs would shortly
be soured by rum they were filled with biscuit and, as Lamb suggested,
molasses—hospitality trade items.[24]

Another unwanted import was disease. Smallpox epidemics had raced
through Columbia River tribes at least once in the waning years of the
eighteenth century,* returning at the turn of the nineteenth. Although
localized, the latter visitation destroyed many Chinooks and Clatsops,
for when the bar was breached by ships it was also breached by disease.
In 1805–1806 Lewis and Clark would note the pock-marked faces of
survivors of a sinister visitation ascribed by Chinooks to the first ship
entering the Columbia.[25] Cannon shots from that craft, they believed,
had sent clouds of lethal smoke upriver and into tributary streams, con-

---

* The Indian population of the Pacific Northwest was at its height before the smallpox
epidemic of 1782–83 which swept the region. The Indian population was nearly back to its
original number by the beginning of the nineteenth century. Of the nearly two thousand
natives living at the mouth of the Columbia in 1780, the population has been estimated as
consisting of 800 Chinooks (including those of Willapa Bay), 300 Clatsops, 300 Wahkiakums,
and 450 Kathlamets. James Mooney, *The Aboriginal Population of America North of Mexico*, Publication 2955, Smithsonian Miscellaneous Collections, LXXX, 7, 13–17. Herbert C.
Taylor, Jr., estimates the Chinookan population on the lower Columbia River from the
Pacific Ocean to the general area of the Cascades (of the river) to have been approximately
5,000 at about the year 1780. These figures are in sharp contrast to estimates of James
Mooney, who for that period put the numbers at 22,000. Herbert C. Taylor, Jr., "Aboriginal
Populations of the Lower Northwest Coast," *Washington Historical Quarterly*, LIV, 4
(October, 1963), 163.

Three Chinook men, drawn by George Catlin, showing their long, straight hair, neck ornaments, and many skin decorations. Although this sketch does not reveal the flattened heads, Catlin drew others which do. The two shields shown are not commonly described as being used by Lower Chinooks.

(Courtesy, The New York Historical Society, New York City)

This Chinook woman and her child, probably copied by the French traveler Abbé EM Domenech from a sketch by George Catlin, shows the woman's flattened head and what is probably a superfluity of tattoos. The infant is undergoing head flattening in one variation of the cradleboard used for the process.

Another type of head flattening cradleboard, in which a strap is tightened across the infant's forehead, is shown in this portrait made after sketches by Paul Kane.

(From George W. Fuller, A History of the Pacific Northwest, *©1931 by Alfred A. Knopf, Inc. By permission of the publisher)*

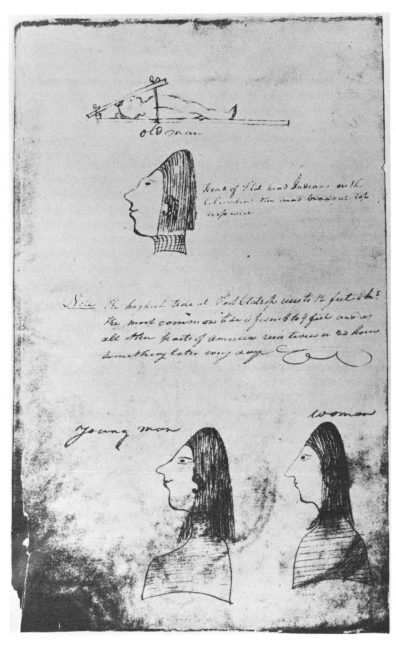

These sketches of flatheaded Chinooks and a cradleboard were made
by Lewis and Clark during their winter's stay among the Clatsops.
(Courtesy, Dodd, Mead and Company)

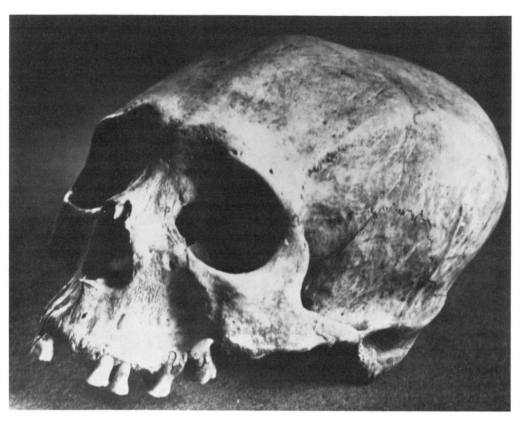

Some six years after the death of Comcomly, perhaps the best-known Chinook chief, his skull was removed by Dr. Meredith Gairdner of the Hudson's Bay Company. Placed in a Portsmouth, England, museum in 1838, the skull lost only its lower jawbone during a bombing of the museum in World War II, and it was returned to Oregon in 1953. After a short trip to the Smithsonian Institution for study, the skull was returned to the Chinook Nation and reburied.
(Courtesy, Oregon Historical Society)

RAMSEY. GEORGE.

George Ramsay (left) and George Washington (right) piloted American and British vessels on the Columbia River. One-eyed Ramsay was probably of Chinook and Scottish parentage. Washington was probably Chinook but may have had Hawaiian and Negro blood as well.

STUM-MA-NU.

A FLAT-HEAD BOY.

Stum-manu, or William Brooks, a Chinook lad orphaned at the age of two, accompanied missionary Jason Lee on a trip to the East in 1838 to speak before missionary groups. He asked for financial help for the Oregon missions and pleaded for an end to the liquor traffic to his people.

(Courtesy, Oregon Historical Society)

This early-twentieth-century photograph is of George A. Charley, a Chinook from Willapa Bay, holding what he claimed was a hand-forged knife given to his people in 1792 by Captain Robert Gray and eventually handed down to him through his father, "Lighthouse" Charley Ma-tote. Charley drowned in 1935 while fishing.

Charles Cultee, informant for anthropologist Franz Boas between 1890 and 1894, spoke both Lower Chinook and Kathlamet dialects.
(Courtesy, University of Washington, Pacific Northwest Collections)

MRS. WILSON, A KATHLAMET WOMAN

This photograph of Mrs. Wilson, a Kathlamet woman, from Franz Boas' *Kathlamet Texts*, clearly shows her flattened head and her ornamental cape containing rows of matched dentalia.

taminating them with death.* White sea and land traders would also spread tuberculosis and venereal diseases, to which natives had no resistance, forcing them to expand their pharmacopoeia to include concoctions of Oregon grape, a fern tea, herbs, and roots to allay their ravages. Chinooks and Clatsops used these and other vegetable compounds for tonics, emetics and cathartics—poultices from the inside bark of skunk weeds, salves from spruce gum mixed with equal parts of beaver grease, and ointments of grease and burned herbs.[26]

In later years white men, lamenting the introduction of their diseases among Chinooks and Clatsops, often forgot that those people had suffered a gamut of diseases long before they had seen white men. Even after the advent of the outsiders, the natives believed their ailments to be caused not alone by them, but also by evil beings who could wither a person's life with a gaze.

Not the least aggravating of precontact ailments were those affecting eyes, lungs, liver, and limbs. Some Chinooks suffered paralysis resulting from strokes possibly caused by their diet of rich, oily marine foods. Some whites believed such attacks were caused by brain damage from head flattening.[27] The addition of new diseases kept Chinook and Clatsop medicine men and their assistants busy beating rafters and house posts and often chanting twenty-four hours at a time while stamping and kneeling on their patients to rid their bodies of evil spirits. To prove their success they cleverly produced from their patients' bodies pieces of wood or stone, alleged evil spirits which they ceremoniously drowned in the river or burned in the fire. Chinooks had the benefit of services of two kinds of doctors—the *keelalles*, sometimes women, who administered medical and spiritual aid, and the *etaminuas*, or priests, who interceded for their patients' souls and their safe passage to the land of the spirits.[28]

Practicing abortions and infanticides at an earlier time, Chinooks and Clatsops did not seriously damage their birth-death ratio, but with newly imported diseases such practices posed a threat to their numbers to the point that a severe epidemic could possibly have wiped them out.

One part of the trading coin, as noted above, would not tarnish until the twentieth century. Then there would be concern for the welfare of the nonhuman objects of the trade—the sea otters themselves. Quite

* The natives did not identify the country from which the vessel came. "A Century Ago," *The West Shore*, V, 6 (June, 1879), 164–65. Blame for the epidemic was tossed like a political football among representatives of the various nations on the Northwest Coast. Ross Cox, *Adventures on the Columbia River, Including the Narrative of a Residence of Six Years on the Western Side of the Rocky Mountains, among Various Tribes of Indians Hitherto Unknown; Together with a Journey across the American Continent*, I, 311.

naturally, those most responsible for their decimation, white promoters and traders who encouraged natives to hunt them by offering enticing trade goods, did not decry such carnage. One of the men who sought these furry animals off the coast, William Sturgis, perhaps expressed the attitude of his fellows toward the object of their enterprise by exuberating that "excepting a beautiful woman and a lovely infant . . ." they are "among the most attractive natural objects. . . ." In eastern America, far from the scene of the slaughter, few, if any, opposed a butchery which came within an eyelash of extinguishing the species. Why should they? The sea otter brought them coveted oriental products. Its own covering, albeit indirectly, covered their women with fine cloths from the Far East. In an age when men thought the physical environment something to subdue, they failed to see that sea otters were as much a part of it as they.

Some time after he had "witnessed the growth, maximum, decrease, and finally, its [the sea otter trade's] abandonment by Americans," Sturgis, in his January 21, 1846, address to the Mercantile Library Association of Boston, would tell how his early visits to the Northwest Coast had "brought to his knowledge the injustice, violence, and bloodshed [to the natives]" which had marked the progress of the trade.[29] Long and far removed from the scene of his trading days, he could safely reveal its evils and his own good conduct in it. Perhaps violence catapulted him into a position of leadership in the Northwest Coastal fur trade. The year following his father's death, 1798, Sturgis, then a mere lad of fifteen, shipped out from Boston aboard the *Eliza* for the Northwest Coast. There, shortly after the mutinous crew of the *Ulysses* held Captain Lamb for a period in his cabin, young Sturgis rose from foremast hand on the *Eliza* to first mate of the *Ulysses*. When the *Ulysses* and the *Eliza* met again, this time in China, he returned to the latter ship as third mate, occupying that post on the homeward voyage which ended in the spring of 1800. Owners of the *Ulysses*, James and Thomas Lamb, impressed by the lad's ability, immediately hired him as mate of the 214-ton *Caroline*, on which he sailed in late 1800 on his second voyage to the Northwest Coast and China. When her master died in 1802 in Honolulu from tuberculosis, Sturgis took his place. His employers, caught in a frenzy of trade, inspired not only by funds but also by fears that trading days were numbered, felt they had little time to waste. So the following year they dispatched Sturgis to the Northwest Coast in charge of the *Caroline*.[30]

To squeeze the most from the trade, Boston merchants owning more than one ship doubled their voyages, ordering some of their craft to China as others traded on the Northwest Coast. So as not to derange the trade, ships of the same company were cautioned not to compete with each other. Six American vessels traded on the coast in 1800. In the quickened pace of the trade, fifteen American ships in 1801 collected some eighteen thousand sea otter skins valued at $275,000. In 1802, eight American vessels collected fifteen thousand skins, which sold for $20 apiece on the China market.[31]

To satisfy native wants in order to stay in the sea otter trade, the owners of the *Caroline*, when dispatching her from Boston in July, 1803, included in her cargo some five thousand ermine furs valued at $43,325.12. On his previous journey Sturgis had observed that the natives had valued these skins so highly that they had made them a standard of exchange, and in response to their requests that he bring them some to trade he had sent home a fine specimen, urging his employers to make every effort to obtain similar ones for the trade. Taking young Sturgis at his word, they had successfully placed an order for the skins at the annual Leipzig Fair, an institution dating from medieval times and drawing customers from around the world. Thus, aboard the *Caroline* heading for the Northwest Coast, ermine from Europe, beautifully white in winter, were like coals shipped from Newcastle. Aboard, they shared space with 650 gallons of rum, a fairly recent trade item finding ever increased space on ships sailing the Northwest Coast. The flow of this commodity would increase to the extent that Boston ships would gain notoriety for the quantities of it they carried to whet the appetites and dull the senses of native consumers.[32] The *Caroline* put into the Hawaiian Islands, where for pigs, yams, potatoes, and watermelons Sturgis exchanged tar and lampblack[33] before proceeding to the coast, which he reached in January, 1804. The date of the *Caroline*'s first entry into the Columbia River is unknown, but it is known that she was there five months into the new year, for on a tree near the river mouth an inscription bore the legend: "Ship Caroline of Boston, May 21, 1804."[34] This was not the only such record carved on trees in Chinook-Clatsop country, for another bore the inscription: "H. Thompson, ship Guatimozin of Boston, February 20, 1804."[35]

In the Columbia River, Sturgis purchased, mostly from Chinook women, 450 beaver skins and 145 clamons.[36] As a mariner, he appreciated the Chinooks' skill in handling their canoes for seeking food, trading goods, and traveling generally. He was particularly impressed by the affection and care given the young by their elders, who, without resorting to corporal punishment, effectively disciplined errant offspring. For example, at one place on the coast a child he saw attempting to eat molasses from an open tub in a canoe was unceremoniously dumped naked, dirt, oil, and all, into the sticky mass.[37] Midwinter plunges of native children into cold water apparently shocked him more than it did them. Even ethnologist George Gibbs, who later would study Chinooks and Clatsops, grudgingly admitted that their mothers, in a "general state of profligacy," showed "a certain degree of affection toward their children."[38]

For a year and a half Sturgis worked the coast peddling his ermines from the Columbia River to Kaigahnee (now Dall), a small island south of Prince of Wales Island in Alaska.* In a single afternoon in those quarters he purchased as many as 560 prime sea otter skins, each worth fifty dollars in Canton, giving for each otter five ermine skins costing less than thirty cents apiece in Boston. In 1804 the 285-ton ship *Vancouver*, Captain Thomas Brown, owned by Theodore Lyman, and the 200-ton ship *Pearl*, Captain John Ebbets, owned by the Perkinses, the Lambs, and Russel Sturgis, carried ermine to the Northwest Coast, helping to depress the market, in which in two years a hundred ermine skins would bring not even one otter skin.

His otter skins safely aboard, Sturgis sailed for China on June 1, 1805. There, subtracting the outward-bound cargo cost of $43,325.12, he realized for the *Caroline*'s owners a net $73,034.32. As good as this percentage of profit was, it did not match that of some more productive journeys, which, with capital outlays of some $40,000, returned their owners over $150,000.[39] Prone to look more at successes than at failures in the trade, hopeful owners jumped into it, and by 1805 a half-dozen or so firms operated several vessels on the Northwest Coast. The large number of ships in the business in 1805, a year which saw 17,445 otter skins taken from the region's rookeries, also insured its decline. Assuming command of the *Atahualpa*, Sturgis left Boston in October, 1806, traded on the coast in 1807, and, sailing via Hawaii and China, terminated his triangle in Boston in June, 1808. At the same time he terminated his face to face contact with Northwest Coastal natives,[40] for after a dozen years at sea he went into business for himself and then formed a partnership with John Bryant. From 1818 to 1825 Bryant and Sturgis would own and operate nine ships in the Northwest Coastal fur trade, quitting that phase of their business in 1829 when it became no longer profitable.†

They and their fellow Yankees had done their share in depleting the

---

* Usually, vessels from 100 to 250 tons burthen remained on the coast from twenty-one months to two years, with but few loading out in a single year, absenting themselves from the east coast for some three years.

† Bryant and Sturgis, however, were engaged as shipowners and merchants in the foreign trade for half a century. From 1810 to 1840 more than half of the trade of the Northwest Coast and China would be conducted by their firm.

sea otter, especially since natives had guns and ammunition, which these New Englanders had been carrying to them in increasing volumes, for their hunting. Sometimes natives turned their guns on the human animal, as happened in 1802 when they massacred Russian traders at Fort Sitka (New Archangel in Norfolk Sound), Alaska.* Most of the murder weapons, complained the Russians, were American, as they had traded none to the natives themselves.[41] Yet the increased numbers of guns in native hands (ten thousand of them in 1802) had enabled the Russians to secure additional furs, with which from 1803 to 1805 they entered China in two ships—about the extent of their direct shipments to that place, as they depended upon Americans to do their carrying.

In his 1846 address before the Mercantile Library Association, Sturgis would assure his listeners that his fortune and those of the Perkinses, the Lambs, Edward Dorr and sons, William H. Boardman, and one Mr. Pope,

> were not acquired, as individual wealth not unfrequently is, at the expense of our own community, by a tax upon the whole body of consumers, in the form of enhanced prices, often from adventitious causes. They were obtained abroad by giving to the Indians articles which they valued more than their furs, and then selling those furs to the Chinese for such prices as they are willing to pay; thus adding to the wealth of the country [United States], at the expense of foreigners, all that was acquired by individuals beyond the usual return for the use of capital, and suitable compensation for the services of those employed. This excess was sometimes very large.[42]

Troubles with Britain at the time of his address would give Sturgis and his listeners additional pride in their Boston heritage. Bostonians would be proud of him, too, as a man "of practical intelligence and sterling good sense," thinking he had done much for their city and country, for as Sturgis would proclaim, "a number of American vessels, and many seamen and others were constantly and profitably employed, for more than forty years—which brought wealth to those engaged in it, and was probably as beneficial to the country as any commercial use of an equal amount of capital has ever been."[43]

It would be of no particular interest to Sturgis' listeners to know that

* Gabriel Ivan Davidov gives the year 1801 for the destruction by natives of the Russian settlement at Sitka. This date seems to be in disagreement with most accounts, which give the year as 1802. At the time the fort was burned, a few American sailors were there. They joined natives in setting fire to the fort. The natives scalped and tortured the Russians in retaliation for cruel treatment they had received. "Extracts from Davidov's Diary by Gabriel Ivan Davidov, 1810–1812," translated from the Russian by Michael E. Affonin, Seattle, Wash., 1932–33, typescript copy of manuscript, Archives of British Columbia.

Chinooks, Clatsops, and others of equal practical intelligence and good sense had also made profits but without risking large amounts of capital, without hiring large crews in fortified ships, and without traveling around the world to do it. Nor would Sturgis mention that for some Bostonians the trade had not only been unprofitable but downright ruinous. Quickly passing had been the time which one fur trader in the Pacific Northwest described as producing "an average clear gain of a thousand per cent. every second year. . . ."[44]

Whether these New Englanders had succeeded or not, thanks to them Chinooks and Clatsops for a first full decade of the nineteenth century regarded as a curiosity a "King George" flag flying from a ship mast. Because of their enterprise in the trade, natives gave the appellation "Boston Men" to all Americans regardless of their place of origin. And, thanks to them, natives had not only guns but also cloth. White sea traders brought them increasing amounts of cloth after 1789. To the white carriers of this commodity Chinooks and Clatsops gave the name "cloth men" (*pâh-shish-e-ooks*).[45]

There is little record that costly Oriental goods adorned Chinook and Clatsop women as they did eastern white women (although the latter also wore utilitarian fabrics such as nankeens).[46] These fineries included taffetas, sinshaws, sarcenets, crapes, pongees, satins, lustrings (soft materials of plain twill weave used for linings), silk velvets, and silk fringes so expensive that they were loaded on ships in China in dry boxes on clear days.[47] Coarser red and blue robes, which eastern Americans would have once gladly worn, were sold to natives of the coast like castoffs handed down to poor relatives. Although not classifying as luxury items, some of the clothing of European origin carried to Chinooks and Clatsops was, in contrast to that of their own manufacture, light in weight, easily dried, and capable of withstanding much crushing, wrinkling, and wadding before wearing out. Seldom carried to the coast, but eagerly sought in eastern America, were dishware and teas.* Differences in

---

* Chinese did not drink green tea, preferring the black. Howard Corning, "Sullivan Dorr, an Early China Merchant," *Essex Institute Historical Collections*, LXXVIII (1942), 162. The outside world was eager for Chinese green tea. Of the various varieties Young Hyson (Uchin) was scarce, requiring close scrutiny by the foreign buyer to be sure that other mixtures were not added. Pickman, "Memoranda from Dudley L. Pickman on Doing Business in Canton," Benjamin Shreve Papers. Young Hyson was made of the inside leaf of the plant picked before rain. Other green teas of the hyson variety were Hyson Skin (Pecha), made of the old, coarse leaves; Gunpowder (Chuca and Imperial), of leaves a degree larger and older than Young Hyson; Gomee, made of the large curved leaves; and Heshon, of leaves taken when the plant was less in leaf. The last was not as strong and was picked before the rain. Of the black teas, those of first quality were Pouchong (that put up in paper); Souchong (fine tea); and Compoi (especially fine, but less than superior). A

white and red American tastes were evident in the fact that while the former sought tea, the latter sought pots, especially those of copper. Thanks to Sturgis and his fellow carriers, Northwestern natives purchased items such as glass beads, which greatly fascinated them. So highly prized were those of blue that Chinooks and Clatsops called them "Chief Beads." White merchants, deferring to these native tastes, strung pennyweights of fifty to seventy beads that sold by the fathom to adorn the necks of chiefs and the ankles and hair of their women. No matter how much native whims may have puzzled white traders, the easterners went right ahead stringing their beads and adjusting to the natives' demands without wasting time or shipboard space on goods which would not sell. Good salesmen, the Yankees probably would have admitted that, no matter how strange, their customers were always right, and scarcely more guilty of conspicuous consumption than they.

With increasing varieties of trade goods such as copper tea kettles, blue beads, blue robes, brass armbands, cloth, and clothing, Chinooks and Clatsops more easily acquired traditional trade items from tribes of the Columbia interior—namely, pounded salmon, bear grass, and roots. By so doing they more firmly controlled the downriver traffic by preventing the interior people from trading directly with ships. As the Columbia mouth was a breaking point in trade, so, in a sense, was the entire river, from which increased traffic diffused its goods to dozens of tributary points. Ship goods, joining traditional ones from the coast, such as shells, were by the early nineteenth century beginning to find their way into the intermontane entrepôts of the Walla Walla and Grande Ronde valleys and others further east.[48] Off the ships came such goods as knives, brass kettles, armbands, and buttons.*

black tea popular with westerners was Bohea, formerly a mixture of Congo (well worked and rolled) and Confu. Chinese coolies drank the last named tea, to which they added Whaping, an inferior tea used by the poor, as was Canton tea, which came from a shrub. Elma Loines, "Hoqua, Sometime Chief of the Co-Hong at Canton (1769–1843)," *Essex Institute Historical Collections*, LXXXIX (1953), 99. Bohea was the only tea packed in Canton. The others were brought from interior China. There was little variation in price of the teas which were packed in chests. Ebenezer Dorr, "Papers of Ebenezer Dorr," manuscript, Peabody Museum, Salem, Mass.

  * The Shoshones in 1804 reportedly had four guns which could have come from several directions. Reuben Gold Thwaites (ed.), *Original Journals of the Lewis and Clark Expedition, 1804–1806*, III, 30n. But Lewis and Clark, traveling in Shoshoni country toward the Rocky Mountains in 1805–1806 saw no guns at all. It was not until they reached the Cascades of the Columbia that they saw one gun among the natives there. *Ibid.*, 194. Although they did not possess guns, natives of the interior, such as Nez Percés, had by 1805 many ornaments of beads, shells, brass, and copper, which most likely had come in trade from the Pacific Coast. *Ibid.*, 78. On the Fraser River to the north, not yet an avenue for the flow of European goods to any extent, Simon Fraser of the North West Company would find in

On May 1, 1804, Captain William Shaler brought the brig *Lelia Byrd* to the mouth of the Columbia after a stormy passage from China in which the ship's hull, foremast, and spars had been damaged.[49] The *Lelia Byrd* had earlier been in the Columbia when owned by Shaler and trader Richard J. Cleveland, but on disposing of their cargo of sea otter skins at a handsome profit, the two dissolved their partnership, which was perhaps fortuitous as the crew was composed of "as accomplished villains as ever disgraced any country."[50] Now Shaler hoped to replace his damaged gear with timbers of this region, which, of all those along the coast, were tall, straight, and slender—well suited for masts, yards, booms, gaffs, and other ship parts. Stormy weather off the bar kept him from making repairs, and after eight days of marking time he sailed to California and on to the Hawaiian Islands, where he sold his ship and sailed to China aboard the *Atahualpa*.[51]

Another vessel arriving at the Columbia (on Saturday, April 6, 1805) was the brig *Lydia*, Captain Samuel Hill, of Boston and recently from the Hawaiian Islands, seeking furs and clamons, coveted as ever by natives of the Queen Charlotte Islands. As Hill put his craft into Bakers Bay no natives greeted his arrival. When he and his supercargo, William Walker, Jr., returned to the brig that evening from a visit ashore, they discovered two canoes alongside. The occupants of these craft had no articles to exchange for those aboard the *Lydia*. The next day Hill and six others took an overnight exploratory trip in a whaleboat. The day after that, true to their usual trading form, the natives sold several river otter and beaver skins to Walker. He thought the slow trading due to inclement weather,[52] when, in fact, it had been due to Chinook reluctance to trade heavily at first contact.

On Wednesday, April 10, Hill, with five hands and a Hawaiian lass he had brought from the islands, left in a whaleboat for Youngs River, leaving Walker to conduct the trade. In Hill's absence the supercargo had "not been able to break trade with the Natives, they holding out for the price that was given by Capt. [Thomas] Browne [Brown] in the

---

1808 that natives just below Fort George (now Prince George, British Columbia) had heard of guns but had seen none. Near present-day Lillooet, British Columbia, Fraser saw a gun of Russian manufacture among natives. Further downriver, near the mouth of the Thompson River, natives dropped from fright at the firing of a gun by the Fraser party. W. Kaye Lamb (ed.), *The Letters and Journals of Simon Fraser 1806–1808*, 64, 83, 86. Yet, two years earlier that party had learned from natives west of the Rocky Mountains in northern Canada that they had communication by water with three portages to a place where natives could obtain guns and ammunition. It was unclear to Fraser just where the point of contact was. In the Beaver Lake area he saw a "pistol brass mounted with powder and ball" gotten at the point of contact from traders. *Ibid.*, 172.

Vancouver during her last voyage."[53] Making it difficult for Walker, then, to melt the ice jamming his trade, was the leniency of Brown, who may have violated the orders of his ship's owners to offer the same prices offered by those of other ships.[54] Most shipowners carefully admonished their captains and supercargoes to follow this fundamental rule of the trade.

Finally, on April 11, true to form, the natives "broke trade"[55] to sell forty-five clamons and several beaver skins, following the next day with more such sales. The types of furs they carried to the *Lydia* indicate that they were finding it easier to collect pelts from land animals such as beavers, foxes, and land otters than from sea otters. Staple items of their trade continued to be salmon and roots, which crews eagerly sought to satisfy their hunger. With apparently no rifles as yet, for bigger game Chinooks and Clatsops used their muskets, which they stuffed with fine gravel when they ran out of shot.[56] This ruinous practice forced them to their bows and arrows to gather not only small animals but larger ones which they had hunted with guns.

Hill returned to the ship early on the afternoon of April 12. His penchant for exploration irritated the nervous supercargo, who from the north the next month would write: "A stranger would suppose that Mr. Lyman had fitted the Brig out on a Voyage of discovery. If I save my life and get to Boston safe, it is more than I at this time expect. The Indians I fear not so long as every Man, under pay on board the Brig is attending to their respective duties on board—At, Columbia's River, at three different times, Capt. Hill with 5 or 6 hands were near being lost."[57]

Trade continued as intermittently as the April squalls chopping up Bakers Bay. On the eighteenth no trading canoes came alongside the *Lydia*, but to get female companions aboard the brig there did appear two canoes for "the convenience of the Ladies." On the twentieth Hill again took off with his Hawaiian lass, increasing the anxiety of the supercargo, who feared for his own safe return to the east coast lest some accident befall the captain. On the twenty-first some Chehalis came in with clamons to sell. The following day, of the dwindling supply of clamons Walker observed that ". . . the Chanoke tribe, I am informed are at work, dressing Moose [elk] hides for sale."[58] Chinook industry paid off, for daily until the brig sailed the natives brought more clamons out to sell. On the twenty-fifth the ship readied to sail, but Hill and his girlfriend had not returned from their outing, much to the chagrin of the supercargo. It was 4:00 P.M. of the twenty-seventh that Hill returned, having gone a considerable distance upriver to the "Great Rapids."[59] Not for a week of bad weather did the *Lydia* get under way, during which time she gathered all the clamons the natives had.

On May 3 the *Lydia* recrossed the bar, and six days later she reached Cape Flattery. At that place Chief Utiller of the Makahs came aboard with a letter from the two survivors of the *Boston*, John Thompson, the sailmaker and gunner, and John Rogers Jewitt, the armourer who had been spared death to work for the natives.[60] Hill sailed north, amid violent clashes with his supercargo, to save the two. In June the *Lydia* met the *Atahualpa*, and it was learned that on June 13 natives had murdered Captain David Porter of that ship, the mate, and eight crewmen. Having stomached Captain Hill long enough, the supercargo transferred himself, furs, and journal to the *Atahualpa*.[61]

In northern waters Hill met other Lyman-owned ships—five in all. To their captains he proposed a mass effort to rescue the two men enslaved at Nootka, ". . . but," wrote Hill later, "they all from Motives and Interest or Fear absolutely refused & represented the attempt as rash & impudent."[62] So Hill went alone to Nootka, where on July 18 he affected the rescue in which a chief was reportedly killed by accident in a *Lydia* cabin by a musket discharge.[63] The captain was proud of his exploit but angered that many of his countrymen, minimizing the feat, "Laughed me to scorn," branding him "a fool or Madman."[64] So worn was he by adverse reaction to his deed that his health was broken for two years, and he became religious. Whether or not he told his wife of his friendship for the Chinook "lady" and the Hawaiian girl is unknown. Any anger she may have had from knowledge of such a relationship could not have hurt Hill more than the taunts that agonized him for the rest of his life.[65]

Hill might have spared himself subsequent woes had his adventure through dangerous primitive country up the Columbia been a one-way trip. Just as his supercargo had feared that it was, so would "Bostons" fear that the trek of their landsmen, the Lewis and Clark party, would be a journey into oblivion. Around every bend of its trail would lurk dangers that would threaten to wipe out not only it, but also with it the hopes of the American republic for westward expansion. Among no peoples, except the Mandans of the Missouri, would the expedition spend more time than among the Clatsops and Chinooks near the mouth of the Columbia River. That the party would survive at all to return home to tell about the trip was due not only to its planning, skill, and intrepidity, but also as much to the disposition of its hosts, among whom it would sojourn a season within the sound of the breakers of the mighty Pacific Ocean beating their fury against the disgorging waters of the Columbia River.

6.   Cloth Men Soldiers

> In traffic they are keen, acute, and intelligent, and they employ in all their bargains a dexterity and finesse which, if it be not learnt from their foreign visitors, may show how nearly the cunning of savages is allied to the little arts of more civilized trade.
>
> Lewis and Clark, *Journals*

B Y ACCIDENT OF history and geography it was not until 1805 that Chinooks and Clatsops at the western edge of a supposed northwest passage were discovered by white land explorers pushing westerly across the American land mass. Sixty-seven years before Meriwether Lewis and William Clark wintered among Mandan Indians of the Missouri River (in present-day North Dakota) en route overland to discover the Columbia River peoples, the French explorer Pierre Gaultier Sieur de La Vérendrye had lived among the same Mandans.* After exploring interior America, La Vérendrye had sent his son to view the Missouri River a few miles beyond, but his party had not followed it to the West.[1] Although the French in the early eighteenth century would build a string of trading posts from Montreal along three thousand canoe miles to the Saskatchewan River (in present-day Canada) within sight of the Rocky Mountains, those peaks, like palisades around a fort, hemmed them out of the Pacific watershed. Their British rivals for North America had wrested an empire from them in 1763 at the termination of the French and Indian War. Now the British traversed old French routes westerly beyond the Grand Portage (from Lake Superior to Rainy Lake in

---

* Unable to obtain financing from the French king, La Vérendrye had turned to Montreal merchants for assistance in exchange for his promise to trade for furs and to explore. In 1731 he and his party, joined by a Jesuit missionary, had passed over the Grand Portage at the western shores of Lake Superior to a vast water route across Canada to the Rocky Mountains. Walter O'Meara, *The Savage Country*, 4.

91

Canada), encouraged by "the lure of 400 percent profit" in the fur trade.[2]

Despite a later eighteenth-century expansion of that trade, much of the American continent from the Mississippi River to the Pacific Ocean had remained unknown to white men. Intercourse of Americans, recently freed from Britain, with natives of the interior had been restricted by Spanish control of the Louisiana country[3] and by strong British influence below the Great Lakes even after that territory, to the Mississippi River, had been ceded to the United States by treaty following the Revolutionary War. In the year of that treaty, 1783, John Ledyard, a Connecticut Yankee and former crew member of Captain Cook's flagship, on returning to the United States had published a small volume of his journeys which,[4] with his other promotional efforts, had helped interest American merchants in the possibility of a Northwest Coast sea otter trade.[5] One of the many with whom he had talked was Thomas Jefferson,* whose interest in the American West had been sharpened by, among other things, British plans to explore it from the Mississippi to California[6] and by the overland journey of North West (Fur) Company trader Alexander Mackenzie to the Pacific. Although in no position at this time to actively project a plan of western exploration, Jefferson's mind had been alive to the possibilities of such an undertaking, which he believed would not only physically strengthen the young republic but have scientific and humanitarian benefits as well.

Then vice-president of the United States, Jefferson had been deeply interested in the original inhabitants of the American continent and especially in their origins and languages. In a June 24, 1799, letter to a Mr. Dunbar, Jefferson had written that for some time he had been interested in collecting the languages of tribes to the Mississippi River. But, he had concluded, "Beyond that river our means fail. . . ."[7] Some day he had hoped to overcome that failure. The following year it had appeared he would have his opportunity of doing that, for he was elected president of his country. On June 18, 1803, he secretly proposed to Congress to send a party to trace the Mississippi and Columbia rivers to the Pacific. Approving the plan, Congress appropriated twenty-five hundred dollars "for the purpose of extending the external commerce

---

* Jefferson was then American minister to the French court. He planned that Ledyard should make trans-Asiatic and trans-Pacific journeys to the Northwest Coast, leaving from France. Once in the Pacific Northwest, he was to explore the western side of the American continent at the latitude of the Missouri River in search of waterways which would connect with that stream. As early as November 26, 1782, Jefferson had expressed interest in "the country between the Mississippi and the waters of South Sea." Frank E. Ross, "The Early Fur Trade of the Great Northwest," *Oregon Historical Quarterly*, XXXIX (1938), 391.

of the United States."[8] Jefferson's secretary, Captain Meriwether Lewis, who had been ordered by the French minister to forego an expedition to the West which had taken him and a botanist as far as Kentucky (after an earlier Jeffersonian proposal to explore the region from the Missouri to the Pacific), was appointed to undertake the expedition, knowledge of which was to be kept from the French, Spanish, and British. In preparing for his journey Lewis was sent to Philadelphia to learn from "distinguished professors"[9] the nomenclature of the natural sciences. He also selected his co-leader for the proposed trek, Lieutenant William Clark, brother of George Rogers Clark, the well-known Indian fighter. Lewis' commission of June 20, 1803, among other things, instructed him to take "Light articles for barter and presents among the Indians" which his party would meet on a journey following waterways which "may offer the most direct and practicable water communication across the continent, for the purpose of commerce."[10] The commission, in part, continued:

> In all your intercourse with the natives, treat them in the most friendly and conciliatory manner which their own conduct will admit; allay all jealousies as to the object of your journey; satisfy them of its innocence; make them acquainted with the position, extent, character, peaceable and commercial dispositions of the United States; of our wish to be neighbourly, friendly, and useful to them, and of our dispositions to a commercial intercourse with them; confer with them on the points most convenient as mutual emporiums, and the articles of most desireable interchange for them and us. If a few of their influential chiefs, within practicable distance, wish to visit us, arrange such a visit with them, and furnish them with authority to call on our officers on their entering the United States, to have them conveyed to this place at the public expence. If any of them should wish to have some of their young people brought up with us, and taught such arts as may be useful to them, we will receive, instruct, and take care of them. Such a mission, whether of influential chiefs, or of young people, would give some security to your own party. Carry with you some matter of the kine-pox; inform those of them with whom you may be of its efficacy as a preservative from the small-pox; and instruct and encourage them in the use of it. This may be especially done wherever you winter. . . . Should you reach the Pacific ocean, inform yourself of the circumstances which may decide whether the furs of those parts may not be collected as advantageously at the head of the Missouri (convenient as is supposed to the waters of the Colorado and Oregon or Columbia) as at Nootka Sound, or any other point of that coast; and that trade be consequently conducted through the Missouri and United States more beneficially than by the circumnavigation now practised.
>
> On your arrival on that coast, endeavor to learn if there be any port within

your reach frequented by the sea vessels of any nation, and to send two of your trusty people back by sea, in such way as shall appear practicable, with a copy of your notes; and should you be of opinion that the return of your party by the way they went will be eminently dangerous, then ship the whole, and return by sea....[11]

It had been the treaty executed at Paris on April 30, 1803, transferring the Louisiana Territory from France to the United States, that further stimulated and vindicated Jefferson's wish to explore this newly acquired territory and beyond to the Pacific. The Lewis and Clark expedition for that purpose got under way from Saint Louis in the spring of 1804. Joining the two expedition leaders were nine young men from Kentucky, fourteen soldiers, two voyageurs, an interpreter, a hunter, Captain Clark's black servant, and fifteen men who "attended on the commencement of the expedition to secure safety during the transit through some Indian tribes whose hostility was apprehended."*[12] Later, a half-blood interpreter, Charbonneau, and his Indian wife, Sacajawea, would join the party. Its baggage consisted of seven bales and a box of Indian presents, clothing, tools, ammunition, and fourteen bales and boxes of Indian trade items of richly laced coats, medals, flags, tools, and ornaments. The nature of the Indian goods indicated that the expedition planners had perhaps discussed with crews of Northwest Coastal trading ships native tastes in trade items.

The party proceeded up the Missouri River to winter, 1804/1805, among the Mandans. During the summer of 1805 it trekked up the Missouri watershed and across the Rocky Mountains into the watershed of the Columbia, on whose broad estuary Clark noted in his journal on November 7, 1805, that they were "inview of the opening of the Ocian, which creates great joy."†[13] Evidence that they were nearing the sea was apparent in the increased numbers of natives wearing clothes and possessing cloth from ships. A Wahkiakum, whose people sold the hungry party pounded salmon and dogs, as had others on the lower Columbia, guided the party downriver on November 7 with such skill that his people won praise from Clark as the "best Canoe navigators." More evidence that they were nearing the sea were English words on the natives' lips, which included profanities, a good indication they had been in contact with sailors. Clark would opine that the Chinookan language

* Charles G. Clarke says that the full complement of the Lewis and Clark expedition was fifty-one members who set out, and seven (including Sacajawea) who joined it en route. *The Men of the Lewis and Clark Expedition*, 71.

† Thwaites notes that the party could not have seen the ocean from their location in the Pillar Rock area, and he thinks that possibly they mistook the great bay of the river as the ocean. Thwaites (ed.), *Original Journals of the Lewis and Clark Expedition*, III, 210n.

as spoken by Clatsops more nearly resembled the pronunciation of English than that of other native tongues and that, unlike those languages, the first syllables, instead of the last ones, were accentuated.[14]

The party proceeded down what it called the "Wappatoe Valley" because of the preeminence of that root in the Columbia watercourse. On November 8 they were at Grays Point. Two days later they reached Point Ellice. Along their route natives visited them almost daily to trade fish and roots. On the eleventh, five natives, one in sailors' clothes, the others in elk skins, traded thirteen bluebacked salmon for fishhooks and some "trifling things." On the thirteenth, George Shannon, Alexander Willard, and John Colter were sent ahead to see what lay downriver. Lewis, with some of the men, followed the next day to explore Cape Disappointment and to see if he could find a white settlement. Colter returned to the main camp that day behind five Indians, confirming Clark's suspicions that some of them had appropriated some of the party's property—a gig and a basket. The guilty yielded the purloined items after Clark threatened them and after some of his men took after them with a gun. On the fifteenth Clark, with a larger group of his men, moved to Chinook Village, then uninhabited save for swarms of fleas.[15] Winds battered the party's canoes, lashing their occupants with rain and soaking them most of the time. Despite inclement weather, the captains maintained their observations of the country and the people about them, noting that one band of Chinooks, down from the north (presumably from winter quarters), spoke differently from the Wahkiakums who had accompanied them to that point on their downriver journey.

On the fifteenth Shannon returned from below to inform Clark that he had met Lewis en route to that area. He brought a warning that the Chinook Indians he had met were a thievish lot, having stolen his and Willard's rifles. Clark promptly ordered the five Indians with Shannon to keep their distance, warning that if they stole anything else he would shoot them. The natives undoubtedly respected the expedition's guns, which brought down fowl almost daily. On the sixteenth several Indians, encamped near the party, were given smokes but no other privileges. The following day, Lewis returned to camp. With Clark, besides keeping an eye on his red retinue, Lewis observed the plant and animal life of their lands, one of the expedition's main tasks.* As the white strangers

* Among the observations was that Chinooks numbered four hundred; Clatsops, two hundred; Kathlamets, three hundred; and Wahkiakums, two hundred. The editor comments that the numbers given for Kathlamets and Wahkiakums were enlarged—by whom or when, he does not say. Presumably, the original figures in the journals of the expedition were altered. Thwaites (ed.), *Original Journals of the Lewis and Clark Expedition*, VI, 117n. James Mooney in his demography gives slightly higher populations for Chinookan tribes,

busied themselves at this, the natives continued about their occupation
—trading their goods from village to village and with the white men
among them. They must have thought these men strange indeed, for
the whites were not interested in trading large volumes of goods, buying
instead only those needed to replace leather goods destroyed by dampness on their way west. In Chinook and Clatsop thinking, real traders
were those who came in ships to Bakers Bay, which anchorage they
pointed out to their visitors. One of these real traders, they claimed, was
a Mr. Haley, for whom Lewis and Clark named that body of water
Haleys Bay.

Hearing of the white men who had come to them overland and not
from ships, several Chinooks came to visit them, including Chiefs Comcomly and Shelathwell, to whom Lewis and Clark gave medals and to
one a flag to insure their good will.[16] One Chinook wearing a sea otter
garment, and certainly aware of the premium American traders placed
on such items, refused for it Lewis' offer of two blankets, saying he
would not take five.[17] Relenting, he exchanged it for a belt of blue beads
from the waist of Sacajawea ("Jane" to the men), who was much trim-
mer now since the birth of her baby back among the Mandans. A Chinook woman, coming into possession of the belt, would retrade it to
the party for some blue cloth.[18] Thus the complex trading game continued. The party continued to purchase cranberries, roots and fish, for
which it thought the natives asked too much, and woven mats and hats.

To the explorers nothing would have revealed more clearly the cultural mixing at work among their new neighbors than their body coverings—two-and-one-half- and three-point blankets* and sailors'
clothes, sea otter robes and skins of beaver, elk, deer, and fox, many
purchased from the Chehalis. The two expedition leaders also noted
among them native blankets of woven goats' wool. Other consequences
of the cultural mix soon became evident to the visitors. Four days before
they would leave Bakers Bay on November 25, a chief's wife made her
debut with six young daughters and nieces with ears, legs, necks, and
wrists adorned with blue beads for the "purpose of Gratifying the pas-

---

indicating that they had nearly recovered from the devastating epidemic of 1783 which
spread from the eastern United States to the coast. *The Aboriginal Population of America
North of Mexico*, 16.

* The points indicate size and weight, averaging three pounds to the point. Clatsops
preferred blue, red, or brown blankets. One maritime trader, giving instructions for the
Northwest Coast, wrote in 1806 that there was "a kind of Blankets imported to this country
term'd Point Blankets these are the best & most profitable wollens which can be sent. tho
best sizes are 2½ & 3 Points. on a common cargo 3,000 would not be too many," to carry
along for trading purposes. William Sturgis to John Dorr, October (n.d.), 1806, in Dorr,
"Collection of letters ship documents and receipts. 1795–1820," Archives of British Columbia.

sions of the men."[19] This was perhaps the same woman whom Sergeant Patrick Gass, carpenter of the party, would record had kept her girls busy at "an easy rate."[20] In time Sergeant John Ordway would forbid his men to associate with the girls after many of the party contracted venereal disease. The mercury treatment given them for it did not prevent the "Old Boud" from trying to extend to these male visitors her own style of hospitality. At the permanent camp which the party established near the Columbia south bank, the men appropriated expedition tools to pay the "Old Boud" and her girls for their services. To meet this crisis, Lewis gave the men pieces of ribbon to give the girls to divert them from appropriation of the much-needed tools. The forwardness of these women, which made the men go to such extremes, Lewis and Clark had not seen among other natives in their long journey west. Yet it should be said that the others had done no business with sailors. None of them had worn such scant clothing, which gave the Chinooks and Clatsops a better opportunity to display for their guests their tattooed arms and legs. Sailors visiting them understood this practice, too, for at least one Chinook woman bore on her arm the inscription of one "J Bowman," who may have been less interested in inscribing letters on the trunks of Chinooks' trees than on the limbs of their women. Like other white men visiting these people, Lewis, Clark, and their men noted the natives' flattened heads. No one could fail to do that.

Clark observed that the Chinooks generally conducted themselves with great propriety from, he believed, no natural goodness on their part but from his warnings to behave themselves. After all, Jefferson had instructed him to treat them in the "most friendly and conciliatory manner," yet only as "their own conduct will admit." On November 23, seven Clatsops came to the expedition camp at Bakers Bay with two sea otter skins to trade and, like Chinooks, knew how much white men coveted such pelts. The Americans could ill afford to pay the price the natives demanded for their goods in fear of depleting their own stores, which were sorely needed for trading throughout the winter and on the way home. Knowing they would live among these people throughout the winter, they traded to them as much as the traffic and good relations would allow. Clark offered the Clatsops a watch, a handkerchief, red beads, and an American coin for their two sea otter skins, but one of their chiefs refused the generous offer, demanding instead "chief beads," meaning, of course, the blue ones.

The next day, after some trading with Chinooks, the explorers discovered that like other natives their hosts sealed transactions in intoxication-inducing ceremonies, inhaling smoke deep into their lungs and stomachs before exhaling it through their nostrils and mouths. Perhaps it was at one of these fumatory sessions that the natives learned that the Americans planned to construct in their lands a fort in which to spend the winter. The Clatsops pulled a coup on the Chinooks when they "tantilized" the Americans into living near them where there were many elk in the hills. In their country, too, was easy access to the Pacific, where salt could be extracted; hoped-for milder weather than on the Columbia north bank; and a better view of ships, one of which the natives said they were expecting in three months. Thirteen, they said, visited them semiannually to trade.[21]

If the whites believed that by moving in with the Clatsops they would be among a people less mercenary than Chinooks, they would soon learn that a river separating the two peoples separated but little their characteristics. Pleased that they had persuaded the party to live with them, the seven Clatsops accompanied the party as it journeyed upriver to a crossing. On November 26, the crossing was made to a Kathlamet village of nine houses,* from which the party and its Clatsop welcoming committee moved down the south bank in blustery weather to encamp until December 7 at Tongue Point (Sookumitséah), which Lewis and Clark named Williams Point. From this place Lewis set off downriver to pick the winter campsite to which the others now moved.† At that place the Clatsops wasted little time in testing the new arrivals for trade, haggling high and backing down when necessary as they did with native and white sea traders.

Some of the travelers were dispatched to fish and to hunt elk and fowl, since the party had too few items to trade the Clatsops for food. As the group prepared to build its post in December it learned that the Clatsop houses to which it was invited were much like those of the Chinooks, as were their furnishings—mats on subterranean floors spread with shellfish, roots, and berries, some of which the natives made into a soup

* The party crossed from Pillar Rock, where they had encamped, on November 25. Thwaites (ed.), *Original Journals of the Lewis and Clark Expedition*, III, 250. Clark says they moved down the south shore five miles to a Kathlamet village. *Ibid.*, 252. John Ordway, one of the party, in his journal says they camped at a Clatsop village, which is undoubtedly in error since Clatsops did not live that far upriver. Milo M. Quaife (ed.), *The Journals of Captain Meriwether Lewis and Sergeant John Ordway Kept on the Expedition of Western Exploration, 1803–1806,*" Publications of the State Historical Society of Wisconsin, Vol. XXII, 314.

† Fort Clatsop, the site chosen for winter quarters, was some two hundred yards from the Lewis and Clark River near its entrance into Youngs Bay. Bancroft, *History of the Northwest Coast*, Vol. II, 55. The location was some fifteen miles down the Columbia from Tongue Point and three miles up the Lewis and Clark River. Quaife (ed.), *Journals of Captain Meriwether Lewis and Sergeant John Ordway*, 315, 316n. The fort site is approximately eight miles from Astoria. Louis R. Caywood, "The Exploratory Excavation of Fort Clatsop," *Oregon Historical Quarterly*, XLIX (1948), 205.

which they served in horn, bone, and wooden dishes. Clark thought Clatsops cleaner than most natives he had seen, for they washed their hands and faces. Good relations continued into the field, where Clark entertained his hosts by sharpshooting wildfowl with his rifle, which was more accurate than the fusees (flintlock guns) used by the Clatsops. They accompanied him partway to the place chosen to make salt by the sea.* Surrounded by swarms of fleas, they felt free to visit the expedition base camp daily, staying overnight to watch those Americans who were not hunting elk perform chores such as splitting planks and hollowing out canoes in Indian fashion. And like Chinooks, these Clatsops never missed a chance to trade, exchanging on December 12 roots and sea otter skins for a few fishhooks and Indian tobacco which the party had obtained from Snake Indians. Wappatoe roots purchased from the Clatsops cost the party dearly; to obtain them from upriver tribes Clatsops and Chinooks often traded their precious blue beads, which understandably would have made the roots expensive. In return for goods sold to the party, the Indians took as many files as they could to sharpen tools, make chisels, and work wood. They also took all the fishhooks and tobacco they could get.

On December 12, following Jefferson's admonition to treat the Indians with as much attention as possible to insure their hospitality, Lewis and Clark presented medals to the principal Clatsop chief, Coboway (Comowool). There is no record that the next ranking Clatsop chiefs, Skanoma and Warkolett, received such awards. Soon Lewis had cause to believe that too much hospitality had been extended the natives, for they crowded around camp, which they believed quite naturally to be theirs as much as their visitors'. Making the situation awkward as well as advantageous for the party was the fact that its home away from home was also a marketplace. In it the men purchased roots and skins well processed by the natives. It could have used well-made native mats to protect itself from the elements, but the price was too high, although no higher than that which ship captains and supercargoes had been willing to pay.

The Clatsops appeared not to have been offended when the men removed planking from an abandoned Indian house to supplement lumber for their buildings, now with walls and roofs underway, possibly because Clatsops and Chinooks often removed house planking from one site to another. However, they would have frowned upon removal of burial properties, which, as Lewis and Clark observed, they regarded with

* The location for making salt was at present-day Seaside, Oregon. Sea water was boiled to extract the salt. P. W. Gillette, "The Site of Fort Clatsop," *Pacific Monthly*, XII, 2 (August, 1904), 93.

reverence. Three days before Christmas, the floors and bunks were completed in seven cabins under construction.[22]

With the buildings nearly completed, the camp became more than ever a gathering place for Clatsops, Chinooks, and others continually dropping by to see the strangers at work. Sacajawea especially interested them as she cared for her baby with its unflattened head, sewed moccasins—novelty items for Clatsops and Chinooks—and helped her husband cook.[23] The day before Christmas, Clatsop chief Cuscalar entered camp, now called "Fort Clatsop," to lay before each white "chief" a mat and a peck of roots. These offerings were scarcely gratuities, for in return he demanded two files. Having none to spare, Lewis and Clark returned the mats and roots, which displeased the Clatsops, as did the failure of the two white "chiefs" to accept the women Cuscalar presented them.[24]

In winter quarters the explorers had ample time to observe their hosts. Lewis noted that they had good memories, were inquisitive and cheerful, but never gay, and were loquacious, their conversation turning on trading, smoking, eating, and women, of whom they spoke intimately without reserve. As had other white men, Lewis observed that the native men did "not hold the virtue of their women in high estimation," being quite willing to "prostitute their wives and daughters for a fishinghook or a stran[d] of beads," and that the men permitted the women to speak freely, "consult[ing] them in their traffic and act[ing] in conformity to their opinions."[25] He also observed that unlike plains Indians, who left their old ones to die, these cared for the elderly.

Natives were at the fort on Christmas day, which the whites announced with volley of gunfire, after which they exchanged gifts among themselves and consumed a dinner of roots, fish, and spoiled elk. Following the festivities, if indeed they could be called that, the party spent the rest of the year drying its clothes, hunting fresh meat, and completing the fort with a timber gate and a wall around—and, of course, dickering with natives over the prices of roots, which looked like the Americans' best bet for food since most of them had taken turns at becoming ill from the meat they had eaten. Quickly divining their need for food, Coboway and four men came two days after Christmas with roots and berries. This gesture won for him from Lewis a sheepskin cap and, for his son, from Clark, ear bobs, a piece of ribbon, and two fishhooks. After some haggling the chief also got a razor, which he perhaps never put to his face. The party had some respite from the Clatsops when the Indians went down to slice thick slabs of blubber from a whale cast upon the beach. While the Clatsops were away a young Wahkiakum chief, accompanied by four men and two women, came with elk skin and wappatoe, a bushel of the roots gaining for him from Lewis a small medal and a red ribbon to tie around his double-coned hat. For other roots the Wahkiakums accepted brass wire and red beads, for which Lewis and Clark may have been happy to find a market.

Completion of the fort two days before the new year, 1806, somewhat altered Indian-white relations at that place. Natives, expecting to encamp overnight within the enclosure, were now warned to move outside after sundown. On hearing this directive they sullenly left the grounds, although they and other Chinookan peoples such as the Wahkiakums came inside to trade on ensuing days. One of those who came was a man of some twenty-four years, of light complexion with a freckled face and red hair—very possibly Jack Ramsay, son of the English sailor-deserter and a Chinook mother.[26]

With considerable traffic to the fort, security was tightened. A sergeant and three privates were ordered to stand guard and to announce the arrival of the "savages."[27] There had been considerable visitation by Chinooks paddling across the river to trade and to appropriate various items without the formality of purchase. To distinguish themselves from their cross-river neighbors, and to stay in the good graces of Lewis and Clark, the Clatsops and some Kathlamets took to announcing their own approach to the fort with the cry "No Chinook!"[28] This Chinook-demeaning sobriquet served as a subterfuge to permit Clatsops to pilfer whenever the opportunity presented itself. Chinook-Clatsop virtues were alike, but so were their vices. Guards, nevertheless, were instructed to abuse no natives unless first assaulted, to eject obnoxious ones, and to deal accordingly with those caught stealing. The expedition leaders thought this policy successful. One, editing Sergeant Ordway's journal, wrote that "The sight of the sentinel, constantly on duty, and the firm tone assumed toward the savages, many of whom had shown themselves 'verry impertenant and disagreeable,' produced an immediate improvement in their conduct."[29] The two white leaders had to be careful not to offend their hosts too deeply, for as winter lengthened so did their dependence upon the natives for sustenance. On January 3 they welcomed Coboway and six Clatsops bringing whale blubber, berries, and three dogs, whose meat tasted better to them than the steady diet of elk, which was more plentiful than venison. The men were eating more than three elks daily. In return for the food Lewis gave the chief a pair of satin breeches, which pleased the native leader very much.

The increasing needs of the men decreased but little Clatsop-Chinook haggling, for these shrewd "higlers" quickly detected their visitors' anxieties in this regard. Every trading session was a lesson to these Americans in native acuity in the trading arts. Any notion they may have held that they were dealing with simple primitives unschooled in commerce quickly vanished. One day Lewis offered a Chinook his watch, two knives, and a considerable quantity of beads for a small, inferior sea otter skin, which Lewis did not much want anyway. Sensing Lewis' response, the Chinook refused to trade further until the quantity of beads was doubled. The next day, with much importunity on the part of the Chinook, Lewis exchanged but a few strands of beads for the same skin. He had discovered that "this trait in their character proceeds from an avaracious all grasping disposition . . . [differing] from all Indians I ever became acquainted with, for their dispositions invariably lead them to give whatever they are possessed off no matter how usefull or valuable, for a bauble which pleases their fancy, without consulting it's usefullness or value."[30] Sergeant Ordway noted that "the general part of them are verry poor and ask a large price for any thing they have to part with."[31]

One item they did not seek was rum, for they appeared to have developed no taste for spiritous liquors. By trading but little rum to them, ship captains had been better able to supply their own crews and other natives on a coast exposed not only to rum but also to other spirits as varied as vino in California and vodka in Alaska. Had they sought rum from Lewis and Clark they apparently would not have gotten any, for on New Year's Day the men celebrated by eating boiled elk and wappatoe, "solacing our thirst with our only beverage *pure water*."[32] The ships, which carried rum, would, the natives told Lewis and Clark, soon be returning for the trading season, which lasted from April until late October. Had any ships wintered that season in Bakers Bay, the explorers would certainly have mentioned it.

A few events transpiring near Fort Clatsop diverted the party's attention from the soggy, flea-ridden winter. On January 6 Clark set out with a group in two canoes to see a whale washed up on a Tillamook beach. Sacajawea insisted on going along, for she had never seen the ocean. By the time they arrived at the beach, Tillamooks had cut most of the flesh from the 105-foot mammal, rendering slabs of its meat into oil in wooden vessels heated with hot stones and storing the sticky substance in the whale's bladder and intestines. Cooked, the whale meat was palatable and tender, resembling in taste that of a dog or beaver. Tillamooks were very possessive of their oil and blubber, trading but small quantities of it; nevertheless, Chinooks and Clatsops went down to trade beads for it.

Shortly after this winter monotony-breaking event occurred another more dramatic. One morning Clark heard a shrill cry from a Clatsop village. His guide told him a man's throat had been cut. One of his men,

Private Hugh McNeal, being absent, the captain sent a sergeant and four men to investigate his whereabouts. They returned with a story that a pretended friend of McNeal's from a distant tribe, so the Clatsops said, had invited him to a lodge for blubber, offering to take him to another dwelling. When a Chinook woman tried to restrain the private, he had broken away. The pretended friend had disappeared and McNeal was freed. The episode, so Clark learned, had been an attempt to murder the American for his blanket.

On January 10 the principal Kathlamet chief, Shalharwarcap, and his followers came to the fort with dried salmon, dogs, wappatoes, and mats to receive in exchange a medal "of the smallest size."[33] They left the next morning for Clatsop villages to barter their wappatoes for oil and blubber recently purchased from the Tillamooks. On January 17 Coboway, with seven of his people, seeking to trade roots and berries, may not have known they were refused trade because the party's supply of goods was in danger due to continual high prices demanded by traders such as they. Wishing goods to make a skimming net, possibly for coming spring runs, Coboway gave roots and berries for an awl and thread. Gigs and hooks, mostly of European manufacture, now replaced the natives' bone hooks, although they still used grass lines for catching fish.

One of Coboway's men was dressed in three lovely sea otter skins but would not trade one of them for six fathoms of blue beads left in the Americans' stores. An offer of a knife would not satisfy him; he wanted ten fathoms of "chief beads" or nothing at all. Such encounters constantly reminded Lewis, as he confessed in his journal, that he had underestimated the natives' preference for blue beads, "the principal circulating medium with all the indian tribes on this river."[34] About the only inexpensive item the Americans could get for trifles were watertight, dye-designed, cedar bark and beargrass baskets. The low prices at which the natives sacrificed these utensils possibly indicated that they were in light demand among neighboring peoples or by mariners in visiting ships. The fact that the women laboriously fashioned them would not, of itself, have increased their value as trade items. Clark would find them of more value than did white sea traders, but never of as much value as did the Indians, who stored fish, roots, and berries in them. The same held for bullrush and cattail flag mats and other culinary utensils of wood and shell.

As early as January the men began preparing for their return home. On the nineteenth of that month they traded their remaining blue beads,* along with some white ones and a knife, for sea otter skins to

* The cheap beads were obtained in strands from China at a cost in England of 13 pence a pound. Lewis knew in advance the natives' preference for blue beads over the

add to their other coverings, such as elkskins, many of which were purchased to make clothing for their homeward journey. Elk served a double purpose—for clothing and for food, of which the party by mid-February had enough to last the rest of the month. Nevertheless, hunters were dispatched to get more, because approaching spring and melting snows would drive the big animals deeper into the hills, where they would be harder to find. Dogs continued to be a reliable source of food. On February 12 a Clatsop brought three of them to pay for an elk he had stolen, but the canines ran away. The stolen elk meant not only less food for the Americans but also one less skin for them to make into clothing for their trip home. The Indians expressed no enthusiasm to trade for the leather clothing the men were fabricating, and they had little use for shoes;[35] they were mainly interested in trading for cloth garments worn by white men on ships.* So eager were they for this commodity that they bartered the favors of their women for it.

It was perhaps more through the trade process than through any other activity that Lewis and Clark had their best opportunity to observe the red men about them. Even through the flora and fauna of the region, many of which the Chinooks and Clatsops worked into items of trade, they learned much about these people, in keeping with their instructions from the president. By contrast, the natives, interested in utilizing instead of classifying the familiar flora and fauna of their country, spent their spare winter time processing food, sculpturing, and working wood with "an ingenuity by no means common among the Aborigenes of America."[36] Importantly, trade gave the explorers an opportunity to meet "influential" chiefs, as Jefferson had wanted them to do.

One of the most influential chiefs of the lower Columbia came in February 20 for his first visit with the "cloth men." He was Taucum, observed to have been bigger than the average Chinook male and about fifty years old. Recognizing his importance, Lewis and Clark presented him with food, a smoke, and a medal, which pleased him so much that he appeared undisturbed when the fort gates closed that evening with his royal person and his followers on the outside looking in. On the birthday of the father of their country Lewis and Clark were presented hats which the natives fabricated to their measurements. These were no mean gifts, for Chinook-Clatsop hats of cedar bark and grass were not

---

white ones, but he failed to take on the expedition enough blue ones to trade. He lamented the fact. Donald Jackson (ed.), *Letters of the Lewis and Clark Expedition, with Related Documents, 1783–1854,* 74 and n.

* They would have had no need to trade for white men's shoes, for Clatsops and Chinooks went barefooted all winter. Quaife (ed.), *Journals of Captain Meriwether Lewis and Sergeant John Ordway,* 319.

only utilitarian in shedding rain but also beautifully designed with colors and figures. One prominent hat style was double-coned and tied under the chin with two strings.* On the hats were black and white and occasionally colored figures of whales and canoe-borne harpooners.[37]

Traffic continued apace at the fort in late February. Besides standard items now, trade was excellent for sturgeon and smelt.† The Indians caught the latter with scooping and skimming nets in the river. On the twenty-fourth, Lewis purchased a sea otter for an old coat and vest. Several of the men wore hats like those presented to their leaders. On the twenty-eighth Private Pierre Cruzatte traded Cuscalar a short cloak for a dog. That Indian, having fared poorly at trading, offered to sell Clark a slave for beads and a gun. Clark refused the offer, a gesture which undoubtedly would have pleased the commander in chief of the expedition, who had written that all men were created equal.

Early March found the food situation at the fort critical as the hunters reported elk moving into higher elevations. The season had been productive, however, with the elk tally from the first of December to the first of March calculated by Sergeant Gass at 131 killed.[38] The men were thus well clothed in elkskin and had 358 pairs of moccasins made up for use on the way home.[39] Plans were to leave on the first day of April, but illness—dysentery, colds, boils, and venereal disease—threatened to delay departure. For venereal disease Lewis treated his men with mercury injections. He noted the ravages of the malady among the Indians but was apparently unaware of any effective cures for it. As the captain went about treating his men he observed its debilitating effects on them and may have regretted his earlier gifts to them of pieces of ribbon to trade to the women for their favors.[40]

Clatsops and Chinooks were happy to have Lewis and Clark treat them for various ailments. One grateful Clatsop woman, whom Clark healed of some disorder, offered herself to him and was "quite mortified" when he refused her generosity.[41] She then declined the solicitations of the men who in her estimation did not match the importance of their "chief."

Positive activity quickened now, Clark making copious notes of the country, Private John Shields busily making elkskin bags to hold them,

---

* Either the hats were trade items from the north or the designs were borrowed from Nootkas.

† Lewis and Clark referred to smelt as anchovies. Natives cured smelt by roasting them. These fish spoiled quickly after being caught if they were not cooked or cured. Sturgeon could be kept for days by being immersed in water. The Indians cooked them by cutting them into pieces, spitting them, and placing them in layers over heated stones that were wetted to produce steam, with green boughs between each layer.

and the party hoarding its food. Last-minute problems occurred, though. On March 11 Sergeant Nathaniel Pryor came to the fort with fish and wappatoes from the Kathlamets for some dwindling fort items, but in a borrowed canoe, for Kathlamet dogs had set his own craft adrift by chewing the thongs tying it to shore. Fortunately Pryor had found the canoe and planned to retrieve it when he returned the one he had borrowed. The expedition had no canoes to spare, having lost too many to winter gales. That the natives showed no inclination to mellow at the marketplace as the Americans prepared to leave helped matters none. On the thirteenth, for example, a Clatsop refused Lewis' uniform coat for a canoe, for which the Indian doubled his price in a manner "agreeable to their usial way of tradeing."[42] Civilian employee George Drouillard would purchase a canoe from Kathlamets for tobacco and Lewis' laced coat, the native equivalent of the price of a wife. The men took one canoe outright from the Clatsops, justifying their appropriation on the grounds that the craft equalled in value six elk stolen during the winter. Also helping matters none as the party prepared to leave was the mid-March appearance of Chinook chief Delashewilt (Shelathwell?) and his wife, now identified as the "Old Boud." Despite Clark's orders to the men to keep their distance from her and her girls, he had little control over these females, for they were free moral, or perhaps in this case immoral, agents seeking to besiege the fort in their own particular way. On March 18 Delashewilt was given a certificate for his, but certainly not his wife's, good behavior. Not only did Lewis and Clark now fear her unwanted trade item and its accompanying venereal disease, but also almost any other item in their wish to hoard the few articles remaining to trade on the plains for horses to help get them home.

As departure date neared, the two explorers presented papers to various chiefs, besides Delashewilt, for their good deportment. One posted on the wall of the fort read:

> The object of this list is, that through the medium of some civilized person who may see the same, it may be made known to the informed world, that the party consisting of the persons whose names are hereunto annexed, and who were sent out by the government of the U'States in May 1804. to explore the interior of the Continent of North America, did penetrate the same by way of the Missouri and Columbia Rivers, to the discharge of the latter into the Pacific Ocean, where they arrived on the 14th of November 1805, and from whence they departed the   day of March 1806 on their return to the United States by the same rout they had come out.[43]

On the reverse side of the papers were maps of the Columbia and Missouri river drainage systems and a sketch of the party's route coming west and the intended route of its return.

It was decided not to leave, as Jefferson had suggested, men to find ship passage to the United States,* although according to the Clatsops there had recently been among the Quinaults three- and four-masted vessels captained by Haley, whom the Chinooks described as their friend, the one who had given natives below the Cowlitz River an iron bow; Moore, who had on board three cows the last time he touched at the Columbia; Callalamet (Callamon?), who had a wooden leg; and Swipton. The four had been buying skins and whale oil. The Clatsops also gave the explorers the names of eight other traders and an elk hunter, Davidson, who visited them on ships.[44] Except for not meeting ships at the mouth of the Columbia, it may be said that Lewis and Clark had completed the objectives of this most westerly phase of their expedition.[45]

They were ready to leave on March 21, the first day of spring, but high winds, oblivious to the date, delayed their departure. This delay gave Coboway and other Clatsops time to come in for last-minute farewells. For his friendship the explorers presented him the fort and its furniture. Were he like most natives, he would have valued the gift less than the certificate, to which the Indians attached almost magic significance.†

* A typescript copy of an anonymous article in the Coe Collection of Western Americana of the Beinecke Library states that the *Vancouver,* Captain Thomas Brown, owned by the Lyman firm, was ordered by President Jefferson to return the party by sea. It is strange, then, that the *Vancouver,* which was on the coast at this time, made no entry into the Columbia River. The article has been placed inside "Log-Book of the Brig Lydia on a Fur-Trading voyage from Boston to the Northwest Coast of America 1804–1805 With Return Voyage by way of The Sandwich Islands Aboard the Ships Atahualpa and Swift 1805–1807," manuscript, Beinecke Library, Yale University. James and Thomas Lamb, owners of the *Derby,* wrote Captain Benjamin Swift from Boston on September 5, 1806, as he prepared to sail to the Northwest Coast: "It is expected by this Government that a party sent to survey the interior of the Country will penetrate the N.W. Coast and may descend the Columbia River. It is commanded by Capt. Lewis and you should meet with him or any of his party you will take charge of any dispatches or render any aid to them which is in your power." L. Vernon Briggs, *History and Genealogy of the Cabot Family, 1475–1927,* I, 407.

† The chief occupied the fort for several years each fall and winter during hunting seasons. The logs of the cabins were in perfect condition as late as 1836, but the roofs had been carried off by natives. Bancroft, *History of the Northwest Coast,* Vol. II, 55n. George Gibbs, who visited the fort site in 1853, wrote that it was yet visible but that the foundation logs were rotting. Then the trail to the coast and salt works were overgrown by brush. Vernon Carstensen (ed.), *Pacific Northwest Letters of George Gibbs,* 43–44. By 1886 not a vestige of the fort remained. Joe Dobbins to Eva Emery Dye, January 21, 1901, Eva Emery Dye Papers. The site was excavated at mid-twentieth century under direction of the Oregon Historical Society. Caywood, "The Exploratory Excavation of Fort Clatsop," 205–10. Today there stands on the grounds a reconstruction of the original fort, having been built by the National Park Service for tourists.

At 1:00 P.M. on March 23, the canoes loaded, the expedition departed Fort Clatsop for the long journey home with crew intact but without any young natives Jefferson had suggested their people might wish to send to the States. They had not gone a mile when Delashewilt and twenty Chinooks, including the "Old Boud" and six girls, came up with various items to sell, including a canoe, since they had heard the men needed one. The departing ones declined the offer but did buy a sea otter skin. They set off again.

On the day they had planned to leave, March 21, the Russian (formerly American) ship *Juno* staggered off the bar as she had off and on for a week.* The same gale that robbed the Americans of their planned-for start for home had also robbed the Russians of an entry to the Columbia River, where they hoped to gain a foothold in the Chinook-Clatsop homeland. The Russians pushed south along the California coast. Their failure would turn them again to the Columbia just as the Lewis and Clark expedition (whose members returned alive to tell about it) would also turn Americans to that stream. It would be several years, however, before Chinooks and Clatsops, or, for that matter, Russians and Americans, would know the ultimate outcome of these Yankee and Muscovite journeys to western American shores.

---

* Eight of the scurvy-ridden crew died trying to sail the *Juno* over the bar. Only a dozen were able-bodied enough to sail the ship. Hector Chevigny, *Russian America: The Great Alaskan Venture, 1741–1867*, 117. Russians purchased the American vessel *Juno* from Captain John Wolf (de Wolf). Rezanov hoped to use it in carrying out plans to secure a commercial treaty with Japan, whose religious leaders opposed his negotiations. Vice Admiral Shischkov, "Russian America: Preliminary Information Regarding the Life of Khvostov and Davidov by Vice Admiral Shischkov, 1810–1812," translated from the Russian by Michael E. Affonin, Seattle, 1932–33, typescript copy of manuscript, Archives of British Columbia, 2.

7. Guardians of the River

> The country was theirs. They had an undis-
> puted right to resist the attempts of any
> person or persons, who should endeavor to
> dispossess them of the country where God
> and Nature had planted them.
>
> William Dane Phelps, "Solid Men of
> Boston in the Northwest"

I T WAS NOT the thrill of exploration that drove the Russians south in the *Juno* in 1806, but two more tangible forces—hunger and increasing troubles with the natives at Sitka.[1] In casting about for a place to re-settle, Count Nikolai Petrovich Rezanov, in a report to the general administration of the Russian American Company, had written of pos-sibilities of exploring the Columbia River,[2] a move conforming to his own dreams of his nation's occupation south of that place.[3] The more practical Alexander Andreievitch Baranov, governor of that same com-pany, would announce: "The Columbia River . . . had forwith [sic] to be explored." Sailing south with sickened crew and insufficient food, the *Juno* was ill prepared to carry out grand designs in a place which for the time being would be less a seat of empire for her owners than a market-place to purchase food to sustain her crew.[4] Chinooks and Clatsops would have supplied them these necessities, as evidenced by large bon-fires they built on the hills to signal the *Juno* into the Columbia River. Had the bar not blocked her entry, the Russians might have confronted Lewis and Clark. Had the Americans been aware of the Russian pres-ence, they most likely would have delayed their departure to the States or would have mentioned the Russian presence near the river. Sailing downcoast to California, the *Juno* did manage to obtain food, but her masters sought a post on the Columbia further from Spanish influence than California. Thanks to British involvement in the Napoleonic wars, Russia's major nonphysical obstacle to unhampered expansion on much of the Pacific Coast was the young American republic.[5]

The aggressiveness of these Americans was seen in Captain Hill's daring rescue of the Nootka survivors and in his relentless pursuit of trade. Following the rescue he sailed in the *Lydia* to the Columbia for a load of spars. The *Lydia* crossed the bar on Saturday, July 12, 1806,[6] to friendlier territory than Nootka, as Comcomly, followed by others, canoed out in a small breeze to welcome her and to trade a few beaver skins, but apparently no sea otter. On Monday the fourteenth ship repairs began. The next day four hands were ashore in squally weather cutting wood. Two others tended the kiln, and two the forge. One carpentered, and the rest performed sundry tasks. Observing the carpenter idle, Hill thundered curses and threats to blow up the ship with all hands. With his "lady," a Chinook belle, another object of his aggression, he cooled off ashore in Comcomly's village, where natives showed him medals given them by Lewis and Clark and placed in his hands one of the papers Clark had left them naming the expedition's departure date, its muster roll, and, more importantly for Chinooks, declaration of their American citizenship.[7]

The next few days saw more fraternizing than trade between crew and the natives. Helping the friendship process along were three dozen thimbles given each crewman to trade as favors to Chinook women. On Friday the eighteenth the carpenter got six dozen of the thimbles to exchange for entertainment to take his mind off hurts sustained in helping natives get out a spar for the ship. Hill did not lack for diversion either, for his "Chenook Lady" came aboard to "Sup with him"[8] and receive as his present to decorate her wrists and midriff some brasswire rings fabricated by Jewitt, one of the men rescued from Nootka. Hill's fashionable Chinook girlfriend was a style setter for her people; the brass, copper, and beads that she wore were beginning to give native shells, bear claws, elk teeth, and feathers for the hair a run for Chinook money. The position of dentalia seemed secure as a medium of exchange and adornment,* enhancing tattoos on thighs, legs, and other parts of the body on special occasions.[9] Paints of earth pigments mixed with salmon grease completed the decoration of the person.

---

* Other native baubles being replaced were those of wood, bone, and quills. The quills were pushed through nose perforations. Lockley, "Chinook and Others," *Oregon Sunday Journal*, June 23, 1929. Dentalia were also used in nose fenestrations as well as in perforations in the ears. Lee and Frost, *Ten Years in Oregon*, 101. The missionary Samuel Parker wrote that it was not the custom, despite reports to the confrary, to slit the upper lip and place wood pieces in it. *Journal of an Exploring Tour beyond the Rocky Mountains, Under the Direction of the A.B.C.F.M.*, 255. Ship's Captain Edward Belcher says Chinook women incised their lower lip, distending it with a piece of wood. *Narrative of a Voyage Round the World Performed in Her Majesty's Ship Sulphur, during the Years 1836–1842*, I, 306. Chinooks used mixed earth pigment and salmon grease to smear their bodies for decoration.

On Monday, July 21, tarrying ashore with his lady (as he had with a similar girlfriend in Atoi, Hawaiian Islands), Hill did not return to the ship until nearly midnight. On July 30 he lavished on the girl a fathom of red cloth, beads, thimbles, four handkerchiefs, and some wire. The other lady in his life, the *Lydia*, also received his attention—work on the mainmast, a new foremast, overhauled rigging, and other repairs. With a blustery advent of August, work continued on the masts as some trade trickled in. More covert activities among the Indians, involving a plot to hold some of the crew hostage for one reason or another, came to light when one of the girls who had gone to the *Lydia* informed the crew of the plan, which she said involved killing them. Thus forewarned, Hill armed the pinnace and blustered ashore, demanding native help in getting the mast to the deck of his ship. "They [the Indians after their plot fizzled] all went Home . . . as Sheepish as a parcel of fools," wrote the supercargo of the affair in his logbook.[10] On Saturday, August 2, the foremast was installed and rigged. The next day found "The Skippers Chenook Lady on board to sleep & tarry till the Brig is ready to Sail."[11] On August 7 the "Chenook Lady," still aboard ship, was joined by the entire "royal family" to attend a farewell dinner. The following day the men hauled wood and water aboard to fill stores which the festivities of the previous day must have depleted. On the ninth tarpaulin hatch covers were stitched. The following day four hands were dispatched "to get the Skippers Lady [and all her decorative hardware] on Shore."[12] On the eleventh the *Lydia* sailed out over the bar just a month after crossing it on the way in.

The *Lydia*'s crew had spent more time repairing the craft and relations with the Chinooks than they had in trade, for in summer business was slower than in spring, when Chinooks traded their winter fur stocks and gathered clamons and land furs. With those of the Columbia added to greater harvests to the north, the value of Cantonese fur imports from American vessels in 1805–1806 amounted to one million dollars— from sale of 17,445 sea otter, 140,297 seal, and 34,460 beaver skins. Americans brought to the China market four million dollars' worth of other goods, including sixteen hundred picules of sandalwood from the Hawaiian and other South Pacific islands and specie directly from Boston, New York, and Philadelphia. During the same period, tea, almost a million pounds of it, was the main Cantonese export aboard American ships, along with Chinaware and silks.[13]

Although Captain Hill may have communicated with Chinook female traders in the language of love, there had to have been a more semantic base for exchange of goods with their people, who knew a few English words at the time—some choice ones from men like Hill—some of which they had communicated to Lewis and Clark. More importantly, they began communicating with traders by means of a white vendor-introduced lingua franca, one day to bear the name "Chinook Jargon." As originally formulated to facilitate white-native trade on Vancouver Island,[14] the trade jargon consisted of Nootkan, Spanish, and English words.[15] Either at contact or earlier it had also taken on, in the north, Russian and Japanese words.[16] It was thus an amalgam, described by a regional historian as "that strange and unique 'Esperanto' of the western Indians,"[17] which had its beginnings in the conduct of the trade.*

One authority maintains that its native origins can never be ascertained, and that, in Topsyian fashion, it just grew. In Pacific Northwestern precontact times, aside from formal tribal languages, there had been regional all-native mixed jargons of sorts developing for the needs of communication among various tribes. Columbia River peoples had formed such a jargon when allied in what has been termed the "Multnomah Confederacy,"[18] using their jargon to facilitate measures for mutual protection from the incursions of tribesmen from east of the Rocky Mountains and bordering plateau lands. Horses under these fast-riding hinterland raiders had given them mobility to strike quickly to threaten the Columbia peoples. Such a form of communication among the latter quite naturally had stimulated their intertribal commerce and other aspects of their culture as well.

Words from such mongrel forms of communication may have contributed to the trade jargon by a flow to the north. Since there had been precontact trade between Chinooks and northern peoples, the two probably used words in common to conduct their commerce. Between the Columbia River and Vancouver Island intermediary native traders such as Makahs and Quinaults may have diluted any drift of the "confederacy" language, which could have filtered toward Vancouver Island where it could have mixed with northern intertribal trade languages; so to what extent any Chinook-used words could have been incorporated originally into the trade jargon cannot be ascertained.

The flow of the trade jargon was from Nootka south to the Columbia. In 1788 Meares discovered that some words of the "Language of King George Sound" (jargon of Nootka) had spread from that place south-

---

* Spaniards with Cayetano Valdes on the Northwest Coast in 1792 used a Spanish-compiled Nootkan vocabulary. *Message from the President of the United States, Communicating the Letter of Mr. Prevost, and other Documents, Relating to an Establishment Made at the Mouth of the Columbia River, January 25, 1823,* House Doc. No. 45, 17 Cong., 2 sess. When rescued from the Nootkas in 1805 by Captain Hill, Jewitt had begun compiling a dictionary of trade words employed by those natives. John Kaye Gill, *Dictionary of the Chinook Jargon with Examples of Its Use in Conversation,* 5.

ward to the Olympic Peninsula. Yet that same year he found natives at Willapa Bay lacking understanding of that language.[19] Where four years later officers of the Vancouver expedition found natives at Grays Harbor familiar with words of the trade jargon used by whites and natives in the north,[20] Broughton, of that same expedition, found natives of the Columbia using words totally unintelligible to him.[21] Following his and Gray's entry to the Columbia, white traders introduced the jargon there. As the trade gradually shifted from the north to the Columbia, the jargon, ever changing to meet trade demands, began to alter rapidly. Chinooks and Clatsops adopted many English words, contributing many from their own tongue.

Whatever its imperfections, the jargon saved white men the task of learning a Babel of tribal tongues, especially the Chinookan language.* This language, despite Lewis' contention that it was most nearly like English of all the native tongues, was, according to one white man who would live among Chinooks, "almost unlearnable."[22] The two races were thus drawn to the trade jargon by its simplicity. By the same token, the jargon was condemned to limited use and was incapable of expressing abstractions.[23] Yet it was an evolving language with words of white vendors added to those of nature, onomatopoeia, when needed.[24] It was a phonetic language of merely eighteen letters, each of which was sounded. It had no moods, verb tenses, noun cases, or comparison adjectives, and only one preposition. Variations in tone and accent served for adjectives and adverbs.[25] It was augmented by sign language,[26] itself an ancient and evolving form of communication. When Lewis and Clark were among the Chinooks and Clatsops it had obtained some form, but not until the advent of land-based fur traders among these people, roughly a decade later, could it be said to have taken on definite form,[27] at which time it would take the name Chinook Jargon.

One Indian trader who helped to mould the jargon was Comcomly, rapidly emerging as the foremost leader among his people and among whites, too, with whom he developed perhaps better rapport than he did with many of his own race. In assuming this place of importance he quickly adapted to the ways of white men while employing Chinookan customs to advantage. His flattened head hindered his intelligence none, nor his powers of recall, for it is said that he recognized ships' officers after absences of several years, one such being the first mate of the *Albatross*. He used his many slaves and his many wives and daughters, whom he encouraged to marry white traders to secure their good will, to

---

* Historian Fred Lockley boldly asserted that only one Canadian fur man ever learned enough of the original Chinook language to speak it. "Extinct Chinook Indians Once Peopled Prosperous Villages along the Columbia," *Oregon Sunday Journal*, July 8, 1928, p. 9.

contact prospective customers. His power did not go unchallenged by others of his race. Clatsops, as did others, resented his power and often threatened to unseat him with force. When confronted by such threats, he cowed his opposition by threatening them with "overwhelming force" of his own, meaning a praetorianlike group that was at his disposal at all times. Native lore has it that it was his custom to point to a large rock atop a high Chinook hill, boasting, "As long as that rock remains in place no one shall question the power of me or of my people!"[28]

Comcomly's position remained more secure than did that of the white coastal traders in a business that was beginning to slacken for various reasons. Less obtainable furs made long sea voyages less profitable at a time when native entrepreneurs like Comcomly were demanding higher prices for them and at a time of lowering China profits in take-home goods. Before the end of the first decade of the nineteenth century trade had narrowed for the most part to three firms—Lyman, Lambs, and Perkinses. In 1807 the Perkinses tried to consolidate the trade but failed.[29]

As Comcomly involved himself in intertribal maneuvering, so did white men maneuver in their own milieu to affect the trade patterns of the world even down to its Northwest Coastal corner. In July, 1807, the British began firing on American vessels, capturing them, condemning them in their courts and impressing American seamen into their navy.[30] On December 22, 1807, President Jefferson imposed an embargo on American shipping, hoping thereby to frustrate both British and French belligerents by withholding American goods from them.[31] During the embargo period, which lasted slightly over a year, only two American vessels sold furs in China, although others on the Northwest Coast apparently combined cargoes or awaited the lifting of the embargo to enter China. The ban helped raise the price of prime sea otter skins from thirty dollars in 1808 to fifty dollars the following year, but the price fell again when the ban was lifted.

During this embargo period a Lyman ship, the *Guatimozin*, gathered furs in the Columbia in July, 1808, as she had previously.[32] Her captain, S. Bumstead, before sailing to China picked up one of the medals Lewis and Clark had left with the Chinooks and Clatsops. In 1807–1808 the Lambs sent the Salem-built 300-ton *Derby*, Captain Benjamin Swift, along the coast for furs.* A good picture of the trade at this time is seen in the Lambs' instruction to Swift to use trade items

* Besides the Lambs, Benjamin Swift and the Perkinses had a financial interest in the *Derby*, which on this voyage was fitted out and supplied for around $100,000, returning her owners $330,000. The good return was made possible to a considerable extent by the Jefferson embargo, which had reduced the number of ships trading and hence the number of

where they will command a high price. . . . From the craving disposition of the savage, you had better keep from them the quantity of each article you carry. . . . Provisions will command the best price early in the season when the Fish & Oil, laid in by the Natives is nearly expended. Activity in moving from one part of the Coast to another is essential to getting many skins. Altho' Sea Otter are the great object yet secure, other furs if it can be done with such trade as will not purchase Sea Otters. . . . Go to Columbia River to dispose of your Copper tea kettles, sheet Copper, thin Cloths & Tobacco. . . . Such violations of the principals of humanity have been exhibited towards the Natives by some of our Countrymen as to call for Government interference. A cautious behaviour and endeavours to conciliate the affections of the Indians will better subserve our interests. We would, however, recommend that you do not place your person, or your ship in their power. Revenge burns in their bosoms.

We authorize your going to Canton, to get a Cargo to return to the Coast, should you think best. In this event you will land at Macao, sell the skins & leave the funds at interest until you return to China. If the price is low, leave the skins with Messrs. Perkins & Co. to dispose of when the market shall rise. . . . As a compensation for your services you will receive 7½ per cent of the net sales of all the Goods shipped by your order or brought by you to America, and $20 per month wages, as per our agreement. Should your owners be deprived of your services by any misfortune, your mate should apply to Messrs. Perkins & Co. who will unquestionably be in China when the *Derby* arrives there. . . .[33]

Swift was also instructed that a stay of less than six to eight weeks of wintering on the Columbia River would bring insufficient clamons to trade with Haidas of the Queen Charlotte Islands.[34] Besides copper, brass, cloth, and beads, the *Derby* carried yet another item for trade with Chinooks for which their sweet tooth had developed a fondness— molasses.[35] Another ship, the 281-ton brig *New Hazard,* shortly after the first decade of the nineteenth century, carried molasses, bread, and rice to exchange for clamons and another item for the natives' use— *shrowton* or *oolachon* grease which Nass River peoples of the coast around north latitude 54°20' extracted from a small fish—the shrow or sa-ow—"in order to re-trade . . . with Indians of those [Queen Charlotte] islands."[36] The *New Hazard* also trafficked in human flesh, callously using it as any other trade good in her quest for otter skins.[37] American and British captains along the Northwest Coast would accuse each other of this practice,[38] in which natives were indeed known to have

furs reaching China, thus raising prices there. Horatio Appleton Lamb, "Notes on Trade With the Northwest Coast, 1790–1810. Made by Horatio Appleton Lamb, from the records of James and Thomas, Merchant Shippers of Boston, 1781–1813," manuscript transcript by Thomas P. Martin, Houghton Library, Harvard University, 49.

been captured by ships' crews and traded for furs.[39] Clamons obtained from Chinooks and Clatsops were known to have brought handsome prices in slaves, who were then profitably exchanged for sea otter skins. Samuel Furgerson, carpenter of the Boston brig *Otter,* Captain Samuel Hill, would record in his journal on February 19, 1811, that Chief Estakhunah, who lived on northern Vancouver Island, brought aboard two boy and two girl slaves. One, "a fine boy about 10 years old," was sold for fifteen clamons, four otter skins, and two blankets.[40]

Other captains traded guns, powder and shot, steel knives, and axes to Chinooks for slaves, retrading them in the north for sea otter skins.[41] Chinooks had no qualms about this ancient and traditional practice, which was then beginning to bother European and American consciences. In 1806 the Clatsops, seeking beads and guns, offered Clark a ten-year-old boy only to have their offer refused.[42] Like furs, humans fluctuated in value. In 1810 a male slave in Chinook-Clatsop country brought ten to a dozen blankets. A good male slave brought up to fifteen blankets, a higher price than for females, although in time the latter would become more expensive than males in that place.[43] To the north female slaves fetched fifty to seventy dentalia, and males seventy-five to one hundred.[44]

Perhaps the most notorious American slave dealer on the Northwest Coast was George W. Eayers (Eayrs), captain of the American ship *Mercury,* who sailed the region in that ship after 1806. On one occasion he spirited a dozen native males from the mouth of the Columbia River, but seven of them escaped by stealing a boat and making for shore.* He traded mainly with Russians, with whom he was under contract to hunt sea otters from the Columbia to the California coast.[45] By terms of his contract hunting was to have been by Aleuts, themselves impressed into service by Russians. On one occasion on the California coast Eayers deserted several of them far from their native lands in the north. On July 15, 1808, he sailed from the Queen Charlotte Islands for the Columbia. Baranov dispatched with Eayers a Mr. Shvetsov, who would purchase 580 beavers from Chinooks before the *Mercury* would leave the river the last day of August.[46] After the ship put into the Columbia the Russian wrote reports to Baranov that they had discovered two officers of the United States government who had come by land with several soldiers and built barracks.† According to his account,

---

* The native who was carried off and sold by Eayers showed his apprehension of sailing vessels years later when an American craft in 1825 came to the coast at Tatoosh off the northern tip of the Olympic Peninsula. Scouler, "Dr. John Scouler's Journal of a Voyage to N.W. America," *Oregon Historical Quarterly,* VI (1905), 205.

† According to the translator of Kiril T. Khlebnikof's manuscript, "Biography of Alex-

the officers had given to natives medals bearing the portrait of George Washington.[47]

Need of food more than furs continued to drive Russians south along the coast, which in 1808 they claimed from Alaska to the Columbia River.[48] Cool climate and stubborn soils around Sitka resisted the agricultural efforts of the Russian American Company. Provisioning that settlement was not only financially prohibitive but physically hazardous as well. The Russian American Company, opined the director of that organization,

> made an effort to find such a place at 46° (N. lat.) near the Columbia River, but there too, just as all along the coast of New Albion to the Gulf of Trinidad, no such place could be found, nor was any sheltered port found for ships. In addition, the inhabitants there were of a savage and indomitable spirit. . . . Furthermore, in the entire expanse of the shore of New Albion, from the aforementioned fortress to the Columbia River, there is not the slightest mark indicating that the land belongs to any European nation, especially there where our settlement is taking place—even the very Indians there inhabiting nomadic or transitory dwellings have not been subjugated by the Spaniards and even now are not submitting to them, but stand against them in hatred. . . . [Further,] There was another no less important purpose, namely, to search between 48° and 49° N. Lat. for the Russian descendants, for, as is known to the government, in 1741, the First Expedition of Captain [Alexei] Chirikov, sent to explore the North American mainland below 55°, never returned home and, on another ship sent in search of them, two sailors sent out remained there.—Their descendants grew to 500 persons. . . .[49]

The Russian company planned settlements south of Sitka in the Strait of Juan de Fuca, Grays Harbor, and the Columbia River. Rezanov thought that "After settling there and making friends of savages . . . it would be easy to move towards California and to become its near neighbors."[50] To make a preliminary survey and to choose a convenient place for a settlement, Baranov in the fall of 1808 dispatched two ships, the *Saint Nicholas* and the *Kadiak* (*Kodiak*), south under commands of Nikolai Bulygin and Ivan A. Kouskov. The *Saint Nicholas* carried Timofei Tarakanov, one of the few to escape massacre at Sitka, "to

ander Andreevich Baranov by Kirl Khlebnikof" (typescript copy of manuscript, Archives of British Columbia), the officers referred to were evidently Lewis and Clark, who had left the river in 1806. The faulty impression given in the manuscript that Shvetsov had been at the Columbia when Lewis and Clark were there may have been due to a poor translation. One author suggests that the Russian may have been referring to the mysterious Lieutenant Jeremy Pinch, thought to have been the one who in 1807 warned British fur traders west of the Rocky Mountains that they were treading on American property. Ross, "Early Fur Trade of the Great Northwest," 397–98.

establish first trade relations with natives at the mouth of the Columbia River."[51] Plans were for Tarakanov to join Kouskov on the *Kadiak* in Grays Harbor and sail with her to the California coast. Both ships were to return with reports before a final decision was made on a fortress location. Tarakanov was to trade and deal with Indians at the mouth of the Columbia, since he had successfully dealt with vengeful Tlingits.

The *Saint Nicholas*, carrying twenty souls, three of them women,[52] sailed from Sitka on September 20 for the Columbia to trade with its natives in keeping with the plan. Sailing toward Grays Harbor to join the *Kadiak*, the *Saint Nicholas* ran into trouble. Near Destruction Island on the Washington coast by the mouth of the Hoh River, a storm disrupted a survey its crew undertook, drifting the ship on November 1 to north latitude 47°56′, where she wrecked.[53] The Russians fired opening shots at that place in a skirmish with some Quillayutes, killing three whose survivors retaliated by capturing some of the Russians. Surviving the winter of 1808/1809, the uncaptured Russians wandered about and in the spring at the mouth of the Hoh River planned to build a boat to take them to the Columbia River and a possible rescue by Americans. Those Russians not captured who survived the winter either surrendered or were eventually captured by natives. Retribution against these enslaved Russians continued, as Quillayutes sold two of the captured women and a number of men to Makahs. Chinooks purchased an Aleut and a Russian from the *Saint Nicholas*.[54]

Death and enslavement of the *Saint Nicholas* crew did not deter Russian American Company plans along the Pacific Coast south of Sitka. Besides Indians, their major opposition in that sweep of coastline continued to be Americans, about whom they had ambivalent feelings. Although rivals, the Americans supplied the Russian company with much of its goods, since those of the motherland had to go either by thousand-mile trans-Siberian sled route, an almost impossible feat, or by ships from the Baltic around Africa or South America to the Northwest Coast.[55] American traders benefitted substantially by supplying the Russian company and carrying its furs to Canton. What few ships the Russians had at their disposal were forbidden to enter that mysterious land,[56] marketing furs there only after a long overland journey through Siberia.* What benefits they could not gain from Chinese they made up by using Aleuts, who, with their seaworthy skin canoes, *baidarkas*, they had been contracting out to Americans since 1803 to poach sea otters in California. One of the first to have contracted thus with Russians was the American Joseph O'Cain. In October 1803,

* The Russian journey to China was across Siberia to K'achta (Kiakta) on the Russian border above Ulan Bator in Mongolia.

O'Cain had arranged to take forty Aleut hunters and half that number of two-man *baidarkas* to California.[57] The California harvest had been evenly split between Russian and Americans.[58] Other Yankees, Jonathan and Nathan Winship, had also contracted with Russians in 1804 to take one hundred Aleuts and fifty *baidarkas* to California.*[59]

In 1809 another American whose name was already a hallmark of the fur trade contracted with Baranov to deliver a cargo of supplies to the Russian post at Sitka.[60] The agreement between John Jacob Astor and the Russian called for the freighting on commission of Russian American Company furs to Canton.[61] For the job Astor outfitted the *Enterprise*, captained by John Ebbets, who was no novice in the China fur trade, having ten years earlier shipped skins to Canton on the *Mary*.†[62] Another American involved in Russian trade was Eayers.[63] In 1808, two years after the Perkinses had proposed to the Lambs that they send a supply ship to trade at Sitka, the Lambs had delivered the goods. Eight years earlier they had carried Russian elkskins to Canton, where the Chinese had found little use for them.[64]

With Gray in 1792, Boit had recognized the suitability of the Columbia as a location of a trading "factory."[65] Across the continent Captain Jonathan Winship of the *O'Cain*, his brothers Nathan and Abiel, and Benjamin P. Horner planned to establish a settlement at the Columbia River. During the winter of 1809/10 an American, Allen Weir, and a party of trappers had been on that river, possibly near its confluence with the Willamette.[66] Unlike the Weir enterprise, the Winships hoped to make their "fur colony" a permanent settlement at a place downstream from Weir's location and some thirty miles up from the Columbia mouth on land to be purchased from the Indians. Well aware of the disposition of these peoples, they planned to build a large two-story house complete with a single trapdoor ladder entrance to the top story,

---

* Baranov's records from the Russian American Company show that the fur harvests which his countrymen received (their half-share) were: in 1809 from Jonathan Winship in the *O'Cain*, using 50 baidarkas, 2,728 skins; in 1810 from Nathan Winship in the *Albatross* using 68 *baidarkas*, 560 skins; in 1810 from William Davis in the *Isabella*, with 48 *baidarkas*, 2,488 skins; in 1811 from William Blanchard in the *Catherine*, with 50 *baidarkas*, 758 skins; and in 1812 from Captain Wentmore, in the *Charon* (number of *baidarkas* not indicated), 896 skins. Kiril T. Khlebnikof, "Russian America: Excerpts from Life of Baranof by K. T. Khlebnikof, 1835," typescript copy of manuscript, Archives of British America.

† The *Mary* arrived in Canton later in the year (1799). She did not go to the Pacific Northwest Coast. Besides furs, Astor also sent in this shipment ginseng, a root used by the Chinese but grown in North America. Astor would write Baranov that he had purchased furs from a Canadian company in the American East, trading them in China for many years before sending his own ships to the Pacific Northwest to purchase furs of its natives. Khlebnikof, "Biography of Alexander Andreevich Baranov," 136.

where cannon and ammunition would be stored and loopholes made for muskets. Natives were to be prohibited access to that level. Over half the crew of the *Albatross*, which was to bring them out and supply the colony, was to be on duty at all times. Plans were also laid for clearing and cultivating land under protection of guns and for collecting sea otters but mostly land animals as beavers, foxes, bears, sables, muskrats, and others.

It may have been when Jonathan Winship in 1810 sold the *O'Cain*'s cargo to Baranov and then accompanied a Russian vessel around the northern end of Vancouver Island[67] that the Russians informed him they were eyeing the Columbia River and intended to build a fort there. Seeing in this revelation a threat to the settlement proposed there by himself and his brothers, Jonathan sent word to Nathan, then trading in the Hawaiian Islands for goats, hogs, and other produce from their king (who forbade trade with his subjects until his family had completed theirs), "to proceed with all possible dispatch to the Columbia River to anticipate any movements of the Russians in that direction."[68]

On May 26, 1810, the *Albatross* entered the Columbia to anchor three miles above Chinook Village. Aboard were twenty-five Hawaiians—or Owhyhees—who planned to become permanent colonists on this portion of the Pacific far from their island homes.[69] As Nathan entered the river, his brother, lying off Point Wales in the north, told Captain Hill of the brig *Otter* that the Russians intended to send an armed force against the Americans for trading guns to the natives, a policy which threatened the Muscovite position among Alaskan natives. Alarmed, Hill visited Kouskov of the *Juno* to validate the statement only to receive the Russian's assurance that he had heard of no such plan on the part of his government—his reply designed to either deceive or becalm the agitated Yankee.[70] As early as 1808 Russia had filed protest with the United States for "clandestine and illicit trade" in arms and powder with natives of the Northwest Coast. The American minister to Russia, John Quincy Adams, had replied that since Americans were not trading with natives under Russian jurisdiction they were not bound by Russian law, as were the natives not so bound. Adams had reasoned that Russia had no right to restrain American trade with the natives, especially since no state of war then existed between the two nations.[71]

From May 26 until the end of the month the men of the *Albatross* with a native pilot sounded the river, inching the craft upstream and anchoring here and there until a safe passage could be assured. On June 1 Nathan and his first mate, William Smith, returned from a whaleboat trip in the evening, having selected an oak- and cottonwood-studded spot for their settlement on the south bank five miles upriver from where the *Albatross* lay at anchor. Wind, rain, and poor conditions of the river, which was nearing its seasonal crest, immobilized them until June 4, when they finally reached Oak Point in the vicinity of their projected settlement.* During the next few days the crew felled trees and broke soil as the tailor fashioned clothes to be left at the settlement after the *Albatross* would depart. They built a log cabin, a most important structure to a fur trader or settler. On June 8 a pouring rain continued all night and the next day, swelling the river and flooding with over a foot of water the cleared and planted land and the floor of the house they had already constructed to a height of ten feet.[72] The location seemed so poor that Smith was ordered out in a whaleboat to find a better one.

Small knots of friendly looking natives visited the men daily, bringing furs and salmon to trade. Although Smith returned without locating another spot, he convinced Nathan to pull the structure down log by log and float it downstream a quarter of a mile to a higher spot on the same side of the river.[73] Twenty-eight men were dispatched to carry out the task. This crew was busily at work on the afternoon of June 10 when several canoes carrying many Chinooks and Chilwitzes, all armed with bows and arrows and muskets, put ashore to inform them that natives nearby had ten months earlier killed a Chinook chief, whose death they had come to avenge. The next morning the crew, extremely apprehensive now, were up and working at daylight but quit before noon when armed natives crowded between part of the crew ashore and part of it on the *Albatross*, a move designed, they believed, to separate the two groups of men. Although the ship's guns were loaded, it is doubtful that the small crew aboard could have moved her without additional help. Men were ordered to board her as the others, under gun cover, were ordered to dump the logs into the river to float down to the new site.

The Chinooks and their allies had also come to express to these strangers their strong opposition to their establishing any sort of trading post upriver from them. Any house built, they said, should be downriver in their territory. Nathan's assistant, William A. Gale, correctly divined their mission, noting in his journal that these Indians were "in the habit of purchasing skins of the upper tribes and reselling them to the ships which occasionally arrive at the River ... [making them] afraid and certainly with reason, that the settlement being established so far up, will tend to injure their own trade, and they are no doubt determined to prevent it if possible."[74] Like others before them, Gale and the Winships had correctly evaluated the commercial role of Chinooks, who delib-

---

* Their location was forty miles from the ocean. Bancroft, *History of the Northwest Coast*, Vol. II, 132. The Oak Point where the Winships attempted to settle is not the present-day Oak Point on the Columbia north bank. *Daily Astorian*, October 26, 1844.

erately prevented upriver peoples from trading with ships at the mouth of the Columbia River.*

To allay fears of the Winships and their men, the mustering Chinooks and Chilwitzes declared their quarrel to have been intra-native in nature. This did little to settle the nerves of the settlers, who were now further on edge and on guard. Nevertheless, the men were sent from the ship back to shore to resume work. This they did for about two hours. The Indians then began regathering their forces after sending their women and children to safety. The would-be settlers were really alarmed. Those aboard the *Albatross* readied to move her downstream. The natives scatter-fired their muskets, chasing the whites to the shelter of the trees. One native, seeking to intimidate Captain Winship, as he perhaps had intimidated other "chiefs" upriver, fired at him as he crouched in the topsail of the *Albatross*. The other men hurried into the ship as she moved downstream to the new location. At that place muskets were loaded, and a crew was sent ashore in a longboat to clear brush lining the bank. The natives followed them downstream, and, as before, "these rascals gathered round with hostile intent," forcing the crew to the ship.[75] Three chiefs and some others came alongside but were prevented from boarding and were addressed concerning their conduct, to which they simply replied that they were not afraid of the whites, who should move downriver into their country. After some consideration, the erstwhile settlers deemed it impractical to remain and do business with natives in such a frame of mind. Informed of this decision, the Chinooks and their allies "appeared quite satisfied and sold us some furs."[76] So, as the Winship party changed its plan, the Chinooks changed their attitude. Forced to yield their plans, the party said it would like to have "punish[ed] these fellows for their insolence as it deserves."[77] As no building was begun at the new location, the ship sailed downriver with the same native pilot who had guided her upstream. Evaluating the situation, the party "determined to abandon all attempts to force a settlement."[78] In reality, it could be said that the decision had not been the party's as much as it had been the Chinooks', for as Gale simply put it: "The country was theirs."[79]

* Chinooks jealously guarded their trade monopoly at the mouth of the river. White fur traders who followed the Winships to the area quickly learned of the Chinooks' tenacity in clinging to their position as middlemen in the trade between natives and whites, who could not buy furs from other natives. Colbert, *Kutkos Chinook Tyee*, 221. Chinooks forced upriver and interior tribes, especially, to channel their furs to them. A Chehalis Indian, for example, as late as 1833 would bring furs to a trading post rather than take them to Chinooks, possibly out of fear of their hold on the trade and fear of their wrath. Clarence B. Bagley, "Journal of Occurrences at Nisqually House, 1833," *Washington Historical Quarterly*, VII, 1 (January, 1916), 66.

On dropping down to Grays Bay, the pilot informed Nathan that the natives had intended to capture the ship upriver.[80] Taking the pilot at his word, the captain put the ship under strict guard. Gale well expressed the frustrations of many white men in their relations with Northwest Coastal Indians as "indeed cutting to be obliged to knuckle to those whom you have not the least fear of, but whom, from motives of prudence, you are obliged to treat with forebearance. What can be more disagreeable than to sit at table with a number of these rascally Chiefs, who, while they supply their greedy mouths from your food with one hand, their blood boils within them to cut your throat with the other, without the least provocation."[81]

Down at Bakers Bay the party aboard the *Albatross* found Captain Eayers of the *Mercury* riding at anchor. From both ships trade was conducted with natives who were quite understandably less hostile now, and parts of both craft were refitted. The two captains, learning of the Russians enslaved by Makahs, decided to show the Chinooks a thing or two by arranging a time to capture important ones of their number to hold as hostages for the release of the Russians. At the same time the two believed such action would serve to punish the Chinooks for their "saucy" conduct toward the party upstream and for robbing and killing some of Eayers' "Kodiaks" when he had been in the river a few months earlier[82] on one of his several sorties into that stream to trade.[83]

It was time for action now; five o'clock in the afternoon on July 8. Eight of several Chinooks alongside the ships were seized and clapped into irons aboard the *Albatross*. In the scuffle attending the capture of the Chinooks one crewman hurt his leg from the recoil of a carronade fired without orders, but no one else was injured and the frightened Chinooks paddled off in their canoes. Informed of the reason for their confinement, the hostages dispatched "without hesitation" orders to their fellows to purchase the Russians in Makah hands,[84] denying having Russians in their villages since they had released one Afanassi Valgusov whom they had purchased earlier. Yet they still held the Aleut purchased along with the Russian.

The Russian slave, formerly in Chinook hands, had indeed been rescued by Captain J. Brown of the Perkins' brig *Lydia* when he was in the Columbia in May. After affecting that rescue Brown had sailed north to rescue the Russians enslaved by the Makahs.[85] For each of thirteen survivors of the *Saint Nicholas* held by Makahs,* Brown paid

* Samuel Furgerson, in his "Journal of a voyage from Boston to the North-West Coast of America, in the Brig Otter, Samuel Hill Commander," manuscript, Beinecke Library, Yale University, entry June 5, 1810, writes that the *Lydia*, anchored alongside the *Otter*, Captain Brown, had on board the thirteen Russians rescued from slavery among the Makahs. Presumably the thirteen included the one released by the Chinooks.

their captors twelve yards of cloth, a saw, a mirror, two knives, five bags of powder, and five bags of shot.[86]

Five days after the Chinooks left for the north to get the slaves, they returned without them, since the Russians had already been freed. The Chinooks then delivered up the seventeen-year-old Aleut prisoner when Captain Winship paid his ransom of twenty-five blankets and tobacco. Now head Chinook chief, Comcomly brought word that some Russians were held by natives on the coast where the *Saint Nicholas* had been wrecked,* but that he had been unable to effect their release.[87] He also brought word that some of them had starved to death.† Taking Comcomly at his word, Winship released four Chinook subchiefs from irons and permitted all to leave but one, who was put aboard the *Mercury*, on which Eayers planned to take him north to verify the release of the Russians. Four other chiefs were released from irons but kept aboard to ensure the good behavior of their people until the two ships left the river.[88]

Both ships sailed on the nineteenth. This would not be the last to be heard from Eayers. In 1813 Spanish authorities would arrest him for trading contraband items at California missions.‡ When taken prisoner he had on board the *Mercury* the Indian lad whom he admitted buying on the Columbia in 1808.[89] For the *Albatross*, her Northwest Coastal venture proved unsuccessful. Not only had the settlement plan failed, but she collected barely three hundred skins along the coast.[90] Pressed by such failure, Nathan hurried to join Jonathan on the *O'Cain* off California to discuss with him the plan of establishing a more permanent settlement. The two would finally give up the idea and in 1812 would begin trading in other commodities, since the fur business had proven unprofitable. With one William H. Davis, Jonathan obtained an exclusive contract with Hawaiian King "Tamashmas" to export sandal-

---

* All survivors of the *Saint Nicholas* had been rescued by this time. None were now held by Quillayutes. It may have been that Comcomly misunderstood the Makahs, or that the ship's crew misinterpreted the Chinook chief's words.

† Seven Russians had died in captivity. One Philip Kotilnikov was taken so far away that he was never found. These, with the Aleut ransomed on the Columbia River and the thirteen released captives, made a total of twenty-two from the *Saint Nicholas*. C. L. Andrews, "The Wreck of the St. Nicholas," *Washington Historical Quarterly*, XIII, 1 (January, 1922), 31. The total does not coincide with Chevigny's statement that the expedition left New Archangel with twenty people—seventeen men, four of whom were Aleuts, and the three women. *Russian America*, 136.

‡ Foreign vessels were allowed to visit the California coast for fuel and water, but not to trade. Because he dealt with Spanish priests, Aeyers' activities were overlooked by Spanish officialdom for some time. May Fidelia Boudinot, "The Case of the Mercury, as Typical of Contraband Trade on the California Coast, 1790–1820," thesis, University of California, Berkeley, 78.

wood to China for ten years, but after four he broke off the business because of the War of 1812,[91] apparently unaware of its termination.

The experience of the Winships in the trade was symbolic of changing trade patterns that were bound to affect the commerce of the Northwest Coast. In addition to buying foodstuffs in the Hawaiian Islands, ships' crews now purchased sandalwood, which was beginning for many traders to supplant traffic in sea otter skins. Decreasing in number, these skins now cost more on the coast yet less in Chinese markets, which were becoming saturated with them.* Although firearms were already beginning to decimate sea otter bands, one of the largest catches ever made was that of the 200-ton *Pearl,* Captain John Suter, out of Boston. Working the coast in 1808–1809, she collected six thousand skins, virtually untouched by competition thanks to the embargo. With the raising of that restriction and the glutting of the Chinese market, some traders disposed of their skins cheaply, but a lingering few, wise to the ways of Oriental business, became rich. Soon seals became the prime target of northern Pacific slaughter as Chinese merchants bought them as well as the furs of land animals. Ships often stretched their voyages from two to three years to increase their trade in these kinds of pelts. All of these changes perhaps affected whites more than they did the Indians, making the latter, if anything, more sophisticated in dealing with white men and more dissatisfied than ever at the marketplace.

American activity on the Columbia caused the Russians to look more eagerly to the California coast to locate a post to forestall Yankee settle-

---

* The Chinese at this time became interested in trading for sandalwood, a scarce, beautiful, fragrant and useful wood obtained first in the Hawaiian Islands. Eventually, some of it pawned off on traders was unacceptable to the Chinese, who used good sandalwood for funeral ceremonies, temple incense, and carved fans, boxes, and combs. Trying to avoid the "spurious or bastard wood" of the islands, traders obtained whale teeth by 1815 in trade from the Pallipagos (Galapágos) Islands, carrying them to the Ingrahams Islands (located by Robert Haswell in "A voyage on Discoveries in the Ship Columbia Rediviva," manuscript, Archives of British Columbia, entry June 14, 1792, when he writes: ". . . at noon saw the outwardmost of Ingrahams Island bearing SEBE ½E my latitude was 51°11' of Long. 129°39' W") and Marquesas Islands for a better grade of wood. James, P. H., and Sam G. Perkins and Co. and John Bryant and William Sturgis to Captain Samuel Hill of the ship Ophelia, June 30, 1815, "Letterbook IX," John Bryant and William Sturgis Collection, 1811–1872, Baker Library. Hawaiians would not accept the whale teeth for sandalwood, wanting instead specie, lampblack, and tar. By 1817 Bryant and Sturgis would be advising their ships' captains to trade brass and fieldpieces to the then Hawaiian king, "Tamiahahmiahia" of Atoi, for sandalwood. Bryant and Sturgis to Captain George Clark of the ship *Borneo,* Boston, December 1, 1817, "Letterbook IX," John Bryant and William Sturgis Collection, 1811–1872. In time, Pacific Northwest lumber and salmon would be traded in the Hawaiian Islands for sandalwood. J. W. Nesmith, "Annual Address," *Transactions of the Eight Annual Re-Union of the Oregon Pioneer Association; for 1880,* 17.

ment in that area.[92] The Russian American Company located its third Pacific post in 1812 at Fort Ross, some sixty miles north of San Francisco at Bodega Bay,[93] when it discontinued the practice of leasing out Aleuts to traders of their countries. American opposition to Russian expansion south of the Columbia had short respite after 1812. During this period Russia seized the opportunity to extend her claims and sent crews to look over, among other places, Shoalwater or Willapa Bay. However, her attempt to place vessels in the trans-Pacific trade to supplement American shipping would prove unsuccessful.[94] The firm of Bryant & Sturgis would begin freighting for Russians in 1815.[95] Under Spanish challenge to their presence on the California coast, Russians in 1817 would sound retreat from the lower Pacific coast.* Shortly, their influence would be withdrawn so that by 1823 they would claim territory only from north latitude 51° northward.†[96]

Russians continued their protests against the American sale of firearms to Alaskan natives, who had lost none of their hostility toward their Muscovite masters.[97] When the American government took no steps to stop such sales, Russia again filed complaints (as she had in 1808), attempting to establish a border delineating areas of Russian and American trade activities. At an October 9, 1810, Saint Petersburg conference, American minister Adams informed the Russian minister, Count Romanzov, that it was impossible to enforce laws against Americans trading with natives and that if the Americans did not trade guns to them the British would. The matter was dropped, but not before Romanzov admitted to Adams that all natives along the Northwest Coast had the right to trade with any country.[98] At the time of Adams'

* In half a century of maritime trade since 1775, Russians were credited with taking over 200,000 sea otters. There are no records of takes by the *promyshleniki* who hunted them earlier. Gordon Speck, *Northwest Explorations*, 163. In an article entitled "Russia and the Declaration of the Non-Colonization Principle: New Archival Evidence," (Basil Dmytryshyn, trans.), *Oregon Historical Quarterly*, LXXII, 2 (June, 1971), 109, the writer, N. N. Bolkhovitinov, states: "In a draft of new privileges, which the Board of Directors of the Russian-American Company submitted to the Tsarist government for approval in the spring of 1819, the 45th parallel north was considered the southern boundary of Russian possessions. Subsequently, however, thanks to the 'appearance of the Americans at the mouth of the Columbia River,' the Tsarist government decided to limit its aspirations to the 51st parallel." In a report to Alexander I, dated September 9/21, 1821, Minister of Finance D. A. Guriev emphasized that "the Company ought to be prevented from disrupting the good relations of the Empire with foreign powers...."

† By treaty with Russia in 1823, Americans were permitted to trade with natives on all parts of the coast except where Russians were actually settled. Russia was restricted by the treaty from making settlements south of north latitude 54°. John Bryant and William Sturgis to James P. Sturgis, April 18, 1824, "Letterbook X," John Bryant and William Sturgis Collection, 1811–1872.

admonition, natives of the north possessed few Russian guns; mostly theirs were American ones. In 1813 a gun of Russian manufacture was reported in the possession of Chinooks.[99]

The opening of the second decade of the nineteenth century marked the end of an epoch in which white men had discovered Chinooks and Clatsops at the Northwest Coastal marketplace. Now, vagaries of the maritime trade—depletion of harvests and international economic and political complications—had caused that commerce to ebb like a Pacific tide. In the new epoch that was about to begin, Chinook-Clatsop trade would be with land-based white traders come to harvest the furry riches of the land just as their ship-borne brothers had harvested those of the sea.

What of these two native peoples at this turning point of the trade? Two decades of maritime trade had produced changes in them. Although they retained basic social cohesiveness, some of their mores had shifted, especially those of Chinook women, chief participants in the trade. Contact with white sailors had intensified their marital infidelity and the contraction of venereal diseases, infecting their men and leaving a mark on their children.[100] Yet through it all Chinook women increased in importance to their people at a time when their men rose to or fell from leadership largely on the basis of their relations with ship traders.

European and American trade had inflated and altered their economy.* Wealth had come to be controlled by those who understood and adapted to the realities of that trade. Evidence of that wealth had begun to change with the adoption of white men's goods, which Chinooks and Clatsops found valuable not only as objects of domestic use but for the things they brought in trade. As important as had been the consequence of the white maritime trade for them, these people remained traditionalists clinging more to the old ways than reaching for the new. But as land traders were about to live among them, the question was whether these newcomers would resume where sea traders had left off, making the Chinook-Clatsop market a place where was exchanged not only goods but a way of life as well.

---

* Joyce Anabel Wike, in her thesis, *The Effect of the Maritime Fur Trade on Northwest Coast Indian Society*, 97–98, disagrees with those who believe a Northwest coast native might elevate his status through increased accumulation of personal possessions. She says the social structure of the Indian was such that the poor might come into possession of larger amounts of personal property through trading with maritime traders, but it was not a personal gain above his rich brothers, only a relative elevation in an inflationary situation. The social structure allowed for an increase in status for one in the society through absolute accumulation of goods. Wike attributes change in one's status to depopulation from epidemics of European origin, which disrupted the inheritance lines.

8. Emporium in the Wilderness

> The Chinooks and other Indians at the
> mouth of the river, soon proved themselves
> keen traders, and in their early dealings
> with the Astorians never hesitated to ask
> three times what they considered the real
> value of an article.
>
> Washington Irving, *Astoria*

IN EARLY APRIL, 1811, the ship *Tonquin*, Captain Jonathan Thorn, out
of New York City, lay at anchor in Bakers Bay. As she rode the swells
of the bay, so, in a sense, on her rode the success or failure of the American fur king, John Jacob Astor, to establish a trading post near the
mouth of the Columbia River for his Pacific Fur Company (a subsidiary
of his American Fur Company) to channel American continental furs
to China. Aboard the craft were Alexander McKay and Robert Stuart,
former North West Company (of Canada) clerks who on June 23, 1810,
had agreed to become Astor's partners in his far western enterprise.[1] As
the two anxiously prepared to send a party to search for two other partners in the Astorian enterprise, Duncan McDougall and David Stuart,
who had become lost while scouting the south bank of the Columbia
River for a site for a trading post, they looked up to see two large canoes
making their way to the ship. The native craft, manned by Chinook
Indians, were bringing in the lost partners. Safely aboard, the two confessed that contrary to warnings from the one-eyed yet weather-wise
Chief Comcomly they had capsized their craft in stormy weather while
trying to cross Bakers Bay to the ship. Fortunately, the natives had
followed to rescue them from a watery grave. Then the Chinooks had
landed them, kindled a fire to dry their clothes, and led them back to
Chinook Village, where Comcomly had received them warmly, offering
everything he could for their comfort. For the natives' kindnesses the
two whites had rewarded them with gifts.

During their three days in the village, composing themselves after their close brush with death, McDougall and Stuart saw a river settlement like those they had seen in the East, vibrating with human existence. The village had not only its own peculiar appearance but also its own sounds—the clucking chatter of its people—and its own smells —odors of fish offal, bones, human excrement, and other refuse swarmed over by insects. The odors would prove more offensive to future white visitors than to these Scot traders, the stoutness of whose stomachs matched that of their hearts. Where eastern cities were rooted in European Christian culture, this village gave but scant evidence that such culture had dented it very deeply. Metal knives, kettles, axes, and guns obtained by the villagers from white coastal traders did not belie to whites what they considered to be the primitiveness of the place. Articles of native manufacture still predominated. Life's most important events—birth and death, were still attended by aboriginal trappings and ceremonials. Medicine men still tried to cure the sick by extorting evil spirits from pain-racked bodies. Marriage partners, although dowered and ceremonialized as in civilized nations, enjoyed a freedom in their relationship that was jarring even to some traders, who as a rule were not overly sensitive to such things. Pleasure seekers in the village, like those of civilized society, found time to play games. Their favorite one was *omintook*, in which four beaver teeth were thrown like dice. In fact, these natives found more time to play than did their white brothers, but they accompanied their gaming with a cadence of sounds strange to the Christian ear.[2]

The Chinooks' welcome to their village of the two rescued partners was in sharp contrast to their reception of the Winships the previous year, possibly because the natives had learned of the partners' plan to establish a post among them near the mouth of the Columbia River and not at some distance away. The generous action of the rescuers was in sharp contrast to that of the nautical despot Captain Thorn. From New York to the Northwest Coast via Cape Horn and the Hawaiian Islands, the American captain had quarreled with the partners and their men. As the *Tonquin* neared the Columbia River his temperament had not improved. A fortnight before the rescue of the partners, as the ship stood off the mouth of the Columbia in a March gale, Thorn had ordered the first mate and four others to proceed in a long boat with bed sheets for sails to sound the bar. In so doing they fell victim as much to his treachery as to that of the river. Two days later he had dispatched an officer and some men to sound again. Their boat was also lost, but two of the men had miraculously escaped. At last, with great difficulty, the *Tonquin* had inched across the bar into Bakers Bay. In far-off New York, Astor had no inkling that these or other events soon to occur would endanger his enterprise, which a rival British trader would term one of "misconduct and disaster."[3]

In mid-April curious natives from the vicinity came to trade and to visit those landed from the *Tonquin* on a "handsome and commanding situation" on the eastern lip of Youngs Bay. Earlier, aboard the *Tonquin,* some of the natives had shown "no disposition to trade," as was their custom when first meeting white men. In deference to Astor, his Scot partners renamed the place Astoria. On the south shore of the river, the site was six miles across the Columbia from Chinook Point. In full view a dozen miles to the west were the bar and breakers of the Columbia—constant reminders of the tragic events of recent days. The Astorians tried to forget by frenziedly attacking thick brush and giant trees to win a stingy clearing in the wilderness to build a fort (Fort Astoria), all the while finding time to reward with trifling gifts the natives who came to watch them out of "curiosity or worse motives."

The mere appearance of these red strangers created a generally unfavorable impression upon the newcomers, who numbered a scant thirty-three souls. The near-naked flatheaded natives strolled among the fur men, who in curiosity eyed the women's fish oil–smeared bodies, pendulous breasts, split ears, perforated noses, and bandy legs. Company clerk Ross Cox, joining the company later, would call them "the most repulsive looking beings that ever disgraced the fair form of humanity."[4] To his colleague Alexander Ross they appeared less repulsive, proving the truth of the old adage that the measure of beauty—or ugliness—in the wilderness as elsewhere was in the eye of the beholder.[5] The Astorians soon discovered what any maritime fur trader could have told them—that Chinook women, despite their appearance, were as active in the trade as their men. Of their industry Ross would comment, "In trade and barter the women are as actively employed as the men, and it is as common to see the wife, followed by a train of slaves, trading at the factory, as her husband."[6]

The Astorians believed their initial friendly meeting with Comcomly and his assurance of fidelity and protection lessened none their need of guns for protection. The natives naturally regarded the bristling weapons as tokens of ill will. The Astorians must have known that friendly Comcomly was a man of authority, based on his ample supply of wives and slaves to paddle his canoe and perform countless other tasks for him. They were soon to learn that his practice of excluding surrounding tribes from trading at the mouth of the Columbia was designed to prevent jeopardy to his authority at that place. This is not to say, however, that the one-eyed chief held a lowly place in Astorian eyes. On the basis of their records, Washington Irving a quarter of a century later would introduce him to the world in *Astoria* as an aboriginal potentate of great importance, albeit one of great craft, wile, and shrewdness.* The newcomers fell short of their estimation of Comcomly's influence if they indeed thought it would provide them a blanket of protection, for they had been on the Columbia but two months when they claimed that Indians killed three of their number.[7] Yet the intellectually and physically powerful chief, with his strong coterie of canoemen, often found at the scene of action, did provide an effective intelligence system not only for his own people but for the Astorians as well. When six of them deserted he returned them to the fort, then under construction, as an object lesson to its builders of his efficiency.[8]

Life was hardly gracious at the post. The unpopularity of headman McDougall, a person of "irritable, peevish temper," was responsible for some of the discontent there. Clerks were hard pressed to hold the enterprise together and sought to do so by trying to stabilize relations between McDougall, his partners, and the men, who were primarily French-Canadian voyageurs and mechanics. Because of the lowly position of the French Canadians, they tended to associate with the Indian people more than did their superiors, and they even added their bit of French to the Chinook Jargon. McDougall was also unpopular with his native clientele, regarding most of them as out for no good, a feeling generally shared by his fellow partners, who believed, for example, that Comcomly had returned the deserters only for "the sordid hope of gain."[9] On one occasion McDougall injured the pride of one of Comcomly's sons, setting back good relations between the groups.[10] A white mariner acquaintance of Comcomly's would write that the chief took goods upcountry to trade with tribes there, bringing their furs to the mouth of the Columbia to sell. Reaping a profit on this business, it was to his advantage to keep his suppliers away from the mouth of the Columbia by telling them that bad men at that place would carry them off and enslave them.[11] The fact that maritime traders had taken Indian slaves to exchange for sea otters on the Northwest Coast gave credence to Comcomly's stories. The effectiveness of his visitations to outlying tribes would come to light when Astorians tried to do business with them.

On learning from natives of a fur post up the Columbia River "above certain rapids" (Spokane House, established by the North West Company in 1810), partners Alexander McKay and Robert Stuart, clerks

* In his "Comcomly and the Chinooks," *Oregon Historical Quarterly*, XXXIII (1932), 270, J. F. Santee states that Irving treated the chief and his followers in a patronizing manner. Of course, Irving was writing in a day before anthropologists had made the study of such people an end in itself. In his *Astoria* his heroes are always Astorians.

Gabriele Franchère and Ovide de Montigny, and Clatsop Chief Coalpo as guide set out on May 2 to find the settlement. Possibly Chief Coalpo may have guided the traders upriver out of gratitude for the establishment of a post in his lands. Such an establishment could receive goods from hinterland natives instead of having them channeled off to some post in the interior that would threaten not only Clatsop and Chinook economy on the lower river but that of the Astorians as well.

Reaching the vicinity of the Dalles, the Astorians gave presents to chiefs and headmen to gain the general good will of the peoples of that quarter, whom whites lumped under the designation "Shoshones." They also learned that there was no trading post near the Dalles, but plenty of trading nevertheless. Natives there employed the natural constriction of the river to charge fees for the portage of goods and, failing that, to pilfer. Partly at least because of their strong geographical position and the general position of inferiority in which they were held by Chinooks and Clatsops, the rapids peoples were on poor terms with those at the mouth of the river. Because of this bad relationship Coalpo refused to lead the Astorians further upstream, fearing that enemies in the villages ahead would kill him. Well should he have been afraid, for on one occasion he had burned one of their villages.[12] The Astorians, believing the trouble to be strictly a native affair, had no such fears, and on their return to Fort Astoria they reported "most favourably of both natives and country." In days ahead, however, they would learn that the place they had visited, although a "great [native] emporium or mart of the Columbia," was also a "general theatre of gambling and roguery."

Shortly after the party returned, another, including Robert Stuart, Ross, and five men, trekked north into the hinterland to put themselves in competition with Chinooks for the trade of that region. Natives there showed the white men a pile of furs destined for the Chinooks. Always on touch and go terms with the Columbia River Indians, the northerners said they would switch their trade from Chinooks to Astorians, whose ample payments caused them "to put their hands to their mouths in astonishment." Never again, they said, would they trade with Comcomly.[13] Soon these northerners would regard Astorians as their enemies as they did the Chinooks, for they would kill an Astorian and later cut to pieces an eight-man party of the white traders.[14]

The departure of the *Tonquin* on June 5 for northern waters to trade with Russians and natives left the infant post with few furs and few men to protect themselves. "When the ship [*Tonquin*] left us," wrote Ross, "not a gun was mounted; not a palisade raised. . . ." Under pressure of fear, the whites became very cautious and labored to complete a log-framed, cedar-bark-covered storehouse, dwelling, and powder magazine. Numerically, the small settlement could hardly match numbers with its neighbors: nearly 1,000 braves—214 Chinooks, 180 Clatsops, 234 of the more remote Chehalis to the north, and 200 Tillamooks to the south.[15]

Natives now moved close to Astoria in greater numbers. Ross confessed nearly forty years later: "We naturally put the worst construction on so formidable an array of savages in arms."[16] The arms to which he referred were mostly of native manufacture. Although the natives had gotten guns from traders, powder was hard to obtain. The environs of Astoria were not conducive to the use of guns, what with their impenetrable undergrowth and the October-to-March dampness that made it difficult to keep the cumbersome weapons in working order.[17] Tillamooks and peoples inland from the coast knew even less than did Chinooks and Clatsops about the use of firearms. It was the natives' skill in their aboriginal weapons that concerned the outnumbered Astorians.

Safely removed from the barbarous Northwest Coast in time and space, Ross would more objectively remember Chinooks and their neighbors as "a commercial rather than a warlike people," with "Traffic in slaves and furs . . . their occupation"—a people "up to all the shifts of bargaining," having learned "the arts of cheating, flattery, and dissimilation [*sic*]" by trafficking with white coastal traders for guns, kettles, and other articles of foreign manufacture.[18] One of the "shifts of bargaining" which Chinooks employed was to secure skins of beavers and other land animals from their close neighbors in exchange for permission granted those peoples to hunt, fish, and trap in Chinook country.[19] Prime beaver skins, involved in Chinook "bargaining" during the Astorian era, ranked with quality dentalia as a medium of exchange. Of the latter on one occasion six fathoms of two-and-one-half-inch shells were refused by a native for a new gun. When buying an article, a Chinook invariably asked the question, "Queentshich higua?" or "Queentshich enna?"—"How many higua?" or "How many beaver skins?"[20]

As foul weather at the river mouth cleared with a northwesterly onshore flow of air, so did Astorian relations with Comcomly clear. The whites were now mildly convinced that the chief was not always canoeing around sowing seeds of dissimilation. For his improved image in their eyes they presented him and a son suits of white men's clothing to hide what had been for the chief nakedness, save for "a short kilt around his waist to the middle of the thigh." (In cold weather he wore a robe of sea-otter skins and other furs.)[21] Offsetting what might have been better public relations between Astorians and natives was the increased incidence of thievery by the latter. Although not above such nefarious activity, Chinook and Clatsop masters often encouraged their slaves to steal for them. With the fate of their very lives hanging on the will of their masters, these unfortunates were hard pressed to do their bidding, whatever nasty business that might have entailed.[22] On one occasion a native, slave or free Ross does not say, pilfered some tobacco at the post only to be caught by McDougall, who had the miscreant incarcerated. Later the native escaped, carrying off his irons and a sentinel's gun. When Comcomly came over to the fort the next day, McDougall, wishing to show the aboriginal "mufti" the power of the establishment, brandished a blunderbuss. The weapon accidentally discharged, blowing a corner off the chief's robe. The frightened Comcomly dashed from the tent minus robe, cap, and gun, yelling for his people to come to his aid. They immediately responded with a war whoop, arming themselves to menace the whites with threats of destruction. Thinking Comcomly had killed McDougall, the Astorians fired after the chief, shouting treason and bloody murder. McDougall and Ross, aware of the situation, placed themselves between the hostile ranks, making signs of peace. After a hectic moment they settled the affair without bloodshed. Now it was Comcomly's turn to be suspicious in the belief a plot had been made on his life.[23]

Near the end of July, Indians hitherto around the fort in great numbers began to thin out. One who had formed a friendship for Robert Stuart told him they were planning to plunder the fort and kill the party. Increasingly apprehensive, the Astorians quickly raised a dwelling house parallel to a warehouse that was already built, erecting shops, palisades, and at each corner bastions with four small cannon mounted.[24] The sudden change of the natives' behavior was occasioned by the arrival from the Strait of Juan de Fuca and Grays Harbor of Indians who "formed a great camp" on Bakers Bay. Having come ostensibly to fish for sturgeon, they had in reality come with the news that disaster had befallen the *Tonquin* in the north. Details of the disaster soon spread to the whites, who at first gave no credence to them but became increasingly uneasy some days later when Chehalis Indians gave as far as the Astorians could understand them, a detailed account of the disaster. The uneasy whites increased their vigilance at the fort and conducted daily drills at that place. With numbers somewhat less than before the *Tonquin* sailed north, and with dwindling supplies, the party was forced from July to subsist on fish and, by the grace of one friendly native, on venison, for which they paid dearly at the rate of a blanket, a knife, tobacco, and powder and ball per animal.[25]

Disturbing as were these developments, the Astorians resolved to continue the trade. On July 22 a party embarked up the Columbia in two Chinook canoes clumsily laden with trade goods to establish a post (Fort Okanogan) at the confluence of the Okanogan and Columbia rivers to collect furs from the interior. (For transporting furs from that place to Astoria company men made light, durable craft of split or sawn cedar capable of carrying cargoes up to a ton and a half.)[26] For all they knew, these traders returning to Astoria might have found it wiped out as the *Tonquin*'s crew had been according to the rumors. Before returning to Astoria, the interior-bound party would have to pass the Dalles and its Wishram village, a troublesome spot where anything might happen—and would happen the following spring when its natives would nearly kill company clerk John Reed with a tomahawk, proving to Astorians as it long before had to Chinooks and Clatsops the treachery of that place, where nature and natives combined to obstruct the river passage. Huddling near their post, the Astorians had no assurance that these hostile natives to the east would not join similar ones from the north to obliterate their small beachhead on a hostile frontier. Perhaps Franchère was attempting to keep up his own courage and that of his fellows by boasting that the fort,* around which guards were posted day and night, "had an aspect sufficiently formidable to make the Indians fearful. . . ."[27] They continued to hope against hope that the persistent rumors of the fate of the *Tonquin* were groundless. Aware that northern tribes in the land to which she had sailed had a reputation for belligerence, they feared that coalesence between these northerners and Comcomly would put Astoria out of business for good.

Had these white men understood very well intertribal relationships on the Northwest Coast, they would have known that its people were too individualistic for such a grand military alliance and that they frequently fought among themselves. One of Comcomly's headmen, Kaloye, for example, reportedly united Chinooks and Clatsops in defense against piratical raids of northern peoples such as the Nootkas from lands

---

* In describing the fort as it appeared in the spring of 1812, Robert Stuart wrote that it was "only about 75 feet by 80 . . . well stockaded with pickets 17 feet long and 18 inches diameter, having two strong Bastions, at opposite angles, so as to rake two sides each . . . ," inside of which were a "framed store, two stories high, 60 feet by 20, with good cellars and a powder magazine.—a dwelling house, one story high, & 60 feet by 25.—a Black Smith's shop, and a large shade [shed] for carpenters, Coopers, &ct. . . ." Kenneth Spaulding (ed.), *On the Oregon Trail: Robert Stuart's Journey of Discovery, 1812–1813*, 28.

where the *Tonquin* had sailed. More threatening to Chinooks and Clatsops than were these distant northerners were peoples closer to the Columbia, such as the Quillayutes,* who occasionally raided the vicinity of the river mouth, often under the leadership of former Chinook slaves, whose knowledge of the dangerous bar and shoals in Willapa Bay made the services of these captives almost indispensable to their Quillayute masters, who prowled southward for spoils.[28] On one of their southern forays they clashed with Clatsops who, according to Clatsop tradition, sent the Quillayute invaders retreating to their own villages carrying their dead in canoes.[29]

There were even bad feelings between Chinooks and Clatsops. Even during peacetime the Chinooks treated such visitors as the Clatsops coldly. After inviting their neighbors to their lodges, the hosts repaired there to wait. Upon the arrival of their guests, all parties sat mutely for several minutes until the partaking of food helped break the silence. As another example, the sister of Chief Coalpo warned Astorians that Comcomly's sore throat, which he wished them to cure, was merely a ruse to capture them. The little knot of traders, fearing such to be the case, kept up their courage by whistling in the November and December darkness while awaiting positive proof and details of the fate of the *Tonquin*. Liquor served at the fort on New Year's Day, 1812, would raise their spirits but temporarily.

The Astorians probed the Columbia that winter, preparing for a springtime resumption of trade. The winter gloom was brightened somewhat by the arrival of the overland brigades, one commanded by Astor's chief agent, Wilson Price Hunt, whom the fur king had commissioned to win the confidence of natives on his journey to the Columbia while seeking out places where posts might be established along the way. When proposed, the Hunt expedition had looked good on paper; on the ground it was a different story. Splintered and nearly starved parties from the expedition reached Astoria in January and February after harrowing journeys. Even after terminating their journeys at Astoria, where Hunt was to take charge, life for them would have been hazardous had not Indians brought fresh fish to sustain the weary travelers.[30]

The arrival of Astor's ship *Beaver*, Captain Cornelius Sowle, on May 10 gladdened the Astorians, for it brought supplies and additional per-

---

* In 1934 a Quillayute Indian, Harry Ho[e]bucket, told of the last battle between Quillayutes and Satsops (Salish) with their Chinook allies. It proved to be a Pyrrhic victory for both sides, for at the battle scene, Grays Harbor, Quillayute canoes got stuck in the mud when the tide went out, and the Satsops and Chinooks lost many men because they were fighting in the open. Harry Hobucket, "Quillayute Indian Tradition," *Washington Historical Quarterly*, XXV, 1 (January, 1934), 53.

sonnel. It also saddened them, for it brought word that the *Tonquin* had indeed gone to a watery grave, carrying with her, besides her crew, Alexander McKay, who left behind at the fort a son, Thomas.[31] That same month one party of dissatisfied men set out for the States, another group to establish a post on the Spokane River, another to explore the Snake River, and still another to explore the Okanogan River near their trading post at that place. These departures reduced the number of men at Astoria, and the natives still appeared unfriendly.[32]

There are no accounts of the activities of Comcomly and his Chinooks that winter. The chief may have spent the winter, as he often did, in a rocky ravine near a creek flowing into the Naselle River, where high wooded hills protected him from blustery Pacific storms. The coming of spring and salmon returned him to his Columbia village for another seasonal round, which included trade at the post.[33] At that place he tried to apprise himself of everything going on, but at this juncture in his relationship with the white traders he appeared to have been on the outside of councils held there. Ironically, he knew more about what was going on than did Astor himself, although the latter, understanding international troubles of the time, had some inkling of potential dangers to his Pacific project. During the summer Astor had written optimistic letters to government officials about the friendliness of Northwest Coastal natives and of the great possibilities in the trade. In reality he had always been suspicious of natives of the coast. In a November, 1809, letter to John Ebbets, captain of the *Enterprise*, sent to explore possibilities of arrangements with the Russians in the north Pacific and to contact natives on the Columbia River and its coastal environs, he had written: "I deem it proper to point out to you in case you should meet with any accident while on the Coast (which God forbid) and which should oblige you to put by distress in any River, Bay or Port among the Natives, to be carefull of them and not permit them to come on board, nor even near the Ship, as I understand several Ships have been taken and with them Crews destroy'd by them."[34] Now, Astor was trying hard to put his Columbia River enterprise in the best possible light while seeking government assistance in protecting it from possible British incursion, especially after June 18, for on that date Congress declared war on Great Britain. Astor believed any British threat to his post to be as great a threat to the United States government as it was to him.

At that post, Comcomly continued to take part in its life and trade. In early May he and his followers had to reckon with an Astorian-based rate of exchange, which on some of the more important items was one half-axe (in size between a regular axe and a hatchet) for four beaver, a hatchet for two beaver, a yard of long cloth for four beaver, one yard of cotton cloth for two beaver, a large knife for two beaver, five leaves of well-twisted tobacco in two rolls for one beaver, and so on. Clerk Donald McGillis, in temporary charge of the post at that time, received careful instructions from Ross to sell no more than one axe to an Indian at a time and no more than seven half-axes, limiting his sale of glass beads, awls, and cloth. He was further instructed to frequently air the leaf tobacco, keep kegs aired, tend the garden, and place unpacked beaver of the store, along with that to be purchased, neatly into the press, on which he was to put over one hundred pounds' weight, changing and repressing it with care. He was to always give his red customers smokes before and after trading. Those bringing nothing were to be given a pipe in the interest of good public relations. He was always to "Assume a certain dignity," keeping Indians at a distance all the time with "a Smilling Countenance" while keeping close tabs on the traffic. He was to make no exchanges, the bane of all clerks, and should his customers object he was to pretend not to understand them. Above all, he was to be kind to those who brought the Astorians something to eat.[35]

The inventory of goods entrusted to McGillis amounted to some $9,541.45 worth of furs accumulated at the post for the Astoria district since April of the previous year. Leading the list were 2,731 large and small beaver skins worth $8,193, followed by nearly 100 large and small sea otter skins worth $755. Land otter skins trailed in value along with a variety of skins of raccoon, lynx, fisher, mink, muskrat, bear, cat (civet cat or cougar?), wolf, fox, and the lowly squirrel.[36]

From May through fall the Indians brought Astorians uninventoried delicacies such as cranberries and oysters. But one product they brought, for which their country would become world famous, was salmon. Robert Stuart wrote that these were "by far the finest fish I ever beheld. . . ."[37] These and other creatures from land and sea had been used by Chinooks and Clatsops mainly for their own consumption and only casually in trade. Wrote Stuart: "The Coast near the mouth of the River, produces a few Sea Otter, and some scattering Beaver, which the Natives, both from inexperience and indolence, seem as yet little inclined to reduce in number, altho' their sole dependence for sustenance is upon Fish, Roots, and what few Animals they can kill."[38] He also noted that Chinooks were "more especially the intermediate traders between the whites and inland Tribes, particularly those to the northward."[39]

Goods from the *Beaver* added more prestige and position to these "intermediate trader" Chinooks with surrounding peoples. (Not all of the *Beaver's* cargo was deposited at the Columbia, however, for some of it was reserved for trade with Russians to the north in keeping with the agreement Astor had with the Russian American Company to furnish it with supplies and carry its furs to Canton to be sold on commission.)[40] The Clatsop-Chinook response to the quality of the goods the *Beaver* brought to Astoria was one of dissatisfaction, and we also know the Astorian response. The Britisher Ross would later express disappointment at the quality of goods Astor supplied his posts. "Instead of guns," he recalled, "we got old metal pots and gridirons; instead of beads and trinkets, we got white cotton; and instead of blankets, molasses. In short, all the useless trash and unsaleable trumpery which had been accumulating in his shops and stores for half a century past, were swept together to fill his Columbia ships."[41] An old hand in the Indian trade, Astor well knew what items were good for it—thimbles, gimlets, files, knives, scissors, buttons and beads, cloth of high color. Like every shrewd trader, he sought to minimize his investment and maximize his profit.[42]

The summer departure of the brigades for the interior to the Spokane, Okanogan, Lewis (Snake), and McKay (Willamette) river districts left the fort poorly manned. Increasingly concerned for its safety, the men constructed galleries inside the palisades, heightened the bastions, and alerted their guards. To Chinooks and Clatsops these physical defenses perhaps seemed less formidable than the economic bastions thrown around it in the form of furs coming to it from the interior. They must have suffered pangs of hostility or at least resentment at being shoved aside as middlemen in a business in which they had at times forced interior tribes to sell furs to them so they could resell them at a profit.

The departure of the *Beaver* on her coasting voyage on August 4 added little to the feeling of security at the fort. The following day the arrival of a native from Grays Harbor with news of the *Tonquin* proved all the more disturbing.* On one of his many junkets to the fort Comcomly had told the Astorians he knew of a native survivor of that ship. Astorians, according to Franchère, had sent to Grays Harbor for him to come down. It was this native, George Ramsay (Lamazu), who now

---

* Locations given for the destruction of the *Tonquin* have varied. It seems rather conclusive from evidence obtained from a Vancouver Island native by Augustine J. Brabant, a Roman Catholic missionary at Hesquiot on the west coast of Vancouver Island, that the site was near the tree and brushwood-covered Lennard Island, called *Eitsape* by the natives, and near the long barren rocky Village Island in Templar Channel leading into Clayoquot Sound. After the explosion, blankets, scarce in those days, were found floating on the water. The natives called them *Cla-o-kwat-skene* (meaning "belonging to Clayoquot"), holding them in great esteem and passing them on to their children. Brabant to John Devereux, May 15, 1896, John Thomas Walbran, "Miscellaneous papers," Archives of British Columbia.

bore the bad news.* By means of voice, gestures, and signs he related details of how he had been an observer at the scene when the ship exploded at Clayoquot Sound on Vancouver Island some fifteen or twenty miles from where Gray and the *Columbia* had wintered in 1791/92. From Ramsay's story it emerged that Captain Thorn had struck one of the principal chiefs, expelling him from the *Tonquin*. Smarting from this insult to their chief, the Indians had sought vengeance by plotting to kill the crew and capture the ship. Subsequently, when a large number of natives were aboard and around her, she had blown up with a terrible noise—arms, legs, heads, and torsos flying in all directions.

Ramsay was well rewarded for his services in relaying the news, and Astorians pondered the event not only in apprehension but perhaps in anger that Thorn had been responsible for the horrid affair, not only because of his brusqueness but also because of his failure to properly defend his ship.[43] When McDougall learned of the tragedy, he sought to control the natives around his fort by calling together several chiefs to show them a small bottle, declaring it to contain the smallpox. This "phial of wrath," as Irving would call it, would be to McDougall an equalizer, since with the *Tonquin* lost, the number of Astorians was more than ever dwarfed by that of the Indians. Remembering the ravages of smallpox of three decades before, marks of which some still bore on their faces, the natives believed the story of McDougall, "The Great Smallpox Chief."[44]

Astorians remaining on the Columbia composed themselves the best they could in the wake of the disaster. Franchère and others went up the Columbia that fall to gather winter food and the skins of 450 beaver and other animals. So successful was the voyage that Comcomly's son accompanied the clerk on a second voyage. Although the second journey was less successful, Franchère found the lad to be intelligent and communicative, helping to make the Frenchman the most versed of all Astorians in communicating with Chinooks and Clatsops. Another party was dispatched from the fort in late November to journey some 150 miles up the Willamette to establish a post whose primary function was to supply venison to Fort Astoria to help offset its almost steady ration of fish.[45] Franchère and McDougall remained at the fort that winter. The latter's illness apparently did not prevent him from having an amorous affair with one of Comcomly's daughters. Franchère kept busy observing the Indians—their languages and customs, their politics, and, when that broke down, their bloodless warring tactics made possible to

* Because Ramsay was thought to have been at the mouth of the Columbia stirring its natives to hostility, some whites would accuse him of implication in the 1814 murder of one "Judge" Archibald Pelton, who had come west with Wilson Price Hunt.

some extent by the clamons or other cuirasses of pieces of wood laced with nettle twine that they wore.[46]

The new year, 1813, came in on an ominous note for Franchère and his fellows. In January Donald McKenzie brought word from the interior, where it had come overland from the East to the Spokane, that America and Britain were at war.[47] To make matters worse, nothing had been heard from the *Beaver*. Had she met the same fate as the *Tonquin*? Trade with the Indians had stopped—not only because the Astorians "no longer had a large stock of goods on hand, but also because we already had more furs than we could carry away" (perhaps overland should the post have to be abandoned).[48]

On April 11 John George McTavish and Joseph La Roque of the North West Company arrived overland at Astoria from the interior. These two, as had other enterprising personnel of their firm, had helped account for its trans-American expansion since its founding three decades before. At the company's annual meeting at Fort William at the head of Lake Superior in the summer of 1812, the Nor'Westers had determined to establish a post at the mouth of the Columbia River to control the trade of the interior, from which they would ship furs to China. McTavish and La Roque had come to further that project as they awaited the arrival of the ship *Isaac Todd*, dispatched by their company to the Columbia River.*

Possibly pleasing to the two visitors was the Astor partners' unhappiness with the trade. Not only were the goods supplied them unfit for that trade and North West Company competition, but also, worse than that, since January the trade had been virtually suspended for want of goods occasioned by Anglo-American tensions and the outbreak of the war. On hand at the first of the year had been fewer than twenty-five hundred furs.[49] Under these discouragements the Astor partners, in a formalized document on June 25, 1813, proposed to their North West Company competitors to divide the trade for the ensuing winter by giving them posts in the Spokane and Kutenai Indian country as well as supplying them goods. These were to be paid for the following spring in

* In 1804 the North West Company had written the British Colonial Office expressing its determination to explore to the Pacific Ocean, requesting a monopoly of any route found across the Rocky Mountains to the "Western sea." Such a monopoly was refused. That same year, Lewis and Clark began their trek. Katharine B. Judson, "The British Side of the Restoration of Fort Astoria," *Oregon Historical Quarterly*, XX (1919), 245. In London in the year of Astoria's founding an enthusiastic Britisher, Nathaniel Atcheson, Esq., had written *On the Origin and Progress of the North-West Company of Canada, with a History of the Fur Trade As Connected with That Concern*, in which he stated (p. 34) that although there were beneficial mercantilist aspects of the Canadian fur trade, they were not as important or as capable of benefits as were those conferred upon Indians with whom the trade was carried on.

horses or "in any other manner which may best suit us at that period. . . ." The foregoing was done on the condition that the Nor'Westers leave the Astorians all remaining "Parts of the Columbia" and forward their dispatches to Astoria by the usual North West Company overland winter express, since the Astorians were in no condition to do so themselves.[50] Many of the Astor men chose to switch their allegiance to the North West Company, but several chose not to.

The advent of summer, usually a pleasant experience for white men whose fate took them to the winter-dreary mouth of the Columbia River, was not pleasant for the Astorians in this year of 1813. By July 1 the *Beaver* had failed to return after nearly a year's absence. On the twenty-eighth of that month Astorian Alfred Seton complained of nearly fifteen months' existence in "this miserable country."[51] The *Lark*, of 300 tons burthen, Captain Northrop, fitted out by Astor with supplies for his Columbia River post, had sailed from New York on March 6. She never reached her destination, wrecking in October in the Hawaiian Islands. To make matters worse, the War of 1812 increasingly stagnated affairs on the Northwest Coast, adversely affecting the two belligerents alike. Furs of the country had fallen short of expectations. Ammunition was running short, and food was too, what with additional Nor'Wester mouths to feed. "In fine," wrote the partners, "circumstances are against us on every hand and nothing operates to lead us into a conclusion that we can succeed."[52] Not the least of their worries was the growing restlessness of Chinooks and Clatsops at the absence of trade goods. Their suppliers feared that should goods and other aid not soon come the red customers would carry out their suspected "ill designs" on the place.[53]

On July 1, in accordance with an 1810 agreement with Astor authorizing them to abandon the project if it proved to be unprofitable within five years, they prepared to leave the country by late spring, 1814. On July 7 David Stuart and J. Clarke, not wishing to abandon the country so soon, returned to their respective Okanogan and Spokane posts. Furs were baled in preparation for shipment, probably overland, at the time the Astorians would abandon the lower Columbia.[54] Not even the return of Hunt the next month on the *Albatross*, Captain William Smith, from the Hawaiian Islands could change their decision to abandon the project, especially since he had brought insufficient supplies with him. It was agreed that he should return to the islands to obtain necessary shipping to remove furs, property, some of the men, and some twenty-five Hawaiians. It had also been agreed that should Hunt not return, the man who was to have sole right to conclude any arrangement with anyone who "may come forward on the part of the N.W. co." was McDougall.[55]

This prerogative only stimulated this man "of a thousand projects," as Irving would describe McDougall, whose stratagems included not only "medicine," as witnessed in the recent object lesson with "smallpox germs," but matrimony. On the basis of his no longer extant "Journal of Astoria," which he closely guarded, Irving, who had access to it, would claim the marriage to have been a great politico-economic stroke to perpetuate good will among McDougall's Chinook in-laws and their people and neighbors in the trade.[56] It is not known when McDougall first took a liking to Illchee (Moon Girl), or "The Princess" (a designation traders gave to Chinook ladies of royal blood), Comcomly's daughter, reportedly by his wife from the "Scappoose" tribe.[57] Had he been smitten by love at first sight, as some suggest, it might have been in her father's village shortly after the Chinooks pulled him out of Bakers Bay. Had it not been such love, the crusty trader would have had time and place to court his beloved, for it was common for native women to come to the fort, some to camp near it in small huts. Some had matrimonial designs; others had intentions incompatible with chastity, which Cox believed to have been "seldom inscribed on the credit side of their account. . . ." Of tribes surrounding Astoria he thought "Cathlamahs [Kathlamets] . . . the most tranquil, Killymucks [Tillamooks] the most roguish, Clatsops the most honest, and Chinooks the most incontinent."[58] Had he been candid he would have admitted that chastity and continence were not so "inscribed" on the credit side of the Astorian paramours who sought favors of Chinook women.

Aware of Chinook protocol in matrimonial matters, McDougall sent two clerks to Comcomly to ask for his daughter's hand in marriage. In Chinook marriages it was customary for a young man's parents, other relatives, or third parties to handle preliminaries, among which was the dowering of a man's intended bride and the return of gifts by her people to equal or surpass those of his. With time, these dowries had become more elaborate. In addition to dentalia and slaves, there were now added, thanks to coastal traders, axes, beads, kettles, brass and copper bracelets, and many other things. Finally, there followed a ceremonious journey by the bride and groom to her home, accompanied by a few old women, to begin a married life.[59]

Early in the afternoon of July 20 a squadron of canoes crossed over from Comcomly's village to Astoria carrying his family and entourage. On this occasion the soon-to-be father-in-law was arrayed in a bright blue blanket, always a favorite of Pacific Northwest natives, and a red breechclout, with extra paint and feathers. A horse waited to receive the regal lady to transport her to the fort. One chronicler records that "by dint of copious ablutions, she was freed from all adventitious tint and fragrance," and thus made ready for a decent ceremony.[60] Had she not been thus freed she might have been in normal July weather somewhat offensive to a white man. But no amount of fixing could alter her flattened head, her "badge of aristocracy,—a sign of freedom" and royalty qualifying her to marry a chief such as McDougall.

The ceremony became more elaborate with the telling. The artist Paul Kane, visiting Chinook country more than three decades later, would record that Comcomly, with unexpected liberality, carpeted his daughter's path from canoe to fort with sea otter skins, which, if true, would have felt the tread of horse's feet, not hers, as one of these animals bore her from the beach. It is doubtful that even the doting Comcomly would have provided such expensive carpeting for his daughter's nuptials.[61] At any rate, the Princess had not come cheaply for McDougall. It would take him nearly a year to pay for her.[62] There is extant a record of numerous items rationed out to him on two separate occasions in October, 1813. It would be interesting to know if any of these came into Comcomly's hands in payment for his daughter.[63] As final payment McDougall had to give his father-in-law fifteen guns and fifteen blankets besides a great deal of other property.[64]

"The marriage tie is not indissoluble," wrote Cox of Chinook matrimony. For McDougall and the Princess it would not be that way either, for he would leave the river and her in 1817.[65] In the interim, Comcomly took advantage of being father-in-law of the chief Astorian by coming almost daily to the fort, where he took an interest in all of its business. He frequently visited the blacksmith shop for forged weapons and tools.[66] His people believed that with a sharp stone their compassionate deity Ecahnie or Ecannum (The Good Spirit of the Waters) had opened man's eyes and given motion to his hands and feet, teaching him to make canoes, paddles, nets, and all other tools from the beginning. Had Talapas made man perfectly, all of this would have been unnecessary.[67] When it came to iron objects, Chinooks had received no similar instructions from their deity; they would have to depend on earthbound Astorian smithies for such things. Like all natives, Comcomly was iron hungry.

Before the Astorian advent, the only tools Chinooks and Clatsops had, as Cox tells it, "consisted of a chisel generally formed out of an old file, a kind of oblong stone, which they used as a hammer, and a mallet made of spruce knot, well oiled and hardened by the action of fire."[68] These were adequate tools for tasks like felling huge trees and shaping them into lumber. Because of Comcomly's importance, his requests for iron tools took precedence over other projects of the smith. The wily chief, hoping perhaps to avoid wearing out his welcome at the fort, supplied it whatever he could with gifts from his people. Nothing was too big or too small for him to bring the traders. From the water he brought sturgeon or smelt; from the land, bear or beaver; from the hands of his people, canoes or caps.

How he would have fared had he not been father-in-law of the fort's headman is hard to say. The marriage of his daughter to McDougall was certainly an important and much-discussed merger overshadowing in story and legend other marriages between Astorians and native women. But there were other such unions which added their bit to the cement binding natives and Astorians together. Soon after reaching the Columbia, William Wallace Matthews, a clerk, married Kilakota (Kelaksta, Kshiah, or Little Songbird), daughter of Clatsop Chief Coboway. Their wedding may have been attended by fanfare, but it was overlooked by most white chroniclers of events at Astoria. Irving, for example, makes no mention of the pair or of her influential father. In 1815 Matthews would depart for the East, leaving Kilakota and a baby daughter, Ellen, behind. Kilakota would marry a French-Canadian Astorian, Louis La Bonte, and the child would be sent east to be educated. Like McDougall's wife and other native women in similar situations, Kilakota would prefer to remain with her people instead of hazarding the uncertainties of "civilized society."[69]

Another Astorian, Benjamin Clapp, a clerk, finding a Chinook woman to his liking, observed the marriage ceremonies of her people and brought her to the fort as his bride. Like McDougall and Matthews, he would later depart, causing her to wonder if he would ever return. There is no record that he did.[70] Some French-Canadian Astorians took more than one mate at a time. Michel La Framboise, long-time fur trader, boasted a wife in every tribe.[71] He had a reputation in those parts as a very good interpreter. No wonder. By no means would all Astorians leave their native women. Their service with the fur company ended, most of them remained at such places as French Prairie in the lower Willamette and Columbia valleys to raise large families.*[72] Roman Catholic priests and

---

* A Philip Degie, who, it is said, came to Oregon with Lewis and Clark, claimed the honor of being the first white man on French Prairie (the twenty-mile stretch of fertile land beginning fifteen miles above the falls of the Willamette River, the bend of which formed the western boundary, and the Pudding River the eastern, of the prairie). Oswald West, "Oregon's First White Settlers on French Prairie," *Oregon Historical Quarterly*, XLIII (1942), 199 and n. Other sources say that Joseph Gervais, a former fur company employee, was the first settler on the prairie. H. S. Lyman, "Reminiscences of Louis Labonte, *Oregon Historical Quarterly*, I (1900), 175. By 1833 at least eight families would form the nucleus of a growing Canadian population, giving to the prairie its designation "French." Dorothy O. Johansen and Charles M. Gates, *Empire of the Columbia: A History of the Pacific Northwest*, 163.

Protestant preachers among these former Astorians from the late 1830's on would seek to legitimatize the marriages consummated under non-Christian custom.

These mixed marriages, especially where Chinook and Clatsop aristocracy were involved, were not as free from conflict as some would have us believe. A visitor at the site of Astoria in 1824 would note that several years earlier the fathers of offspring of such unions had insisted that their infants' heads not be flattened. Mothers, under great pressure from their people, had in some cases murdered their infants rather than have them stigmatized as slaves.[73] There were no white women at Astoria for Chinook or Clatsop males to marry. Had there been, these native men would have sought them; Indian males always did in other such places, and white traders always opposed such unions.

It is not known to what extent Comcomly's new relationship to McDougall provided the chief an understanding of matters being discussed at the fort relative to its prospects. The crafty McDougall would have said nothing to alarm his father-in-law in fear that the influential Chinook might have caused trouble.

Inner councils among the partners were carried on in tones of discouragement deepened by the loss of the *Tonquin*. Just as the fate of that ship had been out of the hands of these Astorians, so were other events taking place, and soon to take place, which would affect not only the fate of the emporium in the wilderness, but with it the fate of its native traders as well.

9. King George's Fort and King Comcomly's Canoe

> Indeed, the indians on the Columbia appear
> to have more aptitude to traffic among them-
> selves than is usual.
>
> John Langdon Sullivan to the
> Secretary of War

J OHN G. McTAVISH on October 7, 1813, returned with a brigade from the interior to Astoria, which he had left three months earlier, bearing a letter from a North West Company partner to the effect that the *Isaac Todd* had sailed from Britain in March in company with a thirty-six gun British frigate, *Phoebe*,[1] Captain Hillyard (Hillyer, Hillier, or the like). As there was a war going on, explained McTavish, the ship was coming to seize the fort, which the British regarded as an important colony founded by the American government. Nine days later, the price of goods and furs at the post being agreed upon, both parties signed an agreement for transfer from Astorians to Nor'Westers of the post with its small quantity of furs, goods, and other stock.* In making the surrender the partners reasoned that were the post to fall to British guns there would not be even that much left.[2]

In the days immediately following the sale, sturdy canoemen paddled Comcomly to Astoria to peddle his salmon. On November 29 he and his men, all armed and agitated, hurried there to report a sail off Cape Dis-

---

* For years Americans believed the sale to have been, if not treacherous, at least in the words of Astor, a "shameful transaction." Yet without the approval of his right-hand man, Wilson Price Hunt, the arrangement made with McDougall could not have stood. Judson, "The British Side of the Restoration of Fort Astoria," 247; Kenneth Wiggins Porter, *John Jacob Astor, Business Man*, II, 1154. In his *History of the Northwest Coast*, Vol. II, 221–23n., Bancroft severely takes Irving to task for stigmatizing McDougall in the transaction. Katherine B. Judson, after searching British Foreign Office records, concluded that there was no intent on the part of Britain to outwit America in claims for the Northwest Coast and the Columbia River. "The British Side of the Restoration of Astoria," 243.

appointment. To McDougall at this time Comcomly said: "See those few King George people [Nor'Westers] who come down the river: they were poor; they have no goods, and were almost starving; yet you were afraid of them, and delivered your fort and all your goods to them; and now King George's ships are coming to carry you all off as slaves. We are not afraid of King George's people. I have got eight hundred warriors, and we will not allow them to enslave you. The Americans are our friends and allies."[3] The chief and his men prepared to conceal themselves in nearby woods from which they would shoot their guns and arrows at the invaders in concert with those at the fort firing their guns.[4]

McDougall tried to set the chief's mind at ease by telling him to lay aside his leather armor and weapons, rewarding his loyalty to the Astorians with a suit of clothing. He told the chief to ascertain whether the ship was British or American. Actually, McDougall and other British subjects at the fort hoped it was the former but feared it might be the latter, knowing that for several years American ships had far out-numbered their British rivals on the Northwest Coast because of Britain's involvement in the Napoleonic wars.[5]

Somewhat confused, Comcomly promised to carry out McDougall's suggestion to disarm, but he had no sooner left the fort than a half-blood interpreter, painted in full Chinook fashion, was called in and sent off to Cape Disappointment to ascertain if a ship had truly been seen. He barely reached the cape when the ship hove into sight, and soon (November 30) it "came dashing over the bar in fine style" to anchor in Bakers Bay. On his return to the fort the interpreter met McDougall en route to the ship to tell him she was the British sloop of war *Raccoon* of twenty-six guns, Captain Black commanding. No sooner had McDougall left the *Raccoon* than his father-in-law, with a "squad of followers," boarded her to extend official Chinook greetings to its captain and, with a curious change of face, to traduce the Americans and extoll the British with expressions of joy that he had lived long enough to see again a great ship of his brother King George enter the river. On the common ground of royalty which British mariners rubbed off on the Northwest Coast, as in other quarters of the globe, the Chinook chief had found identity with the king of England; in fact, white men dubbed him "King George." Consequently, the chief remarked: "The Americacans have no ships to be compared to King George's ships." Then he laid a fine sea otter skin at Captain Black's feet and prepared to debark. The captain called him back, gave him a good bumper of wine and, in return for his new-found loyalty, presented him with an old flag, a laced coat, a cocked hat, and a sword. Then, "His Chinook majesty . . . left the *Raccoon*, and returned to shore as staunch a Briton as ever he had previously been an American partisan."[6] Farcically, Comcomly would sail the next day across to Astoria in full British uniform, with Union Jack flying in the breeze.

Some eighty-seven pieces of assorted items (not a substantial reinforcement), from bales and blankets to casks of beef, were landed from the ship for the post.* At 8:00 A.M. on December 13, shoreside Britishers fired a seven-gun salute to Black, who had come ashore at Astoria the night before. By early afternoon Comcomly had not returned there from a northern journey. After the noon meal, to which Black, a marine officer, four soldiers, and four sailors had been invited, the captain had guns distributed to the Nor'Westers, after which they all gathered on a platform on which a flagstaff had been erected. Ordering a British flag run up, Black took a bottle of Madeira "or something stronger" saved from recent celebrations aboard the *Raccoon* in Bakers Bay and broke it across the staff, declaiming in a loud voice that he was taking possession of the establishment in the name of King George, for whom he rechristened it Fort George. To the assembled Indian chiefs Franchère explained the significance of the ceremony.[7]

Black had hoped to make the foregoing a triumphant event, but it did not turn out that way. Awakening that morning to assay the "few imperfect" palisades of the fort, he inquired of its location, believing that another existed. When told there was no other, he cried out, "Why, is this the fort that was represented to me as so great? Good Lord, I could knock it over in two hours with a four-pounder!"[8] Especially knocking the breeze out of the captain's sails and robbing him of a sporting chance of capturing the place and winning glory and booty was its recent purchase by British Nor'Westers. McDougall, a key figure in the transaction, had even found himself "so ungraciously received" by his countrymen aboard the *Raccoon* that he had been happy to cut short his visit aboard that ship.[9]

It was 3:00 P.M. now. Comcomly had not returned from his trip north. Three guns were fired as a signal to the *Raccoon*. The Union Jack was hoisted. Three cheers were given, and three rounds of musketry were fired by the Nor'Westers and Black's crew from the ship—the ceremony marred when a *Raccoon* marine's gun flashed out on the shore. Finally there was an eleven-gun salute from the fort's four pounders in a toast to

---

* John McDonald of Garth, a North West Company partner arriving on the *Raccoon*, stated that the ship and force had come to fulfill a company duty and was not there as a government measure. "John McDonald of Garth: Autobiographical Notes, 1791–1816," in L. R. Masson, *Les Bourgeois de la Compagnie Du Nord-Ouest; Recits de voyages, lettres et rapports inedits relatifs au nord-ouest canadien, publiés avec une esquisse historique et des annotations par L. R. Masson*, II, 50.

His Majesty's health. The assembled Indians must have been impressed, bewildered, or both at the dramatic succession of events. McDougall, whose place as "nominal chief" at the post it would have been to communicate with the natives on this occasion, explaining to them what was going on, was happy to defer to the French clerk Franchère, who was much more conversant in the native Chinook language than McDougall was, and certainly more skilled in native diplomacy. The clerk directed his remarks to one of Comcomly's sons in the absence of the youth's father.[10]

It would have been difficult for the natives to understand the rapidly moving events of the day had Franchère attempted to explain them in the Chinook Jargon. When it came to matters of trade, that hybrid language was used. Since the appearance of white maritime traders bearing Nootkan words to southern points such as the Columbia River, that evolving language had received numerous additions to facilitate the trade even more. Half-blood Astorians had infused into it Canadian and Missourian patois of the French, a process to be carried still further at Astoria by Nor'Westers and British Hudson's Bay Company men following them. Upriver natives, unfamiliar with the jargon, talked with fur men through the Chinooks and Clatsops accompanying them, apparently to interpret in the trade language.[11] From some of these interior peoples may have come to the jargon words like *moosmoos* from the native word *moosmooschin* (buffalo), now generally applied in the jargon to any large animal. White men's names for certain trade goods of which Chinooks and Clatsops had no previous knowledge, and hence no names, found their way into the jargon, as these people readily accepted terms in use among white traders. Some expressions entered the jargon in bizarre fashion. One, according to a later traveler in Chinook country, was the greeting, *"clah hoh ah yah,"* or *"clachouie,"** a salutation stemming from early times when friends greeted a white man with the words "Clark [of Lewis and Clark], how are you?"[12] Equally bizarre was the word *pehlten*, which came to mean something unusual or absurd because of the irrational behavior at Fort George of one Archibald "Judge" Pelton. Possibly stemming from *pehlten* was the Chinook word *partlelum*, meaning "drunk" or "full of rum" or "lum." It would seem that as the rum-drunken state was new to Chinooks, so was their new word to match it.[13]

Chinook-Clatsop exposure to spirits was becoming more frequent. In fact, these natives witnessed celebrants drinking wine to conclude

---

* In 1825 a Chinook chief saluted the botanist David Douglas with the word *clachouie*, "friend." David Douglas, *Journal Kept by David Douglas during His Travels in North America in 1832–1837*, 138.

ceremonies at the new Fort George. These pale-faced imbibers, or, perhaps more correctly, flushed-face celebrants, had scarcely consumed those spirits when at 5:00 P.M. Comcomly arrived on the scene. His tardiness had spared him sight of events of the afternoon which, after he viewed the Union Jack flying, caused him and his people to believe the British truly intended to enslave the Americans. He knew his own people would eagerly enslave rival tribesmen; he naturally assumed the British would do likewise. Only when Black departed the river at the end of December without slaves would the chief and his followers realize they had misjudged the captain's intent.[14] It was evident that the Indian leader had also miscalculated in assuming most Astorians to be loyal to Astor and the American cause when, with the sale of the post, like its flagpole they showed their true British colors.

McDougall and his men humored the Chinooks and Clatsops, for they knew that any success in their new venture depended on the natives' good will. On the fifteenth they arranged with Captain Black to give Comcomly "a clothing."[15] This gesture paid off, for he and his aides for several days busily shuttled messages to and from the ship. One message from the fort assured the ship's purser that all notes presented by natives at that place for salmon and wild fowl sold aboard the ship (an arrangement made when she entered the river) had been duly honored and would continue to be. With this matter resolved, the white traders continued to pay such notes to their Indian clientele for provisions delivered to the *Raccoon*.[16]

Despite McDougall's kind words and gratuities to his father-in-law, the latter still smarted from the North West Company takeover of the post. There was little love lost between Chinooks and these Nor'Westers, who found the natives less tractable than had the Astorians. But the natives' failure to bring as many goods to the post as its traders may have liked was caused more by the vagaries of nature than by anything else.

The North West Company takeover did not free it from the same problems of the Indian trade that had faced its Astorian predecessors. With keen understanding of the economics of such trade, one John Langdon Sullivan in 1824 would observe the peculiarities that distinguished it from other commerce. What he wrote held true at Fort George as it did elsewhere:

It is not the exchange of the surplus products of the regular industry of one Country for those of another. Besides the dangers which belonged originally, if not always, to the circumstance of traffic with uncivilized men at distances so remote from succor, it was precarious from the uncertainty of vending a sufficient quantity of merchandize to a race whose means of purchase were alone the success of the chase. If very successful, the mercantile operations of the season would be equally so. But if otherwise, a stock of merchandize would lay over and be accumulated by the supplies which were to follow in due time, already ordered, and thus a loss ensue by delay of Sale.[17]

Behind cold economics lay flesh-and-blood white and red traders caught up in its principles and problems. Each confrontation of the two races in the economic process was a story in itself. For example, when Comcomly in late 1813 brought two sea otter skins to Fort George, the parties haggled vigorously over their value in trade. "Mercenary brute," "troublesome beggar," and "niggardly fellow" were epithets used by Alexander Henry, a Nor'Wester partner, for the chief. When McDougall accidently broke one of the chief's dentalia, not even the son-in-law's gift of forty grains of large china beads could satisfy the chaffering chief.[18]

Certainly some of Comcomly's unhappiness was justified. He was understandably apprehensive lest liquor be introduced to his people as an item of trade. The arrival of the *Raccoon* had occasioned the consumption of more spirits than had been consumed in the takeover ceremonies at the fort. Aboard ship there had been an extended period of conviviality with considerable quantities of wine and grog consumed by all, including on at least one occasion the landlubber McDougall. The uneventful passage of tipsy tars from ship to shore through dangerous waters in the wake of these libations during December, when the ship was on the Columbia, was nothing less than miraculous.

Before white traders came to Fort Astoria, and now to Fort George, Chinooks and Clatsops, as noted above, had experienced little exposure to drink.[19] Their aristocracy had a strong aversion to it, if for no other reason than that to them, drinking, especially to excess, was regarded as a weakness of slaves. On one occasion Fort George traders induced one of Comcomly's sons to imbibe a few glasses of rum. The youth, soon intoxicated and sickened, returned to his father's house to sober up. During this time he became an object of laughter to the slaves. The angry father, his pride injured, wasted little time or words in reprimanding those who had sold his son the head-befuddling commodity. This would not be the last exposure of Comcomly's people to liquor. The Anglican Reverend John West narrates the story of a chief, possibly Comcomly, who came to Fort George with his two sons. Company servants made one of them drunk. When the father saw him foaming at the mouth, blabbering, and staggering, he concluded he was mad, exclaiming, "Let him be shot." When the lad regained his senses the chief manifested great joy.[20]

Comcomly's people continued to be amply exposed to drink, since a common passenger on most vessels coming to the Columbia to trade was John Barleycorn or his rum counterpart. He traveled overland, too. When Nor'Westers from the interior annually descended on Fort George to deposit their furs and replenish their provisions, they attracted neighboring natives. Upon the arrival of these brigades there followed a time of "complete carnival," when the riotous *regale* prevailed during a "fortnight of continual dissipation," as voyageurs especially, but not exclusively, sought to obliterate "all recollection of the frozen and lenten severity of the by-gone winter" in a diversion of rum.[21]

Comcomly sought to obtain fewer alcoholic concessions at Fort George, still believing his marital arrangement with McDougall had not lost him a daughter but had won him a son who could secure for him influence with the new company. He got the new year, 1814, off to a good start for himself and his sons by receiving on its first day the "clothing" promised for the lads; he got it off badly for the Nor'Westers six days later by requesting the fort smithie to make a long piece of bar iron into arrowpoints. As noted above, Astorian blacksmiths had done trifling jobs for him; their successors believed the arrowhead project was going too far, especially since they feared the fabricated iron points might return to them on the ends of shafts. This they believed to be a real possibility, since the previous day a canoe carrying David Stuart, John Stuart, Donald McKenzie, and twelve men had reached the fort with word that natives had attacked them.[22]

The attack was a serious threat to the Nor'Westers since it had occurred near the Cascades of the Columbia, where troublesome tribes controlling that portage, and hence passage to the interior, could have disrupted trade with those quarters. On January 9 Alexander Stuart, supported by John McTavish, staggered into Fort George half dead from an arrow, perhaps rattlesnake-venom poisoned, in his left side and shoulder. It could just as well have been a lead bullet in his body, for natives at the portages could have shot him with guns stolen from company traders. To retrieve these arms and other stolen goods and to punish those taking them, should the items not be returned, fort personnel prepared to canoe upriver. The partners consulted Astorians left at the post and Chinooks and Clatsops about how best to proceed with the dangerous project. A canoe was dispatched across the Columbia inviting Comcomly to come over to give the Chinook opinion. The chief failed to respond, presumably on learning that Franchère had been dispatched to the Clatsops to seek their advice, whereas no white man had first been sent to seek his. As it turned out, the main advice came from the wife of Clatsop Chief Coalpo, who explained to them how natives resolved differences by payment of slaves and other commodities for those killed in conflict.[23] In the proposed venture someone could easily have gotten killed, since Coalpo's wife and other lower Columbia Indians were all for wiping out their upriver enemies.

In the words of Ross, the "inglorious expedition" against the freebooting "river pirates," under "a fleet of ten sail," begun on January 10 and ending back at Fort George eleven days later, had "promised . . . much" and "did . . . little." Coalpo's wife and brother-in-law, an Upper Chinookan chief, Casino, who lived near the Willamette mouth and who had assisted in the expedition in retrieving some of the stolen goods, were well rewarded with goods for their part in the undertaking.* In the light of this reward Comcomly might have regretted his decision to stay home.[24]

Late winter brought more natives to Chinook villages across the river, where smoke from their fires signalled potential danger. Fort personnel feared not only attack from these natives but also from "civilized enemies," the Americans, for the War of 1812 was still on. Not only were their persons in jeopardy, but so were their precious stocks of goods and furs. Fears for the security of the fort and a feeling of general unhappiness with its location prompted its management to seek a new site. In February they probed the Columbia as far as the Willamette seeking a new location. The best they could find was at Tongue Point, the high, bold peninsula some three miles east of Fort George. A small station, never as important as Fort George, was established there.[25] Former Astorian and critic of policies of his adopted company, Ross saw in the move to a higher elevation "more fit for eagles than for men" a gesture to match the Nor'Wester mood of grandeur, which to him only masked its great bustling but little accomplishment in the trade.[26]

Increased company trade with upriver tribes easterly from Tongue Point would have deprived Chinooks of the advantage they enjoyed from proximity to the fort. Natives of the Cowlitz River had wanted the Nor'Westers to come up to their villages to purchase beaver skins they had been hoarding instead of bringing them down to the coast, with whose tribes they were on poor terms.[27] Possibly Comcomly and his forces had been responsible for the failure of these Cowlitz to move their furs to Fort George. Just as important a threat to the Chinook trade monopoly were Casino and his people at the strategic Willamette mouth. That chief had gained considerable favor with white traders for services in the recent company adventure near his lands. For that help and

---

* During the expedition the whites paid the troublesome tribes goods "to cover the bodies" of two of their number killed in the skirmishes which had prompted the expedition. Gabriel Franchère, *Adventure at Astoria, 1810–1814*, 98.

continued services he received from the Nor'Westers a flag and an annuity.[28] Although Comcomly recognized in Casino a rival for Nor'Wester affections, the former had no reservations about trading with his rival's people, for on April 18 he dropped by Fort George en route to the Willamette to purchase in Casino's villages horses which may have been driven there by Klickitats or other tribes to the east, who served as middlemen between interior and coastal peoples.[29]

Throughout January natives emerged from winter quarters to journey to the lower Columbia to fish for smelt and sturgeon and drop by the fort. Prominent among the visitors was the omnipresent Comcomly, who came to get wooden boxes of Chinook manufacture he had left there before departing for winter quarters. On January 26 the Nor'Westers made the Clatsop chief and his family remove the body of a slave girl who had died from venereal disease lest the pigs eat it. The natives disposed of the corpse by tying a cord around its neck and dragging it to the beach, where with a wooden paddle they squeezed it into a hole, covering it with stones and dirt.[30]

In early February one of Comcomly's sons, the unpleasant Casacas, "The Prince of Wales," beat up his father for damaging his musket.[31] The old man could not have been too badly damaged in the fracas, for on February 20 he skimmed over to the fort in a large, twelve-paddle canoe to trade sixteen beaver for a new gun.[32] Clearing weather in late February brought large numbers of his people over to trade beaver skins, hats, and smelt.[33] At about the same time, a Nor'Wester crew at Oak Point complained that Chinooks were monopolizing the trade and spoiling the market.[34]

Causing the Nor'Westers further concern was the appearance on March 1 of a brig off the mouth of the Columbia. They scurried to defend their post from an American attack which never came off. The ship proved to be the brig *Pedlar* out of Boston via the Hawaiian Islands under command of Captain Northrop, formerly captain of Astor's ship *Lark*. Although armed, she was on a peaceful mission returning Hunt to what had been his company's post to wind up its affairs there. Aboard the *Pedlar*, performing his usual duties as official greeter, Comcomly welcomed his Astorian friend and received from him a red coat ("New Brunswick Regiment 104th"), a Chinese hat, a white shirt, a cravat, trousers, cotton stockings, and a pair of fine shoes.[35] Had he worn the shoes he would, as so many others of his race did at first exposure to white men's footwear, suffer a gamut of foot troubles from corns to cramps. On one occasion, wearing this or some other military outfit, he marched into a trading post to depart without his trousers—to him, like shoes, an impediment to movement.[36]

Also receiving "a clothing" was his second son, Selechel, "The Duke of York," much friendlier to whites than his older brother and possibly the one who accompanied Franchère on his travels. The old man may have been boycotting Casacas after the thrashing received at his hands shortly before. Besides receiving the clothing, father and son were "handsomely treated at the table with the best of everything." This sartorial shower, followed by a royal feast for the two, sat poorly with Henry. "This may be," wrote Henry, "the way the natives are spoiled on this coast by the Americans. . . ."[37] The women, too, some seventy of them, crowded at the fort to get their share of goods from the *Pedlar*. As Comcomly had gotten his gifts from the ship through his chieftaincy, they sought theirs through their charms, bartering favors to the ship's crew.[38]

Departure of the *Pedlar* about April 1 and departure of an overland brigade to the East on April 4 would remove from Fort George those having no intention of staying on. Relationships the previous winter between freeloading Astorians and former Astorian Nor'Westers and other Nor'Westers had been as smooth as might have been expected, although it was enlivened by needling sessions between the parties, the general good feeling interrupted by "a bit of a turn out between the bullies of the one party and the braggadocios of the other, which only seemed to banish ennui and enliven the scene."[39] Ross thought the Nor'-Westers had exhibited little of the vaunted aggressiveness for which they were noted in the East.

Among those returning east with the brigade was Franchère, whom the Nor'Westers offered £100 annually to remain, partly because of his skill in communicating with natives.* With the brigade's departure, McDougall and Henry were left in charge of the fort.[40] Inactivity of the men the previous winter had posed a threat to the trade in the form of venereal disease. Henry expressed his belief that its prevalence would seriously damage business and attributed its presence to Americans, apparently unaware that Lewis and Clark had found that white maritime traders had already brought it to the Columbia River.[41] It could be said that Astorians' and Nor'Westers' four-year presence there had helped raise to alarming proportions the wages of an unwholesome by-product of the association of Chinook women with white men. Indians as far away as Alaska would call venereal disease "Chinook."

Another threat to the trade was rumor of war among the natives. On March 18 the Nor'Westers learned of a proposed battle to have been

* There were 126 persons at Fort George at the time of the departure of the brigade overland to the East. Seventy-six departed, leaving 50 behind. Coues (ed.), *New Light on the Early History of the Greater Northwest*, II, 856n.

fought in typical marine fashion on the beach at Chinook Point between Chehalis Indians and a band of Chinooks under Chief Taucum. In fact, Comcomly had invited the whites to go over and see the fracas. But it never materialized. Nor'Westers found it strange that contesting natives could gather on good terms after exchanging goods or slaves in a blood-price settlement to assuage the passions of the would-be contestants.[42] One white man noted that "the most formidable of the indian tribes are not so sanguinary as covetous," having "courage without malice, . . . activity when there is occasion, & industry when there is an object."[43]

A continuing problem for the Nor'Westers, as it had been for their predecessors, was the lack of supplies from the outside world, which seriously disrupted the trade. Aggravating the problem was the natives' discrimination in purchasing goods such as Canton beads; even these had to be of a certain size, which meant that unpopular sizes gathered dust on fort shelves.[44] All through spring, the white traders told the natives to retain their furs until the company could deliver the goods. On April 18 Henry carried coals to Newcastle by purchasing a copper kettle from some Clatsop Indians.[45] Had it been used in preparing food it would not have been overworked, what with little to eat for the "no small family" of unsupplied people at Fort George—twenty at the table, eight women and children, and five servants in the kitchen.[46] The Indians would carry their own coals to Newcastle by attempting to exchange beads to fort traders for dried smelt. On May 17 a company shallop brought an actual load of coal to the fort.[47] Its managers assured their clamoring Chinook-Clatsop customers that a supply ship would soon come with the goods. When it failed to arrive they feared that Comcomly, Coalpo, or another important chief would regard them as imposters in contrast to their good "Boston" (Astorian) friends.[48]

Until help arrived the Nor'Westers felt trapped. Speaking for the handful of men at the fort, Henry wrote: "Here we are left the sport of fortune, at the mercy of chance, on a barbarous coast, among natives more inclined to murder us for our property than to assist us, and during a war which any moment may strip us of our all."[49] Ross shared Henry's apprehension, thinking it a particularly dangerous period when Indians threatened to descend on the fort in large numbers to drive away what few people were left there. Actually, the greatest invasion of that place was that of April 19, when a large *cantonée* of women came to barter their favors as they had to the men of Lewis and Clark. They were ordered to keep their distance under pain of being placed in chains. The fort could not afford to have more men ill than the twelve already down.[50] Before fall the women would break through this quarantine to live in huts around the fort when the fall brigades came downriver from the interior. Then these females would besiege the voyageurs "much after the manner which their frail sisters at Portsmouth adopt when attacking crews of a newly arrived Indian fleet."[51]

Within a week of Henry's kettle purchase, and in answer to his prayers, the long-awaited supply ship *Isaac Todd* stood up the north shore of the river on April 22. Ramsay was sent to the ship with a message and to pilot her on the river. He would serve as pilot on most craft entering that stream for some time to come.[52] Shortly, the vessel stood opposite the fort, not alongside it as the partners had wished, with small signal flying at the foretop and large red flag at the peak to receive shoreside gun salutes.[53] Biggest surprise package aboard was Jane Barnes, a Portsmouth barmaid, a "flaxen-haired, blue-eyed daughter of Albion" who "in a temporary fit of erratic enthusiasm" had consented to become *"le compagnon du voyage"* of one Donald McTavish, a former Nor'Wester proprietor now out of retirement to organize the new department of the Columbia. Considering the debilitated condition of the men, a Dr. Swan, arriving on the *Isaac Todd*, was a more valuable, albeit less attractive, addition to the post than was Jane.

Not only was Jane an object of interest to traders, but she also was "the greatest curiosity that ever gratified the wondering eyes of the blubber-loving aboriginals of the north-west coast of America."[54] They named their daughters for her and thronged the fort to examine her various adornment and attire, which she sported in daily evening walks on the beach. Native male royalty sought to prevent a rumored move by McTavish to send her east by proposing marriage to her.* One candidate was Comcomly's son, who came to the fort all dandied up in his best attire, face bedaubed with red paint and body redolent in whale oil, and offered to buy her for a hundred sea otter skins. Were she to have accepted his offer he would have made her his special wife. No hewing of wood and carrying of water and that sort of thing for her—his four other wives could do that. She would have lived a life of leisure, smoked as many pipes of tobacco as she thought proper, and dressed in the manner to which she was accustomed. Rebuffed in his attempts to win her for himself, he plotted with other young men of his tribe to kidnap

---

* Shortly after the *Isaac Todd* arrived from England, McTavish made an agreement with Henry whereby the latter superseded him as Jane's protector, presumably because McTavish, planning to go overland to Montreal, thought the trip too rigorous for the lady. Complications arising from this triangle (Coues [ed.], *New Light on the Early History of the Greater Northwest*, II, 908) were averted by the drowning of the two men when their canoe capsized in the Columbia River on Sunday, May 22. See also Mary Avery, "An Additional Chapter on Jane Barnes," *Pacific Northwest Quarterly*, XLII, 4 (October, 1951), 330–32. For details of the drowning, see Alexander Ross, *The Fur Hunters of the Far West*, 33–35.

her as she took her usual stroll on the beach, hoping no doubt to insure for himself in Tarzanian fashion a happy life in the wilderness with his Jane. Why not? White men had cohabited with his women; this plan would simply be a fair turnabout. In the fall of 1814 Jane would leave the Columbia to receive an even better offer from a nabob of the East India Company. She would later return to the fort after having experienced marriage and motherhood, which one trader thought had improved neither her outlook nor her language.[55]

Cargo from the *Isaac Todd* had been unloaded and shuttled to the fort on the ten-ton coasting schooner *Dolly*, whose frame the Astorians had shipped to the Columbia aboard the *Tonquin*. The craft was renamed the *Jane* for the lady of the hour. On May 16 the men began the laborious task of processing the goods, a chore made difficult by lack of correct accounting of several packages and the admixture of cargo and ship's stores. Some of the cargo unloaded from the arklike ship were pairs of cattle and poultry.[56] On her departure for China the *Isaac Todd* carried a cargo of furs, some of which had been collected in Astorian days. Her presence in the Columbia had served to discourage at least one American ship from landing at that place.[57]

It was at this time that McDougall completed paying for his wife.[58] The recipient of that payment, Comcomly, was, in the opinion of Henry and perhaps of his son-in-law, too, becoming a very pampered chief, especially one day when he walked off in a huff after refusing a piece of goods, saying it was not fit for a Chinook dog.[59] The white traders had no higher regard for the chief's sons, "troublesome fellows" who asked for all they saw while trying, as Henry put it, to get everyone to work for them.[60]

Saving wherewithall to purchase his wife and performing his many duties at the post had kept McDougall's nose to the grindstone. A post trader there at a later period tells how on one occasion the Princess needled her husband for his industry: "You profess to be a great chief; but I see you hard at work every day, behind the counter and at the desk, and your time is so fully employed that you have scarcely time to eat your food, or to enjoy the society of your wife a moment. . . ." Pointing to a pig in a puddle, the Princess chided, "See there, that is the true chief; he has no labour to perform, like a slave; when hungry, his food is served up, he fills himself, he then lies down in the soft mud, under the influence of the warming rays of the sun, sleeps and takes his comfort."[61]

Rumors continued to float around the mouth of the Columbia that a Chehalis flotilla of forty or fifty canoes was en route there to battle the Chinooks. On May 6 natives informed fort personnel that the

Chehalis had finally come to Chinook Point for their showdown. Typical of times of these native confrontations, business continued as usual. Several Chinooks canoed up to Tongue Point preparing to catch sturgeon, which did not change their migrations to conform to the machinations of men.[62] The arrival of Chehalis war canoes embarrassed the Chinooks considerably because of their own troubles with Clatsops, some of whom had recently killed a Chinook. Should the trouble occasioned by that killing be unresolved, the Chinooks were in danger of conflict on two fronts. On occasion the Chinooks besieged rival Clatsops in their homes, but such action at this time would have only tied up war parties in Clatsop country and weakened them for action against the Chehalises. As it turned out, the Chehalis-Chinook showdown was resolved without serious blows. The Chinooks satisfied Chehalis demands by payment of slaves and goods after a harmless exchange of shots.[63] These formalities observed, the two parties resumed their normal routines. The Chehalis, who had come down to trade as much as to fight, joined their erstwhile and temporary enemies at Fort George.

At that place, about a month after the departure of the *Isaac Todd*, Donald McTavish, a person of "bold decided character," gathered several influential chiefs and chieftainesses to lay plans to track down some murderers and to serve on a jury with fort traders to condemn them to death.[64] The accused, said to have been Tillamooks or Klatskanies, had murdered the half-witted Astorian "Judge" Pelton while he was out making charcoal, in revenge for an Astorian attack on one of their number some years before.* The suspects were tracked down and executed. After the executions McTavish gathered the natives in the grand hall of the fort to reward them with presents and smokes for their services. Meanwhile, mourning relatives carried away their dead.[65] Shortly after this nasty business, on Sunday, May 22, the mourners may have believed that a retribution was at work, for on that day McTavish, the cause of all their sorrow, was drowned when his canoe capsized in the Columbia River. Joining him in a watery grave was Alexander Henry, whose last official act was to clothe a Clatsop chief and invest him with "a writing." The American "writing" which the native carried Henry threw into the fire in British contempt for Yankees.[66]

Impact was given to Henry's action when a North West Company ship, the 185-ton schooner (formerly American) *Columbia*, outfitted by a London firm, slipped across the bar with native help in July and ran with the tide into Bakers Bay. As stories of the ill-fated *Tonquin* still rumbled among visiting white mariners, the *Columbia*'s crew, on the

---

* Ross states that the murderers were hanged for the killing of three Pacific Fur Company (Astor) men. *Fur Hunters*, 32–33.

natives' approach to the ship, readied her ten nine-pounders and ran up boarding defenses around her bulwark, an action that surprised the natives, as recent ships in the river apparently had not exhibited such posture. The natives had harmlessly wanted only to exchange some berries for buttons and knives. Among those coming to the ship to officially welcome her and receive her biscuit and molasses were Comcomly's sons, Casacas and Selechel. Two days later their father, his wives, and others of the royal family visited the ship at anchor off Fort George. Her sails signaled neighboring Indians to her side to trade aboard their beaver and sea otter, the latter item, with an "assortment of other articles," fetching a slave.[67] Plans of the crew to have Indians trade aboard their ship were unsuccessful, for they were under strict orders to refuse pelts; under company regulations that was the prerogative of the fort. The same restriction seemed not to have applied to salmon and sturgeon, then in season.[68]

For the next three years the *Columbia* would sail from the river of her name to Californa and Alaska, the Hawaiian Islands, and China. From California her crew would carry to Fort George flour, beef, and tallow; and in Alaska's Norfolk Sound they would exchange powder and shot for furs, which, with those from Columbia, they would sell in China.* Returning to Fort George via the Hawaiian Islands, the ship would carry pork and Hawaiians to work for the company.

The *Columbia* would truly help sustain the fort in its particular position. The sea on which she sailed linked the fort to markets of the outside world just as her namesake river linked the post with a vast interior land mass from which it gathered furs. From the fort's immediate environs came furs, too, but also a flow of fish and other provisions to help sustain it. Its importance and that of the North West Company it represented might have been even greater had not the British been forced to rely on American ships to bring supplies and carry furs out of the upper Northwest Coast, where Yankees continued to be favored by the Russians controlling that region. The position of the fort might also have been strengthened if the company had had a favorable position in trade to China. There the British East India Company monopoly denied the

---

* When the *Columbia* was in Norfolk Sound in 1815, Peter Corney wrote that there were "four American vessels lying there, from whom we learned that the war with America was at an end. The names of the Americans were the *Okean* [*O'Cain*, W. D. Alexander], the *Isabella*, and the *Albatross*, formerly under the Russian flag, in the sea otter fishery on California; the schooner *Liddy* [*Lydia*], with a cargo from Canton for the Russians, and the brig *Pedlar* [*Pedler*], commanded by Mr. [Wilson Price] Hunt, the individual who crossed the Stony [Rocky] Mountains. The *Pedlar* was seized by the Russians for selling powder to the natives in the Sound, but was given up before we sailed." Peter Corney, *Early Voyages in the North Pacific, 1813–1818*, 132.

Columbia and other company ships a license to carry tea and other Chinese products to European markets in return for what furs they sold in the Orient. This competition, dogging Nor'Westers from one Pacific shore to the other, as one of them observed, "ruined the coast trade" and "completely spoiled the Indians."[69]

To evade these crippling restrictions, the company in 1815 entered into an agreement with the Perkins firm under which arrangement supplies of British manufacture for posts west of the Rocky Mountains were shipped from England to Boston, from where the American firm dispatched annual ships to the Columbia to gather furs for China.[70] For services in lieu of freight the American firm received a joint and undivided interest of one-fourth part of the furs so shipped. The last vessel to arrive in the Columbia River (June, 1816) before those coming under the Perkins' contract was the British brig *Colonel Allan.* An American ship sailing under the new arrangement, the brig *Alexander* of 270 tons, would enter the river in mid-April, 1817. After depositing her goods at Fort George she would load furs for China, where the beaver she carried would sell at six dollars and the sea otter at thirty-three.[71] She would carry furs to China on a second trip in 1821, with proceeds from the sale of her cargo invested in Oriental produce to the extent of over $70,000.[72] The *Alexander* in 1821 would be the last ship to fulfill the annual contractual arrangement between the North West Company and the American firm.[73]

The 340-ton, Boston-built Perkins ship *Nautilus* would sail from Boston on October 20, 1818, reaching Fort George on February 11, 1819. This passage of 115 days would be said to be the fastest voyage ever made by a sailing vessel between the two ports. On May 25, 1820, another American Perkins ship, the 244-ton *Levant,* Captain Charles Carey, after discharging goods at Fort George would clear the Columbia for China with 13,414 beaver, 860 otter, 266 beaver coating, 6,770 muskrat, 259 mink, 104 fox, 116 fisher, and 37 sea otter. The *Hoqua* of 339 tons burthen, Captain Joshua Nash, last of the American ships to carry furs to China and the vessel named for the prominent merchant of that land, would sail from Boston for the Columbia in late 1821 and on to Canton. The foregoing ships served the North West Company well in the China trade, rounding Cape Horn and Cape Hope and touching landforms as diverse as the barren Aleutians and the verdant Hawaiian Islands.[74]

The North West Company's arrangement with the American firm brought it virtually no change in its trading methods of previous years. Yet it continued to hold its Fort George beachhead at the western edge of its empire facing the vast Pacific and China. When Alexander Ross in 1816 on its behalf handed an American captain on the Columbia company regulations regarding the Indian trade, he did so ostensibly to facilitate good relations between Britishers and Americans, but the action served to show that Britishers took precedence over their rivals at that place.[75] Americans, however, proved to be persistent. In August, 1818, Captain James Biddle, implementing an aggressive American policy,[76] arrived aboard the twenty-gun sloop of war *Ontario* at the mouth of the Columbia to exert his nation's claim to the region. Not wishing to hazard a crossing of the bar in his ship, he proceeded to cross it with three boats well armed and manned by more than fifty officers and men. In Bakers Bay, in the presence of several natives, he displayed the American flag, turned up a "sod of soil, and giving three cheers" nailed to a tree a lead plate bearing words claiming his possession on behalf of the United States. The Indians could not have read the words; they were meant for the British. As this was going on, the *Ontario* fired a salute. Ceremony concluded, Biddle proceeded up to Chinook Village to visit its chief and thence crossed the river to Fort George. On seeing the Americans in their boats, the British raised their flag, as now chief trader James Keith had received word by the ship *Levant* that the Americans were sailing to the Columbia River. In a remote spot one-half mile from the fort Biddle had a board nailed to a tree with a message declaring his possession of the place in the name and on behalf of the United States. The North West Company had protested that the post had been acquired by purchase, not conflict, and was not on American soil (the Treaty of Ghent of December 24, 1814, which ended the War of 1812, provided for restoration of nearly all locations taken by military action by either party in the conflict),[77] but as a consequence of various diplomatic exchanges American claims had been recognized and ceremonialized by actions like those of Captain Black. These actions were not to have been construed as affecting possessory claims of either nation to the lower Columbia region.[78]

On October 1 special United States agent John B. Prevost arrived aboard the British sloop of war *Blossom*, Captain Frederick Hickey, to hoist the Stars and Stripes in token of American possession and sovereignty at that place. Prevost notified James Keith that his firm could continue to occupy and protect the fort under the American flag until the United States should order its withdrawal. Neither would have known that Anglo-American negotiators had consummated on October 20, 1818, what has been through common usage termed a "joint occupation" agreement—meaning that citizens and subjects of the two powers could enter the region for a ten-year period without prejudice to either nation's claim to title to the land. Prevost continued to Monterey to file a promising report of the Columbia and its environs but wrote nothing of its fur prospects. He described its natives as inquisitive, cheerful, and sagacious, with few of the vices such as scalping that were usually associated with the "savage."[79] After he departed, the flag he had hoisted very likely came down.

Occupation at the fort in 1818 would continue for two clerks, a surgeon, an overseer, seventeen *engagés*, mostly Canadian, some twenty-nine Hawaiians performing much of the menial work, an Indian boy, sixteen French-Canadian and Iroquois trappers, and women and children, most kept by Canadians.[80] The tiny knot of humanity sought protection inside an area about two hundred yards square surrounded by pickets some fifteen feet high.* Around the settlement was a walkway to facilitate a strictly kept night watch. Armament consisted of fourteen eighteen-pounders and many small arms and cutlasses, but only two guns were mounted. Around about lay a wilderness of river, sea, and forest except for two hundred cleared acres, twenty of them given to potatoes and the rest to forage for livestock imported from California. And more to be feared than this wilderness were its natives, who were as hostile as ever. Casacas, often advising his father to attack the place, had lost none of his hostility.[81]

As unsettled as were Nor'Wester managers from recent experiences with Americans, their primary concern was to maintain a friendly posture among natives of the region. They perhaps had less difficulty maintaining that posture with the time- and trade-tested Chinooks whose chief had shunned suggestions to make trouble for his white friends than they had with Casacas and his kind. Making it difficult for the Nor'-Westers to achieve their peaceful objectives were not only edgy Indians

* In late 1817 Corney wrote of Fort George: "The Northwest Company's Establishment lies about seven miles from Point Adam [Adams], on the south side of the river, above a small bay, where ships are in great safety out of the strength of the tide. There is a very good wharf with a crane for landing or shipping goods. . . . The grand entrance is through a large double gate on the north side, above which there is a platform for the sentry to walk; on this are several swivel mounted. As you enter the fort, or square, there is a two-story house, with two long 18-pounders in front of it on the south side; on the east is a range of low buildings, where the clerks have their apartments; and in the same row stands the grand hall, where the gentlemen assemble for dinner, etc. The houses for the men are on the same side, and behind the two-story or governor's house; in the S.W. corner, is the magazine well secured; along the west side stands a range of stores, tailor's shop, and Indian trading shop; in the S.E. corner the blacksmith's and cooper's shops, and on the N.E. corner a granary for the corn. In the N.W. corner stands a very high flagstaff, erected by the crew of the *Columbia*." Corney, *Early Voyages*, 175–76. An account of conditions at the fort at this time may be found in Josiah Sturgis, "Extract from the Journal of Josiah Sturgis kept on board the Ship Levant on a Voyage from Boston to the North West Coast and China in the Year 1818," typescript copy of manuscript, Oregon Historical Society.

of the region but also those in company employ—the Iroquois who, although brought west to expedite fur gathering by their example, had proven warlike and refractory. Of their activities one Nor'Wester wrote, "The Natives of the country, consider them as intruders. As they are mere rovers, they do not feel the same interest, as those who permanently reside here, in keeping the stock of animals good, and therefore they make great havock among the game, destroying alike the animals which are young and old. . . ." A few defected to native villages, marrying their women;* others caused all kinds of trouble among those of their own race along the Columbia as they forgot why they had been brought west in the first place.[82]

During the winter of 1817/18 the company had patched up a "rude treaty" with Willamette natives after a company hunter, most likely an Iroquois, had killed one of their number.[83] To add to the troubles brought on by these Iroquois in 1817, the fort had stood alert, fearing that a dissident company blacksmith, defecting to the Clatsops, would lead those people in reprisals against the establishment. His capture and incarceration did little to ingratiate white traders with the Clatsops.[84] In 1818 interference of Iroquois hunters with native women on the Cowlitz resulted in the killing of a dozen natives there. An equal number of Indian men in the Umpqua region of southern Oregon also fell victim to the villainy of these company traders. With native help company men tracked down, tried, and executed some Klatskanies who at Oak Point had killed four company hunters in their sleep, possibly in reprisal for some injustice done them by company traders.[85]

Chinooks and Clatsops were hardly bystanders to all these events. Following usual practice, they helped the company track down its foes and got involved in other ways. Shortly after the Cowlitz killings, Keith brought a Cowlitz chief, How How, to Fort George, where traders sought to appease him by arranging a marriage between his daughter and one of the men. Then some Chinooks fired on How How and his braves. Men at the fort, thinking How How and company were attacking it in retaliation for the Cowlitz killings, turned the bastion guns on them, wounding one.[86] Just a year previously a "Shoshone" of the interior had loosed an arrow at Comcomly, who was bathing in the river.

---

* The few Iroquois who married native women dissolved into Indian villages. Their action would contrast with that of French-Canadians who married Indian women, established farms, and had their children educated. Most Iroquois returned to their homes in Ontario. Richard T. Conn, "The Iroquois in the West," *Pacific Northwesterner*, IV, 4 (Fall, 1960), 59–63. Nevertheless, considerable numbers of Iroquois, deserting the fur hunter ranks, settled among the Flathead Indian tribe in present-day Montana. Francis Norbert Blanchet, "Historical Sketches of the Catholic Church in Oregon during the Past Forty Years (1838–1878)," *Catholic Sentinel*, February 7, 1878.

The chief had dispatched his number one slave to run down the attacker, which he did, laying him low with a bludgeon and finishing him off with a dagger.[87]

Comic and not so comic opera scenes at the fort and in the field in one year deprived the company, in the opinion of Ross, of four thousand beaver, worth six thousand pounds sterling, and, worse than that, deprived the firm of its image.[88] Attempts of the partners to improve this image, and their expansion into new trapping grounds in the beaver-rich Snake River country, provided no permanent solution to the ills affecting their operation in the Columbia River watershed. Neither could they escape the problems facing their company at large. The War of 1812 had impeded movement of personnel to the West. Jealousy and bickering among partners had hampered the trade. Lax and wasteful methods that had developed when the country was rich in furs had not been shaken off. But perhaps the most serious problem had been the nagging rivalry between the North West Company and the Hudson's Bay Company—a rivalry in which blood had recently been spilled on the Canadian soil each was trying so hard to win.

Under pressure from the British government a merger was effected between the two companies on March 26, 1821, just ten years to the week after Astorians had entered the Columbia to establish a post. Since then Astorians had been forced to yield their Columbia foothold, and now the Nor'Westers had to do the same. Soon the Chinooks would be paddling across the river to Clatsop country to find a new company tending the store. The new owners, bearing the Hudson's Bay Company standard, entered a new chapter in that company's history. On the Columbia the firm of the "Governor and Company of Adventurers" would depend on the British crown, and the crown, in turn, on them. But no less would their fate depend on other royalty, whose fate would likewise depend on them. These were the royal natives and their subjects west of the Rocky Mountains on the Columbia River by the western sea.

10. Merchants and Chiefs

> The Chinooks never take the trouble of
> hunting and rarely employ their Slaves in
> that way, they are however keen traders and
> through their hands nearly the whole of our
> Furs pass, indeed so tenacious are they of
> this Monopoly that their jealousy would
> carry them the length of pillaging or even
> murdering strangers who come to the Estab-
> lishment if we did not protect them.
>
> George Simpson, *Journal*

IN NOVEMBER, 1824, after a long journey from York Factory on Hudson Bay to the Columbia River, George Simpson, governor or "superintendent" of the Hudson's Bay Company Northern Department, assayed
Fort George. Before him stood, as he saw it, "a large pile of buildings
covering about an acre of ground well stockaded and protected by Bastions or Blockhouses, having two Eighteen Pounders mounted in front
and altogether an air or appearance of Grandeur & consequence which
does not become and is not at all suitable to an Indian Trading Post."[1]
Despite the superintendent's assessment, workmen had faithfully built
and fortified the fruits of their labor. And thanks to ships of the American Perkins' firm the fort had been well supplied with provisions.[2]

There had thus been on hand at Fort George ample supplies of American flour, butter, salt pork, beef, tea, mustard, pepper, pimento, rum,
and wines in addition to fifteen hundred bushels of potatoes raised at
the fort.[3] But food shortages after 1822, occasioned by the reorganization of the firms and failure of other ships to supply the establishment,
had forced parties from that place in the summer of 1823 to sail upriver
to various Indian camps to purchase fresh salmon, and even dogs, to
eat. In his journal a company clerk, John Work, tells how on May 18,
1824, in Chinook villages natives demanded of the hungry traders nearly
twice as much for salmon as those Indians could get for the fish at Fort
George. To show the red merchants that the whites were not at their

mercy for food, the traders brought out rations of flour and grease, whereupon the natives lowered their prices.*

Simpson complimented the post for its "appearance of grandeur and consequence," but also deprecated it as "not at all suitable to an Indian Trading Post." To him, like everything else on the Columbia River *"except the Trade,"* it was "on too extended a scale." This observation, like an epitaph over a grave, foreshadowed the demise of the place in the company scheme of things. Like his Nor'Wester predecessors at that place, he thought the post should be removed, and for about the same reasons—as he explained it—to render "ourselves independent of Foreign aid in regard to the means of subsistence. . . ." Such a move, he believed, would occasion no great loss of trade in that quarter. Yet he expected no miracles in an extractive enterprise promising little increase with time. Returns at Fort George in 1822 had been some 6,000 beaver; in 1823, 5,500; and in 1824, 5,000.†

The post's politics were as important in the proposed removal as were its economics. The British government wanted the company governor and committee, from whom Simpson took his orders, to remove "to avoid all risk of collision with Citizens of the United States, whose Government by some ambiguity of the Treaty of Peace [ending the War of 1812] claimed this scite [sic] as a public Fort. . . ."[4] On July 22, 1824, the governor and committee ordered chief factors of the Columbia Department to move to the north side of the Columbia because Americans were to have possession of Fort George whenever they pleased.[5] Just where on the north side of the river the traders should move they did not say because of their ignorance of the geography of the country.

Simpson hoped that the removal of Fort George would not jeopardize a native trade greater than any he had seen in other parts of North America. Potentials for trade were great, he opined, provided the natives of the interior Columbia country could be wrested from their overdependence on the chase, and those of its lower reaches from their overdependence on the bounties of river and sea. He noted, for example, that

* A later employee of the company, Dr. William Fraser Tolmie, tells of an expedition in search of food at this time. Tolmie based his information on notes of an old friend in company employ. "Letter From Dr. Tolmie," *Transactions of the Twelfth Annual Re-Union of the Oregon Pioneer Association for 1884*, 31. It is possible that he may have been referring to the journal of his father-in-law, John Work, who was on such a party scouting for food. John Work, "Journal April 15–November 17, 1824," typescript copy of manuscript, Oregon Historical Society.

† For the first three years after removal of Fort George activities to Fort Vancouver, annual proceeds would be some two thousand fewer furs. E. E. Rich (ed.), *Simpson's 1828 Journey to the Columbia*, Publications of the Champlain Society, 67–68, and John McLoughlin, "Fort Vancouver Report," Appendix A in *ibid.*, 236.

"Thousands of Sea Otter" abounded off Chinook coasts, where its natives never troubled themselves to hunt them.[6] Concerning him specifically was whether the principal chiefs of the lower Columbia, where stability in the trade would first have to be maintained, would favor the move. Chiefs involved were primarily Comcomly at the key river entrance, Schannaway, a Cowlitz whose village lay astride the route leading down to the Columbia from the populous Puget Sound country, and Casino at the Willamette mouth gateway to a vast Oregon hinterland. Simpson was banking hard on the continued loyalty of Comcomly, as noted above, but there was always the possibility that the chief would revert to his pro-Americanism of Astor years and channel his goods to some reborn American settlement in the vicinity of Fort George. His loyalty would lessen none his sharp dealing, for he continued to keep his one good eye open for a good deal. Casino perhaps would remain loyal to the British traders, for he catered to them, treated his slaves kindly in their presence, and proclaimed his "King George" citizenship. Moreover, he did not want to do business with some American post a hundred miles downriver from where he lived.[7]

Simpson hoped that Comcomly's ties with the traders through the marriage of his daughter to Britisher McDougall would keep her father loyal, although her husband had left her in 1817. On the other side of the marriage coin, Chinook and Clatsop royalty continued to offer their daughters to secure material benefits for themselves and their people. Although company rules did not require its male employees to make permanent unions with Indian women, it did require them to accept responsibility for the care and support of their dependents. These marriages were now producing children. Two such offspring were born at Fort George in 1824. One of them, Ranald McDonald,* was the offspring of the Princess Sunday, Comcomly's daughter, and company clerk Archibald McDonald. Years later Ranald would recall how the "King" had held him in his arms and how his grandmother (after the early death of his mother) had called him *qua-ame, qua-ame,* meaning "my grandchild." Neither could he forget that the one they called the Princess (his aunt—Comcomly's daughter Chowa, perhaps)

---

* The story of Ranald MacDonald is told in Lewis and Murakami (eds.), *Ranald Mac-Donald*. Ranald would claim that at the marriage of his parents two hundred "Elites" had lined up from the canoe landing to the dwelling place of his mother's father. Both of his parents, he claimed, were adorned with the most valuable furs. Donald Ross to Eva Emery Dye, May 21, 1904, Eva Emery Dye Papers. A half-brother of Ranald, Donald MacDonald, stated that Ranald was taken by his mother's aunt, Carcumcum (Comcomly's sister), to a lodge at Fort George, where they were kept for a year or two. William S. Lewis (ed.), "Narrative of Benjamin MacDonald," *Washington Historical Quarterly,* XVI, 3 (July, 1925), 186.

had scarcely noticed him.[8] Another offspring of these marriages was William Cameron McKay, son of Thomas (grandson of Alexander McKay, who was killed on the *Tonquin*) and a Chinook woman, Timee, who he claimed was "closely related" to both Comcomly and another Chinook chief, Chenamus.[9]

Association, marital or otherwise, with white men raised Chinooks and Clatsops in the eyes of their own people. This is one reason Comcomly offered to place in Simpson's care his nine-year-old grandson, a child of Casacas (Romanized by Simpson as Cassicus). The lad's uncle, who Simpson identified as Sachla (Selechel), was still second to Casacas in line for the Chinook "throne." The superintendent wanted the lad as part of his harvest of chieftain sons for the (Anglican) Missionary Society School at Red River (Fort Garry—present-day Winnipeg) in response to evangelical-humanitarian concern in Britain for the welfare of benighted natives around the world.[10] At that time Britishers were reading the just-published book of the Reverend John West, late chaplain to the Hudson's Bay Company. In it West appraised mission prospects among the Chinooks, who afforded "facilities, with other surrounding tribes for the benevolent attempt of introducing the knowledge of Christianity among them. . . ."[11]

Simpson refused Casacas' and Casino's requests to put their sons in school because the lads were too delicate to hazard the long transmontane journey to Red River, on which some accident befalling them might prove offensive to Casino and Comcomly, "the principal Men below Walla Walla."[12] Perhaps it was with special regret that he denied the request to educate the son of Casacas, for he may have believed the Christianizing influence of the Missionary School could have made the boy into a better man than his father, "a cruel Tyrannical blood thirsty Villain who has formed several plans to cut off the Fort. . . ."[13] Casacas' adverse influence had indeed spread some distance from that place. In November, 1824, John Work, with a company expedition to the mouth of the Fraser River, reported that the Chehalis along the route threatened the party by brandishing bows and arrows. Their agitation stemmed from a Casacas-spread rumor that the party had come to attack them.[14] To show that it had no such designs, the party presented the Chehalis chiefs a little tobacco, the importance of which in the trade at the time was expressed by a company official who implied that his firm's short supply on the Columbia might jeopardize its trade in that quarter.[15]

As much as he and his men of the "Bay" depended upon Casacas' people for the trade, the superintendent's regard for them scarcely exceeded that of his opinion of that young man, for he wrote:

The Chinooks never take the trouble of hunting and rarely employ their Slaves in that way, they are however keen traders and through their hands nearly the whole of our Furs pass, indeed so tenacious are they of this Monopoly that their jealousy would carry them the length of pillaging or even murdering strangers who come to the Establishment [Fort George] if we did not protect them. To the other tribes on the Coast they represent us as Cannibals and every thing that is bad in order to deter them from visiting the Fort; and in order to strengthen their commercial relations men of consequence or extensive traders have sometimes as many as half a Doz[en] Wives selected from among the best Families of the Neighbouring tribes and each of those is entrusted with a small Outfit and sent on trading excursions to Her Friends & relatives and this is her constant employment.[16]

Simpson apparently did not subscribe to the theory that his Chinook customers were always right. Neither did he apparently see how as middlemen between the company and other tribes they could help the trade. Yet it was a Chinook, speaking the "Nootka Tongue," who enabled Hudson's Bay Company traders to deal with those powerful peoples of the north.[17]

Just as Chinooks did not consult company officials when making their moves, the company had not taken them into its counsels when discussing its proposed move. Yet they had to be told. That responsibility fell to Simpson. When on March 16, 1825, he officially broke the news of removal to them, Comcomly wept as he shook hands with the "White Chief" at the water's edge, and the "fair Princess 'Chowie' " (Chowa) had appeared as moved as her father. Both had been somewhat consoled by his promise to see them again soon. The old chief's tears may have been genuinely shed at prospects of his friends' departure; they may also have been shed at the thought of the inconvenience such a move would mean to him and his people.[18]

For his part, Simpson had failed to understand the sentimental and social attachment Chinooks placed on their homelands. So eager, he believed, were they and other coastal natives to barter furs that they would bring them to the Cascades of the Columbia or as far beyond as Fort Nez Percés, which the North West Company had built in 1818 at the confluence of the Walla Walla and Columbia rivers.[19] He was apparently unaware that countless Columbia floods rushing from the Cascades and the Dalles to the sea had not covered bad blood between Chinooks and Clatsops and the portage peoples who stood between them and Fort Nez Percés.

Not one to let tears stand in the way of fulfilling company policy, Simpson had already set the wheels in motion for the move. A chief factor, Alexander Kennedy, and Dr. John McLoughlin had examined

the north bank of the Columbia to near a place that Lieutenant Broughton had named Belle Vue Point. The two had searched no further, for
it was the first spot on the river where the banks were neither too steep,
high, or rocky nor so low that they flooded in high water.[20]

On March 19, 1825, the superintendent christened the new post Fort
Vancouver with the traditional breaking of a bottle of spirits on the
flagstaff. This climax of his western trip accomplished, he was off the
next day for the East. His superior, Governor J. H. Pelly, kept British
foreign minister George Canning apprised of these developments in a
December 9, 1825, correspondence in which he wrote that Simpson had
named the new establishment Fort Vancouver "in order to identify our
Claim to the Soil and Trade with Lt Broughton's discovery and Survey."[21] All true, but lower Columbia River peoples many years before
had claimed the place and named it Skitsotoho.[22]

Simpson had no difficulty convincing almost everyone except the Chinooks, Clatsops, and their neighbors of the rightness of the move. These
would not have understood the company's need for agrarian self-suf-
ficiency, more of which it hoped to find on the gentle prairies around
Fort Vancouver than in the harsh surroundings of Fort George.[23] Fort
Vancouver also provided better docking for ships than did Fort George.
This, however, was of no consequence to lower Columbia River peoples,
who landed their canoes on any beach. Some Chinook women, however,
always trade-oriented, clustered around the new Fort Vancouver. At the
"Kanaka (Owhyhee) Village" near the fort after 1827, women speaking
the Lower Chinookan dialect made up about one-third of their sex residing there. Apparently most Owhyhees returned to the islands when
their terms of service with the company were over, leaving their half-
blood children on the Columbia.[24]

The move to Fort Vancouver would not lessen company need to keep
land and sea routes open to the outside world or to the vast Columbia
hinterland. Simpson happily reported that natives guarding the entrance
to that interior world at the Cascades and the Dalles portages had been
tamed over the years by "conciliatory yet firm and judicious conduct of
the traders...."[25] Native merchants at places like these could not exact
the high tolls of an earlier period, but their treacherous waters would
exact far higher ones in the lives of company men shooting downriver on
their annual brigades to Fort Vancouver.

There was always the Columbia bar, that "nest of dangers" whose
shifting shoals over recent years had made it, if anything, more dangerous than ever. The move to Vancouver had not obviated the need of
company ships to cross it. Simpson was critical of inadequate efforts of
the company's Marine Department to meet its challenge—their failure

to understand it and build craft to conquer it. Chinooks and Clatsops had great respect for and a reasonable fear of that treacherous passage, but over the years they had made their peace with it, adjusting to its dangers as well as their technology and seamanship would permit. Even sea-bred Hawaiians in the company more successfully coped with the bar than did the Britons, and along with Chinooks like Ramsay they were often used as pilots on the lower river. Simpson complained that until 1824, when James McMillan led an expedition to the mouth of the Fraser River,[26] no company traders had ventured further than twenty miles along the coast in either direction from that bar. This failure, in his opinion, tended to limit company success in those quarters and certainly did little to check inroads of the "few contemptible American Adventurers" then able "to Monopolize the Trade of our Coast, and through that channel extract the Riches of our interior country."[27]

Simpson was concerned not only with waters flowing over the bar but also with another liquid he believed to be just as dangerous. Removal to Fort Vancouver would lessen none the need to dry up liquor sales at Fort George, for that place, retained as a subpost, was like a cork controlling the flow of spirits into the Columbia bottle. The *regales* were as boisterous as ever. Three traders leading a fifty-man expedition up the Columbia into the interior in six loaded boats in early August had allowed the men to pause a few miles from Fort George to have their *regale*. The traders may have purposely scheduled the celebration at that place to remove from natives at the fort the sight and example of such an event. Wrote John Work, one of those in charge of the brigade: "In a short time the greater part of the men were drunk and began to quarrel, when several battles ensued, and the afterpart of the day was spent drinking and fighting." None of the men was much injured, observed Work, because they did not make "good use of their fists."[28]

But this had happened shortly before Simpson came. Thus, it was with pride, but also with naïveté, that he announced that with his arrival on the Columbia the liquor flow had dried up on that stream. In his thinking, liquor tended to deprive Chinooks of the will and wherewithall to continue their role as dealers and agents to the various tribes. This, in turn, he believed, hampered their gathering furs and garnishing themselves with "Woolens and other useful British Manufactures which will in due time become necessary to the Natives from habit, when they must and will work to supply their wants. . . ."[29]

There would thus be for Chinooks, observed Simpson, changes in "habit." But these changes came no faster to peoples of the Columbia River than to other men; during the time white traders had been among them Chinook culture had changed, but slowly. More inhumane practices such as killing slaves had tapered off somewhat with white influence, but during Simpson's presence on the river even Comcomly had killed a slave with the excuse that the wretch was dangerously ill.[30] In the technical field the superintendent noted that even imported tools would have been in greater demand had not the natives skillfully made wood products in their own fashion with sharp-edged flint tools.[31] John Scouler, a British physician to company personnel on the lower Columbia from 1824 to 1826, observed that Chinooks could not be induced to raise potatoes or breed pigs and poultry despite the example whites had set for them.[32] There was even some question of how good that example was, at least as far as hog raising was concerned. Simpson complained that "the good people of Fort George have been so averse to the rearing of live Stock and so dainty that they would not Eat their sucking Pigs but by way of keeping down the Stock and for want of more rational pastime actually used to amuse themselves in practising Pistol Shooting by making War on the poor little Grunters at Twelve paces distance. . . ."[33] Most of the participants in the hog slaughter were perhaps Canadian half-bloods, for they had a reputation for such things.

Scouler ascribed the "inferiority" of Columbia River tribes to the vast numbers of salmon and sturgeon at their disposal as well as to "natural indolence," a view hardly acceptable to scientists of a later day.[34] Botanist David Douglas, traveling among them in 1823–27 while collecting and classifying the rich plant life of their lands, thought Chinooks and their neighbors "much prejudiced in favor of their own way of living." He did note that a few spoke English tolerably well and fabricated articles in imitation of those imported by whites. They retained their own counterparts for imported goods such as kettles, knives, buttons, needles, beads, and awls, but with their limited technology it would have been nigh impossible for them to have duplicated certain imported goods such as guns, powder, and looking glasses. Oval-gilt and pocket-cased looking glasses were available to them at Fort George, but the spectacles Douglas carried must have been a novelty to them, for when he placed them upon his nose the Chinooks, in their usual gesture of dread or astonishment, clasped their hands tightly to their mouths. Of equal wonder was the botanist's lens which he used to light his pipe from the sun. This demonstration earned for him the appellation *olla-piska*, meaning "fire." They also called him "The Grass Man" and "King George's Chief." With his razor he shaved Tha-amu-u, or "The Beard," Comcomly's brother, because the old man wanted to look like a "King George Chief."[35]

Imports of which Chinooks and Clatsops wanted no more were diseases such as smallpox, about which they spoke with great fear. Unlike natives removed from white contact in the interior, they wanted the medicine (vaccine) that protected whites.[36] This protection, of course, meant no abandonment of their own "medicine" administered by their own practitioners. Fort George Indians also succumbed to apoplexy, which struck freeman and slave alike. Scouler attributed the malady to their heavy diet of fish and oil. Few natives lived as well as did Chinooks, Clatsops, and other Northwest Coast peoples, but, as in other societies, unwise eating of nature's bounties took its toll.[37] In fact, when Scouler was on the Columbia two natives dropped dead in transit across the river. Although Scouler attributed their deaths to possibly oily foods, he performed no post-mortem on them; thus, he never knew for certain the cause of their deaths. They may have been poisoned, a not uncommon way of disposing of enemies along the feud-ridden lower Columbia River.

Simpson as trader and Scouler and Douglas as scientists viewed Chinook-Clatsop customs through eyes less moralistic than those of burgeoning evangelical-humanitarian reformers in their homeland. If most traders and scientists experienced cultural shock at what they saw, they did not outwardly show it. With typical British calm, Simpson made little moral judgment of the debilitating effects of "Imported Diseases" or of native customs such as the wearing of "Kilts or Petty Coats" by the women, their sexual promiscuities, and their head flattening custom. Other practices recorded by his objective pen were those of the shamans and canoe-burial, a more civilized practice than the nonburial of slaves, who in death, as in life, were at the disposal of their masters as they had been before the white man came. Sometimes dogs and crows picked the bones of these unfortunates, who had even been stakes in the stick and stone games of their masters along with such items as dentalia and blankets. It may have been of little moment to Simpson that after death slaves were denied the privileges of heaven. He implied that unorthodox religious beliefs could have been altered or at least tempered by regular Sunday visits to Fort George, where at the reading of public prayers (as would be ordered by Article 138 of the company Indian policy, resolved in July, 1825), they had conducted themselves with "great decorum."[38] What provision there would be for religious instruction at Fort George after removal of major operations to Fort Vancouver Simpson did not say. The exigencies of the trade came first; removal had been top priority.

After Kennedy and McLoughlin returned to Fort George from their reconnaissance to Fort Vancouver, a party had been dispatched to begin building. Every effort had been made to leave Fort George as soon as possible, but the move would not be completed until June 7, 1825.[39]

Hostilities among Fort George natives delayed removal. Company personnel feared that a pullout during such turbulent times would invite natives to loot the place of its goods. As many as fifteen to thirty of them occupying a dozen houses on a low sandy beach a little westward of the fort might have moved in to appropriate its properties. To guard the stores, men were dispatched from Fort Vancouver. Their involvement in guarding the post and its contents slowed removal and, by the same token, work on the new Fort Vancouver, although at that place by March 18, 1825, sturdy pickets had surrounded nearly three-quarters of an acre, enclosing a dwelling, two stores, an Indian hall, and temporary quarters for workers. "It will," Simpson had boasted, "be the finest place in North America. . . ."[40]

Trouble at Fort George began when Comcomly placed two sons under the care of a neighboring shaman chief, not an unusual practice among Columbia River tribes. Despite the shaman's incantations, the two had reportedly sickened and died. The Chinook finger of guilt had pointed to the shaman, whereupon Casacas, the unpleasant one, had ordered one of his slaves to assassinate the unsuccessful practitioner. The slave had carried out his bidding, and the wounded shaman had died.*[41] A short time before, the killing of two company employees by natives had made the situation all the more ominous, spurring removal by prodding company men to load their furs for shipment to Fort Vancouver on boats sent from there.[42] Fears that an American man-of-war might enter the river gave more urgency to workmen to finish their task. As was their custom, the Canadians did not work on Easter Sunday (April 3), but chief post trader McKenzie and John Work did, in their haste to finish the job. On Monday all hands hurriedly packed and loaded the boats, whose poor condition only slowed removal.[43]

On April 14 the Indians held a war dance near Fort George. As Scouler recorded it:

> About 50 men paraded from the vicinity of the fort to the beach, they moved at a most grotesque pace, keeping their feet in the same position with respect to another as nearly as possible. On their progress to the beach they fired their fowling pieces & set up the most disagre[e]able howling I ever

* McLoughlin identifies the murdered shaman as a chief of the Chinooks, with whom, as did Simpson, he groups the Clatsops. E. E. Rich (ed.), *McLoughlin's Fort Vancouver Letters: First Series, 1825–38*, Publications of the Champlain Society, 5. The fact that Fort George in Clatsop country was the scene of the gathering for war, and the fact that Chinooks were then preparing for battle against Clatsops, might further tend to indicate that the trouble was between these people rather than among Chinooks themselves. In John Work's narration of the incident he states that the slave of "Cassernses" (Casacas) killed a native of the fort named "Tet [sic] Plume." John Work, "Untitled journal," typescript copy of manuscript, Oregon Historical Society. See also, Douglas, *Journal*, 58, 137–38.

Chinooks and Clatsops made many utensils from wood. Lewis and Clark noted that they carved bowls and troughs of different forms and sizes, usually from solid pieces of wood. In them they boiled food by means of hot stones immersed in water.

(Courtesy, Smithsonian Institution)

Such Chinook-carved ladles as this one, though usually made of ash or cedar, were sometimes made of bone.

(Courtesy, Smithsonian Institution)

This sheep's-horn bowl was imported to the Columbia River from interior tribes. From the headwaters of the river also came buffalo-skull dishes, which the Chinooks sometimes traded to northern coastal tribes. The horn was carved and fashioned after steaming and boiling.

(Courtesy, Smithsonian Institution)

These harpoon points were made by Chinooks from European materials. Before the contact period bone was used. The detachable points were mounted at the ends of long poles and were used to catch sturgeon.

(Courtesy, Smithsonian Institution)

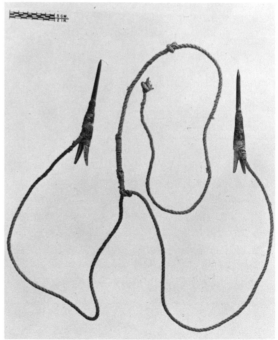

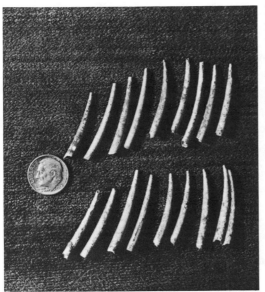

Dentalium shells, called *hiqua* in the Chinook Jargon, were used by many Pacific Northwest tribes as a medium of exchange. Quality as well as quantity of the shells determined their value in trade for slaves, canoes, salmon, and other trade items. These dentalia are small, numbering eighty to the fathom, whereas the standard, more highly valued shells counted forty to the fathom.
(Courtesy, Norma Lee Kayler)

Chinook-Clatsop adzes, like the one at left, were made from bone and stone in early times and were used for dressing many wood articles. After white contact, iron was used.
(Courtesy, Smithsonian Institution)

This copper sword (right) was found in a Chinook burial site on the lower Columbia River. Its overall length is forty-four and one-half inches. In 1793 Chinooks traded a sea otter pelt for such a copper sword.
(Courtesy, Robert J. Wiles)

OUTSIDE OF AN INDIAN LODGE.

Above, this interior view of a Chinook lodge was painted by Paul Kane. The wood carvings give the dwelling a ceremonial air, yet the recessed fire pit and the sleeping platforms are typical of Lower Chinook housing.
(Courtesy, Stark Foundation)

Above left, the outside of a Chinook lodge and Chinook canoes drawn by James Gilchrist Swan, a settler on Willapa Bay.

Below left, the Chinooks lived in wooden houses grouped into villages long before the whites came to their lands. The windowless houses, lodging from three to fifteen families, had openings in their ceilings to permit smoke from open fires to escape. Bunks lined the walls, and meat and roots hung from the rafters to dry.

SALMON FISHING AT CHENOOK.

Lower Chinooks made one-hundred-foot nets of plant fibers weighted with rocks to seine for salmon. They observed strict tabus in catching, preparing, and eating the fish, which was the main item in their diet.

This sketch, made by George Gibbs in 1850, shows a Chinook canoe with a sail. The use of sails was first introduced by white men.

(Courtesy, Smithsonian Office of Anthropology, Bureau of American Ethnology Collection)

This Chinook burial scene appears in an 1857 work by Henry Rowe School-craft. Bodies were not disemboweled or rubbed with grease or preservatives, but they attained a mumified state in the damp climate after being painted with ochre and water and wrapped in several folds of mats or blankets.

(Courtesy, J. B. Lippincott Company)

Chief Comcomly was first laid above ground in a canoe burial near Point Ellice on the north side of the Columbia. After his skull was removed, his body was buried in this grave behind Astoria, across the river from his own land.

Prow of dead Canoe on Bank of Columbia R. at mouth of Chanous Creek — Oct 30 – 1850

This Upper Chinook canoe burial sketch by George Gibbs shows the wood carving which was an important part of Chinook culture.

(Courtesy, Smithsonian Office of Anthropology, Bureau of American Ethnology Collection)

heard; they then formed a circle round theirs, & continued their dance, making a general yell every two or three minutes. Many of them were armed with fowling pieces others had bows & arrows & all of them had knives. They each of them [wore] a war dress consisting of dressed elk skin, which went over them like a shirt without sleeves. This war dress, although a poor defence against fire arms, is said to be arrow proof. The warriors were painted of every sort of colour, but principally black, red & yellow. Their music consisted of a number of shells of *Pecten marina* tied to a stick, which they rattled during the whole of their manoeuvres.[44]

There were no deaths on this occasion, but the mass dancing and brandishing of weapons suggested to whites in Chinook-Clatsop country that some great internecine war was about to erupt. The previous year John Work and a thirty-five-man party on a salmon purchasing expedition had thought so. At a Chinook village they visited Comcomly's sons, and a fifty-man war party all decked out in their best fighting clothes had performed "an awkward kind of dance, accompanied by yellings and gestures not of an entertaining description."[45]

Just three days before the demonstration described by Scouler, the company brig *William and Ann*, Captain Henry Hanwell, had stood at anchor opposite Fort George, bringing vital supplies for Fort Vancouver and new hopes for the trade.[46] An outbreak of hostilities among the natives might have frustrated her mission. The belligerents, instead of taking their wrath out on white men and their ships, generally took it out on each other, and with more vituperation than violence. Observed Scouler: "The Indians continue to behave very peac[e]ably toward us, although it is apparent that the utmost distrust prevails among themselves."[47] They guarded their white guests. When in mid-July Douglas stepped into the midst of the continuing Chinook-Clatsop feud, his host, Cockqua, whom he described as chief of the "Chenooks and Chochalii [Chehalis] tribes," was extremely solicitous for his safety. Cockqua's concern did not unstring the botanist, who watched prewar ceremonials (like those recently held at Fort George) in which three hundred warriors on the beach prepared to meet an expected Clatsop invasion to settle old scores. Several people would subsequently be killed and wounded. On the morning after the demonstration one of Cockqua's men showed the visitor his skill with bow, arrow, and gun in the manner of shooting matches which, according to Chinook legend, were an ancient practice.[48]

It was Comcomly's strategy to frighten his adversaries by threatening to field twice as many warriors as they. But none of his well-calculated stratagems could preserve from death those of his own kin. Within two years (until September, 1825) the chief, then in his sixtieth year, buried eight of his family at Point Ellice. The wide, sandy beach between that point and Chinook Point had long been favorite Chinook grounds, but now Comcomly and most of his people had abandoned it to the dead. Occupying one canoe for the journey to "The Land Beyond the Sea" was his son Shalapan (Sachla or Selechel?), apparently one of the victims of recent Chinook-Clatsop feuding. Had he not died, maintained Scouler, he could have made this world a better one for his people because of his search for knowledge and his acquisition of some proficiency in reading, writing, and ability to speak English fluently. His people never spoke of him without shedding tears. Comcomly's third son, the "Duke of Clarence,"* apparently succumbed at the same time, possibly the son who with Selechel fell victim to feuding.[49]

Chinook survivors of those buried at that time numbered 350 free males and 200 free females. (There were 100 male and 70 female slaves.) The Clatsops, whose head chief was still Coalpo, had 50 free males and 50 free females against 50 slave males and 40 slave females for a total of 190.†[50] The Chinook and Clatsop living were happy in the knowledge that their deceased had gone well accoutered in laced coats, silks, and beads to the great beyond, hopefully to "The Land of the South," but if not, to a desolate region controlled by an evil spirit, the Black Chief. Comcomly's sons went to one or the other well protected with fowling pieces at their sides and loaded pistols in their hands. As these possessions tempted thieves, the chief occasionally exposed the bodies to see that all ornaments and possessions were in good order, covering them when necessary with new blankets and matting.[51] Chinook dead on their nightly visits would have been angered to find their property being used by others. No one spoke the names of the dead in fear that they might return to harm the living. The survivors were understandably angered when two of their deceased went headless to the other world for the cause of craniology and phrenology in this one. Dr. Scouler, their conveyor, wisely waited until his last night ashore to appropriate the heads.[52]

To add to his other woes, Comcomly found removal of the fort a hardship unlike any he had experienced when trading at his own bailiwick, Fort George. It looked like he might never trade there again when in early September natives were "rapidly reducing it to a state of ruin &

---

* The trader Josiah Sturgis, in his "Extract from the Journal," identifies Comcomly's third son as "the Duke of Clarence."

† Similar statistics for Chinooks and Clatsops, classified as Chinooks, living near Point George are provided by Simpson. Including eleven other bands, he gives a total population for lower Columbia River peoples as 1,140 free males and 950 free females with 395 male and 275 female slaves for a grand total of 2,760 souls. Merk (ed.), *Fur Trade and Empire*, 170.

filth."[53] Over the next two years they would reduce it still further and burn it down.[54] It must have angered the chief that after a decade and a half of pampering by white traders at Fort George, his position had passed upriver to Casino, who now had a trading post in his own front yard. The marriage of Ilchee, McDougall's wife, to Casino had done little to cement relations between Comcomly and her new husband. Guarding his newly found importance, Casino raised a fuss because the company had assured Comcomly's passage upstream beyond his village some six miles below Fort Vancouver on the Columbia north shore to trade with the British. Now chief factor at Fort Vancouver, McLoughlin warned Casino that the company could not stand by and let his guns obstruct Chinook flotillas en route to the fort. A big man in most ways, McLoughlin spoke with the authority of his understanding of the native mind gained from experience in the trade that had consumed nearly half his forty-one years. The crafty Casino countered McLoughlin's proposal by one of his own—namely, a free river in the vicinity of the fort, which in effect would have given him a much stronger position on that stream than any enjoyed by his Chinook rivals far from their home villages. McLoughlin, believing the Comcomly-Casino feud to have blocked nine-tenths of the native trade that summer, diligently sought to effect a truce between the contending parties. In this he was apparently successful.[55]

Just as Casino wanted no opposition on the river from rivals of his race, McLoughlin wanted none from those of his race either. He was alarmed when sailors of the *William and Ann* offered "any price" to natives for furs, inducing them, in his words, "to suppose we deal unfairly with them [making them] discont[ent]ed with us."[56] He was less apprehensive of British tars aboard the *William and Ann* than of Americans who had been trading on the river for more than three decades. This apprehension he revealed in an October 6, 1825, letter to his superiors in London: "If the Americans grant a Monopoly of the Trade of the South Side of the Columbia there is no place on the North Bank that will pay the Expence of keeping up a Post and it will secure to them all the advantages to be derived from the Fur Trade in the Columbia."[57]

When the brig *Owhyhee*, 116 tons burthen, Captain John Dominis, in the service of the Boston firm of Marshall and Wilde, appeared in the river on June 4, 1827, McLoughlin was under the impression she had come for wood and spars, which indeed she had, although Dominis had been under orders to entice the natives to bring him their furs.[58] Ten days later the *Owhyhee* left the river. McLoughlin had not seen the last of her. On February 22, 1829, she was back at anchor in Bakers

Bay, her captain wasting no time on his mission. Two days later that mission was obvious when he purchased six river otter and seven beaver.* Not relying on Indians alone to bring furs to his ship, he dispatched parties from it up- and downriver, peddling and collecting furs from tribes along that stream as the Chinooks had once done. His ship soon became a trading post afloat, and he, a chief trader on the deck of that post, collecting from four to forty beaver skins daily as well as land otter, muskrat, raccoon, and others, at a rate much lower than that of the Hudson's Bay Company. Dominis had begun trading at a rate of a gun for six skins and a two-and-one-half-point blanket for two pelts. At that time the company had given a gun for eighteen skins and a blanket for five guns, but now the Dominis competition served to drive its "tariff" down to a quarter of its former rate.[59] "Fine picking for the mercenary Chinooks," complained a company official at this new development.[60] Leading trade goods that Chinooks could now buy cheaply off the *Owhyhee*, besides blankets and muskets, were powder, shot, scarlet and blue cloth, beads, duffel, fearnaught (thick, stout woolen cloth), trunks, and traps. The temporary reduction in its prices to one-quarter of its former schedules was for the company a needed sacrifice to retain its trade ties with the natives and a bitter pill for it to swallow, especially since a beaver at that time "was equal to five in days of yore."[61]

The foregoing statement reveals somewhat the exploitation of this animal in the Pacific Northwest. For two decades land-based traders had made it the prime object of their aggressive quest just as maritime traders had the sea otter. Weighing some thirty-five pounds when fully grown, it supported dark brown, stiff-haired fur over a shorter layer, soft, thick, and beautifully glossy. Well known for the power of its jaw in gnawing wood for its lodges, it was found in the numerous tributaries of the Columbia. A compliment to its importance was paid it by the Hudson's Bay Company, which used it as a rate of exchange in the trade.

Men of the company had certain advantages over their Yankee rivals —their knowledge of the country and its people, a knowledge and control facilitated not only by their own physical aggressiveness but by mental acuity, which helped them communicate with their native customers. Nevertheless, they left nothing to chance, dispatching parties in all directions to keep the Indian trade out of American hands. Dispatching these parties was nothing new for McLoughlin. From the previous year parties of up to fifty Canadian trappers, with women, slaves, horses, and equipment, would journey from Fort Vancouver to

---

* River otter are the *Lutra canadensis*. Beaver are the *Castor canadensis*.

as far south as 40° north latitude,[62] and particularly to the Sacramento
Valley of California.* Clerk Donald Manson and a few men had been
dispatched in the spring of 1829 to the site of old Fort George, where a
tent was pitched and later a house was built to restore the post. Four
years earlier McLoughlin had said he would get a temporary hut built
there to strengthen Hudson's Bay Company–British claims to occupancy on the river.[63] Now, the building of that house had economic as
well as political immediacy. From his Point George lookout, Manson
kept McLoughlin informed of their competitor's moves. Manson also
acted as intermediary between McLoughlin and the Indians in an attempt to keep the trade out of American hands.[64] He had also been
instructed by McLoughlin to keep an account of the number of salmon
salted by Americans.[65] Some Americans, with the depletion of furs on
the Northwest Coast, would trade salmon instead of furs. Instead of
hardware, ammunition, clothing, and blankets, which they once sold
natives, they would increasingly sell liquor. Among forerunners of this
new salmon trade, the crew of the *Owhyhee*, although collecting furs,
salted some of these Chinook-caught delicacies,[66] which Americans, as
the Britisher Robert Stuart before them, believed to be the finest fish
in the world.† Some American traders, with changing patterns of the
coastal trade, began selling their hardware and clothing to missions in
California.‡

Seriously disrupting McLoughlin's attempt to cope with his American
competition and creating a shortage of goods was the March 10 breakup
on Clatsop Spit of the inbound *William and Ann* at the very time that
the *Owhyhee's* consort in the trade, the *Convoy*, Captain D. W. Thomp-

---

* In his *Northwest Coast*, 313–14, Swan writes: "The wife of Mr. [Rocque] Ducheney
[Princess Mary, married to him in 1844], the agent at Chenook for the Hudson Bay Company, who is a very intelligent woman, informed me that her father was a Frenchman, and
her mother a Walla Walla Indian, and that, when she was quite a child, she recollected going
with her mother and a party of her tribe to the south for a number of months; that they
were three months going and three months returning; that they took horses with them, and
Indian trinkets, which they exchanged for vermilion and Mexican blankets; and that on their
return her mother died, and was buried where the city of Sacramento now stands. I asked
her how she knew where Sacramento was, and she replied that some of her friends had
since gone to California, to the gold mines, and that on their return they said that it was
at Sacramento where her mother was buried."

† Since the United States claimed no exclusive ownership of the Columbia River, fish and
furs from its environs, shipped to that country, had been subject to duty as foreign imports.
Joseph Anderson, Comptroller of the Treasury, to David Henshaw, April 22, 1831, in
Samuel Eliot Morison, "New England and the Opening of the Columbia River Salmon
Trade, 1830," *Oregon Historical Quarterly*, XXVIII (1927), 130.

‡ This trade increased after Californians were freed from Spanish rule in 1821.

son, had entered the river.* Comcomly's daughter, the Princess Chowa, reportedly apprised Manson of the tragedy in which the ship's cargo had been washed ashore; worse than that, all hands had been lost. With Chowa and three men, Manson left for Clatsop Point to find ship litter and goods on the beach and many natives wildly appropriating the seaside bonanza for themselves. Some had appropriated rum from broken casks, staggering on the beach and refusing to comply with Manson's demand to surrender the goods, all the while claiming that whatever the ocean cast upon their shores and was saved by their labor belonged to them. The company in this instance did not agree with the natives' practice of claiming all properties washed up on the beach— an obvious conflict between it and them in the matter of possessory rights. Joined by natives from Chinook Point, the Manson party fired a few shots into the air, and Manson broke a couple of rum casks to disperse some Indians, but apparently he retrieved no goods of a more solid nature.[67]

Half-way believing the Clatsops had murdered the *William and Ann* crew,† McLoughlin, still in a punitive mood from the previous year when he had dispatched a party, including two Chinook slaves, to chastise Clallam Indians for killing five company men,[68] sent down a fifty-man party, including an interpreter, to join Chief Factor William Connolly, down from New Caledonia (the lake region beyond the headwaters of the Peace River in Canada), who had gone ahead to investigate and recover the goods. The saucy Clatsops returned Connolly's demand for the goods by sending him by messenger "an old Brush and a Swap." In response the expedition killed four natives, two of them at Chinook Point, and burned Clatsop Village as punishment for what a later writer would term their "aggressive impudence, rather than . . . murder."[69] Word would go out that not just four but several natives had lost their lives in this company retaliation which, according to stories making the rounds, sent a chief's head to Honolulu.

On August 4, returning to the river (which he had left on April 23) after trading on the Northwest Coast, Dominis planned to match Manson's housebuilding at Fort George. Three days later from the *Owhyhee,*

---

* A Hudson's Bay Company employee on the Columbia at the time described Captain Thompson as a man "of fine social qualities, a skillful navigator, a lively trader . . . [who] knew little of Indian character." Willard H. Rees, "Donald Manson," *Transactions of the Seventh Annual Re-Union of the Oregon Pioneer Association; for 1879*, 60–61.

† In 1899 Silas Smith, on the basis of the word of a Felix Hathaway, a crewman of the nearby *Convoy*, claimed that the murder charge against the Clatsop Indians for killing the passengers of the *William and Ann* was utterly groundless. "Mr. Smith's Address," *Morning Oregonian*, December 11, 1899, p. 9.

anchored one-half mile off the fort, he sent the mate and some of the crew ashore to build a house and deposit trade goods for Captain Thompson. The *Owhyhee* proceeded upriver later that month. There, Dominis visited Fort Vancouver, where McLoughlin tried to buy him out with lumber, but Dominis demanded furs and sterling exchange. Outward pleasantries between the two scarcely masked McLoughlin's discomfiture with his competitors, who from their ships were boldly challenging the "Bay" with a trade they had going all the way from the Dalles to the sea. It was little comfort to McLoughlin that the *Convoy* in September sailed to the Hawaiian Islands, for the *Owhyhee* remained. From their location near Fort George throughout the winter and well into the following summer the Americans collected furs and dispatched supplies and trade goods, especially blankets, around the river. Trying to keep on as good terms with their customers as did their rivals, they extended such favors as repairing their muskets.[70]

In late summer an American visited the coastal area near the mouth of the Columbia River on a mission considerably less mercantile than that of his countryman Captain Dominis. He was Jonathan S. Green of the American Board of Commissioners for Foreign Missions, searching out mission possibilities on the "dreary N.W. coast," as he recorded it. Aboard the *Owhyhee* Green had met a Chinook Indian with whose appearance he said he had been pleased. The condition of his soul was another matter, for Green noted that he and his people had learned all the vices but none of the virtues of their white neighbors. Natives all the way from Norfolk Sound to the Columbia had breathed the spirit of trade; Green wanted them to breathe a new spirit. But not for seven years would missionaries of his board travel from eastern America to minister to natives of the Pacific Northwest, and then to natives of the interior rather than to those of the coast. To Green, as to many others, Cape Disappointment was a symbol of his own discouragement; the captain of his ship feared to challenge the bar to carry to natives in their villages behind it the challenge of his faith.[71]

Dominis had no such noble aspirations. His *Owhyhee* and Thompson's *Convoy* were still in the river in 1830, busily trading as ever. When on July 29, 1830, Dominis finally left the Columbia and the coast, after several months of trade for him and trouble for McLoughlin, he carried furs which would never find their way to company posts at Forts George and Vancouver.[72]

But what of some of the carriers of these furs—the Chinooks—at the end of the first quarter of the nineteenth century? At that time they suffered threats to their trade as great as those faced by the company. Now they met ships to barter mostly salmon and items of their own manufacture and skins only occasionally. In his own person Comcomly seemed to reflect this and other troubles of his people. His own hopes had been dashed several years before with the death of Selechel, on whom he had bestowed his own name and pinned his hopes of making him one day chief of the Chinooks. The deaths of others of his family had further saddened the old man as he went around mourning in his poorest clothes.[73] Once friendly to whites, he was now growing suspicious of them. As Fort Vancouver had upstaged Fort George, Comcomly had been shunted aside by white men and their ships, which once had entrenched him as the "greatest chief upon the river."

The appearance of one of these ships, the *Owhyhee*, and her Captain Dominis had been the greatest threat to the Hudson's Bay Company in nearly a decade of operation on the river. But the appearance of that ship and her captain would prove an even greater threat to Comcomly, his people, their Clatsop neighbors, and other peoples of the lower Columbia. Just how this happened makes one of the strangest chronicles of man's history along that stream.

11. The Cold Sick

> Take the wings
> Of morning, pierce the Barcan wilderness,
> Or lose thyself in the continuous woods
> Where rolls the Oregon, and hears no
> sound
> Save his own dashings; yet the dead are
> there.
>
> William Cullen Bryant, *Thanatopsis*

I<small>T WAS THE</small> practice of mariners entering the Columbia River to sometimes set markers in that stream to delineate its deceptive channels. Chinook tradition has it that Captain Dominis followed this practice when on the river. A few hours after the markers were set, according to that tradition, an Indian pulled one up and took it to his village. Scarcely had he reached shore when a strange feeling came over him. He began to tremble and complain of being cold. His fellows built a fire and had him hug it, but to no avail. Nor could skins and blankets thrown over him still the chattering of his teeth. A medicine man and some shamans were called to examine him but could not diagnose the illness. At length his fellows examined the marker, "found it guilty," beat it with clubs, and dragged it over the rocks and through the water. Finally, they placed it over a fire, slowly reducing it to ashes, which they carefully gathered and threw upon the water to destroy its evil spirit in the belief that the Tlchachie (spirits of the dead) did not like dust or ashes and would not pass through them.[1] The victim died. His body was placed in a burial canoe, joining others in their sepulchral craft for their journeys to the other world.*

* During this time, Indians of the lower Columbia believed, as they had for years, that many of their fellows stricken by fever had gone to the place of ghosts, from which they may or may not have returned depending on whether or not they recovered. The informant for Franz Boas, Charles Cultee, tells of the visit of his grandfather to these spirits at the time of a great plague, very possibly the intermittent fever. Boas, *Kathlamet Texts*, 247–51. Sickness was not, however, the only cause of such journeys, as seen in a Kathlamet account

Two events of the contact period had strengthened in the minds of the lower river peoples the belief that disease was in some way associated with white men and ships. It was, they said, from the first ship riding at anchor in the river that they saw a flash of lightning, the angry flash of the eyes of the great spirit bird, and heard thunder, the loud flapping of his wings among the clouds as smoke carried seeds of pestilence and death to strike people from the face of the earth.[2] Thunderbird, descending from his abode in the sun, was as vengeful as he had been in the beginning when pursuing the Old Giantess who broke the eggs he had laid on a mountaintop near the mouth of the Columbia. Each of Thunderbird's eggs had become a native.* The other tradition fresh in the Indians' minds was that of McDougall's virulent vial, which they associated with diseases borne by white men.

A misunderstanding Chinooks had with Captain Dominis in the trade caused them to point the finger of wrath at him. As some would subsequently relate it to white men, the "King George" people (of the Hudson's Bay Company) had told them to bring in large beaver and other skins but to give the captain the smaller ones. Learning of this policy, and that he was giving them more for the small skins than the company was giving them for the large ones, Dominis had become *hias silix* ("very angry") and had told them they would all soon die. Then, in McDougallian fashion, he had opened his vial, releasing the fever. In one version, instead of placing sticks in the channel he had hung an evil sail in a tree.[3]

The native, carrying the stick ashore only to expire, had died from what his fellows called the "Cold Sick." Did they associate the fever with the marker because the words *sick* and *stick* sounded alike to them? Indeed, peoples of the lower Columbia attributed great power to sticks. In healing sessions their doctors used sticks which were grease-smeared, striped, painted, feathered, and in other ways embellished, rhythmically beating three- or four-foot-long ones against the frameworks or rafters of their houses. Sometimes "power sticks" moved about in their hands with such force that they stopped the vibrations only by throwing out their hands and blowing at the same time.[4]

Thus, from Dominis and demons the "Cold Sick" spread its contagion along the lower Columbia River,[5] producing high fevers, chills, muscle cramps, intestinal upsets, and coughs.[6] By 1830 it unleashed its

---

of a warrior who did not return from the ghosts because he had died when accompanying them on a battle campaign. *Ibid.*, 182–76.

* In Boas, *Kathlamet Texts*, 221–24, appears the story of Thunderbird, who carried away a young girl from Saddle Mountain. Clatsops who laughed at Thunderbird were consumed by fire.

full fury, raging its worst until 1832 but appearing intermittently thereafter through the 1830's.[7] During its worst years, the few surviving natives of the lower river could no longer bury their numerous dead in their usual manner. Corpses, denied canoe interment, piled up along the shores to fatten carrion eaters, and famished dogs wailed pitifully for their dead masters. Surviving natives dared not remove or care for the bodies as they normally so meticulously did. Nor dared they molest markers in the river in fear of more fever.[8] Natives burned their villages attempting to destroy the contamination.[9] For years skeletons of victims would bleach on gaunt and dreary shorelines like so many pieces of driftwood.[10] How many succumbed to the disease will never be known, but eyewitnesses recorded pictures of vast devastation. The statement of one that "scarcely one of the original race is now to be seen" is not as overdrawn as might appear at first glance.[11] "But how the scene is changed!" lamented that observer.[12] Another wrote, "The aspect of things is very melancholy."[13]

As Indians mourned their dead, blaming their demise on Dominis and demons, white men who assayed the carnage had their own explanation for it. A special agent of the United States, which was beginning to challenge the Hudson's Bay Company position on the Columbia, was under the impression that company agents had blamed Americans for the disease, foisting on natives "this absurdity, for reasons . . . most obvious!"[14] Unlike McDougall, McLoughlin of the company would have been out of character peddling such a story. Workmen in his employ would not have been. Any trouble involving Dominis, who was, in the words of a company doctor, "a gentlemanlike person,"[15] would most likely have been no more serious than normal disagreements between parties in the Indian trade. Boston schoolmaster Hall J. Kelley, wishing to challenge the British by promoting American settlement on the lower Columbia at the time of the epidemic, said it was caused by "the excessive filth and slovenly habits of the inhabitants of the British settlement at Vancouver . . ." (a place naturally healthful enough on its own). His Anglophobia would not have permitted him to see that in the hardly antiseptic American Astoria no such violent fevers had broken out.[16] To balance the record, a company employee attributed the advent of the disease to "Americans of the United States" coming overland from that country to the Columbia.[17] Why it could not have been equally carried by Nor'Westers overland from Canada he did not say.

Less nationalistic and less scientific explanations of the tragedy were advanced by others. A shipmate of Dominis said it coincided with the cultivation of soil at Vancouver, which sent a virulence into the air.[18] Another said it proceeded from "miasmata pervading the atmosphere" and "foul exhalations from low and humid situations."[19] A Roman Catholic priest who assayed the carnage in 1839 believed it to be a manifestation of the wrath of God because of the natives' "abominable lives." Yet it would have been as easy to prove that in a decade the fever had lost some virulence as to prove that natives' lives during the same period had become less "abominable." The priest held out more hope for survival of the natives at Fort George, whom he heard had sent a delegation to Fort Vancouver for the "French Priests," than he did for corrupted natives at the latter place, where the contagion was at its worst.[20] At that fort a schoolteacher boasted that he had "no superstitious fears about it" as did natives. True, they had the superstition; he had apparent immunity, as did his non-Indian associates at Fort Vancouver.[21]

There were British and Americans who, although not subscribing to the punishment-of-God theory, believed the epidemic to have been ordained by higher powers. Wrote one Britisher: "Has the fiat, then, gone forth, that the aboriginal inhabitants of America shall make way for another race of men?"[22] The capstone to this type of thinking would be set in 1844 by commissioners of a Pacific Northwestern local government: "This country," they would write, "has been populated by powerful Indian tribes, but it has pleased the Great Dispenser of human events to reduce them to mere shadows of their former greatness. Thus removing the chief obstruction to the entrance of civilization, and opening a way for the introduction of Christianity where ignorance and idolatry have reigned uncontrolled for many ages."[23]

Although the epidemic wreaked a disparate havoc on whites and Indians, the former, composed largely at the time of members of the Hudson's Bay Company, did not escape its attacks. Right after the heaviest onslaughts, McLoughlin reported to his superiors that while the disease had carried off three-quarters of the Indians in the vicinity of the fort, nearly every employee there, although sick, had survived.[24] Fort personnel sought to check the ravages among themselves by administering well-known remedies such as quinine and a quinine substitute from the bark of the dogwood tree.[25] In his reports McLoughlin referred to the disease as "The Intermitting Fever," apparently under the impression, as this and the remedies would suggest, that it was malaria. Others called it the "fever and ague," which has also been associated with malaria. Present-day students of the plague are not in agreement about its cause. Some have also concluded that it was perhaps that disease carried by the mosquito.[26] Others, after examining sources and symptoms, have concluded that it may have been a form of virus influenza,[27] a conclusion of Dr. Meredith Gairdner (a Hudson's Bay Company doctor who came to the Columbia with Dr. Tolmie in 1833) and also of an 1857 report to the British Parliament.[28] Other supporters of this view believe the disease to have followed trade routes to the Northwest Coast overland from Canada or by ships touching alternately in China. They point out that an epidemic characterized by symptoms similar to those on the Columbia had broken out in Europe in 1827 as in previous centuries, one such having girdled the globe in 1557 from Asia via Europe to America. Continuing outbreaks of Asian flu to the present, they claim, give weight to their opinion.[29]

Partly at least because of the epidemic, the company faced a sagging native market potential, already in decline for at least a decade. It also delayed for a while its plans to widen that market by enlarging its trade perimeters on the Northwest Coast at Nass Harbor just below Alaska while at the same time checking American traders in that quarter.[30] To add to its other woes at the time was the loss of its ships the *William and Ann* in 1829, the *Isabella* the following year, the *Vancouver* in 1834, and bateaux in treacherous waters of the Columbia River.[31] Trade went on nevertheless. Business might have been worse had the company by 1830 not sent out trapping and trading expeditions, obviating dependence on local natives and their environment as the sole source of furs. Expeditions to points as distant as California had to be alert to native attacks in the interior regions in contrast to operations on the lower Columbia, where disease had lessened company fears of Indian outbreaks in that region. The greatest danger to an expedition to the Bonaventura (Sacramento) in 1832–33 was the "fever," which literally plagued it coming and going.[32] Of that expedition the leader, John Work, wrote to a friend: "Ah! Ned, the dangers among the Blackfeet are bad enough God knows, but them and all the other troubles in my most troublesome part of this savage country are not to be compared to the calamity of a whole party being thus attacked with sickness in a wilderness far from any aid or means of procuring remedies. God keep me from ever experiencing the like again."[33]

Just as the supposed causes of the disease became a factor in the growing rivalry of Britain (and its Hudson's Bay Company representative in the Pacific Northwest) and the American republic, so did other factors constitute a deterioration of Chinooks, Clatsops, and other tribes of that region. Hall Kelley wrote that while he was at the mouth of the Columbia River in 1834 he had seen "little there but darkness and blackness and desolation; heard but little more than the sighs and cries of the misery in the perishing remnants of the Clotsop and Chenook tribes, and the roar and rage of mighty waters."[34] In fact, wrote Kelley, all Indians below Vancouver were living "in the most brutal, sottish, and degraded manner."[35] Inspired first by Lewis and Clark's journals, published in 1814, and then by the attention the Pacific Northwest had received in the 1820's through the efforts of people such as Congressman Dr. John Floyd of Virginia to have the United States occupy that region,[36] Kelley had sought to establish an American colony on a "Donation of Land" at the mouth of the Columbia River, envisioning exclusive possession by Americans on that stream. In his plan, possession would follow trade with the Indians, whose wants would be stimulated by concourse with Americans and the introduction of agriculture. Very fine; but in his plan it was not by chance that in a proposed town at the mouth of the Columbia Chinooks were to live on the back streets.[37]

Kelley hoped to rectify on the Columbia the effects of Astor's failure there.* So did other Americans. On March 6, 1819, Sir Charles Bagot, British minister to the United States, wrote to Lord Castlereagh, British Foreign Minister, warning of plans of the United States government to send a small expedition in connection with some establishment at the mouth of the Columbia River to secure the fur trade and promote an American whale fishery in the South Seas.[38] Kelley's frustration in attempting to realize his project at the mouth of the river had undoubtedly sharpened his awareness of the evils into which the natives under British influence had fallen. Besides disease, for which, as noted above, he held Britain accountable, there was also drink. Aboard a company ship he claimed to have seen its captain dealing out "rum by the bucket" in exchange for wild game; afterwards, a chief and his family

---

* Kelley would continue to equate his own efforts at colonization with what he hoped were those of the U.S. government on the Northwest Coast. In the 1840's he would petition that government for a tract of land as "reward for his labors and sacrifices." Specifically, he associated his own efforts with those of Captains Gray and Kendrick, who received deeds from Vancouver Island native chiefs to tracts of land in that region for their company and for themselves. Details of these arrangements may be found in "Letters and Documents" in Fred Wilbur Powell, *Hall J. Kelley on Oregon*, 375–402. In 1854 Kelley would estimate the value of the deeded territory, some 5,000 square miles, at $8 million. Because of Gray's and Kendrick's discoveries on the Columbia River, Kelley would also include that region in the deeded area, although claims there were nebulous, as were others below the Strait of Juan de Fuca. See Kelley to Asa Caldwell, July 8, 1854, Hall Jackson Kelley, "Correspondence re Oregon Land Claims," manuscript, Archives of British Columbia. In 1832 Kendrick's heirs conveyed to Kelley deed to one-fourth part of the land purchased, apparently attempting to guarantee success of their quest for satisfaction of claims with the Kelley project at the mouth of the Columbia River in an area more likely to someday become American territory. Subsequently, Kelley yielded a large percentage of his interest to some of Kendrick's heirs and a college. Hall Jackson Kelley, "Quit claim to the heirs of Capt. John Kendrick in the ownership of lands in Oregon 1838," manuscript, Archives of British Columbia. As with Gray and his heirs, Kendrick and his, and Kelley, would be unsuccessful in receiving satisfaction from the U.S. government.

of eight were intoxicated by this "besom of destruction" from the Britons.[39] Had he wished, Kelley could have cited numerous sales of spirits by Americans on the Northwest Coast.

As in other parts of America where Indians and liquor did not mix, a Chinook at the mouth of the river, detecting differences between the preachments and the practices of white men, said to one of them: "You tell us Rum is no good, but you take a tolerably fair quantity yourself." The white man was hard pressed to explain how his people usually imbibed in moderation.[40] Once Columbia River natives developed a thirst for drink, they could not see why, if a small dram were good, a big draught would not be better. Perhaps it was a good thing that the liquor they got in trade was diluted. In reality, perhaps no other official of a fur company had tried harder than McLoughlin to curb a practice so entrenched in the trade.[41] Under his leadership the company also cooperated with some Americans in the Willamette Valley in the 1830's in preventing a distillery from going into business.[42] Yet he was no miracle worker. It was easier for law-abiding Americans in their embryonic Willamette community to take an abstinence pledge than it was for company workers to forgo their traditional "high-strung convivialities" at Fort Vancouver. At that place temperance pressures closed company liquor stores except mainly on special occasions such as Christmas.[43]

Especially critical of company influence along the Columbia was special United States agent Lieutenant William A. Slacum, who was there in late 1836 and 1837. He was critical of the British firm not only for the drunkenness of the Indians, but also for slavery among them, overlooking the fact that the practice had prevailed long before the company came to the river. He noted that the price of a slave in this traffic in human flesh was from eight to fifty blankets.[44] Some half-dozen years later, a white traveler would note that slaves were going for four or five woolen blankets, either plain or gaudily striped—or for two pounds of powder[45]—and that women slaves were in high demand by company personnel, who took them for wives.[46] Wishing not to greatly upset native mores, the company had permitted its employees to marry free slaveholding Indian women, slaves, and slaves who, in accepted native tradition, owned slaves themselves. These arrangements would have brought little criticism from native women, especially the slaves, whose marriages to company men freed them from some of their former drudgery.[47]

Always close to the natives of the Columbia, the company understood the practice much better than did its critics. Although aware of certain evils attending that practice, it also knew that slaves often worked with their masters, shared the same food, although eating separately, and often advised them in various matters. It would also have known that slaves, like their masters, sought guardian spirits and sometimes achieved freedom through purchase and acquisition of shamanistic powers.[48] For Slacum or most other Americans to have attacked slavery on the coast would have been like a pot calling a trading kettle black, for slavery was a recognized institution in the United States. One Britisher (whose empire abolished slavery in 1833) wrote that should war ever erupt between the two countries his would never relent until as a condition of peace there would be "total abrogation and abolition of slavery in the States, where the lustre of the charred standard is dimmed by its red stripes."[49]

Company clerk John Dunn, critical of what he termed American "buccanneering commerce" on the Northwest coast, which in his words had done its share to demoralize its natives, boasted that the Hudson's Bay Company had done much to civilize those in its commercial care. He wrote that as clerk at Fort George (in the 1830's) he had been charged with stopping barbarous native (secret society) practices like the "impostures of priests," who, to show divine approbation, stuck daggers into flabby parts of their patients without drawing blood.[50] Dunn may have slowed some of the more barbarous practices at Fort George, but he had worked no great reformation there, for James Birnie, in charge of that place from 1838 on, wrote that Indians of that quarter were "the most abandoned and profligate set of people on the Columbia River."[51] An American trader concurred, calling them "a rum set."[52]

Taking issue with Dunn was his countryman the Anglican Reverend Herbert Beaver, who came to Fort Vancouver in 1836 and left it after two and one-half years of attacking policies of the company, which he believed had failed its moral and economic responsibilities to the Indians with whom it dealt. Wrote Beaver: "Of articles bartered by the Company for peltry and other native produce, one half may be classed as useless, one quarter as pernicious, and the remainder of doubtfull utility...."[53]

Against another evil involving Chinooks, Clatsops, and other Columbia River peoples—that of petty intertribal wars—the company, Dunn implied, had made some progress.[54] It had certainly tried hard to quash such outbreaks because they were no good for the trade. McLoughlin, for example, breathed more easily in the fall of 1838 when hostilities between Chinooks and Tillamooks were "hushed up" after three of the latter were severely wounded.[55] In so doing he was trying to protect what was left of a trading empire. To maintain it, Slacum believed the company had persuaded the natives to trade solely with it just as its rum had befuddled them. Not only that, but the company had also sold Indians guns, which one day could be turned on Americans. An American sea captain observed, "Their [the company's] resources are immense, and their ambition unbounded."[56] And so was their experience, he might have added. Unlike so many American enterprisers on the Columbia, the company understood the native mind, notwithstanding occasional lapses like its importation of manufactured dentalia of ivory, at which natives turned up their noses.[57]

One American enterpriser who stumbled over the position and initiative of the company on the Columbia was Nathaniel J. Wyeth. He first came west in 1832 with his Pacific Trading Company to challenge the trade and status of the company, but his firm dissolved through attrition. Two years later, returning to the Columbia with a newly organized firm, the Columbia River Fishing and Trading Company, he sought to rechallenge the men of the "Bay."* He was defeated in his undertaking, for among other reasons the superiority of the company to which the Indians were so closely associated forced him to dispose of his goods and chattel to his competitor and leave the country a second time, "a disappointed adventurer."[58] Even natives in 1834 gave a poor reception to a Captain James Lambert of Wyeth's supply ship *May Dacre*, fearing that like Dominis' ship *Owhyhee* it carried contagion.[59] Ironically, the United States, whose cause he had hoped to advance on the Columbia, had charged import duties on fish and furs from that quarter.[60]

As Americans in the 1830's devoted increasing attention to salmon fishing on the lower river, the company used to advantage the Chinooks' skill in fishing. As soon as these natives caught cargoes of fish, they canoed them to the nearest company post. After the number of fish was ascertained, Chinook women received tickets which at the close of the season they exchanged for ammunition, tobacco, beads, cottons, calicoes, blankets, and so on. Until they cashed their tickets they prepared the salmon, in a rather complicated pickling process, for the company to ship to the Hawaiian Islands.[61]

Although in Chinook-Clatsop territory fish were surpassing furs as the major product purchased by the company, that firm remained primarily in the fur business in the Pacific Northwest. In 1840 at Vancouver it would collect eighteen thousand beaver.[62] Beaver pelts were shipped annually to London, where the fur was pounded into the finest felt for quality hats[63] until the styles changed at about the time of the depletion of the furry animal. Besides pelts, the company shipped wheat

---

* Mariners involved in the enterprise were forbidden by contract to trade with natives without express permission of the company. Such a contract was that between Nathaniel J. Wyeth and Joseph Thing. "Articles of Agreement," manuscript, Beinecke Library.

to Russians in the north and lumber, salmon, shingles, and hoop poles to the Hawaiian Islands in return for sugar, salt, and coffee.[64]

Chinooks and Clatsops tried proudly but pathetically with numbers reduced by plague and by flight to other tribes to maintain their pre-eminence in trade at the mouth of their river. Wishing to bypass them, a Chehalis chief in mid-July, 1834, showed up at the company's recently established (1833) Fort Nisqually (Sequallitchew), at the lower end of Puget Sound, to trade otter and beaver.[65] The establishment of that fort and of Fort Langley on the lower Fraser River (in present-day British Columbia) in 1827, involving the company with trade from Vancouver to northern Puget Sound, tended to upset all the more the Chinooks' historically strong position of trade along the lower river and northward along the coast.[66]

Although Chinooks and Clatsops had suffered a lower mortality in the plague than had peoples some hundred miles up the Columbia in the Cowlitz River and Fort Vancouver areas, where the disease seemed to have wreaked its greatest havoc,[67] ravages of the epidemic nevertheless had indeed cut deeply into the ranks of these two proud peoples. An 1824–25 Hudson's Bay Company enumeration of Chinooks under Comcomly had placed their numbers, including slaves, at 720 souls.[68] A company official there in 1840, after a decade of disease, would place their numbers at 75 men, 88 women, 69 children, and 58 slaves for a total of 280.[69] These figures are very close to those which natives furnished a white man, placing their numbers, including slaves, in three villages at 288.[70] The disease and subsequent decimation would virtually destroy the Chinooks about Willapa Bay, permitting Chehalis Indians to expand their territory there, where they took possession of village sites.[71] Helping further to reduce numbers of natives there and on the Columbia was the return of old diseases such as smallpox, which broke out in the north in 1836, spreading to the Columbia country, whose natives had not learned from the "Cold Sick" that hydrotherapy was unsuitable treatment for fever.* Hall Kelley believed that what was commonly called the "intermittent fever" had stripped the Clatsops of tribal existence, their survivors seeking shelter among surviving Chinooks.[72] Despite Kelley's suggestion that the Clatsops had lost their identity, a small cluster of them existed precariously near Point Adams under their "chief," Kotata (Kate-ya-hum).[73] In their village a palisade of thick planks surrounded a few lodges to protect their inhabitants

---

* The epidemic seriously hampered business at Fort Vancouver. A company official at Fort George said it did not wreak as much havoc near his post as it did in the epidemic-prone environs of Fort Vancouver. Rich (ed.), *McLoughlin's Fort Vancouver Letters*, 269–70; Hinds, "Journal."

from the frequent attacks of hostile Indian neighbors.[74] Because whites would settle in their lands before they would in those of the Chinooks, conflict between the two races would erupt there first.

Clatsops still hunted elk in their lands and beachcombed as had their ancestors once for the copper and fastenings of wrecked ships. For years they and the Chinooks would trade coins and sell pottery and other items gathered from wrecked ships like the Japanese junk that beached near Cape Flattery in 1834.[75] In a school which young Ranald Mac-Donald attended at Fort Vancouver were three survivors of that junk, who were held by Indians until McLoughlin had them brought to his fort.[76] Their presence helped inspire Ranald to journey in 1848 to the mysterious land of Japan.*[77] The Oriental adventure would provide him an education more exciting than that of the Fort Vancouver school or that of his subsequent continuing formal education, which his father sought for "my young Chinook."[78]

It is believed that the plague in its early onslaughts took with it one of the most eager of all Columbia River traders—Comcomly.[79] He was buried in a canoe in the family burial ground near Point Ellice. The legend persisted that many times he had pointed to a rock resting on the summit of Chinook Hill, proudly asserting that as long as it remained no one would question his power or that of his people. After his death the rock disappeared. Certain Clatsops and Tillamooks reportedly shook it loose, and it rolled down the hill.[80] In 1835, at a time when, in keeping with ancient Chinook belief, he had become a star in the heavens, a portion of Comcomly's mortal remains, his once proud head, so full of schemes and stratagems, was sent by Dr. Gairdner to Britain for scientific analysis. In years to come it would be not only the most famous item exported from Chinook country but also the most controversial, at least as far as the funerary Chinooks were concerned. Quite naturally they were angry at the theft, and they placed the body in a long box which was eventually located in the woods behind Fort George.† In the Hawaiian Islands Dr. Gairdner, author of the first chapter in the "saga of the skull," died from tuberculosis, which natives

* Ranald's grandniece claimed that he set off for Japan on learning that, unlike his brothers and sisters, he was half Chinook. Interview with Nellie Lynch Stanton, Chesaw, Wash., July 29, 1970.

† Some present-day Chinooks doubt that Comcomly eventually was buried in the land of the Clatsops, whom the chief disliked. Stephen A. Meriwether to authors, January 9 and 20, 1973. Three early sources, however, report the chief's burial as being behind Fort George: Hiram Martin Chittenden and Alfred Talbot Richardson (eds.), *Life, Letters and Travels of Father Pierre-Jean de Smet, S.J. 1801–1873*, II, 442; Charles Wilkes, *Narrative of the United States Exploring Expedition during the Years 1838, 1839, 1840, 1841, 1842*, IV, 321; Dunn, *History of the Oregon Territory*, 131.

might well have believed to be a retribution for his disturbing the dead. In its saga, the skull, after resting nearly 120 years in England, where it came near to being a casualty of the blitz in World War II, would be returned to the Clatsop County Historical Society in Astoria, Oregon. In 1956 it would be sent to the Smithsonian Institution for study and shortly returned to Astoria before burial in 1972 in the Ilwaco Community Cemetery.[81]

Lieutenant Slacum believed Comcomly's passing removed a big curb to drunkenness and instability among his people.[82] His daughter, the beautiful Princess Charlotte (Chowa?), although exhibiting his sharp talent for trade and diplomacy, had a "passion for intoxication and extravagance." After passing a season of concubinage trading furs and favors to company "gentlemen," she had by 1833 married a petty portage chief who, as Dr. Tolmie recorded, frequently banged her with a paddle or butt end of a musket—rough treatment for royalty.[83]

According to the Reverend Samuel Parker of the American Board of Commissioners for Foreign Missions, in the mid-1830's tragedy also attended other royalty at the mouth of the Columbia River. One of Comcomly's daughters, the wife of one whom Parker identified as "Calpo, an influential chief of the Chenook village near Cape Disappointment," on losing a daughter in 1829, possibly to the plague, killed two female slaves to attend the daughter in the spirit world.[84] Tragedy also dogged another of Comcomly's daughters, the former wife of McDougall who later married the powerful Casino.* That chief sought to kill her, thinking she had caused the death of their son. After a period of refuge at Fort Vancouver under McLoughlin's protection she returned to her people at the mouth of the river.[85] Recrimination of this kind among the natives certainly gave little encouragement to whites to administer medicines to them for fear of similar treatment. This very situation would be the cause of the 1847 massacre near the Walla Walla River (a Columbia tributary) of the Reverend Marcus Whitman, a missionary of the American Board of Commissioners for Foreign Missions, and his party during a measles plague. That massacre might have been avoided had Whitman heeded McLoughlin's warnings of danger inherent in treating the natives.[86]

On Comcomly's death his leadership passed to Chenamus, often called his brother but possibly a cousin. From his village Qwatsamuts, at the mouth of the Wallicut River on Bakers Bay, Chenamus claimed

---

* Parker, in his *Journal of an Exploring Tour beyond the Rocky Mountains*, 191, claimed that Casino could muster a thousand warriors before the epidemic. Wilkes would state that about 1840 he could muster but four or five hundred. Wilkes, *Narrative of the United States Exploring Expedition*, IV, 369–70.

authority over peoples all the way to the Cowlitz, although he was challenged by Kathlamet Chief Squamaqui (Scummague, Skumaquea, Skamakewea, or the like) for supremacy of the country from Grays Bay to the Cowlitz, despite the fact that Squamaqui had lost many people to the plague.[87] Two men traveling in the Pacific Northwest in 1843 would write that Chenamus at that time held sway over all tribes between the Pacific Ocean and the Cascade Mountains and beyond, and between the Umpqua River of southern Oregon and Puget Sound, a position no one could fill after his death, if indeed he filled so great a position in life.[88]

As Comcomly and his wives had before them, Chenamus and his favorite wife, Sally (Aillapust), acted as official greeters of ships entering Bakers Bay. Because of increased jockeying between Britain and the United States for position on the river, most ships they would greet were of those countries. On at least one occasion they did not know the national origin of the ship they were greeting. Hitting the deck of the American brig *Loriot*, chopping at anchor in the bay one 1836 December night, they asked: "Is this King George or Boston ship?"[89] Another ship greeted by the royal pair was H.M.S. *Sulphur*, Captain Edward Belcher, which crossed the bar on July 29, 1839, to extensively sound and survey it as part of Britain's increased reconnaissance and surveys of the region. From the pen of Dr. Richard Brinsley Hinds, the ship's assistant surgeon, we have a most intimate account of his Chinook hosts now nearing the fourth decade of the nineteenth century. "The Chinook chief," wrote Hinds, "is a sedate, discreet, dignified man when sober, but is as fond of 'Lum' as the rest of them, and forgot himself so far last night, as to get quite drunk."[90] Trade in other commodities, however, observed Hinds, had been good for Chenamus' wardrobe, from which he sported for the occasion a shirt, neckerchief, waistcoat, and trousers. Hinds found Sally to be "a very useful character" who spoke "a convenient share of English" and who was "a ready pander" to the desires of officers and crew and, from her contacts with Europeans, a lover of money. Like other Northwest Coastal women, she was more at home aboard ship than was her male counterpart, and consequently she spoke a more "convenient share of English" than he, although he spoke more of it when rum loosened his tongue. Hinds was struck by the quickness of Chinooks to adopt English words and to string them together in sentences with pronunciation better than intonation. With her understanding of shipside morals and manners, Sally washed herself before meals and appeared shocked when her spouse surrendered his knife and fork at the meal for his time-tested fingers, pitching into salmon smothered with anchovy sauce and washed down with rum.

Aboard ship on August 4 was a bevy of Chehalis women whom the crew at first could not distinguish from their Chinook sisters. The Chehalis had come down to fish, a move causing some resentment among their hosts, whose thinning numbers increasingly regarded their Chehalis rivals with apprehension, feeling their encroachments not only on the Columbia but at Willapa Bay. White traders and mariners, aware as were Chinooks of the aggressiveness of Chehalis males, dared not let them board their ships.[91] The crew of the *Sulphur* had no such fear or resentment against their female visitors, and like typical mariners they were glad to see girls in any port. Like Chinook women, Chehalis females had both the rum and run of the ship, where they were given rooms and cabins. Some wandered aft, where rooms were set aside for native chiefs. Whatever their other faults, they kept their deft mat-weaving fingers from pilfering, so a mat of welcome was always out for them.

Returning the crew's hospitality, Sally conducted Hinds, dubbed "Docta" by her people, on a guided tour of her village as her husband had three years earlier guided another doctor, John K. Townsend, whom he had regaled with finest foods—sturgeon, salmon, wappatoe, and cranberries. Hinds agreed with Townsend, who wrote: "Whatever may be said derogatory to these people, I can testify that inhospitality is not among the number of their failings."[92] Hinds found it to be a failing of their canine companions—"fierce brutes, who are not half as hospitable as their masters." Their wolflike appearance, with sharp noses and long, bushy tails, as Dunn described them, did not endear them to strangers. Hinds's hosts were too polite to overtly take offense at his threats to shoot the curs. Inwardly they may have been offended, giving credence to the lines of Alexander Pope in his "Essay on Man" that an Indian's "faithful dog shall keep him company."

En route to the house of Chenamus and Sally, Hinds peered into others to see infant heads being flattened. Once inside the split-wood, twenty-family longhouse, the "docta's" eyes met those in every corner, which peered at him as brightly as coals in the ten fires of unfailing wood from the beach burning opposite pairs of bunklike berths. To the visitor the natives appeared to have ample food and other necessaries of "civilized" life and were "not without their portion of happiness," although (unlike Europeans) they "appeared to live under no government and proper control."[93] Chenamus had no great power, but he did have great pomp, sitting at the rear of the dwelling on a platform backdropped by a board painted in high relief of colored rings, and behind this, a gigantic red and black figure against which he customarily sat to cast off evil spells.[94]

The eerie appearance of this symbolic figure must have put Hinds in an appropriate mood as he left the stuffy house to visit the burial grounds—the highlight of any tour of a Chinook village. His guide ran a calculated risk by taking a doctor to such a place, for, as others of his profession had, the visitor could have returned at night to appropriate another head for science. In the interest of good will, Sally was willing to take that chance. She showed her visitor a canoe tomb of the chief's recently deceased son and the burial of one of his wives. At the end of her canoe hung a blanket and, over the craft, pans and shoes she had once highly prized. Increasingly, white trade goods like tin cups, kettles, clothes, brass buttons, and rings mingled with dentalia and other native ornaments to decorate Chinook tombs.[95]

Hinds and Sally returned from the graveyard showing their friendship by walking arm in arm along the beach. One gossip spread the word that Sally had become his wife. The rumor caused him considerable concern not so much for his own safety as for hers, for he knew that Chenamus loved her but in a jealous rage could have sent her to the graveyard for good. This did not happen, and Hinds and the *Sulphur* left the river in mid-September.[96]

Chenamus, Sally, and their people must have known that their lands at the Columbia gateway to Oregon were becoming an international prize. Early in the year, when the *Sulphur* was on the river, Congressman Churchill C. Cambreleng of New York wrote Senator Thomas Hart Benton of Missouri that the British company settlement on the lower Columbia was the center of an immense fur trade and that unless the United States took some step to place American traders on an equal footing with the British the Americans would have to surrender the entire Indian country.[97] An American general, Thomas S. Jessup, saw not only that a post at the mouth of the Columbia would be good for trade and defense, but also that the entire Northwest Coast would be "an admirable nursery for seamen."[98] Very popular with Americans was Slacum's suggestion that a United States customs house and military post be established at the Columbia mouth to offset the British Hudson's Bay Company monopoly there.[99] Slacum did not designate which side of the river the post should be on, but fervent Americans wanted it on the more British north shore; again, restraints imposed by joint occupancy tended to check official government policy.

The Hudson's Bay Company and Britain maintained a visible toe-hold on the lower river at Fort George. There Indian trade continued, but the post now served more as a crude port of entry than anything else—a lookout for approaching vessels, a place from which to assist company ships waiting to clear the bar, and a communications center to send and receive messages from Fort Vancouver.[100] It stood unpretentious in the 1830's, one principal house of an attendant and a few cottages perched on a green knoll close to the beach where the Clatsop village stood. Very unpretentious, but it was visible; not so the symbol of American failure on the Columbia, the fur post Astoria, now overgrown by a voracious wilderness. From James Birnie, the Fort George manager, Hinds had received a picture of its neighborhood clientele as the decade of disease came to a close. Birnie attributed their small numbers to intermittent fevers, liquor, syphilis, infanticides, and abortions.[101] They now brought fewer furs to ships than formerly not only because there were fewer people to bring fewer furs, but also because the main traffic in furs had been channeled off to Vancouver and Nisqually. To ships now coming to the river mouth on other than fur-gathering missions, Chinooks and Clatsops brought items as varied as baskets and beeswax.[102]

Perhaps the best analysis of what had happened to these people was expressed by Birnie when he told Hinds that "the prosperity of Europeans had struck deeply at the root of the[ir] customs"—his way of saying that time and Pacific tides had brought increased numbers of foreigners and their culture to their shores. Birnie noted, for example, that under foreign influence even the old custom of carving rude images of men and animals had begun to wane, and the women, although still doing handiwork, were substituting more and more foreign goods for their own.

In those foreign places from which these goods had come, men were taking increased interest in the Columbia River empire. But in their rising interests they gave more interest to nationalistic position than to native peoples. Yet there were missionary forces at work seeking to elevate the natives from what were termed "darkness and oblivion." One such force would result in the arrival of the "Great Reinforcement," whose promoters hoped would bring a new day to the plague-riddled children of the river. Shortly, Chenamus and Sally and Clatsops across the river would be meeting a new ship. Would it bring for them a new day?

12. The Great Reinforcement

> Let a branch of Christ's kingdom be estab-
> lished here, with its concomitant expansive
> benevolence exerted and diffused, and this
> place would be a centre, from which divine
> light would shine out, and illumine this re-
> gion of darkness.
>
> Samuel Parker, *Journal*

On May 21, 1840, the *Lausanne*, Captain Josiah Spaulding, inched across the bar to anchor in Bakers Bay. Aboard was the "Great Rein-forcement" of the Missionary Society of the Methodist Episcopal Church arriving via the Hawaiian Islands from New York, which it had left in October the previous year.[1] Aboard were some fifty-one persons, among whom were six ministers, four young women teachers, a physi-cian, a cabinetmaker, a steward, and a number of farmers and mechanics and children.[2] Leading the reinforcement was Jason Lee, who had helped recruit it in order to strengthen a mission of the church which he and his nephew, Daniel, had established one-half dozen years earlier pri-marily in the Willamette Valley but with branch missions at the Dalles and Fort Nisqually. Also returning was an Indian lad, Thomas Adams, a Kalapuya from the Williamette who had accompanied Lee east in 1838. Missing, however, was William Brooks (Stum-manu), a Chinook youth who had also accompanied Lee to the East. Believed to have been born at Chinook Village and orphaned possibly by the plague, William had been trained at the Willamette Valley Methodist Mission School, which he had entered in 1835. He had been an important member of Lee's team to promote his missions, acting in the capacity of what one writer has called a "Chinook Publicist."[3] William's younger brother, Ozro Morrill (Klytes), had also entered the school, as had his sister, Harriet Newell (Tapal).[4] Death on the eastern tour, possibly a result of some tubercular infection, had denied William Brooks any further education. The death had given poignancy to his words at various meetings, in which he had denounced the white men who carried rum to his people and eastern clergymen who were more interested in the economic than the spiritual resources of his homeland. His words had helped raise both cash and conscience among his listeners.[5]

Chinook half-bloods William Cameron, Thomas, and Alexander McKay, sons of Astorian Thomas McKay and their Chinook mother Timee, had been en route east in a fur company brigade when they left it to join Lee's party. (The lads had been cared for by Dr. McLoughlin, whom they called their grandfather because of his marriage to the widow of Alexander McKay, who had been killed on the *Tonquin*.) William McKay was to have left for Scotland to study medicine. His brothers were to have remained in the East. They had, however, been persuaded by missionary Marcus Whitman to abandon the brigade in order to study in the United States. As Whitman had offered to pay for his education, William had entered Fairfield College in New York to study medicine. His brothers had entered a Methodist training school in Wilbraham, Massachusetts.

It did not take long for members of the reinforcement now arriving on the *Lausanne* to learn that they had their work cut out for them. As soon as Sally, decked out in calico dress, neckerchief, and red woolen shawl, boarded the ship on May 21, she lumbered to the cabin in the forward style of Chinook women to ask, "Where is the lum?" On being informed there was none, the "queen" nodded her head in surprise, exclaiming "Oh!"[6] That same day her husband, Chenamus, told Jason Lee that he was very angry with "King George" people for refusing him rum and that if he, Lee, came among them he would impose a similar prohibition and no doubt would make the natives free all their slaves. " 'And then,' asked Chenamus, 'Who would get wood and water and catch salmon?' "[7] None the less shocking to Lee's fellow missionaries was the arrival on deck of a band of Clatsops, "savage in their appearance," all painted and singing and dancing on the fore part of the ship.[8] This welcoming exercise must not have received the response its participants had hoped it would. Neither had their leaving their nearly naked slaves alongside the *Lausanne* to shiver all night in their canoes.[9]

With the *Lausanne*'s arrival, missionary traffic was heavier at the mouth of the Columbia than ever before. The very day the ship arrived, so had the Reverend Modeste Demers. With Reverend Francis N. Blanchet he had come to the Pacific Northwest the previous year from eastern Canada to rescue Columbia River natives from barbarity and to restore company employees whose isolation from the church had tarnished their Roman Catholic faith. On May 22 Demers from Astoria crossed the Columbia to the Chinooks. There, as numerous historians of his exploits would write, "with a little bell in one hand and a 'Catholic Ladder' in the other" he continued his mission for three weeks, "instructing the adults, baptizing the children and doing much good."[10] He instructed in the Chinook Jargon, the only immediate vehicle of communication he found to overcome the almost insurmountable Chinook languages.[11] Equally insurmountable to him were their polygamy and mercantilism, in which, as he saw it, they would barter any Christian faith they might have had for a shelter or a shirt[12]—or baskets and beeswax which they traded aboard the *Lausanne*.[13]

To cross the bar, that ship had carried a Hawaiian who claimed to be familiar with that dangerous stretch. Once inside the river, Birnie piloted the ship to Fort George. On the twenty-third most of the party went ashore to meet Birnie's half-Chinook, half-Tillamook wife and family and to ramble around,[14] somewhat disappointed in the savage appearance of Irving's "New York of the West" but happy in prospects further upstream, where they were told a thousand Indians had recently learned to pray.[15] After the ship ran aground, Alexander Lattie, a company employee, guided her as far as Pillar Rock,[16] which natives called Taluaptea. Then Ramsay (he now called himself "King George") took the helm.*[17] The next day the *Lausanne* was met by a boat bringing food and another pilot, George Washington ("Old George"), called variously a Chinook, a Hawaiian, and a Negro, to pilot them on to Fort Vancouver.†[18]

At Vancouver in early June members of the reinforcement received their appointments to their various stations.[19] Appointed to the Chinook-Clatsop station was the Reverend John H. Frost. He and Daniel Lee were back at Fort George on July 12. The following day they crossed the Columbia to minister to Chinook and Chehalis peoples, among whom Frost immediately set down some ground rules to the effect that his primary purpose in coming was to teach them how to worship the Great Chief and trade for beaver and salmon only so much as he might need for food. Like Demers before him, he noted that his listeners never acted from a higher motive than that of temporal gain.[20]

Like fur traders also before him, Frost on July 14 chose to make his future residence among the Clatsop Indians, possibly because of greater

* In 1840 Ramsay had only one eye. Wilkes, *Narrative of the United States Exploring Expedition*, V, 114.

† George Washington married a Chinook woman, a sister of the wife of one John McClure, who would take up a claim joining the Astor site on the west. This land would later become the principal business section of Astoria. In the 1850's McClure sold out to a Judge Cyrus Olney. The Hudson's Bay Company also used Hawaiian Islanders as river pilots in the 1830's. P. W. Gillette, "Early Pilotage on the Columbia River," *Pacific Monthly*, VI, 1 (June, 1901), 5.

possibilities of sustaining the mission on the fertile Clatsop Plain. After journeying to Vancouver for his family and effects, he returned to the Clatsops on August 6.[21] Shortly he was joined by Solomon Smith and his wife, Helen (Celiast),* daughter of Chief Coboway.[22] Frost soon found himself in the middle of a hornets' nest of Indian troubles, which, buzzing for years, now added more attrition to lower river tribes to that already brought on by the plague. At this time Birnie apprised Frost of the census of Chinooks as provided by Chenamus. His Clatsop parishioners numbered 160 souls.[23] Current troubles were those Daniel Lee had reported on his return to the Dalles on August 3 after a visit to the Chinooks. In those disturbances, Lee had reported, a Clatsop had killed another native, whose friends had avenged the death at Fort George by literally cutting a woman to pieces. Within the month, Clatsops had killed several of their own people.[24]

Within a fortnight of Frost's arrival at Fort George, word came that natives at the fishery at Pillar Rock had murdered a young Briton, Kenneth McKay, and an Indian companion in the latest incident of long-festering bad white-Indian blood at that place. "A gloomy commencement of our missionary work," wrote Frost on receipt of the news.[25] Birnie immediately dispatched a letter by canoe to Fort Vancouver and sent Indians across the river to invite Chenamus, who had a reputation of friendliness to whites, to come over with his men to guard Fort George lest it become an objective of some Indian conspiracy. Chenamus immediately canoed over to the fort with fifteen or twenty warriors, each armed with knife and musket. Three of his men were dispatched to Fort Vancouver as the rest stood guard. After being supplied with fresh ammunition and regaled with biscuit and molasses, they declared themselves to be in the true spirit and tradition of Comcomly, whose bones rested nearby, and ready, as he had always been, to protect

---

* Solomon and Celiast (Helen) had been "married" at Vancouver without benefit of clergy, the union later solemnized by Jason Lee. Celiast was born the year before Lewis and Clark came to the Columbia. She had previously been "married" to one Porier, a French-Canadian baker at Fort George, and bore him three children. In 1824 they moved to Fort Vancouver, where McLoughlin, learning that her husband had another wife in Canada, advised Celiast to leave the Frenchman. She subsequently did, taking her children with her, and took up residence with a sister, Yiamust, who also had married a fur company employee, Joseph Gervais, and lived on French Prairie. Another sister of Celiast, Kilakota, now called "Margaret," was deserted by Matthews, married fur man Louis La Bonte, and settled on French Prairie. Of the Solomon-Celiast union there were six children. The couple raised three others, including a Hawaiian girl known as Jessie Bill, whom Celiast bought from a sailor as her slave. Emma Gene Miller, *Clatsop County, Oregon: A History,* 57; Elwood Evans, *History of the Pacific Northwest: Oregon and Washington,* II, 571; S. A. Clarke, *Pioneer Days of Oregon History,* II, 419. Their best known offspring, Silas, was born in 1839. Evans, *History of the Pacific Northwest,* II, 570.

their white neighbors. Of some comfort to Frost was word that sailors of the brig *Maryland* out of Newburyport, Captain John H. Couch, were nearby, as was a party under Dr. Tolmie just in from Fort Vancouver to avenge McKay's death.[26]

On the morning of August 24 the search for the murderers got under way. Two wives of two headmen of the clan living at Pillar Rock were taken along as guides-hostages, it being assumed that a slave of one of their husbands was one of the murderers. A sister of the two women departed with two other women and the child of one of the guides-hostages for Youngs Bay, singing the death song as they went. Then Chief Squamaqui (who had assisted Frost on his initial journey to Fort Vancouver) came down to declare his innocence and help in the search. He brought along a Quinault Indian and the suspect slave, who were declared indicted as perpetrators of the crime. The Quinault promised to remain at Fort George, and Squamaqui returned home. On the twenty-sixth, after an initial search for the killers, Tolmie left to join McLoughlin aboard a barge brought down from Fort Vancouver and lying off Pillar Rock. On the next day a canoe from the party searching for the killers arrived at Fort George carrying a slave girl with a ball lodged in her shoulder. She would die the next day, in Frost's words a victim of "heathenism." The canoemen said that a slave, one of the murderers, discovered by an Iroquois party, was shot through the head.

In the meantime the Quinault had escaped. A bounty was offered for his recapture, which Squamaqui effected, redelivering him, this time to McLoughlin, who brought him to Fort George on the morning of the twenty-ninth. It was now decided by the whites present that the Quinault, believed to have been as deeply implicated as the slave, was one of the murderers and that, as it was necessary to prevent further killings, an example should be made of him. Consequently, "according to the laws of Great Britain & America" he was adjudged worthy of death. At 1:00 P.M. on the twenty-ninth, by order of McLoughlin, he was hanged by the neck until dead. Assembled Indians were told that whites wanted to live with them in uninterrupted peace; should that peace not be maintained, warned the whites, such a scene would reoccur. As a footnote to the episode, the women retained as hostages were permitted to search for their husbands under instructions to say to them, when found, that if they would come in and make it appear that they were innocent of the crime of which their slaves had been found guilty they would be permitted to return to their homes in peace. About two weeks later, the slaves' owner and his brother came to Fort George to assure the whites that they had no knowledge of the murder and were innocent of it. On the Columbia the next year Lieutenant Charles Wilkes of the United

States Navy Exploring Expedition would claim that the master of the slave kept himself aloof from all company posts until the matter should be forgotten.[27]

After this flurry of tragic excitement Frost attempted to settle down to a routine, if such a thing could be said to have been possible. On September 1 with Dr. Tolmie and Calvin Tibbets, an American settler from the Willamette, he set off to visit the Smiths. Crossing Youngs Bay in a canoe, they followed the Skipanon River a few miles to the head of navigation and crossed Clatsop Plain by walking to the beach at the southern end of the plain. There, at the mouth of Neacoxie Creek, they found the Smith family living in a small cabin near Clatsop Indians gathered at their ancient fishery. The next day the men returned to Fort George.[28]

As far as the Clatsops were concerned, Frost was just another white man in their midst, and they behaved before him just as they had before others of his race. He responded, quite understandably, with greater shock at native practices than had the mariners and traders. On September 18, for example, he told with great poignancy of a Clatsop mother walking the beach on her way to bury her dead child, which was wrapped in a mat slung on her back, singing the death song as she carried out her mournful mission. A clergyman on the lower river observed that natives loved to sing.[29] But not death songs. With a knife another woman cut off the mother's hair, a sign of mourning.[30]

Later that month the missionary welcomed a fellow member of the reinforcement, the Reverend W. W. Kone, to help him convert Chinooks and Clatsops from these kinds of practices. With Kone and Smith, down from Fort George, Frost set out for Clatsop Plain to put up a house "in a wild region, where the foot of the white man had seldom troden . . . surrounded by Indians . . . ignorant, superstitious and barbarous."[31]

An event transpiring at Neacoxie at the time of salmon runs further confirmed in the missionary's mind the barbarity of that place. An Indian hunter brought an elk into camp. As food was scarce, he invited his fellows to his lodge to eat it. One ate too much and paid for his overindulgence with heavy breathing and groaning. His sister and others of his lodge, discovering him ill, set up a cry that he was dying and should be buried without delay, for should he lay dead above ground the salmon would all leave the river and there would be no food. Some of the natives hurried to Smith's house for a shovel to bury the man. Celiast, a Christian convert, rushed to the house to find the man very much alive, and she sought to persuade his relatives to postpone the pagan burial until the next morning, by which time she thought he would recover. Her appeals were in vain. They rolled him up in his blanket and mat, as was their custom, and took him to the burial place. There, despite the continued pleas of Celiast, they buried him alive. "No doubt," wrote Frost, "as they had a great abundance of salmon, they felt satisfied that they had done a good work."[32] This would not be the last of such untimely deaths which sacrificed Clatsops on the altars of ancient tabus.[33]

Frost was aware that other unusual Clatsop deaths had occurred before—and at the hands of white men, too—but he did not dwell on them at any length. When some Clatsops came to help him and Kone put up their cabin, he thought their headman, Kotata, no chief in the traditional sense, as the last real chiefs had been wiped out by Hudson's Bay Company recrimination for the supposed murder of the *William and Ann* crew.[34] The cabin neared completion with everyone pitching in to help except Kotata, who thought it beneath his dignity to perform such menial tasks. He did promise, however, to listen to the words of the missionaries and keep law and order among his people. Until the families came from Fort George, natives occupied the place. Afraid of throwing them out lest they become offended, the two clerics built another cabin in the form of an Indian lodge to accommodate them. Winter, with its usual rain, made extremely difficult the task of removing the families and their household effects and supplies from the fort. There was, however, no record of complaint by Wallace, a black man who assisted in the removal; he had deserted the *Maryland* when she was in the river.[35]

That winter Mrs. Kone was ill and expecting. Her husband talked of leaving the country, as did Frost in the belief that his effort to survive there prevented him from effecting the work he was sent to do. One bright spot that winter occurred when Smith brought down a pair of horses to help in farming on the plain and to make the mission less dependent on the Willamette headquarters, thus providing a better-provisioned base from which to minister to Clatsops in their winter residence at Neacoxie and to Tillamooks further south. With approaching spring the families moved near Youngs Bay to be near Indians gathering there for salmon fishing. As Frost had previously visited lodges to converse with their people about the faith, he now requested them to meet in Kotata's lodge on a Sabbath to hear him explain the Bible, hoping, no doubt, to accustom them to regular attendance at services on that day. That Sunday they showed up; the next one they did not, for they had scattered to shoot wild fowl and to fish. The only ones left for Frost to preach to were Kotata, his wives, and slaves.[36]

On April 23, 1844, Wasulsul, a Clatsop headman, invited his missionary guests to his lodge for a salmon feast. First the fish was carefully cut in compliance with tabu. As it was set to roasting, the braves could have told how Talapas (Coyote), maker of Clatsop lands, on finding his people with only bear, deer, and wild fowl to eat, made salmon for them, after which he left a seine in the Columbia River for them to catch the fish and meticulous instructions on how it should be prepared and who should eat it. Talapas had also instructed the people that "Murderers, those who prepare corpses, girls who are just mature, menstruating women, widows and widowers should not eat salmon."[37] Such a "barbarous" practice had not spoiled the missionaries' dinner. With Birnie they walked to Point Adams to visit Clatsops, lounging, gambling, and chattering in smoke-darkened lodges. In early July Kotata sent Frost word that the *Peacock* of the Wilkes expedition had lost her mast and wrecked on the northern breakers. Frost preached twice to her rescued crew. Relations between that group and the Clatsops were on a less spiritual basis. True to their mercantilism the Clatsops sold their guests eight or ten salmon for a cotton shirt or its value in red or green baize. Before long they raised their prices by one-half. In the presence of the expedition crew the Indians proved that the spirit of speculation of the marketplace, carrying over to their gaming, was so deeply ingrained that Wilkes believed it would continue until they should be wiped out as a race.[38]

Another routine-breaking experience for the missionary occurred in August and September when he, Smith, an Indian, and a former sailor journeyed to the Willamette via Tillamook country, topographically dangerous country along the sea and dangerous there in other ways, too, as Tillamook chiefs there were on poor terms with their Clatsop rivals. Collecting livestock in the Willamette, the party, now increased in size, returned to Clatsop country with the help of Tillamook Chief Kilches, a bitter enemy of Kotata.[39]

Shortly after the rainy season set in, Reverend Kone and his family left outbound on the company ship *Columbia*. He was satisfied that he "could effect nothing as a missionary in this dark land."[40] Frost felt the same way about himself but hung on, struggling clumsily with the Chinook Jargon to communicate to his flock the truths of the gospel. Natives came to him winter-hungry with nothing to eat save roots. Beached whales, which often mitigated their improvidence by supplying them with food and oil, were scarce this year, and from either sloth or snows they did not hunt elk. Their poverty was matched by the paucity of their numbers. Of some ten Clatsop children born between the previous November and February, 1842, only two survived. The major cause of these deaths was infanticide, which a Clatsop woman explained as an attempt to free her sisters from burdensome chores like preparing the food their husbands demanded on returning from hunts.[41] Continuing disease and internecine squabbles further decreased their numbers. Seeking to perpetuate the Methodist mission, Jason Lee would happily report that if it had not done anything else it had stopped all petty Indian wars from the Dalles to the sea.[42] Members of his board in the East would have believed this by reading over-optimistic reports calculated to save the missions as well as by reading guidebooks for emigrants bound for the Pacific Northwest Oregon country. These publications played down Indian troubles as, in the words of one of their writers, "little else than a mere farce."[43]

To natives and whites in Clatsop-Chinook country the troubles were more than mere farce. On some days fire from natives' muskets was heard from morning until evening,[44] and a few primitive weapons helped bring death as surely, albeit more silently, than firearms.[45] On July 11, four or five native women were wounded in skirmishes, and a man was injured apparently in the same fracas. Frost extracted a ball from him, but within a week he was dead.[46] On another occasion, after Kotata or someone else took his hatchet, Frost sent an Indian to retrieve it. This the Indian did after tracing the implement to Kotata's lodge. Angry over the detection of the purloined object, Kotata sought to kill the missionary. Finding him working in his garden, Kotata took a bead on the cleric, but before he could fire his musket the friendly Wasulsul diverted him. Shouting to Frost to run to his house, Celiast caught the enraged Kotata by the hair and threw him backwards. As she had saved Frost this day, so would she save others by cooling hot blood among her people and whites, thus preventing more of it from being shed among the Clatsops. In so doing she was friendly toward whites yet protective of her people, for whom she set aside in her house a room to receive them.[47]

At the root of most of the troubles were white men, who continued to bring with them, as they always had, vices to corrupt the natives. Two travelers in Oregon country at the time aptly observed that wherever those of their race mingled with Indians, almost without exception it had tended both morally and physically "to degrade, sink, and destroy" the red men.[48] Earlier, Frost had gotten a pledge from the captain of a rum-carrying American ship to not give or sell spirits to natives. In exchange for the pledge the American had been furnished a house from which to trade for salmon. As the captain had brought the liquor to trade with natives for salmon, he soon broke his pledge. In the rowdiness resulting from that breach of faith, an Indian was shot. Of these whites an Indian said to Frost, "Hias peshock mika tilacum shicks," meaning, translated from Chinook Jargon, "Your people are very bad, friend."[49] William Brooks had said he must put word in the newspapers to white men not to carry rum to his people. "He makes it himself," said William, "he must *drink* it himself, these Yankees."[50] Unfortunately, his words went unheeded.

Control of the liquor traffic on this faraway Oregon frontier was nearly impossible due to lack of government law enforcement. Under presidential appointment as federal Indian subagent for Oregon, Elijah White would write Birnie in March, 1843, that in White's absence Birnie was to visit vessels arriving on the lower Columbia and read them the laws of the United States pertaining to the introduction and vending of ardent spirits in Oregon.[51] White had been appointed under the Linn Bill, which among other provisions sought to force settlement of the boundary issue between the United States and Britain by extending American laws below the 49th parallel. In reality, he was acting without authority, for the Linn Bill failed to pass. Under the Oregon Provisional Government, organized in 1843, a law was passed on June 24, 1844, to prevent the introduction, sale, and distillation of ardent spirits in Oregon.[52] The law could not have been well enforced on the Columbia, for on August 16, 1845, the persistent Elijah White would inform the provisional government that Indians, after receiving drinks aboard the American brig *Chenamus*, named for the chief whose likeness protruded from her bow, in their carousing and fighting had forced white men to dodge their bullets in a no-man's-land in the territory of the provisional government,[53] itself a no-man's-land somewhere between United States and British territories. Curbing liquor sales to the Indians would be more difficult in 1847, when the provisional government legislature would amend the statute permitting liquor sales under certain restrictions, an action inspired by the Hudson's Bay Company, which by then would accede to that temporary government for mutual protection from lawless elements and which held stores of liquor at its Fort Vancouver.[54]

Believing it the will of God and morally wrong to do otherwise, Frost, with his family, decided to abandon his mission, blaming part of his failure to "Their language [which] is so defective, that thereby it is impossible to acquaint them with the nature of the law."[55] Aboard the British bark *Diamond* (Captain Fowler), departing "the land where I have experienced many trials," Frost put out to sea on August 21, 1843, under the frowning Cape Disappointment, trying to convince himself that the natives were better off than when he came.[56] His replacement, Josiah L. Parrish, a blacksmith of the *Lausanne* reinforcement, down from the Willamette mission to the Clatsop mission shortly before Frost departed it, was scarcely more effective among his native parishioners than was his predecessor, but he was more optimistic. He also found it difficult to preach in the jargon. On first arriving among the Clatsops he secluded himself from his family to live with those natives and master the jargon, boasting that he could learn it ten times faster than the Clatsops could master English.[57] Jason Lee happily reported that in the short time Parrish had been among Clatsops several of them had become "praying men."[58]

On July 31, 1844, another "Great Reinforcement" entered the Columbia—that of the Roman Catholic Church aboard the *Infatigable*. Frightened that she entered the river through a dangerous unused southern channel, the Clatsops rent their garments in mourning for those whom they believed would surely drown. The *Infatigable*, living up to its name and aided by "Divine Pilotage," successfully escaped treachery of not only the bar but also Chinooks, whom they thought were flashing signals from Cape Disappointment to trap them. In reality they and Birnie were only trying to guide them into the river. Clatsops and Chinooks boarded the ship, displaying their adornment as they always did, bringing gifts of fresh salmon and potatoes and evoking from the passengers an evening *Te Deum*.[59] Taking over the helm from the "Divine Pilotage," Birnie steered the ship to Fort George. From there the new reinforcement continued up the Columbia and Willamette rivers, from where it would go to various points in Oregon. Before the end of the decade a priest would labor among Chinooks on the lower river.

White traffic, especially American, at that place was heavier now than ever before. One of the few concessions these whites made to its Indians for their takeover was the naming of the ship after Chenamus. In 1844 under Captains John H. Couch and Avery Sylvester, deferring to natives' salmon tabus, the *Chenamus* took on salmon from the lower river (Couch had commanded the brig on the river the two previous years; Sylvester had been there in 1843 commanding the brig *Pallas*) at eight to twelve per dollar to fill 250 barrels, worth five dollars each and ready to ship to the Hawaiian Islands to be sold at a very good advance. In March, 1845, the *Chenamus* crew would take on 50,000 board feet of lumber at a mill completed in the summer of 1844 twenty miles from Fort George,[60] across the Columbia from present-day Cathlamet and some four hundred yards from the river.*

Captain Sylvester noted that Parrish, on failing to civilize the natives, had taken to farming, at which the captain thought he should do better,[61] for during his ministry several natives had become "preying" rather than "praying" men. In late 1844 Kotata murdered his youngest wife, a Chinook, to set her people on the warpath against the Clatsop

* This mill belonged to Henry H. Hunt and Ben Wood. In 1846–47 another lumber mill would be erected on the south side of Clatsop Plain. "Mr. Smith's Address," *Morning Oregonian*, December 11, 1899, p. 9.

leader. On learning of the deed, Parrish refused to shake Kotata's hand.[62] With the closing of the Oregon Methodist Mission in 1844, those left at its Clatsop station pretty much disengaged themselves from the Indians to create as never before a biracial culture in Clatsop-Chinook country. In a school Parrish opened on Clatsop Plain in the winter of 1844/45 he taught white children,[63] as did Brother W. W. Raymond in a second school during the winter of 1846/47 after having moved four years earlier from the Willamette to the Clatsop as an aide to Frost.[64]

Migration of Americans to Oregon (some seven thousand of them from 1842 to 1847) increased Anglo-American tensions over that region. In July, 1844, His Majesty's Sloop *Modeste*, Captain Thomas Baillie, entered the Columbia to guard British subjects from possible attack from Americans, not Indians, primarily.[65] British lieutenants Henry J. Warre and Mervyn Vavasour of the Royal Engineers on their "secret mission" to Oregon in 1845–46, struck by the strength of American presence there, recommended for their government sites for military installations on the lower Columbia to protect their countrymen from white Americans more than from red ones.[66]

Tensions at the international level became personalized in Oregon in conflicts between individuals of the two nations. An American, James Welch, for example, in the spring of 1846 moved to Astoria, where, in defiance of company personnel, he built a home.[67] That same year Lattie, the bar pilot who replaced Birnie as Fort George clerk, came to blows with an American, John McClure, who took up a claim adjoining old Astoria and lived with a woman said to have been a direct descendant of Comcomly.[68]

To help offset American influence on the lower river, company trader Peter Skene Ogden was instructed to occupy for his firm a claim at Cape Disappointment he purchased in 1846 from an American, a move some Americans believed to be as shrouded and bold as the headland itself. At that place the company apparently constructed no more than one building to function presumably like Fort George should the international boundary be set at the Columbia River.[69] Until word was received of that settlement, Fort George continued in operation. Its clerk was directed to send intelligence of ships coming and going on the river, to maintain the "tariff," as there was plenty of pressure by natives to change it, to be kind to them, to exhort them to industry in the salmon trade, and to offer freemen's (free hunters') prices to residents of the countryside should they bring in furs to trade.[70]

Further bifurcating the old pattern of white-Indian relationships in the Oregon country were the 1846 boundary settlement at the 49th parallel to the north of the Columbia River, the August 14, 1848, act of

Congress establishing Oregon Territory, and the March 2, 1849, declaration of territorial government with the arrival of Governor Joseph Lane in Oregon that year, which cinched American control there. At the mouth of the Columbia Chinooks and Clatsops sank deeper as white traders plied them with more and more liquor in the salmon and fur trade.[71] Their plight might have been worse had Clatsop country churchmen Solomon Smith, Calvin Tibbits, and W. H. Gray (the latter a former American Board of Commissioners for Foreign Missions lay worker) not labored in their behalf.[72]

Like so many other deliberations involving the fate of North America, those of the 1840's in the Oregon country had been effected without consulting its native inhabitants. Whether Indian women knew it or not, even their marriages to white men helped give the latter and their fellows a foothold in Indian country. For example, in Clatsop country Robert Shortess "claimed" two miles along the Columbia and inland one-half mile, including all of Tongue Point, by virtue of the Organic Act of the Oregon Provisional Government and hereditary title through his native wife.[73]

In 1848 some company people remained in Astoria occupying a cluster of houses, one a store and the others dwellings. The year before, the post office, Astoria, had been established. By act of Congress, on August 14, 1848, Astoria was made a port of entry, and a customs house was shortly established there.[74] In 1849 Astoria noted some growth, boasting about a dozen log and frame houses, including that of the customs collector. Prices were high, and lots twenty-five feet by one hundred feet were selling for two hundred dollars in the town they were calling "the future New York of the Pacific."[75] White population in Clatsop country in 1850 was 462, of which 249 lived in Astoria.[76] Doing their part to advance civilization in the town were men of a new breed of white settlers, of whom there were now an increasing number, like Messrs. Welch and Shively, who frowned on John McClure for having an Indian wife.[77]

Diffusing life into Astoria was the 1848 discovery of gold in California. No gold was uncovered in Clatsop-Chinook country, saving it from a big influx of miners, the cause of so much trouble for other western Indians. Chinooks and Clatsops knew that white men kept their eyes open for "colors," and some natives brought to Fort George platina and silver ore from as far away as the northern Queen Charlotte Islands.[78] The two peoples did not escape the California gold excitement from the time the brig *Honolulu*, a fast sailer, came to Oregon Territory to return with picks, crowbars, and irons for the diggings.[79] Many recently arrived Americans in the territory laid aside their settlement plans to scurry to California, as did many company people. The gold rush proved the undoing of a former Chinook slave called by whites "Chinook." Escaping his captors, he got into numerous scrapes and was hanged in Shasta City by forty-niners.[80] Returning miners infused the Oregon economy with gold, of which the company received "a fair proportion."[81] A Fort Vancouver visitor in 1848, however, thought that its glory was declining,[82] and a story in the *Morning Oregonian* in nearby Portland on July 27, 1861, would report its utter desertion and near ruin at that time. Natives in the Astoria vicinity, the chief staging area for the California mines, discovered more money in selling potatoes to goldseekers than in selling salmon and sturgeon,[83] but when the rush was over they soon abandoned their agrarian ways, of which they were never very fond.

Astoria was an important staging area for the California mines and a port of call for ships entering the river, for they now entered by the south channel to anchor at that port. This is not to mean that the bar had lost its treachery. Whites believed that the first examination of the Columbia mouth by the United States Coast Survey of 1850 and the installation of the Cape Disappointment Lighthouse (obviating the building of bonfire beacons, and first exhibited in October, 1856) had come none too soon. The *Oregon Spectator* (Oregon City, Oregon Territory) of January 24, 1850, reported the loss of the *Josephine* on the bar and placed the blame on a drunken Indian pilot. Possibly the editor, by making the Indian look bad, was attempting to make the bar look better, which Oregon promoters were wont to do.[84] As early as 1846 the Oregon Provisional Government had passed a law authorizing it to appoint a pilotage commission. The first pilot under this law was granted a license the following year.[85]

What of Chinook-Clatsop destiny in the face of this burgeoning white settlement in their country? It was well evaluated by one who at this time wrote: "Their inexhaustible resources have been taken from them, their bows are unstrung, and from 'lords of the soil,' they have sunk to the degredation of slaves."[86] The Great Reinforcement had failed to rescue them. As a result of fast-moving Anglo-American developments of the 1840's they would soon be covered by an American blanket. Again, the question might have been asked concerning some four hundred Indians near the mouth of the Columbia River: "Could this in any way have ushered in for them their new day?"

13. Tansey Point and Beyond

> The poor Indians are fully aware of the
> rapidity with which, as a people, they are
> wasting away. . . . They are fully sensible
> of the power of the Government, admit that
> they cannot be killed and exterminated, but
> they say they cannot be driven far from the
> homes and graves of their fathers.
>
> Anson Dart to Superintendent
> of Indian Affairs

BEFORE THE MIDDLE of the nineteenth century, Americans made no
rush north of the Columbia River to settle. For one thing, the Hudson's
Bay Company remained there, seeking, as one American of that region
put it, "to extort from the American government a fabulous price for
their old log forts and rotten trading houses, and, through their em-
ployés, or those formerly in their employ . . . to poison the minds of
the Indians against the Americans. . . ."[1] By 1850 most of the settlers
venturing north of the Columbia were former company people who were
familiar with the country and married mostly to native women. Birnie,
like another company man named Anderson who had preceded him
north of the Columbia near a place Birnie called Cathlamet,* had
seemed like no intruder to Indians when he moved there in 1846 and
they helped him clear his land.[2] Birnie and John McLean, living upstream at Oak Point, had been by 1848 virtually the only whites between Chinook Point and the Cowlitz River. Below the latter stream by
1850 lived a Mr. Abernethy,† who ran a sawmill.[3] Down the Columbia
John Pickernell had settled at the mouth of the Wallicut River sometime about 1842.[4] Shortly thereafter burly James Scarborough,[5] a com-

---

* A post office was established at Cathlamet, Oregon Territory, on August 8, 1851,
with James Birnie as postmaster. Guy Reed Ramsey to authors, August 22, 1972.

† A tombstone in a graveyard some fifteen miles downstream from present-day Kelso
and Longview, Washington, bears an inscription of one Alexander S. Abernethy "who
Pioneered the Lumber Industry . . . of This Region. . . ." Ralph G. Taylor, "Historic
Abernethy Cemetery," *Cowlitz County Historical Quarterly*, VI, 2 (September, 1964), 9.

pany employee, had settled at Chinook near the foot of a hill (formerly Chinook Hill) which came to bear his name (Scarboro). By 1848 he had established a farm there thanks in large measure to hard work by his Chinook wife, Ann Elizabeth (Ketalutsin), whom he had married in 1843. Under the Donation Land Act of 1850 he filed for his land, which, as finally patented, consisted of 643 acres extending about a mile on the Columbia north bank.* On the peninsula at Willapa Bay as early as 1841 had lived one John Douglas, who was married to a Chinook woman, Judith.[6] Not far from the Scarboroughs lived an American sailor named Edwards who had an Indian woman and a nine-pin alley.[7] Also in the vicinity, as noted above, had lived Peter Skene Ogden and Captain James Johnson, bar pilot, who earned extra cash by peddling liquor to Indians and white wayfarers and cargo salvaged from wrecked ships.[8]

Even though settlers did not rush north of the Columbia, some early ones nettled their Chinook neighbors. The latter complained that Captain Johnson had forbidden them use of portages through "his" lands.[9] There was also friction between them and a white man, George Washington Hall, who had taken up with a Chinook slave woman, Jane (Methusnah).[10] For a time he had been on good terms with those of her race at Chinook Point on a claim received from them in a December 12, 1848, agreement witnessed by Roman Catholic clergyman Toussaint Mesplié and signed by two Chinook chiefs. One of the chiefs was Elwahco[11] (Elwah, Ellewa, or the like), son of Comcomly's sister Carcumcum;[12] the other was Chenamus (another, not the well-known chief who had died a few years before). Under the questionably legal agreement, Hall was not to sell the land unless the United States should purchase Indian title to it.[13] In another agreement with Hall on February 24, 1851, the Chinook tribe was permitted to draw water from a stream on his place.[14] Within ten days of that agreement Hall claimed that natives had broken down his garden fence, cut down his fruit trees, and committed other damage for which he wished the offenders punished.[15]

In the face of white encroachments Clatsops and Chinooks at midcentury clung to little village beachheads. At the upper end of Chinook Village at the mouth of the Chinook River were four houses under a chief Comcomly, son of Tatoosh.† A little way down from there were

---

* Under provisions of the Donation Land Act, a white, married individual, settled on land before September 1, 1850, could claim 640 acres of public land, while a single man could claim 320 acres. Each single male had to be eighteen and a citizen of the country or declare his intention of becoming one before December 1, 1851. The act provided that those settled between December 1, 1851, and December 1, 1853, were entitled to but half the acreage for a claim.

† In 1902 testimonies Samuel Mallette and Catherine George substantiated the fact that a Comcomly (not the chief), perhaps this one, was a signer of an 1851 treaty with the U.S.

four more houses, and near the southeast extremity of the village, two, for a total of ten houses sheltering some 40 people, who still abandoned the villages in winter. At Qwatsamuts village, under the leadership of Kulchute, were 20 people in four houses. At the Chinook River mouth, under Chief Narchotta (Narkarty) lived 10 people in four houses. Further upstream at Grays Bay lived 20 Wahkiakums and Kathlamets under Selawish, who wintered on the Nemah River. At that river was one permanent dwelling of 20 souls under Tletah. On the nearby Naselle River was a seven-house village of 40 people under Quewish. On Willapa Bay 35 Chinooks lived in two villages under Chiefs Seyehkehul and Kanqualth. The total number of these Chinooks, Wahkiakums, and Kathlamets was 185 people living in thirty-seven houses.[16]

As they had from the time of promoter Hall Kelley, white men sought to build towns of their own on the lower Columbia. Thinking Oregon City (in the Willamette Valley), the major Oregon white settlement, too far from the sea, Dr. Elijah White in March, 1848, from a donation land claim in Bakers Bay, projected a future metropolis, Pacific City. Platted in 1851 by J. D. Holman, it was an object for wild speculation, rivaling that of San Francisco and making faces at its rival, Astoria, across the river. One critic called the project the product of White's "disordered brain," but it never had a fair chance of survival. By 1852 the president, under an act of Congress authorizing him to reserve 640 acres for military purposes, would order the establishment of a military post, first called Fort Cape Disappointment and later Fort Canby Reservation, incorporating the townsite of Pacific City. Like a large hall reportedly burned there by soldiers, Pacific City would be doomed.[17]

The failure of Pacific City meant that for a while longer the north side of the Columbia (unlike Astoria, which grew rapidly in the 1850's) would retain its primitive character. Recently (1846–47), artists of note such as the Canadian Paul Kane and the American John Mix Stanley had captured by brush a people who believed that the two, by painting their likenesses, had taken something from them, and the women, that they had exerted unlimited influence over them.[18] Whites were shocked when a revenge-seeking party of Chinook braves caused a shaman to jump a white man's ship, after which they killed him.[19] Shortly after this, natives at Chinook Village tried to starve a little girl to death, but they failed at the intervention of white citizenry, who offered to redeem her.[20] At Willapa Bay whites rescued from a chief a slave girl he had tried to kill.[21] And Elwahco, possibly under the influence of drink, shocked

government. *Rolls of Certain Indian Tribes in Oregon and Washington. House Exec. Doc.* No. 133, 59 Cong., 2 sess., 24, 28.

white settlers by mistreating Dolly, one of many slaves brought to him by his wife Jane, daughter of a chief.[22]

Seeking to rescue the Indians from such barbarities were two Roman Catholic clerics, Toussaint Mesplié (working first as a novice) and J. Lionnet, called by the natives "Les Plates," the nearest they could come to pronouncing the French *les pretes*. On December 28, 1847, Lionnet had been sent to establish a mission at Astoria,* but instead he had founded it on the more primitive Columbia north shore.[23] With approaching winter, in letters to his superior Lionnet cataloged the difficulties of his task—ill health, meager food (mostly salmon obtained from the Chinooks in exchange for blankets purchased at Fort George, of which he had only one left), worn out shoes and trousers, a flimsy windowless house, and back-breaking work clearing land. Less concerned for himself than for his flock, he saw them threatened by many evils, one of which was their fear of baptism because several of their children, formerly given this sacrament, had died. "But their greatest obstacle," he wrote, "that we hold against this nation is their drinks which they get in abundance from the Americans." He continued: "It is sad and lamentable all the mess which occasions their disorders. Because when drunk these poor people strike each other. . . ." To him "not less disgusting" was gambling, which "inspired them to behave rowdily among themselves."[24]

Like the Protestants, Catholic clerics such as Lionnet found the "Chenook Gibberish," as Dr. Tolmie termed it, "too defective for the conveyance of Christian ideas."[25] Additions to it of words from the Chehalis language, because of increased association of Chinooks with those people, did nothing to further its utility to clergymen. Nevertheless, Catholic churchmen, like Demers in 1838 and 1839, had diligently composed a Chinook Jargon dictionary of catechisms, prayers, and hymns, which Reverend Francis N. Blanchet would revise and update in 1867.[26] Because of French traders on the Columbia, most Spanish words of the jargon had been replaced by French words, and it was easier for Indians (many of whom spoke considerable French because of their contact with Canadians) to learn that language than it was for priests to teach them the jargon. Before mid-century, Chinooks were singing French songs taught them by missionaries.[27]

In his correspondence Lionnet revealed an attempt to be optimistic amid obstacles to his work. "My savages," he wrote, "begin to communicate with the grace. God had put his arms around them and their

---

* The register of the mission, the Stella Maris at Chinook Point, for 1848 consisted mostly of half-bloods. M. Leona Nichols, *The Mantle of Elias: The Story of Fathers Blanchet and Demers in Early Oregon*, 333.

frightened course is opening to the light of the truth." Again he wrote, "Your Grandeur wants me to go on with them and shortly Marie will see growing in the hearts of the Chinooks the adoration of her son." In his correspondence he also cited the major cause of the abandonment of his mission, presumably in 1852, when he penned: "At this moment our savages are few in number and several of them who remain are now traveling so that there are only small numbers to whom I teach the catechism." On first coming to the Chinooks he had gone around instructing them in their own lodges. With the building of his station he had believed they would gather there for instruction. As his words indicate, events had not worked out that way.[28]

In 1852 an envoy of the French government would find his countryman Lionnet hanging on at the point in his cabin "perched like a house for the shipwrecked," rescuing his fellowmen like those plucked from the sea—all the while surrounded by burial canoes, the symbols of death. At that time, Lionnet's only companions were two small *métis* (half-bloods) rescued on the death of their parents—the two raised in the vestry as "geniuses of civilization compared with the Indian tribes, which, although washed by holy water, continued no less savage."[29] An American traveler talking with Mesplié and Lionnet stated that the fathers confessed their lack of progress because their neophytes were "rather thick headed!"—a characterization coming out rather badly in translation from the French.[30]

An American, Patrick McGowan, purchased half of Lionnet's land for nine hundred dollars—a reasonable price considering that some of it was a wide stretch of beach. McGowan would later testify that the priest, yielding his land because he did not wish to become an American citizen but to remain French, told him that the natives among whom he worked "had dwindled away so that, as Shakespeare said, 'His occupation was now gone' and he wanted to get out."[31] As with Reverend Frost on the south side of the river, how much permanent good Lionnet on the north side accomplished only heaven knows. One American thought he knew when he wrote: "All of them [the natives] had a general idea of the Christian religion, but not one believed it, although several had been considered, during the residence of the priest at Chenook, as exemplary members of the Church. But when the restrictions of the Church were taken away by the absence of the priest, they all returned to their old heathenism again."[32] Shortly after the purchase of the priest's land, McGowan settled at the southeast end of Chinook Village (southeast of Chinook Point, which was earlier a bulging shoreline from Point Ellice on the south to as far north as the present town of Chinook, Washington). McGowan well knew that the stretch of river from Chinook River to Point Ellice was ideal for fishing. The Chinooks had known this for years, and so had their neighbors the Chehalises, who lived in what was perhaps a temporary village near Chinook Point, and the Clatsops, in such a village a little further north.[33]

Chinook Point beach buzzed with excitement during fishing seasons. To meet the challenge of salmon migrating from the ocean into the Columbia off its north shore,[34] Indians, half-bloods, and French Canadians loaded into their skiffs seines, one end of which was fastened or held to the shore. When the skiffs semicircled to shore a few rods below, the trapped salmon darted and plunged in all directions, as did the fishermen trying to kill them with short heavy clubs, half-bloods and Canadians outdoing the Indians in the slaughter.[35]

Chinook Village now became the center of the commercial salmon business. To symbolize its new image it took the name Chinookville, in deference to the village of Indian houses there. In about 1852 Rocque Ducheney (De Cheney, Duchene, or the like) would run a store there for the Hudson's Bay Company, trading mostly with Indians and half-bloods.[36] A post office would be established there on October 19, 1852, with Washington Hall as postmaster.*[37] Contributing to the excitement of fishing seasons at Chinook Point were human conflicts, such as "a little war" breaking out there in 1847. Happenings of this kind were nothing new, but the introduction of liquor was adding to them a volatile dimension. At that place the same year some Chinooks tried to kill a medicine man who had treated a young girl. When she died they plied the doctor with as much liquor as he could hold, and when he passed out they stabbed him "in many places."[38] Aware of what firewater was doing to their people, Elwahco and Chenamus had included in their agreement with Washington Hall a provision that he stop the sale of spirits to them. As on the Astoria side of the river, the liquor flow did not dry up, and prosecutions were too few and far between. There were some prosecutions, however, for United States Marshal Joe Meek wrote the Solicitor of the Treasury that a five-hundred-dollar fine paid to him by a defendant for selling liquor in Clatsop County, Oregon Territory, had been expended in discharge of debts already incurred in the necessary costs of his office.[39]

* Present-day Chinook, Washington (where a post office was established on March 17, 1892), is four miles northwest of the old Chinook post office. Chinook territory was in Pacific County, established by the Oregon Territorial legislature on February 3, 1851. The intended county seat had been planned for the expectant Pacific City but, due to the latter's failure, was transferred to Chinookville. Oysterville, Washington, first settled by R. H. Espy and I. A. Clark on Willapa Bay in 1854, was designated county seat of Pacific County in an election in May, 1855. In the November, 1892, election South Bend would become the county seat.

In early 1850 Lieutenant W. E. Jones, in charge of federal troops stationed at Astoria, wrote Governor Lane that it appeared that Chinook Indians had murdered a passenger lost from the ship *Forrest* and that two natives involved in the foul play had been arrested. Jones reported that their fellows, while drunk, had threatened violence if their comrades were not released. Believing his command inadequate to cope with the problem, Jones dispatched a message to territorial officials for help.[40] What he did not report in that message was that some of his troops, given to drink themselves, were none too scrupulous about selling whiskey to the Indians.[41] In receipt of Jones's letter, an Oregon territorial official wrote Major J. S. Hatheway of the 1st Artillery at Fort Vancouver (a military post established in 1849 and known first as Fort Columbia and later as Vancouver Barracks) for help, stating: "Inasmuch as there is no civil power here adequate to the emergency, I respectfully submit the matter to your consideration and invoke such aid as it may be in your power to afford, in placing the murderers [one of whom escaped] within the reach of justice." Hatheway assured territorial officials that a party had been dispatched from Fort Vancouver to Astoria on March 18 with orders to apprehend all persons suspected of implication in the murder and to bring them to Fort Vancouver until they could be arraigned before a civil tribunal for trial. In poor health and unsure of his responsibilities in such matters, Hatheway was in no position to provide aggressive leadership in apprehending the allegedly guilty and following up on the warning of Oregon Indian Superintendent Anson Dart to stop the liquor flow at the mouth of the Columbia.[42]

Some officials believed that one way to protect Indians from such vices as the liquor traffic was to confine them on reservations. There was perhaps less question among those officials of the propriety of shunting Indians onto the confines than there was about where the confines should be located. Under the pressure of white settlers who wanted to rid themselves of Indians, Governor Lane, under appointment not only as territorial governor but also as superintendent of Indian affairs, recommended that Indians be paid for their lands and be removed from the settlements. He also recommended that an agency be established in the fertile Grande Ronde Valley (in present-day eastern Oregon) and a subagency further east at Fort Hall (in present-day southern Idaho). He recommended an agency on Puget Sound and a subagency in the Umpqua Valley for areas west of the mountains in sparse white settlements, but already whites were beginning to appropriate those areas. The first Oregon territorial delegate to Congress, Samuel Royal Thurston, urged that body to enact legislation to move Indians from west of the Cascade Mountains to east of that range. This suggestion was met with anger by natives on both sides of the mountains—those of the west not wishing to leave their ancestral homes and the graves of their people, and those of the east fearing an influx of coastal Indians who might bring diseases and upset the delicate balance of nature under which man survived in that arid interior. The act creating Oregon Territory had provided that $10,000 be appropriated for presents to Indians; a further appropriation of like amount was authorized by Congress on May 15, 1850, under the urging of Thurston, for presents to be given the Indians until the government should purchase their lands.[43]

Pleas of western Oregon Indians to retain their homes fell on deaf ears, for an act of Congress on June 5, 1850, provided for the negotiation of treaties and the appointment of three commissioners to treat with Indians west of the mountains to remove them to the interior. The act also provided for extension of laws regulating trade and intercourse with Indians east of the Rocky Mountains to those of Oregon and the creation of the Office of Superintendent of Indian Affairs of Oregon, which was separated from the office of the governor. The superintendent of Indian affairs was instructed to pay attention to the work of civilizing the Indians, part of which task was to be accomplished through cooperation between the Indian service and missionaries. Under the act, three agents were to be appointed.[44]

From Astoria on February 5, 1851, the acting subagent at Astoria for Chinook and Clatsop Indians, Robert Shortess, provided a pretreaty census of these peoples. Of Chinooks there were 171 souls—99 full-bloods, 36 half-bloods, and 36 slaves; of Clatsops, 80—54 full-bloods, 18 half-bloods, and 8 slaves.[45] For lower Columbia River peoples from the Cowlitz River downstream he recommended a reservation (on which there were but few white settlers) lying north of the Columbia and west of the Wahkiakum village, extending north to the Chehalis River, and with a portion of land running into Willapa Bay to secure fisheries occupied by Chinooks.[46] Shortess' friend, George Gibbs, with whom he must have discussed the proposal, had recommended for the lower Columbia River peoples a similar area—a tract of land on the north side of the Columbia, south of the Chehalis River and between the Cowlitz River and the Pacific—about fifty square miles with good salmon grounds on the Columbia and enough area near the coast for natives to fish and raise animals and crops.[47]

Shortess suggested meeting with the Indians out of range of whiskey peddlers at Astoria or on the Chehalis River in early April when the Indians would be gathering for salmon fishing but before the season was in full swing.[48] Officials hoped that the increasing anger of western Oregon Indians at the loss of their lands by removal could be quieted by distributing various gifts to them. In 1847 Lieutenant Neil Howison,* on an American naval reconnaissance expedition to Oregon, had suggested annual distributions to them of a few thousand flannel frocks and good blankets, "for an Indian would rather go naked than wear a bad one."[49] Concerned lest natives believe the gifts were from the Hudson's Bay Company, government officials quickly instructed their agents to dispel the misapprehension by purchasing them instead from American merchants wherever possible.[50] This did not raise the quality of goods in the natives' thinking, for they continued to favor company goods over American ones. "Whoever had traded with an Indian," wrote an early American settler, ". . . must have often heard the remark, *"Wake close okoke Boston mámoke, wake car'qua King George, quánisum close kon'away icktas King George mámoke*—This is not good, this American manufacture; it is not like the English; that is always good."[51]

On April 22, 1851, Dart reported to Shortess that he was sending for the latter's Clatsops and Chinooks six pieces of 221 yards, of which he was to disburse 7 yards to each woman.[52] Since no council had been arranged to treat with them in April, Shortess awaited an opportunity for some gathering like those at Chinook Village to distribute the goods.[53] In early May he received the yardage and some twenty blankets, but he requested a few more of the latter so there would be one per person, since some, on not receiving them, had gone away dissatisfied. An Astoria firm offered to meet the blanket supply by selling some they had on hand at New York cost and freight.[54] Some of these blankets would perhaps cover the dead. Three years later a white man at Chinook would state that natives placed an elderly Indian in a large trunk buttressed by as many blankets as they could pack in, after which they piled logs and effects around him and burned his house and canoe, leaving his old "cloocherman" [wife] homeless. "This, he would write, "is their custome. . . ."[55] And of course there would be the inevitable trading of clothes and blankets for whiskey.[56]

On receiving from Anson Dart, the now very busy superintendent of Indian affairs for Oregon Territory, a copy of the act of Congress regulating trade and intercourse with the Indians, Shortess had written him on November 18, 1850, that he had held a talk with traders and shopkeepers at Astoria about the liquor traffic and that when instructed they had expressed willingness to have bonds and take licenses; ". . . but," Shortess had concluded, "the grogsellers grumbled."[57] Like

* When Howison was on the Columbia he learned of the boundary settlement between Britain and the United States at north Latitude 49°. Neil M. Howison, *Report of Lieut. Neil M. Howison, United States Navy, to the Commander of the Pacific Squadron*, 3.

most other Indian agents married to Indian women, Shortess, with the interest of his wife's people at heart, sympathized for a wronged and injured race which, as he put it, until then had been almost wholly neglected by the government. "It is impossible," he had written, "not to feel indignant."[58] The liquor flow made it much easier for Indians of the lower river, like those elsewhere in America, to part with their lands and fisheries and to believe the promises of whites that the Great Father would compensate them for their loss or that they would feel his wrath should they not yield to him. Especially pitiful on the lower Columbia was the plight of half-blood children. When their parents died they fell victim to squatters who dispossessed them of farms and homes, thus making them derelicts between the races and "servants or stumpets" in their own lands.[59]

As the white-red treaty council showdown for Indian removal neared in western Oregon, Shortess increased his pressure on his superiors to protect those in his care. To Dart on February 5, 1851, he wrote: "It is my opinion that if brought together upon a reservation, secluded from the influence of the whites, and affording all means of pasturage and agriculture that they can be materially improved in character and condition."[60] The best way, opined Shortess, for Indians to respect the government was for it to pay them for their lands. "For myself," he wrote, "I have so long preached patience and hope to them that I am almost ashamed to do so any longer."[61] Yet he believed the government could salvage itself in their eyes, noting, as had others, that the Indians were friendlier to whites than they were to each other. Aware of this fact, Indian Commissioner Luke Lea wanted Indians to enter into written treaties of peace and amity among themselves, referring their misunderstandings to the "umpirage" of proper representatives of the United States government.[62]

The commission, established under the Indian Treaty Act of 1850, had negotiated six treaties with Willamette Valley Indians after (but before they knew that) its authority was transferred to Dart.* It was Dart's task to treat with those living near the mouth of the Columbia and elsewhere in Oregon Territory. The secretary of the interior requested troops to accompany Dart to the lower river, as was often the practice in treaty negotiations, but the War Department informed the secretary that the only troops in the general area were two companies of artillery—one stationed on Puget Sound (at Fort Steilacoom, established in 1849) and the other dividing duties between Astoria and Fort

---

* The six treaties were made with the Santiam, Tualatin, Yamhill, and Lakmiut bands of the Kalapuya tribe and with two Molala bands.

Vancouver.[63] Unable to fortify himself with federal troops, Dart armed himself for his forthcoming treaty making with an array of gifts which Chinooks and Clatsops customarily received from traders—clay pipes, cotton handkerchiefs, molasses, tobacco coils, and the like.

On August 1 Dart reached the place chosen as the council grounds, Tansey Point, some eight miles downstream from Astoria, a spot marked by sand dunes, low marshy ground, and sandy beach. Assisted by the Reverend Henry H. Spalding, agent; Josiah Parrish, subagent; W. W. Raymond, interpreter; and N. Du Bois, secretary, Dart prepared to treat with what he termed the "bands" of Chinook Indians to remove them east of the mountains out of the way of whites. From the first treaty, signed on August 5, until the last, one week later, he would effect with headmen representing 320 Indians the cession to the United States of all country from Willapa Bay to Tillamook Head—more than one hundred miles along the coast and sixty miles up the Columbia River, a tract of more than three million acres—at a cost of $91,300 payable in annuities over a ten-year period.*

Dart treated first with the Clatsops. All men, women, and children of the band were present—a contrast to attendance of only portions of tribes at treaty councils east of the Cascade Mountains, where not all chiefs signed for the tribes. Fascinated with "writings" received from time to time from whites, Clatsop men were anxious initially to sign or "make their mark." When they discovered that Dart wished them to yield their lands, they objected vociferously, complaining of injustices done them by the government, who they said had taken their lands without compensation.† Whites, these Clatsops complained, were farming those lands, selling them for as much as six thousand dollars, from which the Indians had received nothing. They said they would not talk until Dart stopped ships from entering the Columbia and destroyed two sawmills they said were frightening the fish away. When the superintendent told them frankly he could not meet their demands, they agreed to withdraw them on condition that they be given two reservations of

* This acreage, added to that ceded by three more treaties which he effected (with natives of Port Orford and Clackamas Indians in the Willamette Valley), would give the United States more than six million acres of land. Dart to Lea, August 15, 1851, Microcopy of Records in the National Archives, *Oregon Superintendency of Indian Affairs*, No. 2, Roll 3; Anson Dart "Report [to Luke Lea, November 7, 1851] concerning treaties negotiated as Superintendent of Indian Affairs, Oregon Territory, with Chinook and other Tribes," photocopy of manuscript, Bancroft Library.

† Because whites coming to Oregon wanted the Indian land, the Oregon Provisional Government enacted legislation for the staking and recording of settlement land claims. Under the law an individual was allowed to claim up to 640 acres, providing he occupied and made improvements on the particular land.

some ten square miles each. On Dart's objection to this, they held councils with neighboring bands in which they agreed to settle for one reservation if it would cover Clatsop burial grounds and lodges at Point Adams in a space three and one-half miles long, two miles wide at the northern end, and one mile wide at the southern end. For this they ceded some one-half million acres, including the already white-occupied fertile Clatsop Plain. With regard to the loss of most of their lands, some have cynically noted that Article 4 of the treaty permitted them to "pick up whales that may be cast away on the beach."[64] Contrarily it is one of the best things the government could have done for them. Their forefathers believed the huge mammals had been sent to their beaches by supernatural beings on the far side of the ocean, and all the people in return observed strict tabus in cutting and processing these gifts.

Following the council, in a letter to the commissioner of Indian affairs, Dart made no mention of the promise of goods to the Clatsops, but in following years they and their Chief Tostow would complain that he had failed to deliver the goods he had promised them at Tansey Point or somewhere else.[65] In a more positive vein, Clatsops, Chinooks, and others with whom Dart would treat would be spared the removal they and other western Oregon Indians opposed as unsettling not only to them but also to the spirits of their dead. Worshiping in church buildings, white men had no understanding of what the land meant in a religious sense to the Chinooks and Clatsops as a resting place for their dead, but neither did they understand what the land meant to the Indians as a spiritual arena for the living. Natives believed that each of its myriad objects had a soul. To many of its prominent places their youth went questing for their spirits, their *tamanawas*. When successful in seeking visions and dreaming dreams on their lonely vigils, they took their spirits from the first objects they saw before they returned to paint and carve boards that would protect their lodges in life and their graves in death.

On more materialistic grounds than all of this, Indians of the lower Columbia would be spared removal. Dart, for example, thought they should be so spared, for he found them industrious, moreso than many of their white neighbors,* at tasks like rail splitting, farming, and boating, and he noted that they were willing to work for much lower pay than

---

* Patrick McGowan would later testify that "The white laborer was not a very good class, mostly hunters and men who lived in the mountains." "Copy of Testimony taken in 1902, in Astoria in support of a claim of *Chinook Indian Tribe against the United States* for land in the State of Washington, near the mouth of the Columbia River. Containing historical material relating to the Chinook villages and the people, with some reference to the Clatsop Indian Tribe in Oregon," manuscript, Oregon Historical Society, 69.

that demanded by whites.[66] In the 1840's Chinook Indians did farm work for white men, receiving for a week's labor a white man's shirt worth 83 cents.

On August 7 Dart and his agents had a graphic example that they were treating with mere remnants of once populous bands. On that day they treated separately with one Wallooska—head of a Clatsop family of seven,[67] only survivors of the Nucqueclahwemuck villagers. Lands which he ceded to the government, beginning at the eastern end of Ahwahpinpin Point near Astoria on the eastern boundary of Clatsop lands bordering those of Kathlamets, extended south as far as Saddle Mountain, west of the Lewis and Clark River, north of its mouth, and east along Youngs Bay to the place of beginning. It was valuable for choice timber and a mill site on the Lewis and Clark River. Wallooska was also permitted to live out his days there and was promised $1,500 and $300 in cash and merchandise, clothing, hardware, and miscellaneous items to be delivered.[68]

Like Wallooska, other natives of the lower Columbia were, as Dart reported, "fully aware of the rapidity with which, as a people, they are wasting away," on which account "they could not be persuaded to fix a time beyond ten years to receive all of their money in exchange for their lands." Most of the tribes, thus, were promised annuities within a decade, with a percentage of them in cash, although this plan was contrary to instructions given Dart, who believed the Indians would waste money and clothing in excess of their yearly needs. Thinking that their oily fish diet should have killed them some years before, Dart sought to temper it with payments of bread and flour.[69] He also included payments of clothing to protect them from inclement weather, having earlier informed the commissioner of Indian affairs that nearly all Chinook Indians dressed as nearly like whites as "their means will allow."[70] At about this time the Chinooks abandoned personal tattooing. The only adornment embellishing their white men's clothing was a sort of band of black ostrich feather purchased from the Hudson's Bay Company and worn around their caps.[71] Farm tools and cooking utensils Dart had included for them would not, in themselves, have ensured their longevity.

After Wallooska, Dart made treaties (August 8) with Konniacks (Upper Chinooks), whom Lewis and Clark had called "Skilleuts,"[72] and with other "bands" he erroneously called Chinooks—the (Salish) Tillamooks (August 6 and 7), and the (Athabaskan) Klatskanies (August 9). On August 8 Dart concluded a treaty with Wahkiakums, who ceded lands along the north side of the Columbia in exchange for a $700 annuity for ten years, $100 in cash and the remainder in goods; the privilege of occupying their place of residence and fishing on the Columbia and two small streams; the privilege of cutting timber for building and fuel; hunting rights; and the usual clothing, hardware, and miscellaneous items.[73] On the ninth Dart treated with "Wheelappas" (Willopahs) and "Quillequeoquas" (Kwalhioquas),* whom he erroneously designated as "Chinook" but who were in reality Athabaskan peoples.[74]

In the August 9 Kathlamet treaty those people ceded lands (on which stood Astoria and Fort George) from Ahwahpinpin Point forty miles east along the south side of the Columbia, running southerly into the interior some twenty miles. Also reserved from sale were two small islands in the Columbia River.[75]

Signing the treaties on the same day, August 9, were twenty headmen of the Chinooks proper (whom Dart called the "Lower Band of Chinooks"), the largest of the tribes treated with—in Dart's words "[once] the most powerful Nation upon the Pacific coast; now wasted to a few over three hundred souls."[76] The Chinooks ceded a large area north of the Columbia River.† In exchange for their cession they were to receive a $2,000 annuity for ten years in the form of $400 in cash, clothing, hardware, tobacco, soap, molasses, a keg of powder, and some rifle caps—all of which reads like a bill of lading of a ship on the Northwest Coast or the inventory of a trading post on the Columbia River. They

---

* In this report Dart speaks of the "Wheelappas and Quillequeoquas." The latter name is mentioned in the treaty, Article 6, stating that the land cession of the Wheelappas in Article 1 embraced land formerly owned by Quillequeoquas. Dart was apparently dealing with two groups of Athabaskans (or one Athabaskan and one Salish). (See note *, page 5 chapter 1.) Gibbs, in his *Tribes of Western Washington and Northwestern Oregon,* 164, calls these groups Willopahs (the same as the river along which they lived), stating that the linguist Horatio Hale termed the same peoples Kwalhioquas. Much mixing of terminology arose after Dart erroneously called all Indians with whom he treated at Tansey Point "Chinook." The fact that the apparent last vestiges of Chinooks proper living on Willapa Bay were often referred to as Willapas has further added to the confusion in distinguishing Chinook Willapas from Athabaskan (Salish?) Willopahs.

† The land area ceded by Chinooks proper is defined in the treaty made with them, as are land areas ceded by other tribes outlined in their treaties. These land areas correspond roughly to the actual land areas of each tribe. Attorneys who prepared a petition of Chinook claims for the Claims Commission in 1951 erroneously stated: ". . . no treaty was entered into with the Chinook (Proper) consisting of the Willapa or Shoalwater Bay Chinook and Waukiakum Bands." *Before the Indian Claims Commission of the United States: The Chinook Tribe, the Wauhkiakum Band and the Willapa or Shoalwater Bay Bands of Chinook, the Kathlamet Tribe of Chinook, the Clatsop Tribe of Chinook, and the Nucqueclahwemuck Band of Chinook, Petitioners,* vs. *The United States of America, Defendant,* Docket No. 234, Petitioner's Findings of Fact and Brief, 26. Copies of the treaty may be found in "Copies of certain treaties made Aug. 8–9, 1851, at Tansey Point," photocopy of manuscript, Bancroft Library. Copies of the treaty appear as well in C. F. Coan, "The First Stage of the Federal Indian Policy in the Pacific Northwest, 1849–1852," *Oregon Historical Quarterly,* XXII (1921), 75–78, 81–83.

were permitted to reserve trom sale certain small tracts of land for their residences, where they could build, fish, graze stock, cut timber, pick cranberries, and cultivate land.

In the treaties the Indians acceded to a stipulation that those white men claiming land under the "Oregon Land Bill" (Oregon Provisional Government Land Law, stimulated by the Linn Bills, providing a section of land with no requirement of proof of claims other than a description of boundaries) be allowed to hold their claims.[77] It appeared that Indians of the lower Columbia with whom Dart dealt had less attachment to the land than did many other American Indians, but it was perhaps with some exaggeration that an early settler would write: "If I or any of the settlers had been allowed to have purchased the Indian titles to the land when we first went there, the whole tract from the Columbia to Fuca Straits could have been bought for a few trifling presents."[78] In the East, one C. T. Chamberlain, two years before the Tansey Point treaties, had written a letter to President James Polk claiming that his wife was heiress to a large tract of land purchased by her grandfather, Captain Gray, from natives at the mouth of the Columbia River. Chamberlain claimed to have seen the deeds to it covering some six million acres. His pleas, largely unsupported, were to no avail, for he was informed that the United States had exclusive right of purchasing land from Indian tribes and that no sale was valid which may have been made by Indians unless recognized and sanctioned by the government and them.[79]

An exception at Tansey Point to the granting to settlers of permission to retain land claims was that of Washington Hall. His case proved to be one of the most troublesome problems at the councils. Adamant for his removal, the Chinooks refused to "talk" in council unless it were assured, forcing Dart to agree to Hall's removal on pain of discontinuing negotiations altogether. The superintendent found it easy to concur with the Chinook assessment of this man he called a "whiskey trader."[80] Chinooks had grievances, other than liquor sales,* against Hall for laying claim "to the ground covering their whole village," from which, in violation of his agreement, they alleged that he had sought to exclude them,[81] insulting them further by marrying a slave woman. Behind the proposed removal of Hall lay various facts which quite naturally were not included in the treaty. Although Hall, as noted above, had entered into a legally questionable agreement with Chinook Indians for his land, which he had "bought with gold their good will to it," Shortess claimed

* In testimony, Mary Kelley claimed that Hall had sold liquor to Indians. "Copy of Testimony . . . in support of a claim of *Chinook Indian Tribe against the United States*," 81–83.

it belonged to that agent's own regal wife.[82] Whether Shortess, popular with his wife's people, even supporting some of them in his own household,[83] had gained the ear of white and Indian principals at the Chinook treaty councils for Hall's removal is unknown. It would appear he had. On September 6 Dart notified Hall by letter that he was to be removed. Hall responded on the fourteenth, blaming Shortess for the treaty provision for his removal.

Dart hurried the treaties off to Washington, D.C., but no action was taken on them. Perhaps no one was more pleased by this nonaction than Washington Hall. In analyzing nonratification of the treaties, Dart thought one possible reason had been the provision for Hall's removal. He believed another to have been occupation by two settlers of the proposed Clatsop Reservation at Point Adams, and a third reason the fact that no other official had accompanied him when he negotiated with the Clackamas tribe. Perhaps a more valid reason, as a student of the treaties has pointed out, was that "in most cases they were made with insignificant bands,"[84] and another more likely reason might have been that Dart had failed in the original purpose for negotiating with Indians, which was to get them to agree to remove east of the Cascade Mountains where they would be out of the way of white settlers.

Never given to elaborate preparations for winter, Chinooks and Clatsops faced posttreaty months with more "improvidence" than usual in consequence of awaiting their promised payments. Expecting income in this form, they had not sold fish and cranberries to whites to get a little money. Even had they wanted to, they would have sold few furs, for that trade on the lower river was "substantially extinct" by midcentury.[85] Shortess' replacement, Raymond, reporting from Tansey Point on October 17, 1853, expressed fears that the failure of Chinooks and Clatsops to receive goods had made them indolent and easy victims of liquor. In his annual report that year, the new Oregon superintendent of Indian affairs (appointed in March, 1853), Joel Palmer, would claim that gifts presented to the Indians to help keep them quiet until the treaties were ratified had made them indolent.[86] Awaiting the government to fulfill its promises, Chinooks and Clatsops suffered extremely in the years following the Tansey Point councils as omnipresent liquor did its work, inflaming them to continued acts of violence. Agent Raymond's suggestion of banishment of those found intoxicated offered no solution.[87] Superintendent Palmer's suggestion, because of the nonratification of the treaties, that punishment of lawlessness among natives be tribal rather than individual, may have had some merit, but it likewise offered no real solution to their problems.

In 1853 the Chinooks and Clatsops, separated for ages by a river, would be separated at that stream by territorial jurisdictions. Whatever this separation would involve, it could scarcely work less evil to them than forces already at work. While white men made these changes, Chinooks and Clatsops continued to live in "perpetual peace and friendship" with the United States as they had promised at Tansey Point that they would. But one year after they signed the treaties it was evident that the United States might not do likewise. After the president sent the treaties to the Senate on August 3, 1852, they were read and printed. From then on they would gather dust. Thus, as it would turn out, Tansey Point was a symbol of Indian faith and trust moreso than American.

14. From River Bar to Bar of Justice

> Thus we see that Humanity and Patriotism both require and demand immediate and energetic action. Let all, then, who cherish these noble and ennobling virtues, rally round the standard of the suffering Red man, until the tramp of gathering millions shall shake the land to its center; and in the thunderous volume of concentrated power, send forth the truest expression of a great People's Will. And this will be nothing less than an act of self-preservation; for, in restoring freedom to others, we shall forever consecrate and protect our own.
>
> John Beeson, *Plea For the Indian*

CHINOOKS AND CLATSOPS were separated into differing political jurisdictions on March 2, 1853, when President Millard Fillmore signed the bill creating Washington Territory. It was organized that year under its governor and superintendent of Indian affairs, Isaac I. Stevens. Under the new organization Chinooks came under the Southern Indian District of the new territory. In 1854 their agent, William H. Tappan, visiting them at the mouth of the Columbia River, "the stronghold of their fathers," noted that they had been reduced (to 126 souls) more than had interior tribes from white men's drink and disease. Smallpox reappeared the year of the changing political jurisdiction, reducing Chinook numbers still further as though in fulfillment of their own prophecies of imminent extinction. Appearing first at the mouth of the Columbia, the disease spread south of Clatsop Plain, northerly to the Chehalis River, Puget Sound, and Olympic Peninsula areas, and up the Columbia to the interior. It dropped Chinook-Chehalis numbers to some seventy souls at Willapa Bay, where in some lodges on the southern peninsula corpses were found wrapped in blankets like people asleep. The death toll might have been higher had not some natives taken to the hills to escape contagion.[1] Mrs. Julia Russel in 1902 would maintain that all Chinooks proper signing the Tansey Point treaty were dead and that at least one-half dozen of them had succumbed to smallpox.[2] In reply to Stevens' request for a census of Chinook Indians, a white citizen of Cathlamet, Washington Territory, on January 12, 1854, provided the governor a numbering of all Indians from the mouth of the Cowlitz to that of the Columbia. From Cape Disappointment to Chinook he reported a mere thirteen men, nine women, eight slaves, and three children, and from that point upriver but eleven men, fourteen women, fifteen slaves, and six children (Wahkiakums and Kathlamets). All of these lower river peoples, he reported, continually shifted residence up and down the river, posing no hindrance to white settlement and only requiring from the government assurances that they be permitted to live and die where they were.[3]

From Chinook, a white man in June, 1854, wrote of a dozen of his race at that place; there were no white women nearer than three-quarters of a mile, but "no end to the Indians."[4] He should have lived there before the intermittent fever, had he wished to see many Indians. Lining the Chinook beach were several white houses, which from Astoria looked like a row of rocks.[5] One white man thought business dull there and money scarce along the lower Columbia.[6] Business was not so bad that whites did not purchase delicious cranberries from Chinooks, who gathered them in the fall and winter on the settler-free peninsula between Willapa Bay and the Pacific Ocean. In 1854 natives sold a bushel of the berries for fifty pounds of flour costing $2.50 in Astoria or $3.00 in Portland.[7] Another equally delicious food whites found hard to resist was oysters, which Chinooks gathered in nearby Willapa Bay. As early as 1852 an extensive trade in oysters was developed on the northern margin of the bay by three or four California companies, which purchased them of Chinook and Chehalis Indians for the San Francisco market.[8] By June, 1853, nineteen ships had entered the bay, some several times, carrying oysters and mostly miscellaneous cargoes such as pilings and furs.[9] An 1854 report from San Francisco estimated that the Willapa Bay oyster business amounted to more than one hundred thousand dollars yearly.[10] Shortly, annual oyster shipments would reach some thirty thousand bushels.[11] By 1860 white residents, irritated by territorial government regulations of the industry, would have the nerve to warn all "foreign Indians," such as those coming, as they had for years, from points as far distant as Puget Sound, to cease collecting oysters for sale.[12]

Partly because of the oyster trade, Chinook habitation had shifted somewhat from the Columbia River to Willapa Bay, where in 1854 lived seventy-one of their tribe. Over old trails between there and the Columbia, traffic was as heavy as ever, and even heavier than ever in liquor. At Willapa Bay, Indians traded oysters for liquor by the barrel. This they drank and traded to other natives of the Columbia and Chehalis rivers.[13] Members of the white community viewed this trade with alarm not so much for what it did to Indians as for what it did to whites.* One of their spokesmen, the editor of the *Oregonian*, complained bitterly of drunken Indians plundering the brig *Vandalia* some five miles north of Cape Disappointment.[14] Over at Astoria temperance advocates, with Indian as well as white sobriety in mind, had been unable in 1854 to prevent the deaths of "four fine young [Indian] men" returning to Chinook drunk from Astoria and never heard from again. In Astoria they had sold salmon, three dollars worth of which at that time went for a thirty-cent bottle of whiskey.[15] Lamented Elwahco of such occurrences: "The children are learning to drink, to gamble, to cheat and lie. Soon they will be like the Astoria white traders."[16]

Governor Stevens wanted to rescue Chinooks and Chehalis from this kind of white influence and at the same time reserve for these same whites the lands to be thus taken. Armed with a federal appropriation of $45,000 for fiscal year 1855 to negotiate treaties and furnish goods and provisions to Indians of his territory, he set about to treat with them for their lands.[17] On December 26, 1854, at Medicine Creek on lower Puget Sound, he first negotiated with Nisquallys, Puyallups, and other tribes living around the sound and adjacent inlets, telling them that in pity he had asked the Great Father to provide them farms and education if they would sign the paper. At the same time he was careful to assure them that the gifts he was dispersing in council were not payments for their lands.[18] This treaty, although unpopular with settlers because of the establishment of reservations near the settlements, would be ratified by the Senate and proclaimed by President Franklin Pierce on April 10, 1855.

Undoubtedly aware of Stevens' treaty making in the northern territory, Chinooks in the south were apprehensive and upset at treaty makers and settlers encroaching in the shadow of promises unfulfilled from Tansey Point. Early January, 1855, found them especially sullen and unwilling to talk with Agent Tappan, whose word they believed "unavailing as the wind that blows." Instead of using the jargon to communicate with him, they conversed among themselves in their own tongue. At Willapa Bay they received him just as coldly, partly, he believed, because of "recent interference of white men who have Indian

---

* There was a growing discrimination against Indians by whites. Soon after the creation of Washington Territory, its legislature passed a law declaring void any marriage between a white person and an Indian of more than one-half blood. Marriages of such combinations entered into before the passage of the act were permitted to remain. *Acts of the Legislative Assembly of the Territory of Washington, Passed at the Second Regular Session, Begun and Held at Olympia, December 4, 1854.*

wives." They told him they would sell their lands and move to a reservation, but to none further north than the Naselle River, where on a small piece of land they would fish, raise potatoes, and gather cranberries. Under no circumstances, they insisted, would they move north to Grays Harbor or the Quinault country because of food shortages there and the unfriendliness of the people.[19] Shortly, with every possible excuse, they refused to come to Grays Harbor to a late January council planned by the governor for that place.[20]

During that period Stevens made treaties on January 22 (Point Elliott), 26 (Point-No-Point), and 31 (Neah Bay) with other tribes in the northwestern part of his territory. Proclamations of these treaties would be deferred until April 18, 1859.[21]

Stimulated by the success of his efforts, Stevens prepared for a treaty council with Indians mainly of southwestern Washington Territory to be held on February 25, 1855, on the Chehalis River some ten miles from its mouth at Grays Harbor, to which he ordered Agent Tappan, Colonel Henry D. Cocke, and Sidney S. Ford to summon the natives. James Swan and Doctor James Graham Cooper, invited to the council, came there from Grays Harbor with some twenty canoe-loads of Indians to camp on the council grounds, a bluff bank of the river. Although it was a cold morning when they arrived, the Indians washed, combed their hair, dressed in their best clothes, and painted their faces. The women wore bright shawls and put on their beads and trinkets. The council began with fourteen white men and 350 Indians representing Chinooks, Upper and Lower Chehalis, Quinaults, Satsops or Satchaps (Salish), and Cowlitz—a total of 843 people. To the Indians, who had drawn into a large circle, the governor made his customary warming-up speech, which was translated by Colonel B. F. Shaw into the Chinook Jargon, from which Indians of each tribe translated it into the language of their people, who in turn discussed it—in all a lengthy process of great concern to Stevens but not to the Indians. The next day the treaty was read line for line.

A believer in the one big reservation concept, Stevens proposed one extending from Grays Harbor (whose lands the Chehalis claimed)[22] to Cape Flattery. Once gathered there, the Indians were to receive forty thousand dollars and an additional four thousand dollars to clear and fence the land. They would have teachers, doctors, carpenters, blacksmiths, and others. Liquor and slavery were to be forbidden.

The next morning, after a speech from the governor, the treaty was reread. Chinook chief Narchotta, for whom a town (Nahcotta) on Willapa Bay would be named, expressed the feelings of his people to the proposals:

When you first began to speak we did not understand you; it was all dark to us as the night; but now our hearts are enlightened, and what you say is clear to us as the sun.

We are proud that our great father in Washington thinks of us. We are poor, and can see how much better off the white men are than we are. We are willing to sell our land, but we do not want to go away from our homes.

Our fathers, and mothers, and ancestors are buried there, and by them we wish to bury our dead and be buried ourselves. We wish, therefore, each to have a place on our own land where we can live, and you may have the rest; but we can't go to the north among the other tribes. We are not friends, and if we went together we should fight, and soon we would all be killed.[23]

More palaver followed, after which the Quinaults agreed to sign. They could afford to; the reservation was to be on their lands. Chinooks and Chehalis held out. Swan opined that Stevens might have gotten signatures from their headmen had it not been for the antics of one Tleyuk, son of an old Chehalis chief, Carcowan. Ambitious to be the great chief of the tribes to be confederated, Tleyuk wanted the reservation to include his own lands. Failing this, he stirred dissension among the assembled tribesmen, a process carried further by his father, who smuggled whiskey onto the council grounds, defying a prohibition by Stevens, before whom he appeared quite drunk. The next day Tleyuk said that he had no faith in the governor's words, as he had been told by mostly Hudson's Bay Company employees that the United States intended to put the Indians aboard steamers and ship them out of the country. That night Tleyuk refused to sign the treaty and with his fellows did a great deal of shouting and shooting.

The next morning Stevens saved some face in this unexpected turn of events by severely reprimanding the unruly Tleyuk, tearing up before the assemblage a paper recognizing him as chief. Tleyuk had the last word, for his action symbolized the refusal of his people to sign the treaty. The council broke up on March 3. Later that year Stevens would save more face from his week-long effort on the Chehalis treaty making with the Quinaults et al. July 1, to establish the Quinault Reservation north of Grays Harbor. In assessing the governor's failure to achieve the treaty settlement he wanted on the Chehalis, Swan believed an underlying cause was his attitude that because the natives with whom he was treating were mere remnants of once powerful bands, they could be concentrated on one reserve.[24] It would have been as logical for him to have believed that since they were so fragmented and diminished they would need no concentration or confinement at all and could be assimilated into the white community. Just as Stevens had underrated Chinook-Chehalis attachment to the graves of their dead, so had he overrated their willingness to accept his promise of the white men's civilization, which emphasized goods more than it did graves.[25]

As the Chinooks were escaping a reservation, so were their Clatsop neighbors in Oregon Territory. In an 1855 treaty negotiated by Superintendent Palmer with various tribes of Indians, extinguishing title to their lands lying west of the summit of the Coast Range in that territory, they and Tillamooks of all bands involved held out from signing.[26] The treaty was not ratified by the government because some of the territory was set aside for a reservation by executive order on November 9, 1855, five days before the treaty reached the office of the secretary of the interior. A portion of the reservation, known as Coast Range Indian Reservation, would be restored to the public domain by executive order on December 21, 1865, and separated into two parts with an intervening strip between. The northern portion would become known as the Siletz Indian Reservation, and the other would be called the Alsea Indian Reservation. Forty miles apart, they would also be separated by Yaquina and Alsea bays.[27] There was no great effort by whites to remove the Clatsops from the lower Columbia, not only because they had already been dislodged from most of their lands but also because, as the Oregon superintendent of Indian affairs would put it in 1861, they posed no threat to the "good morals and safety" of the white community. Ironically, it had been bad morals adopted from whites which had reduced their numbers in the first place to make them threatless.[28]

As Chinooks on the north side of the Columbia returned from the Chehalis council, Governor Stevens prepared to journey east of the Cascade Mountains to treat with interior tribes. Since the Tansey Point treaty council, word had passed from the coast to the interior of governmental attempts to take Indian lands. As early as 1852 the Reverend Charles Pandosy, O.M.I., missionary to the Yakima Indians, had heard that all natives on the Columbia left bank from the Blackfeet at the head of the river to the Chinooks (and Clatsops) at its mouth were to assemble to make war on the whites for taking their lands.[29] Now, in the spring of 1855 from the coast to the interior passed accounts of Stevens' treaty making to dislodge the Indians of western Washington so that white men could take their lands.

Before the year was out, interior tribes took to the warpath because of unhappiness at the treaties negotiated by Stevens with them at Walla Walla in May and at the violation of their lands by miners and settlers. The war spread to Puget Sound, where in the fall of 1855 natives wiped out some settlers on the White River and in January, 1856, briefly besieged Seattle. In early April, 1856, interior Indians visited the Chinooks and other natives of western Washington and tried to entice their coastal brothers into war, threatening to exterminate those remaining friendly to the whites.[30] Special agent Travis Daniel, on April 12, 1856, reported to Stevens that the Indians of Willapa Bay had been very excited at the news of the victory of the interior tribes over Major Granville O. Haller in the Yakima country on October 10 of the previous year. Down at Chinook, Daniel, possibly on receipt of news of a March 26 Indian attack on a white settlement at the Cascades of the Columbia, had feared war might spread down that river. A blockhouse in the Cascades area had been attacked, but one completed early in 1856 on the Chehalis River escaped a similar fate.

As at Willapa Bay, natives at the mouth of the Columbia lacked numbers, unity, ammunition, and proximity to the scene of action to make war. Chief Carcowan's boast that "King George" men, still at Fort Vancouver, would help them drive off the "Bostons" was wishful thinking, for the company would do no such thing, and it even curbed sales of guns and ammunition to its red customers.[31] A white man on the lower Columbia in May, 1856, wrote, ". . . we feel nor have no particular fears from the war, or any of the Indians, unless it is that they wont bring us half salmon enough. . . ."[32] All of this did not mean that there was no possibility of conflict among the Chinooks. This was evident in July, when they threatened retaliation against whites after one of that race, named McGonegal, shot his Indian wife. Government authorities hustled McGonegal off to Vancouver for safekeeping.[33]

White authorities, however, took no chances on the friendliness of their red charges. To restrain those of southwest Washington Territory they adopted a policy of separating nonhostile from hostile Indians, placing the former under the surveillance of local agents. This policy, credited to an agent, John Cain, and continued by another, Michael T. Simmons, received department approval in Washington. At the outbreak of the interior Indian war, Cain had collected natives such as Klickitats at Vancouver, Cowlitz near their river at Cowlitz Farms, and Chehalis at the places of Agent Ford and B. C. Armstrong on the Chehalis River.[34] Officials wanted to keep close tabs on their internees because of their ties with hostile Klickitat, Yakima, and Puget Sound Indians. Besides confining them, the agents took their guns and ammunition, as teachers would slingshots from errant pupils, until peace should be restored.[35]

On December 9, 1858, Agent A. J. Cain (not John Cain) reported to Oregon Superintendent of Indian Affairs James Nesmith, "I have nothing to report of an unsatisfactory character. . . ." By then the war was over, having broken out in its final stages in the more remote Spokane country earlier that year. There, under the vigorous efforts of Colonel

George Wright commanding federal troops, it had been crushed. With war's end, white officials and others of their race on the Washington territorial frontier did not rest easily. A "war" had recently been patched up between Lower Chehalis and Quinaults. Under the passion-inflaming influence of liquor others could easily have erupted.

Made belligerent by such outbreaks, and strong by their victory over natives in the recent war, certain whites bullied the vanquished, especially nonreservation ones like the Chinooks. Several natives at Willapa Bay, their numbers reduced by disease and drink, retreated under white pressures to the Quinault country to survive, often returning to Chinook for the whiskey available there. A number of people of Chinook ancestry would be allotted on the Quinault Reservation, claiming membership in the organized Quinault tribe. Today few of them live there.

Across the Columbia near Points Adams and Tansey, Tillamook Indians caroused and stole fish. Perhaps unaware that they had come there for years, the whites wanted them removed so that, as a group of them in Tillamook country put it, "we may sleep in peace without fear of our buildings being set on fire, or our cattle killed." Fearing their own removal for Tillamook misbehavior, the Clatsops asked Solomon Smith if they, too, were to be removed. Perhaps one reason they were not was because of Smith's strong defense of, and influence over, his wife's Clatsop people.³⁶

Eventually, remnants of the Clatsops and other tribes on the lower Columbia south bank with whom the government had treated at Tansey Point would go to the Alsea, Siletz, and Grand Ronde reservations. The last was established in the western reaches of Yamhill and Polk counties of western Oregon Territory by executive order on June 30, 1857.³⁷ Many Indians, avoiding the reservations, remained along the lower Columbia and the coast. Whites were mistaken if they believed they had seen the last of Indians going to reservations, for in June, 1861, settlers on the lower Columbia south bank complained of those from Siletz en route to Washington Territory causing trouble while attempting to get liquor.³⁸ The presence of two jurisdictions, Oregon and Washington, made law enforcement difficult, as a United States commissioner revealed in an 1858 complaint to the Oregon superintendent of Indian affairs. Indians of his jurisdiction from Cathlamet, he claimed, had gone in salmon season to the Oregon side of the Columbia, where liquor had subverted both them and the law. Captain M. Maloney of the Fourth Infantry, commanding Fort Chehalis, Grays Harbor, Washington Territory, on February 21, 1861, wrote to Acting Governor Henry McGill stating his opinion that liquor should not be sold in that part of the country until Indian titles to the land were extinguished, only to receive the following response from McGill:

> Although no provision has yet been made for the extinguishment of the Indian title to the lands occupied by the Cowlitz, Chehalis, Grays Harbor, Shoalwater Bay and Chenook Indians, yet by the Organic act, and the laws of Congress regulating the sale and disposition of the public lands, this country has been opened up to settlement, and the citizens residing therein are entitled to all the privileges accorded to those of any other portion of the Territory. I do not therefore consider this country as Indian country, within the meaning of the 20th. Section of the act of 1834.[39]

In August, 1865, one Chenamus (Tanamus, Cacnamis), a "dissipated Character" and "chief" of a small band between Grays Harbor and Willapa Bay, perhaps under the influence of liquor, was stabbed through the heart by a white man during an argument, whereupon his people choked the killer to death with a chunk of wood.[40] As at Willapa Bay, natives at Chinook and in the town which in 1873 would bear the name Ilwaco (Washington Territory) more than ever depended upon whites for their sustenance, sometimes even sending their slaves with berries to exchange for bread and sugar.[41] At Willapa Bay Indians continued "oystering" and "cranberrying" for white employers in their former beds and bogs, and they passed on to these whites their skills in obtaining food from nature. Old Elwahco, for example, taught whites the Chinook way of "grasping for sturgeon" in Bakers Bay by impaling the fish with long spear-hooks as they lay feeding in the mud.[42]

A white traveler in the 1860's wrote that Chinook was still a busy place. When the hundred French-Canadians, half-bloods, and inter-married descendants of all finished processing their daily catches at that place they "frolicked" at day's end, punctuating the air with sounds of a patois, a French and Indian jargon interlarded with some Scottish and a little English. They canoed fresh or dried and salted salmon in half-barrels to Astoria, selling them for six dollars per hundred pounds in that marketplace,[43] which had grown from its fortress days to an emporium "wilderness of wharves." Chinooks loaded half-barrels of salmon onto canoes and under sail glided upriver to sell their cargoes in Portland.[44] Sometimes Indians sold sea otter furs at that place for prices averaging $6.50 each[45]—not a very big price. One Hudson's Bay Company trader stated that skins costing $40 in 1860 would, at the beginning of the twentieth century, go for as much as $400 on the white man's market.[46] Because the company had slackened its fur purchases, since the 1850's there had been an increase in most fur-bearing animals all the way from the Columbia to the Strait of Juan de Fuca.[47] High prices were

Fort Astoria shortly before the takeover of that post by the British North West Company during the War of 1812. The site of the fort is present-day Astoria, Oregon.

This drawing, by Captain Sir Edward Belcher, R.N., in 1839, is of Fort George, which replaced Fort Astoria when the latter post fell into the possession of the North West Company in 1813 and which was taken over by the Hudson's Bay Company in 1821 after the two firms merged.

This view of Astoria was made in 1841 by one of United States Navy Lieutenant Charles Wilkes's party. The main Hudson's Bay Company fur post was then at Fort Vancouver.

Captain Robert Gray was more fur trader than explorer, but as the first navigator to enter the Columbia River, Gray also held another distinction—that of the first American to sail around the world under the United States flag.
(Courtesy, Alfred A. Knopf, Inc.)

In 1792 the *Columbia Rediviva*, commanded by Robert Gray, was the first vessel to sail into the Columbia River. Although most Chinooks had probably never seen a white man's ship, there were some among them who already understood the process of fur trading.

Captain Meriwether Lewis (left) and Lieutenant William Clark (right) led
the first party from the United States to the western coast of the continent to
trace the Columbia River to its mouth and to find a western land trade route.
They wintered among the Clatsops in 1805/1806 before beginning their return
trip.

(Courtesy, Independence National Historical Park)

Hoqua, chief of the Canton, China, security merchants of the Co-Hong, was the most popular of the group with the Americans who brought Chinook-gathered furs to China to trade for tea, chinaware, and silk. Although frugal, Hoqua was extremely wealthy.

John Jacob Astor founded his fortune in the fur trade. He began the first permanent settlement at the mouth of the Columbia River—the fur post Astoria. His profits from various fur ventures he invested in farmland on Manhattan Island. This portrait is by Alonzo Chappel.

Gabriel Franchère, one of the "scribbling clerks" with Astor's Pacific Fur Company, left valuable accounts of early-day life at Astoria among the Lower Chinooks.

(Courtesy, Alfred A. Knopf, Inc.)

Alexander Ross, also a clerk for Astor's company, later switched loyalties and became manager of the North West Company's Fort Nez Percés.

(Courtesy Alfred A. Knopf, Inc.)

George Simpson, field manager for the Hudson's Bay Company, was sent to Oregon to whip the lagging Columbia fur trade into shape. In 1824 he moved the company's headquarters from Fort George upriver to Fort Vancouver.

(Courtesy, British Museum)

Dr. John McLoughlin, a Scotch-Irish physician, came to Fort George in 1824 and later became chief factor at Fort Vancouver. He married the Chinook widow of Astorian Alexander McKay.

(Courtesy, Alfred A. Knopf, Inc.)

due to a sharp decrease in sea otters, which natives hunted for white men from Grays Harbor to Point Grenville. Before 1860 the company had generally given Chinooks and Clatsops trade goods for furs obtained from northern natives, but after that, with American competition, it was forced to adopt the American policy of giving them money or anything short of liquor. Indians would carry furs from points as distant as the Quinault country to the company store at Chinook, which would continue operations until about 1870.[48]

The American government, whose soldiers had defeated the Indians in the recent wars, continued to assert its official power throughout the Pacific Northwest. The Chinook-Clatsop remnant felt its force even more in peace than it had in war. In the 1860's it watched the building of Fort Canby.[49] In 1859 government officials selected a tract of land at the Chehalis–Black River confluence in southwestern Washington Territory as a reservation for natives of that region, including Chinooks. By executive order of September 22, 1866, a small (355-acre) reservation was set aside on the north shore of Willapa Bay for some thirty or forty Chinook families admixed with Chehalis who for some years had lived around that body of water, claiming the country adjacent to it as their own.[50] Eventually, the few Indians residing on this, the Shoalwater Reservation, would be allotted land on the Quinault. In 1889 a William F. Prosser would report that remnants of Chinooks, Chehalis, Clatsops, and others on the Shoalwater Reservation knew little of the early history of the tribes to which they belonged.[51] The Shaker religion, which originated among Squaxin Indians at the upper end of Puget Sound, made its appearance on that reservation at the turn of the century. The land on that reservation was not especially desirable and never heavily settled,* many Indians preferring to remain off the tract, fitting their way of life to that of white men around the bay, perhaps because both races were involved in similar economic activities.[52]

---

* In 1927 three families would remain on the reservation, although all members of these families had been allotted on the Quinault Reservation with the exception of four children. Under the date April 6, 1927, the president would grant authority for allotting the Shoalwater Reservation to these children in accordance with an act of February 8, 1887 (24 Stat. 388), as amended. The allotments would not be made immediately, and persons who would have been entitled to them on the Shoalwater eventually took allotments on the Quinault. Authority for making the Shoalwater allotments was then revoked by the president in December, 1932. The Indians, since they went there for fishing, had asked that the Shoalwater not be allotted but be kept for an Indian village. A number of Indians from neighboring reservations, principally Quinaults, would go to Shoalwater Bay to fish. In January, 1932, the superintendent of the Tahola Agency on the Quinault would report that eight families had permanently located on the Shoalwater Reservation. *Ccreation of An Indian Village, House Report* No. 1098, 73 Cong., 2 sess., 1–2.

After the Chehalis Reservation was established by executive order of July 8, 1864, Washington Superintendent of Indian Affairs I. J. Mc-Kenny sought to bring onto that confine all nonreservation Chinook, Willapa Bay, Chehalis, and Cowlitz Indians. To hurry them along to what he hoped would be their new home, he ordered his agents to lure them with gifts of every kind from timber to trinkets. He also held government-sponsored "potlatches" where gifts were dispersed just like the Indians had given them in similar celebrations for years.[53] McKenny hoped that reservation life would gradually eliminate among these un-confined Indians "bad habits," the worst of which, to his thinking, were gambling, drinking, sorcery, head flattening, and polygamy, all of which prevailed into the second half of the nineteenth century.[54] By 1870, despite government attempts to herd them onto the Chehalis Reserva-tion, there was no great rush to go there among the nonreservation rem-nant of the Chinook band—87 men, 60 women, and 73 children.[55] By the beginning of the next century the Shaker church, a native religion advo-cating strict morals made its appearance among the Willapa Bay Chi-nook.

With the passing of old Chiefs Comcomly, Chenamus (later ones bore these names too, as noted above), and Coboway, the Chinook and Clat-sop Indians were virtually leaderless. Solomon Smith would maintain that tribal organization had died out in the 1850's, after which each In-dian acted for himself in gaining a living and "anything like that."[56] In the early twentieth century Chinooks would claim that Princess Sally, at about the time of the Tansey Point treaty, had been appointed queen of the Chinook tribe. Although enjoying considerable prestige among her people, as women traditionally had, she had not signed that treaty. In white American fashion, its signers had all been males.[57] At century's end an *Oregonian* writer would state that "Princess Mary" (Mary Ron-deau), claiming to be a granddaughter of old Comcomly, held court in his former empire on these lower Columbia ancestral lands.[58] But her power and influence were but a shadow of those of earlier Chinook leaders. In 1864 she and a second husband, Solomon Preble, signed a quit claim deed renouncing their interest in the Scarborough claim pur-chased by her former husband, Rocque Ducheney, company clerk at Chinook. The princess and a third husband, John Kelly, a fisherman, clung to the land as home, living there during fishing seasons "when they cannot find any other place."[59] It was on the former claim, which would become Chinook Point (Military) Reservation, that shortly before 1900 Fort Columbia would be built.*[60]

* In 1864, after several years of obtaining and clearing the land titles, the Fort Colum-bia area was turned over to garrison troops. One year later Fort Stevens at Point Adams

On Willapa Bay in August, 1876, a Chinook bearing the name Ma-tote, or Light House Charley, would be recognized as "chief." One of the last to have a flattened skull, his behavior did not match his "regal badge." Chenamus had been surplanted by one Coolidge, who was "deposed" because of blindness. Light House Charley, with supposedly much vision, was, as far as the government was concerned, to keep his people in line and away from drink. He might better have accomplished that mission had he refrained from drink himself. He finally drowned in the Columbia River.*

In its columns on November 29, 1893, the *Oregonian* would carry a story of "Clatsop's Lawful King," Ranald MacDonald, whose kingdom and authority, according to the editor of the *Spokane Review*, had been first usurped by the Oregon Provisional Government. Calling attention to MacDonald and his lost kingdom was word that President Grover Cleveland was about to restore the Hawaiian queen to her throne. Ranald did not hold out much hope of regaining the Chinook throne. On his return from Japan he lived out his days on the upper Columbia away from the home of his royal ancestors and the scenes of his travels. In those travels he had entered a foreign country, as other strangers had entered his, to introduce Chinooks and Clatsops to a new world. He had taught English to Japanese, just as white strangers had taught English to his people, and had influenced those island people to open their country to commerce of the West (in advance of Commodore Matthew Perry's visit to Japan) and the adoption of its ways.

By century's end, word would circulate that the person ascending the Chinook chieftaincy on the death of Chenamus in the 1840's was William McKay, son of Thomas, married to Comcomly's daughter.[61] Whether he was actually chief or not, his qualifications were imposing. After his medical education in the East he had returned to open a mer-

was ready for occupancy. But the urgency for military occupancy at the mouth of the Columbia was relieved with improving Anglo-American relations, so the forts lay idle until 1895. Then the War Department prepared to mine the river and construct modern facilities there and at Fort Canby as well. By 1904 construction programs were complete. The facilities remained so until after World War II. The first troops were sent to Fort Columbia in 1898.

* Agent Robert Huston Milroy wrote: "If I find any more bad reports about him ["Light House" Charley] I will dismiss him as head chief." Milroy to [illegible] Peterson, April 5, 1877, Letterbook, Vol. I, February 19, 1877, to November 18, 1878, manuscript, Suzzallo Library. On Ma-tote's death the mantle of leadership would pass to his son, George A. Charley. After Charley's death, his son, Roland, would be recognized leader. Subsequent leaders, designated "chairmen," would include Roland's daughter, Myrtle Charley Landry, and, more recently, Roland Charley's grandson, Dennis Baker. "Shoalwater Reservation Centennial from Carcowan through the Charleys—100 Years," *The Sou'wester*, I, 3 (Autumn, 1966), 44–45.

cantile business in Oregon City before going to the California gold fields in 1849. On McKay Creek, near present-day Pendleton, Oregon, in the tradition of Chinook mercantilism, he engaged in raising, trading, buying, and selling cattle.[62] Focusing attention on McKay as Chinook leader was a well-known court case involving his citizenship. In an election in the East Dalles precinct his right to vote was challenged by election officials since he was born of "an independent political community" —the Chinook, on his mother's side. Besides that, he was a British subject on his father's side. Many other "bloods" of similar background had been allowed to vote, but a judge in the United States District Court for the District of Oregon on November 7, 1871, ruled against McKay, opining that "public opinion [which had permitted him to vote] is not any authority on a point of law." In the case, as in so many others, it appeared, in the judge's words, "that common consent is sometimes in common error."[63]

Chief or not, McKay, living out his years as Umatilla Indian Agency physician, was helpless to check the continuing appropriation of the lower Columbia River by whites. Red men there were forced to yield more and more of their fishing as they watched whites introduce into that industry new types of nets and traps and gigantic fish wheels that caught salmon at a ravenous pace.[64] These former masters of the river complained that they had to buy the very land on which they lived and could not even catch salmon or sturgeon without a license. Gone were the days when they had been relatively free to earn a living. Gone were many of their old company friends who might have helped them. In 1864 death claimed James Birnie, described as a man "of some note [who] kept a good many Indians around him."[65] As far as the Indians were concerned, no greater tribute could have been paid a white man. By the late nineteenth century white men would build salmon canneries near old native fisheries at places like Points Oak, Chinook, Ellice, and Tansey and near towns such as Ilwaco and Astoria.[66] At the turn of the century these canneries[67] on the lower Columbia would be less numerous than in the 1880's, when they totaled some forty in number.* Chinese, instead of Indians, labored in these establishments, where historian Frances Fuller Victor observed them, armed with long, sharp knives, disemboweling and beheading salmon and pushing offal into the river at the same time.[68] In their mercantile rush the white canners would have regarded first salmon ceremonials, once so meticulously observed, a waste of time. Even Chinooks under white influence neglected

* At Chinook and other places near the mouth of the Columbia it was estimated that no less than 1,500 barrels of salmon were put up in 1866. *Morning Oregonian*, March 10, 1867, p. 3.

these ceremonials, which had once meant so much to them.[69] Mrs. Victor noted that Indians of the lower river, "dissipated by the beams of civilization," had deferred to white men, profaning not only ancient burials but also recent ones in their search for plunder.

Not all white men were as solicitous for Indians as were members of the Quaker-oriented Whealdon family, which in 1863 gathered Chinook bones to give them a decent burial in a big box.[70] This action of the Whealdons caused little stir among Chinooks. Nearly a hundred years later Chinooks would respond much differently to the disturbance of the bones of their dead. Then, under the aura of renewed tribalism, they would become very protective of relics and artifacts. Some of these relics accidently unearthed by men excavating in 1953 near Willapa Bay would cause Chinooks to institute a fifty-thousand-dollar lawsuit against the property owners, who offered to turn the material over to a university.[71] But most white men of the nineteenth century, with little fear of natives or lawsuits, were careless with Chinook and Clatsop bones. "Alas!" wrote Mrs. Victor, "nothing of one race is sacred to another. . . ."[72] The lines of a poem (substituting the word "cedar" for "birch") seemed appropriate on the West Coast as they had in other parts of America which succumbed to white men:

> Behind the squaw's light birch canoe,
>   The steamer rocks and raves;
> And city lots are staked for sale
>   Above old Indian graves.[73]

Death from conflicts resulting from commercial rivalries on the river added to the graves. One occupying such a burial was Rocque Ducheney, killed in a fight between a salmon packing company and a fishermen's group.[74]

The graves were fitting monuments to Chinooks and Clatsops near extinction. Writers of the time, influenced by stories of lost tribes, believed them to have been an extinct race. A correspondent of the *San Francisco Chronicle*, in a June 1, 1884, article, wrote, "We name the Chinooks and Clatsops among the lost tribes of Oregon, not because they are the only ones lost, but because they were the most conspicuous coast tribes, and in all respects a superior race of aboriginees. . . ."[75] As noted above, Franz Boas, near the end of the nineteenth century, discovered the Chinook remnant living on Willapa Bay. These Indians had adopted the more expressive and flexible Chehalis dialect just as Clatsops had adopted the Nehalem dialect of the Tillamooks.[76] It was from two elderly survivors of this remnant that the anthropologist Ray gleaned his information on ancient Chinook culture.[77] The quickened pace of archaeological studies of the last half of the twentieth century will undoubtedly yield new information on the early history of these people. Boas noted that they still clung to the Chinook Jargon, which prevailed among them and whites until the twentieth century. Despite its utility to Pacific Northwestern frontiersmen, whites continued to poke fun at it. One of them in the late 1870's noted: "The most popular hymns have been translated into metrical Chinook, so we find every red-man indulging in psalms when he is seized with a fit of devotion. They render them somewhat incongruous, if not ridiculous, however, quite frequently, by uniting with them an erotic or bacchanalian ditty, composed by some political white scapegrace whose ideas of propriety might be considered open to criticism."[78]

Following Boas, Edward Curtis, in his early-twentieth-century work on the American Indian, dealt primarily, as far as the Chinookan peoples were concerned, with upriver ones, very possibly because they were more numerous than those lower down on the Columbia.[79] Perhaps white men believed that since there were no Chinook or Clatsop reservations there were none of those people left. But around the turn of the century remnants of the two tribes began stirring for compensation for their lands under unfulfilled government promises made to them in the mid-nineteenth-century treaties. In 1897 the Nehalem "band" of Tillamooks (including Indians of Clatsop and Chinook blood) were awarded $10,500 in settlement of a claim against the government for the unratified August 6, 1851, Tansey Point Treaty.[80] This settlement may have encouraged Chinooks and Clatsops to press for similar awards. On March 2 and 28, 1899, the Indian Office submitted to the Department of the Interior for approval claims prepared by attorneys of these people.[81] Because the body (to ultimately approve appropriations for compensatory payments for such claims) did not generally approve Indian claims, the department reacted unfavorably to the Clatsop claim. Nevertheless, with Chinooks, Wahkiakums, and Kathlamets they continued to seek compensation.* Pressure on behalf of these tribes brought Congress in 1905 to appropriate funds to investigate the numbers of Clatsops, Chinooks proper (including Willapa Bay Chinooks, often designated Willapas, who are named for the bay and are not to be confused with Athabaskan [Salish?] Willopahs or Wheelappas, as has been frequently done), and Kathlamet heirs to the 1851 Tansey Point treaties.[82] In 1906 Supervisor Charles E. McChesney, conducting the investiga-

---

* When in 1901 the Kathlamets submitted a claim to Congress, the Senate took the position that since the 1851 treaties had been unratified there was no reason to recognize the claim. In 1902 the attorney for the Chinooks proper (meaning that tribe as distinct from Lower Chinook tribes) sought for his clients compensation for their lands.

tion, found many descendants of the 1851 groups, most of whom had no reservation addresses.

In 1906 Senate bills were prepared for Nucqueclahwemucks and Wahkiakums providing for referral of their claims to the Court of Claims for a hearing. Congress, in that same year, authorized funds to investigate the "validity of the . . . claims against the United States."[83] Acting Commissioner C. F. Larrabee mistakenly reported that "nearly all the Indians who were parties to the treaties of 1851 and 1855" were on the Siletz Reservation, and "some" were on the Grand Ronde Reservation.[84] In the investigation, the Office of Indian Affairs reported in 1907 that although Chinooks, Clatsops, Wahkiakums, and Kathlamets had ceded certain lands in 1851, the act of cessions did not mean ownership of the land, and that if the treaties and correspondence setting forth their needs did not provide sufficient merit to justify ratification in 1852, "it would seem preposterous to give them any recognition fifty-five years afterward. . . ."[85] The Court of Claims saw it differently, handing down a decision for compensating the tribes. Congress, by action on August 24, 1912, awarded each tribe payments for their aboriginal lands.*[86]

After the 1934 reorganization of the Office of Indian Affairs, the concept of an Indian Claims Commission was realized on August 13, 1946.[87] The law establishing the commission provided for an *identifiable* tribe or band of Indians to petition the government for claims of treaties, contracts, and agreements which had been revised on grounds of fraud, duress, unconscionable consideration, and so on. Not until 1951 would all Lower Chinooks combine to press that body with a claim. Chinooks were encouraged to think that their 1912 award for an "unconsionable consideration" was an indication, said their attorney, "that Congress [had] recognized and thereby established the identity of the foregoing Tribes and Bands of Chinook Indians as being the aboriginal owners of their respective Tribal lands and that the consideration was tendered as compensation for claimants' aboriginal title." The press for Chinook "band" claims had what one attorney would call "a rather hectic his-

---

* Clatsops were awarded $15,000; Nucqueclahwemucks, $1,500; Kathlamets, $7,000; Wahkiakums, $7,000; and Chinooks proper, $20,000 (37 Stat., 518). Many western Washington Indians, dissatisfied with government failure to respond satisfactorily to their claims, petitioned the Court of Claims en masse. Despite their 1912 award from the court, the Chinooks joined these other Indians, whose claim was asserted in United States Court of Claims, Cause No. F-275, *Duwamish et al* vs. *United States*, 79 Court Claims 530. The court dismissed their case on June 4, 1934, on grounds that the tribes' right to land occupancy had been unrecognized by the United States and furthermore that the court would be unable to determine the extent and value of any right as it existed in 1851. *Before the Indian Claims Commission of the United States: The Chinook Tribe and Bands of Indians, Petitioner*, vs. *The United States of America, Defendant*, Petition No. 234 (Filed August 8, 1951), 7, 8.

tory"[88] for these nonreservation Indians.* The Chinooks' claim (Docket 234) was filed with the Indian Claims Commission before the deadline prescribed by law for filing such claims. From then on it was still touch and go for the Chinooks, not so much on the basis of governmental recognition of their right to original ownership of the land surrounding the lower reaches of the Columbia River as to their providing proof of being an *identifiable* group of Indians. Since most claims filed with the commission after the 1934 reorganization of the Office of Indian Affairs (renamed in 1947 the Bureau of Indian Affairs) had been by reservation Indians who were permitted to adopt constitutions, there was in such cases less of a problem of their establishing recognized organizations than there was for their nonreservation fellows.†

Prepared by attorneys, the original Chinook petition, in which John Grant Elliott swore to being chairman of the General Council of the Chinook Tribe of Indians, was filed on August 8, 1951, with the Indian Claims Commission to meet the August 13 deadline.[89] With no previous council organization, the Chinooks "banded" solely to bring suit against the government. Not for ten days after the filing was a general meeting of Chinooks called,‡ and then not until September 22 were delegates elected at Skamokawa, Washington, to sign the contract on October 11 with their attorneys, who had prepared the filed petition.

* Three attorneys served the Chinooks. There was a division, leaving but one working on their behalf. He was, himself, replaced by another in time.

† Those of Chinook, Clatsop, Wahkiakum, and Kathlamet blood who were reservation Indians were included in petitions of tribes of various reservations on which they were allotted. Those of the Chehalis Tribe were included in a claim of *Upper Chehalis et al.*, Docket 237, filed August 8, 1951, and were named in the petition. The commission received from the Chehalis plaintiffs on November 5, 1953, a motion to file an amended petition deleting the Chinooks by name and any claim for original Chinook territory. Chinook tribes had been included in the original Chehalis petition at the request of the Bureau of Indian Affairs, but the claim for members of the Confederated tribes of the Chehalis Reservation was for Chehalis lands and automatically included members of Chinook blood belonging to that reservation. *Before the Indian Claims Commission: Upper Chehalis, et al, Plaintiffs vs. The United States, Defendant*, Docket No. 237, Defendant Motion to File Amended Petition. Those of Chinook blood who are members of other reservation tribes were included in *Kalapuya tribe et al.* and *Grand Ronde Community*, Docket No. 238; in *Tillamook band et al., Grand Ronde Community*, and *Confederated Siletz Indians*, Docket No. 240; and in *Quinaielt* (Quinault) *Tribe*, Docket No. 242. Those of Chinook blood, however, could elect to exclude themselves from these petitions and be included in the Chinook claim, Docket No. 242, if they so chose.

‡ Those elected to office at the general meeting were John Grant Elliott, chairman; Myrtle Woodcock, secretary-treasurer; and local representatives Mildred Colbert, Charles C. Larsen, Oscar McLeod, and Claud Wain.

Heirs of the once powerful peoples at the mouth of the Columbia organized as the Chinook Nation,[90] but there were Chinook complaints that mostly silence followed the initial meetings, and notices of meetings were so late that many living at a distance could not attend.[91] Because of this situation a meeting was finally called at Bay Center, Washington, on Willapa Bay, for May 3, 1953, by Secretary-Treasurer Myrtle Woodcock. Those present elected new officers, calling themselves the Chinook Indian Tribe.* A split in Chinook government occurred when Elliott, absent from the meeting, insisted that his organization, the Chinook Nation, would remain as it was until the claims settlement was reached. On June 13, 1953, the two groups held separate meetings. Two days later the Chinook Indian Tribe incorporated under state laws. Elliott's group, now commonly referred to as the "Skamokawa Council," met to fill the vacancies of those who had left that organization.† Each group continued to function separately from then on, formulating its own identity. One Chinook wrote that the "differences in basic philosophy of the two groups [is that] neither group is all 'black' or all 'white' in its purposes, most Chinooks belong actively to both."[92] The Chinook Nation continued on its primary course to settle the claim. The Chinook Indian Tribe, Inc., assumed promotional and watchdog functions for the tribe. Through the latter group, dental service for tribal members was obtained, housing and education programs were promoted, and (in traditional Chinook fashion) commercial ventures were projected, one of them being a salmon fishing enterprise. It had cultural objectives as well.

Both groups were well aware that the 1951 Chinook petition had asked thirty million dollars' compensation for the loss of 762,000 acres, the loss of hunting, fishing, and forest lands, and the loss of big game, berries, and roots from which had come the fibers for their existence—clothes, mats, cords, ropes, canoes, and houses.‡ On November 4, 1971,

---

* Roland Charley, chairman; Myrtle Woodcock, secretary-treasurer; Lewis Hawkes, vice-chairman; and Jack Petit, Claud Wain, Charles Larsen, and Paul Petit, directors.

† The slate of officers then were Elliott, chairman; Kent Elliott, his son, vice-chairman; and Frank Quigley, secretary-treasurer. Deciding not to incorporate or recognize the Chinook Indian Tribe, which they considered a social organization, the "Council" filed suit to gain recognition as the "true Government" of the Chinook Indians. No ruling was obtained. Elliott's group drafted a constitution on April 3, 1954.

‡ The petition claimed that the government had paid the Hudson's Bay Company $25 an acre for land, and that some Chinook and Clatsop lands by 1850 had gone for as much as $400 an acre. Subsequent to the 1951 petition, the Chinooks asked compensation for mineral rights. *Before the Indian Claims Commission of the United States*: Docket No. 234, Petitioner's Findings of Fact and Brief, 38. The Indian Claims Commission on April 16, 1958,

the commission made its final award* decision on the Chinook claim at the "fair market value of the subject tract" of $75,000, which, after deducting $26,307.95 of that paid in the 1912 award, which had been "unconscionable," left a balance of $48,692.05 for the plaintiffs.[93]

Present-day descendants of Lower Chinooks, with perhaps a higher quantum of white blood than most Pacific Northwest Indians because of their longer and closer association with white men, hope that proven genealogical ties will mean material gain for them. Some of this gain, unlike that of the past, will perhaps come less from red and white traders than from the government itself. Besides trying to strengthen their economy in the modern world with projected fishing enterprises, an industry as old as the tribe itself, they attempt to keep alive tribal spirit and heritage through celebrations and plans for a Chinook museum and cultural center.

White men have been unable to completely tame the environment in which Lower Chinooks once moved. By jettys and other navigational aids they have lessened the dangers of the bar, but their mariners and pilots still respect it as did their Chinook counterparts in the past. We respect these people, who made a mariner's peace with nature and a mercantile peace with men. We retain the memory of a remarkable people who left us the Chinook hallmark in a wind, a language, an incomparable salmon, a canoe which some have believed to have been the inspiration for the clipper ship,[94] ships of a more modern type, aircraft, vehicles, hostelries, other business establishments, and countless other things that bear their name.

When old-time Chinooks were asked from whence they came, they answered, "We have always been here." If by some magic they could be

entered its findings and opinion and interloculatory order on the first phase of the petition, agreeing that there had been tribal land ownership before 1851 (Jerome K. Kuykendall, Chairman, Indian Claims Commission, Washington, D.C., to Senator Warren G. Magnuson, September 9, 1971) but stating that there was lack of evidence to support the petitioner's valuations on this land. The commission also agreed to Chinook ownership of 76,630 acres, valuing them at just under a dollar each, which they said was the 1851 price. It also decided that the timber then (in 1851) had no commercial value and declared no tribal right to "free swimming fish." *Before the Indian Claims Commission of the United States*: Docket No. 234, Defendant's Requested Findings of Fact, Objections to Petitioner's Proposed Findings of Fact, and Brief, 4, 5, 45; Frederick W. Post, formerly attorney to the Chinooks, to the authors, July 19, 1972.

* The Chinooks' attorney filed a notice of appeal with the Court of Claims on January 19, 1971, orally arguing the case on November 29, 1971. E. L. Crawford to the authors, August 1, 1972. The Court of Claims handed down its decision on December 3, 1971, affirming the decision of the Indian Claims Commission. The commission's final award of $48,692.05 was reported to Congress on June 18, 1972. Norman E. Timko, Deputy Clerk, Indian Claims Commission, letter to authors, January 11, 1971.

contacted in the better land to which they were carried in their incomparable canoes, to ask their wish for their descendants in that earthly home of river and sea, we might hear them say, "May they, too, always be there."

> To Be, contents his natural desire,
> He asks no angel's wings, no seraph's fire.
>
> Alexander Pope, "Essay on Man"

Notes

CHAPTER 1
A Cloud-Topp'd Hill

1. Robert Rogers, "Petition of Major Robert Rogers," Oregon Historical Society, Portland. The historian T. C. Elliott uses the spelling *Ouragon* for the river which Major Rogers hoped to reach. "The Origin of the Name Oregon," *Oregon Historical Quarterly*, XXII (1921), 102.

The Jesuit missionary Le Jeune, as early as 1633 and again in 1634, recorded the words *Ouragana* and *Ouragan*, stating that they referred to bark dishes used by the Indians. Reuben Gold Thwaites (ed.), *The Jesuit Relations and Allied Documents: Travels and Explorations of the Jesuit Missionaries in New France, 1610–1791*, V, 97, and VI, 285. The word *Ouragan* was subsequently used to refer to "The River of the West" in a letter from the French governor of Canada in the early eighteenth century. One Baron Louis-Armand de Lom d'Arce Lahontan heard from natives, as did the French explorer Charlevoix in 1721, of a great western river running to the ocean. John E. Rees, "Oregon—Its Meaning, Origin and Application," *Oregon Historical Quarterly*, XXI (1920), 325.

Rogers proposed in 1772 to lead an expedition to the Pacific via the "Ourigan." Elliott, "Origin of the Name Oregon," 108. For a long time it was believed that French and Indian war veteran Captain Jonathan Carver had given the name Oregon to the Columbia River. He had used the name Ourigan on May 6, 1767, but only after a meeting with Rogers, from whom it is now suspected he learned the name. T. C. Elliott, "Jonathan Carver's Source for the Name Oregon," *Oregon Historical Quarterly*, XXIII (1922), 60. By the time Carver's book appeared in 1778, he had simplified the name to Oregon.

Travels through the Interior Parts of North America, in the Years 1766, 1767, and 1768, 76.

One authority states the word is Algonquin. Vernon F. Snow, "From Ouragan to Oregon," *Oregon Historical Quarterly*, LX (1959), 446. Another authority says that it cannot be an Indian word. T. C. Elliott, "The Strange Case of Jonathan Carver and the Name Oregon," *Oregon Historical Quarterly*, XXI (1920), 349. Many others speculate about the meaning of the word, some giving contractions of the Chippeway words *owah*, meaning "river," and *waken*, meaning "slave," hence "river of slaves." Elsie Frances Dennis, "Indian Slavery in Pacific Northwest," *Oregon Historical Quarterly*, XXXI (1930), 181. Still others use the Shoshoni words *ogwa*, meaning "water" and *pe-on*, meaning "west," hence "river of the west." It has been suggested that Carver heard these Shoshoni words from the Sioux. Rees, "Oregon—Its Meaning, Origin and Application," 319. The Cree word *othagan*, meaning "platter" has been suggested as the origin, since the Crees' name for the Columbia River was Othegansiki, or "Platter River." John Stuart, "Oregon or River of the West," Folder XVI-2, Kenneth L. Holmes Collection, 3.

Some say the root word *Oregon* is French—*Ouragan* for windstorm, blizzard, or tornado; *Organan* for wormwood; or *Ouracane* for hurricane. Elliott, "Strange Case of Jonathan Carver and the Name Oregon," 351, 354; Snow, "From Ouragan to Oregon," 440. Since Spain has long been associated with the Pacific coast, certain Spanish words have been suggested as roots of the word *Oregon*, such as *Aragon* (Elliott, "Strange Case of Jonathan Carver and the Name Oregon," 351); a corruption of explorer Martin d'Aguilar's name (*ibid.*, 353); *huracan*, meaning "hurricane" (*ibid.*, 354); *oye-el-agua*, meaning "hear the waters" (William H. Galvani, "The Early Explorations and the Origin of the Name of the Oregon Country," *Oregon Historical Quarterly*, XXI [1920], 338); *ore-jon*, meaning "big ears" as applied by Spanish explorers to Indians (*ibid.*); and *os regos*, Spanish for "large ears" (*Catholic Sentinel*, December 17, 1879, p. 3).

2. George Davidson, *United States Coast and Geodetic Survey, Pacific Coast: Coast Pilot of California, Oregon, and Washington*, 456.

3. Barbara Coit Elliott, "Cape Disappointment in History," *Washington Historical Quarterly*, XIV, 4 (October, 1923), 263.

4. F. N. Blanchet, et al., *Notices and Voyages of the Famed Quebec Mission to the Pacific Northwest; Being the Correspondence, Notices, etc., of Fathers Blanchet and Demers Together with Those of Fathers Bolduc and Langlois*, 217.

5. Frederick Webb Hodge (ed.), *Handbook of American Indians North of Mexico*, I, 273.

6. A. L. Kroeber, "The Tribes of the Pacific Coast of North America," *XIX International Congress of Americanists*, 391.

7. See Melville Jacobs, "Historic Perspectives in Indian Languages of Oregon and Washington," *Pacific Northwest Quarterly*, XXVIII, 1 (January, 1937), 55–74.

8. Verne F. Ray, *Lower Chinook Ethnographic Notes*, University of Washington Publications in Anthropology, VII, 2, 36. Anthropologist Leslie Spier places the Athabaskans further back on the upper waters of rivers tributary to the Columbia. *Tribal Distribution in Washington*, General Series in Anthropology, No. 3, 22.

9. Jacobs, "Historic Perspectives in Indian Languages of Oregon and Washington," 62.

10. For a study of the Upper Chinook, see Leslie Spier and Edward Sapir, *Wishram Ethnography*, University of Washington Publications in Anthropology, III, 3, 563.

11. Ray, *Lower Chinook Ethnographic Notes*, 38.

12. *Ibid.*, 39.

13. *The Oregon Territory, Consisting of a Brief Description of the Country and Its Productions; and of the Habits and Manners of the Native Indian Tribes*, 45. The author seems to have based his conclusions on the fact that the four tribes were ethnically similar. Washington Irving, in his *Astoria; or, Anecdotes of an Enterprise Beyond the Rocky Mountains*, 83, quotes fur man Robert Stuart when he writes that the Wahkiakums had split from the Chinooks. Abbé EM. Domenech, in *Seven Years' Residence in the Great Deserts of North America*, II, 16, claimed that Kathlamets, Wahkiakums, Chinooks, and Clatsops were four clans of the same tribe which fragmented in the mid-1700's because of quarreling village chiefs.

14. George Davidson uses the spelling *Wallacut*. *United States Coast and Geodetic Survey: Pacific Coast*, 459. F. W. Howay uses the spelling *Woolquot*, "Early Followers of Captain Gray," *Washington Historical Quarterly*, XVIII, 1 (January, 1927), 16.

15. Davidson, *United States Coast and Geodetic Survey: Pacific Coast*, 459; Howay, "Early Followers of Captain Gray," 16.

16. The hill known as Scarboro (Scarborough) Hill by Hudson's Bay Company personnel was named Chinook Hill by the United States Exploring Expedition in 1841. Davidson, *United States Coast and Geodetic Survey: Pacific Coast*, 460.

17. S. A. Clarke, *Pioneer Days of Oregon History*, II, 420.

18. T. C. Elliott, "The Chinook Wind," *Oregon Historical Quarterly*, XXXIII (1932), 243–49; "The Chinook Wind," *Oregon Historical Quarterly*, XLI (1940), 103–106. See also Ella E. Clark, "Bluejay Brings the Chinook Wind," in *Indian Legends from the Northern Rockies*, 98–100. For legends of the origin of the Chinooks, see Ella E. Clark, *Indian Legends of the Pacific Northwest*, 135–36. For the legend of the origin of the Chinooks at Shoalwater Bay, see Isaac H. Whealdon, "Stories and Sketches from Pacific County," *Washington Historical Quarterly*, IV, 3 (July, 1913), 187.

19. Clatsop villages are listed by J. Neilson Barry in "The Indians of Oregon—Geographic Distribution of Linguistic Families," *Oregon Historical Quarterly*, XXVIII (1927), 55, 56. Chinook and Wahkiakum villages are listed in the same article on pages 149–50. Lower Chinook villages are listed

in Ray, *Lower Chinook Ethnographic Notes*, 38–41, and in Spier, *Tribal Distribution in Washington*, 21–24. Chinook villages on Shoalwater Bay are listed by Jean Hazeltine in *The Historical and Regional Geography of the Willapa Bay Area, Washington*, 50–51.

20. Don Greame Kelley, "Trees of the Totem Culture," *American West*, VIII, 3 (May, 1971), 18.

21. E. Sapir, "The Social Organization of the West Coast Tribes," *Transactions of the Royal Society of Canada, Section II*, 2d ser. IX (1915), 357.

22. Philip Drucker, "Rank, Wealth, and Kinship in Northwest Coast Society," *American Anthropologist*, n.s. XXXXI, 1 (January, 1939), 56.

23. Philip Drucker, *Cultures of the North Pacific Coast*, 174.

24. George Gibbs, *Tribes of Western Washington and Northwestern Oregon*, 185.

25. John Minto, "The Number and Condition of the Native Race in Oregon when First Seen by White Men," *Oregon Historical Quarterly*, I (1900), 300.

26. Gibbs, *Tribes of Western Washington and Northwestern Oregon*, 198.

27. Minto, "Number and Condition of the Native Race," 299.

28. Paul Kane, *Wanderings of an Artist among the Indians of North America from Canada to Vancouver's Island and Oregon through the Hudson's Bay Company's Territory and Back Again, by Paul Kane*, 130.

29. Ray, *Lower Chinook Ethnographic Notes*, 51.

30. Dennis, "Indian Slavery in Pacific Northwest," 286.

31. Fred Lockley, "Chinooks and Others," *Oregon Sunday Journal*, June 23, 1929.

32. Franz Boas, *Chinook Texts*, Bureau of American Ethnology *Bulletin 20*, 252.

33. *The Oregon Territory, Consisting of a Brief Description of the Country and Its Productions*, 52.

34. James C. Strong, *Wah-Kee-Nah and Her People: The Curious Customs, Traditions, and Legends of the North American Indians*, 133.

35. "The Lost Tribes of the Chinooks and Clatsops," *San Francisco Chronicle*, June 1, 1884.

36. H. A. Yarrow, "A Further Contribution to the Study of the Mortuary Customs of the North American Indians," *First Annual Report of the Bureau of American Ethnology to the Secretary of the Smithsonian Institution 1879–'80*, 179. For a discussion of the Chinooks' belief in the soul and life after death, see Franz Boas, "The Doctrine of Souls and of Diseases among the Chinook Indians," *Journal of American Folk-Lore*, VI, 20 (January, 1893), 39–43.

37. Ray, *Lower Chinook Ethnographic Notes*, 49.

38. Franz Boas discusses the potlatch in his *Chinook Texts*, 268–69.

39. Verne F. Ray, "The Historical Position of the Lower Chinook in the Native Culture of the Northwest," *Pacific Northwest Quarterly*, XXVIII, 4 (October, 1937), 368, 370; Ray, *Lower Chinook Ethnographic Notes*, 49.

40. "Bancroft's Native Races of the Pacific States," *Atlantic Monthly*, XXXV, 208 (February, 1875), 168. An explanation of the use and significance

of crests may be found in Franz Boas, *The Social Organization and the Secret Societies of the Kwakiutl Indians*.

41. Richard Brinsley Hinds, "Journal," Kenneth L. Holmes Collection, Oregon Historical Society; Albert Buell Lewis, *Tribes of the Columbia Valley and the Coast of Washington and Oregon*, Memoirs of the American Anthropological Association, 173–74; Mildred Colbert, *Kutkos Chinook Tyee*, 220.

42. Ray, "Historical Position of the Lower Chinook in the Native Culture of the Northwest," 370. The anthropologist Melville Jacobs suggests that the power spirit, Blue Jay, a zany actor, stirred Chinooks to laugh at the mere mention of his name, for he was a projection of their anxiety about men resorting to antisocial behavior in a preposterous manner because of their "venomous rivalrousness and anguish about low status." The Chinooks, states Jacobs, "feared such men and knew that ever so often they turned up in one's own household or lineage." Melville Jacobs, "Indications of Mental Illness among Pre-Contact Indians of the Northwest States," *Pacific Northwest Quarterly*, L, 2 (April, 1964), 50.

43. Ray, "Historical Position of the Lower Chinook in the Native Culture of the Northwest," 371.

44. Kane, *Wanderings of an Artist among the Indians of North America*, 275; John Dunn, *History of the Oregon Territory and British North-American Fur Trade, With an Account of the Habits and Customs of the Principal Native Tribes on the Northern Continent*, 139.

45. There are accounts of Chinooks catching sturgeon by means of wooden hooks fastened to lines of twisted tree roots. Dunn, *History of the Oregon Territory*, 135; Kane, *Wanderings of an Artist among the Indians of North America*, 275; Mildred Colbert, "Naming and Early Settlement of Ilwaco, Washington," *Oregon Historical Quarterly*, XLVII (1946), 186; Bon I. Whealdon, "On Whealdon Hill (Ilwaco, Wash.) Eve of July 16, 1860," Oregon Historical Society, 4.

46. Hubert Howe Bancroft, *The Native Races*, Vol. I, *Wild Tribes*. Vol. I of *The Works of Hubert Howe Bancroft*, 232; Avery Sylvester, "Voyages of the Pallas and Chenamus, 1843–45," *Oregon Historical Quarterly*, XXXIV (1933), 359.

47. Boas, *Chinook Texts*, 262–63; Myron Eells, "The Worship and Traditions of the Aboriginies of America; or, Their Testimony to the Religion of the Bible," Victoria Institute, London, *Journal of Transactions*, XIX, 22–23.

48. L. R. Williams, *Our Pacific County*, 42.

49. Charles Wilkes, *Narrative of the United States Exploring Expedition during the Years 1838, 1839, 1840, 1841, 1842*, V, 119.

50. Bancroft, *Native Races*, Vol. I, *Wild Tribes*, 232.

51. Hollister D. McGuire, "Columbia River Salmon," *Pacific Monthly*, I, 2 (November, 1898), 45–51.

52. Gibbs, *Tribes of Western Washington and Northwestern Oregon*, 194–95.

53. Albion Gile, "Notes on Columbia River Salmon," *Oregon Historical Quarterly*, LVI (1955), 141; "Copy of Testimony taken in 1902, at Astoria, in support of a claim of *Chinook Indian Tribe against the United States* for land in the State of Washington, near the mouth of the Columbia River. Containing historical material relating to the Chinook villages and the people, with some reference to the Clatsop Indian Tribe in Oregon," Oregon Historical Society, 71.

54. The character of many beaches became unfit for the type of clams the Chinooks once harvested. *Morning Oregonian*, December 11, 1899, p. 9.

55. Vernon Carstensen (ed.), "Pacific Northwest Letters of George Gibbs," *Oregon Historical Quarterly*, LIV (1953), 212; Ella E. Clark, "The Mythology of the Indians in the Pacific Northwest," *Oregon Historical Quarterly*, LIV (1953), 171.

56. Elwood Evans, *History of the Pacific Northwest: Oregon and Washington*, II, 570; Charles De Wolf Brownell, *The Indian Races of North and South America*, 477; Kelley, "Trees of the Totem Culture," 21.

57. Paul Kane, "Incidents of Travel on the North-West Coast, Vancouver's Island, Oregon, Etc.," *Canadian Journal*, III, 12 (July, 1855), 276.

58. Leslie M. Scott, "Indian Women as Food Providers and Tribal Counselors," *Oregon Historical Quarterly*, XLII (1941), 215–16.

59. For a discussion of the distribution of the plank house, see A. L. Kroeber, "American Culture and the Northwest Coast," *American Anthropologist*, n.s. XXV, 1 (January, 1923), 13.

60. Lockley, "Chinooks and Others"; Frederick Merk (ed.), *Fur Trade and Empire: George Simpson's Journal*, 95.

61. Fred Lockley, "Extinct Chinook Indians Once Peopled Prosperous Villages along the Columbia," *Oregon Sunday Journal*, July 8, 1928, p. 9. For a discussion of the location of pits under houses, see T. T. Waterman, "Some Conundrums in Northwest Coast Art," *American Anthropologist*, n.s. XXV, 4 (October, 1923), 440.

62. Ross Cox reports houses to have been ninety feet long and forty feet broad. *Adventures on the Columbia River, Including the Narrative of a Residence of Six Years on the Western Side of the Rocky Mountains, among Various Tribes of Indians Hitherto Unknown; Together with a Journey across the American Continent*, I, 327.

63. Lockley, "Extinct Chinook Indians Once Peopled Prosperous Villages along the Columbia," 8; Merk (ed.), *Fur Trade and Empire*, 103; Gibbs, *Tribes of Western Washington and Northwestern Oregon*, 214.

64. Ronald L. Olson, *The Quinault Indians and Adze, Canoe, and House Types of the Northwest Coast*, 13.

65. Gibbs, *Tribes of Western Washington and Northwestern Oregon*, 188.

66. Dunn, *History of the Oregon Territory*, 125; Gibbs, *Tribes of Western Washington and Northwestern Oregon*, 192.

67. Frederic W. Howay, "A Yankee Trader on the Northwest Coast, 1791–1795," *Washington Historical Quarterly*, XXI, 2 (April, 1930), 84.

68. Lewis R. Williams, *Chinook by the Sea*, 30–33; John Donovan, "Chinook Victory," *Cowlitz County Historical Quarterly*, II, 4 (February, 1961), 22, 23.

69. Charles Bishop, "Commercial Journal Copy's of Letters and Accts, of Ship Ruby's voyage to the N.W.T. coast of America and China, 1794, 5, 6," Archives of British Columbia, 162–63.

70. "Chinooks at the Cross Roads," *Sunday Oregonian*, November 28, 1937, Sec. 6, p. 2.

71. Olson, *The Quinault Indians*, 19.

72. Drucker, *Cultures of the North Pacific Coast*, 172.

73. Philip Drucker, *Indians of the Northwest Coast*, 66–67.

74. Ray, *Lower Chinook Ethnographic Notes*, 102.

75. Williams, *Chinook by the Sea*, 32, 53; Wilkes, *Narrative of the United States Exploring Expedition*, V, 133; E. Ruth Rockwood (ed.), "Letters of Charles Stevens," *Oregon Historical Quarterly*, XXXVII (1936), 249.

76. Herbert C. Taylor, Jr., "John Work on the Chehalis," Washington State Library, 12a.

77. Olson, *Quinault Indians*, 88.

78. "Copy of Testimony . . . in support of a claim of *Chinook Indian Tribe against the United States*," 121, 124.

79. Helen Peterson interview, Neah Bay, Washington, August 7, 1970; James G. Swan, "The Indians of Cape Flattery at the Entrance of the Strait of Fuca, Washington Territory," *Smithsonian Contributions to Knowledge*, XVI, 8, 30; Olson, *The Quinault Indians*, 68.

80. Thomas Bulfinch, *Oregon and Eldorado; or, Romance of the River*, 162; Scott, "Indian Women as Food Providers and Tribal Counselors," 217; Gile, "Notes on Columbia River Salmon," 142.

81. Frederic W. Howay and T. C. Elliott (eds.), "Vancouver's Brig Chatham in the Columbia," *Oregon Historical Quarterly*, XLIII (1942), 324; J. Neilson Barry, "Spaniards in Early Oregon," *Washington Historical Quarterly*, XXIII, 1 (January, 1932), 26; Gibbs, *Tribes of Western Washington and Northwestern Oregon*, 220; Clarke, *Pioneer Days of Oregon History*, II, 420; J. Neilson Barry, "Columbia River Exploration, 1792," *Oregon Historical Quarterly*, XXXIII (1932), 144, 153.

82. Drucker, *Indians of the Northwest Coast*, 51.

83. Drucker, *Cultures of the North Pacific Coast*, 169; Kane, "Incidents of Travel on the North-West Coast," 276; Spier and Sapir, *Wishram Ethnography*, 222. The nor'Wester David Thompson, among the Chinooks and Clatsops in 1811, noted: "These people had many Slaves, all that I could learn of them was, that they were prisoners taken in their marauding expeditions along the sea shore, most of them youths when taken; they appeared as well off as their masters, except their paddling the Canoes, and hauling the Seine Net, in which their masters took a share of the labor." Richard Glover (ed.), *David Thompson's Narrative 1784–1812*, 363. Cited hereafter as *Thompson's Narrative*.

84. *Ibid.*, 222, 227.

85. Elliott Coues (ed.), *New Light on the Early History of the Greater Northwest: The Manuscript Journals of Alexander Henry, Fur Trader of the Northwest Company, and of David Thompson, Official Geographer and Explorer of the Same Company, 1799–1814*, II, 753; D. Lee and J. H. Frost, *Ten Years in Oregon*, 101.

86. Dunn, *History of the Oregon Territory*, 134.

CHAPTER 2
Those Who Drift Ashore

1. Edward P. Vining, *An Inglorious Columbus*, 54–55, 68–69. While some historians discredit the validity of Hwui Shan's voyage, Robert Wauchope in his *Lost Tribes & Sunken Continents*, 91, points out that one investigator believed Hwui Shan reached only the coast of Japan. There are "numerous evidences" that Asians reached western shores by water several centuries before Europeans "and produced an effect on the life of the inhabitants." See Charles Edward Chapman, *A History of California: The Spanish Period*, 21–30.

2. Frederick W. Howay, "William Sturgis: The Northwest Fur Trade," *British Columbia Historical Quarterly*, VIII, 1 (January, 1944), 21n.

3. Vining, *Inglorious Columbus*, 27.

4. Gordon Speck, "The Journey of Hwui Shan," *Pacific Search*, V, 1 (October, 1970), 11.

5. Thomas Jefferys, *Voyages from Asia to America, for Completing the Discoveries of the North West Coast of America*, v.

6. Charles Wolcott Brooks, *Japanese Wrecks Stranded and Picked Up Adrift in the North Pacific Ocean*, 7.

7. John Keast Lord, *The Naturalist in Vancouver Island and British Columbia*, II, 216.

8. Coues (ed.), *New Light on the Early History of the Greater Northwest*, II, 854–55.

9. Dorothy O. Johansen and Charles M. Gates, *Empire on the Columbia: A History of the Pacific Northwest*, 22–23.

10. Hubert Howe Bancroft, *History of the Northwest Coast*, Vol. I. Vol. XXVII of *The Works of Hubert Howe Bancroft*, 146–47.

11. See *ibid.*, 127–36 for a discussion of the many maps produced representing the outline of the Pacific Northwest coast.

12. Bancroft, *History of the Northwest Coast*, Vol. I, 147.

13. Harry Hobucket, "Quillayute Indian Tradition," *Washington Historical Quarterly*, XXV, 1 (January, 1934), 53–54.

14. S. J. Cotton, *Stories of Nehalem*, 55.

15. For a discussion of the Manila galleons, see William L. Schurz, *Manila Galleon*.

16. Cotton, *Stories of Nehalem*, 50.

17. Clarke, *Pioneer Days of Oregon History*, I, 157.

18. Gibbs, *Tribes of Western Washington and Northwestern Oregon*, 236.

19. Clarke, *Pioneer Days of Oregon History*, I, 156.

20. Gibbs, *Tribes of Western Washington and Northwestern Oregon*, 238.

21. One source says 1725. *Morning Oregonian*, December 11, 1899, p. 9. Another date given is 1750. Clarke, *Pioneer Days of Oregon History*, I, 158.

22. Other spellings are *Tio hon nipts*, "those who drift ashore" (*Morning Oregonian*, December 11, 1899, p. 9), *Tlehonnipts*, "castaways" (J. F. Santee, "Comcomly and the Chinooks," *Oregon Historical Quarterly*, XXXIII [1932], 277).

23. Boas, *Chinook Texts*, 277–78.

24. Barry, "Spaniards in Early Oregon," 25.

25. Gibbs, *Tribes of Western Washington and Northwestern Oregon*, 236–37.

26. Gabriel Franchère, *Adventure at Astoria, 1810–1814*, 51.

27. Clarke, *Pioneer Days in Oregon History*, I, 158.

28. *Ibid.*, 145–47.

29. *Ibid.*, 173.

30. J. Neilson Barry, "Astorians Who Became Permanent Settlers," *Washington Historical Quarterly*, XXIV, 4 (October, 1933), 298.

31. Fur man Alexander Henry, at Fort George in 1813, writes of a red-haired man of about thirty years of age. Coues (ed.), *New Light on the Early History of the Greater Northwest*, II, 768. Presumably this was the same young man of about twenty-five years of age Lewis and Clark had seen eight years before. Reuben Gold Thwaites, *Original Journals of the Lewis and Clark Expedition 1804–1806*, III, 301. Ross Cox, who arrived at Astoria in 1812, mentions seeing a red-haired young man. Cox, *Adventures on the Columbia River*, I, 315. According to age, the red-haired Chinook seen by John Keast Lord in 1837 at Fort Vancouver may have been Young Jack, judged by Lord to be sixty years of age. Lord, *The Naturalist in Vancouver Island and British Columbia*, II, 230.

32. One of those was said to be the son of a Captain Crelleman. Silas B. Smith to Eva Emery Dye, October 3, 1900, Eva Emery Dye Papers. This may have been Captain Callamon, who was in the area in the first decade of the 1800's. James K. Hosmer (ed.), *History of the Expedition of Captains Lewis and Clark 1804–5–6*, II, 153.

33. *Sunday Oregonian*, October 4, 1970.

34. O. F. Stafford, "The Wax of Nehalem Beach," *Oregon Historical Quarterly*, IX (1908), 39.

35. Cotton, *Stories of Nehalem*, 49.

36. Stafford, "Wax of Nehalem Beach," 25.

37. William S. Lewis and Naojiro Murakami (eds.), *Ranald MacDonald: The Narrative of His Early Life on the Columbia under the Hudson's Bay Company's Regime; of His Experiences in the Pacific Whale Fishery; And of*

His Great Adventure to Japan; with a Sketch of His Later Life on the Western Frontier, 1824–1894, 122n.

38. Clarke, *Pioneer Days of Oregon History,* I, 175.

39. The Indians have traditions of several wrecks off the Chinook-owned coast. Clarke, *Pioneer Days of Oregon History,* I, 172.

40. So coveted was copper from wrecked ships among peoples of the lower Columbia that it appears in Kathlamet mythology. Franz Boas, *Kathlamet Texts,* Bureau of American Ethnology *Bulletin 26,* 39–44.

41. Bruno de Hezeta, "Diario de la navegacion écha por el Teniente de Navio de la Real Armada, D. Bruno de Hezeta, a explorar la Costa Septentrional de Californias. Año de 1775," Bancroft Library, University of California, Berkeley. The translation has been made by Charles Walters, Instructor of Languages and Latin American History, Wenatchee Valley College, Wenatchee, Washington.

42. A bibliography in the Washington State Library, Olympia, Washington, erroneously reports that the thesis prepared by Mary Gormly states of the Hezeta diary: "This diary contains the first account of the Chinooks seen at the mouth of the Columbia River." "Early Culture Contact on the Northwest Coast 1774–95: Analysis of Spanish Source Material," Suzzallo Library, University of Washington, Seattle, 73.

Harry M. Majors, who has done an extensive research of the early explorations along the Pacific Northwest Coast, writes July 25, 1971, in a letter to the authors, "There are six diaries for the 1775 Hezeta voyage, but only one of the two ships visited the Columbia River. That was Hezeta's frigate *Santiago,* which carried the diarists Hezeta, Pérez, Campa and Sierra. Pérez died during the voyage (his diary terminates 23 June 1775). Thus, only three diaries document the discovery of the Columbia River: Hezeta, Campa and Sierra. . . . None of them mentions seeing any Indians, Chinook or otherwise, at the mouth of the Columbia River." It is likely, as Majors explains, that natives encountered north along the Washington coast may have been confused by readers of the diaries as being natives at the mouth of the Columbia. Majors documents Spanish voyages in the Pacific Northwest. "Science and Exploration on the Northwest Coast of North America 1542–1841," John Carter Brown Library, Brown University.

Translations of the three diarists for entries of August 17, 1775, may be found as follows: Hezeta in Robert Greenhow, *The History of Oregon and California and the Other Territories on the North-West Coast of North America,* 430–33 and in Francisco Antonio Mourella, *Voyage of the Sonora in the Second Bucareli Expedition to Explore the Northwest Coast Survey the Port of San Francisco and Found Franciscan Missions and a Presidio and Pueblo at that Port,* 86–88; Campa in John Galvin (ed.), *A Journal of Explorations Northward along the Coast from Monterey in the Year 1775,* 54–55; and Sierra in Henry R. Wagner, "Fray Benito de la Sierra's Account of the Hezeta Expedition to the Northwest Coast in 1775," *California Historical Quarterly,* IX, 3 (September, 1930), 235.

43. T. A. Rickard, "The Sea-Otter in History," *The British Columbia Historical Quarterly*, XI, I (January, 1947), 19.

44. Bancroft, *History of the Northwest Coast*, Vol. I, 161.

45. Erna Gunther, *Northwest Coast Indian Art*, 24.

46. T. A. Rickard, "Drift Iron: A Fortuitous Factor in Primitive Culture," *Geographical Review*, XXIV, 4 (October, 1934), 525–26.

47. For an account of Vitus Bering's and Alexei Chirikov's voyage of exploration for Russia to the Pacific Northwest coast, see Jefferys, *Voyages from Asia to America*, 39–50.

48. Katharine Coman, *Economic Beginnings of the Far West*, I, 199.

49. Coues (ed.), *New Light on the Early History of the Greater Northwest*, II, 790.

50. Williams, *Chinook by the Sea*, 52.

51. Leslie M. Scott, "Indian Diseases as Aids to Pacific Northwest Settlement," *Oregon Historical Quarterly*, XXIX (1928), 145.

52. Cox, *Adventures on the Columbia River*, I, 312.

53. Gordon Speck, *Northwest Explorations*, 83.

54. At this time the natives cared little for beads. Bancroft, *History of the Northwest Coast*, Vol. I, 154.

55. Rickard, "Sea-Otter in History," 28.

56. Bancroft, *History of the Northwest Coast*, Vol. I, 154.

57. *Ilwaco Tribune*, March 13, 1953.

58. Blanchet, et al., *Notices & Voyages of the Famed Quebec Mission to the Pacific Northwest*, 221.

59. Speck, *Northwest Explorations*, 103.

60. Rickard, "Drift Iron," 541.

61. William Duncan Strong, "The Occurences and Wider Implications of a 'Ghost Cult' on the Columbia River Suggested by Carvings in Wood, Bone and Stone," *American Anthropologist*, n.s. XLVII, 2 (April, 1945), 252.

62. Barry, "Columbia River Explorations," 144.

63. James Strange, *James Strange's Journal and Narrative of the Commercial Expedition From Bombay to the North-West Coast of America*, 26.

64. Frederic W. Howay, *Voyages of the "Columbia" to the Northwest Coast 1787–1790 and 1790–1793*, 395.

65. Howay, "A Yankee Trader on the Northwest Coast, 1791–1795," 144.

66. "Copy of Testimony . . . in support of a claim of *Chinook Indian Tribe against the United States*," 147.

67. Jean Francois de Galaup, comte de La Pérouse, *A Voyage Round the World Performed in the Years 1785, 1786, 1787 and 1788*, I, 371.

68. See Adele Ogden, *The California Sea Otter Trade, 1784–1848*, 3–9.

69. Bulfinch, *Oregon and Eldorado*, 2.

70. There were numerous unofficial published accounts of Cook's third voyage which helped excite interest in the fur trade. James Stirrat Marshall and Carrie Marshall, *Pacific Voyages*, 33.

71. Rickard, "The Sea-Otter in History," 26.

72. Bancroft, *History of the Northwest Coast*, Vol. I, 182.

73. Bishop, "Commercial Journal . . . of Ship Ruby's voyage to the N.W.T.," 152.

74. *Ibid.*, 152–53.

75. When later claiming ownership to the Pacific Northwest, the British would claim that Barkley had traded in the vicinity of the Columbia River mouth. E. E. Rich (ed.), *Simpson's 1828 Journey to the Columbia*, Publications of the Champlain Society, 172.

76. The south entrance to the bay he called "Low Point." The north entrance had a high bluff which he called "Cape Shoalwater." John Meares, *Voyages Made in the Years 1788 and 1789, from China to the North West Coast of America*, 163–64.

77. *Ibid.*, 164.

78. *Ibid.*, 165.

79. *Ibid.*, 168.

80. J. Neilson Barry, "Who Discovered the Columbia River?" *Oregon Historical Quarterly*, XXXIX (1938), 156.

When negotiating with the United States over ownership of the area, Britain would also claim that it was Meares who discovered the Columbia River. Clinton A. Snowden, *History of Washington: The Rise and Progress of an American State*, I, 115.

CHAPTER 3

White Sails on the Oregon

1. Kenneth A. Spaulding (ed.), *On the Oregon Trail: Robert Stuart's Journey of Discovery*, 42.

2. Dorothy O. Johansen (ed.), *Voyage of the Columbia Around the World with John Boit, 1790–1793*, 52. John Boit wrote: "It [destruction of the village of Opitsatah] was a Command I was no ways tenacious of, and am grieved to think Capt. Gray shou'd let his passions go so far." Edmond S. Meany (ed.), *A New Log of the Columbia by John Boit on the Discovery of the Columbia River and Grays Harbor*, 25.

3. Frederic W. Howay and T. C. Elliott (eds.), "John Boit's Log of the Columbia—1790–1793," *Oregon Historical Quarterly*, XXII (1921), 307.

4. Howay, *Voyages of the "Columbia" to the Northwest Coast*, 395.

5. Gibbs, *Tribes of Western Washington and Northwestern Oregon*, 238.

6. Howay, *Voyages of the "Columbia" to the Northwest Coast*, 397.

7. Frederic W. Howay, "Captains Gray and Kendrick: The Barrell Letters," *Washington Historical Quarterly*, XII, 4 (October, 1921), 247.

8. Frederic W. Howay, "The Ballad of the Bold Northwestman: An Incident in the Life of Captain John Kendrick," *Washington Historical Quarterly*, XX, 2 (April, 1929), 119n.

9. Promoters were Joseph Barrell, Samuel Brown, and Charles Bulfinch of

Boston, Crowell Hatch of Cambridge, John Derby of Salem, and John Pintard of New York. Bulfinch, *Oregon and Eldorado*, 2–3.

10. For a history of the China trade, see William C. Hunter, *The Fan Kwae' at Canton before Treaty Days, 1825–1844*, 96.

11. Coman, *Economic Beginnings of the Far West*, I, 214.

12. John Fiske, "Oration," in *Transactions of the Twentieth Annual Reunion of the Oregon Pioneer Association for 1892*, 71.

13. Barrell to Gray, September 25, 1790, "Voyage Aug.–Nov. 1790 Ship Columbia," Massachusetts Historical Society.

14. Edmond S. Meany, *Vancouver's Discovery of Puget Sound*, 233.

15. *Ibid.*, supplement "A New Vancouver Journal," 40.

16. *Ibid.*

17. *Ibid.*, 5.

18. T. C. Elliott (ed.), "Journal of John Work, November and December, 1824," *Washington Historical Quarterly*, III, 3 (July, 1912), 206; Wilkes, *Narrative of the United States Exploring Expedition*, V, 132; C. L. Andrews, "The Wreck of the St. Nicholas," *Washington Historical Quarterly*, XIII, I (January, 1922), 28.

19. John C. Ewers, *The Blackfeet Raiders on the Northwestern Plains*, 51–52.

20. Howay, *Voyages of the "Columbia" to the Northwest Coast*, 397, 436.

21. Meany, *Vancouver's Discovery of Puget Sound*, 71.

22. Howay, *Voyages of the "Columbia" to the Northwest Coast*, 399.

23. *Ibid.*

24. Bancroft, *Native Races*, Vol. I, *Wild Tribes*, 224; Lee and Frost, *Ten Years in Oregon*, 102; John Scouler, "Dr. John Scouler's Journal of a Voyage to N.W. America," *Oregon Historical Quarterly*, VI (1905), 164; A. N. Armstrong, *Oregon: Comprising a Brief History and Full Description of the Territories of Oregon and Washington*, 103; Dunn, *History of the Oregon Territory*, 122.

25. "Bancroft's Native Races of the Pacific States," 168.

26. Bancroft, *Native Races*, Vol. I, *Wild Tribes*, 226.

27. Robert H. Ruby and John A. Brown, *The Cayuse Indians: Imperial Tribesmen of Old Oregon*, 15.

28. The practice also existed among the ancient American tribes such as the Natchez. Domenech, *Seven Years' Residence in the Great Deserts of North America*, II, 294. Among those of Peru before the Spanish conquest head flattening was practiced. John Scouler, "Observations on the Indigenous Tribes of the N.W. Coast of America," *Journal of the Royal Geographical Society of London*, XI (1841), 223–24. The custom also prevailed among the Mayans. Wilton Marion Krogman, "Medical Practices and Diseases of the Aboriginal American Indians," *Ciba Symposium*, I, 15 (1939), 15. Samoans flattened heads. "Samoan and Chinook Head-Flattening," *Frank Leslie's Popular Monthly*, II, 4 (October, 1876), 448.

29. Emma Gene Miller, *Clatsop County, Oregon: A History*, 60.

30. Armstrong says ten days after birth. *Oregon: Comprising a Brief History and Full Description of the Territories of Oregon and Washington,* 105.

31. Zechariah Atwell Mudge, *Sketches of Mission Life among the Indians of Oregon,* 80.

32. Bishop, "Commercial Journal . . . of Ship Ruby's voyage to the N.W.T.," 160.

33. Armstrong, *Oregon,* 105.

34. One author says the hinged method of head flattening was practiced more among Upper Chinooks. "Artificial Deformities," *Chambers's Edinburgh Journal,* X (1840), 111.

35. John K. Townsend, when on a visit to the mouth of the Columbia River, made an illustration of a cradle board he collected which shows loops for ties used to hold the body in a fixed position. T. D. Stewart, "The Chinook Sign of Freedom: A Study of the Skull of the Famous Chief Comcomly," *Annual Report of the Board of Regents of the Smithsonian Institution Showing the Operations, Expenditures, and Conditions of the Institution for the Year Ended June 30, 1959,* II, 569.

36. Marguerite Eyer Wilbur (ed.), *Duflot de Mofras' Travels on the Pacific Coast,* II, 181.

37. "Samoan and Chinook Head-Flattening," 448.

38. Mudge, *Sketches of Mission Life among the Indians of Oregon,* 28.

39. Harold Mackey, "Siuslaw Head Flattening," *Oregon Historical Quarterly,* LXIX (1968), 173.

40. "Voyage Aug.–Nov. 1790 Ship Columbia," Massachusetts Historical Society.

41. T. C. Elliott (ed.), "The Log of H.M.S. 'Chatham,' " *Oregon Historical Quarterly,* XVIII (1917), 236.

42. Jean Hazeltine, "The Discovery and Cartographical Recognition of Shoalwater Bay," *Oregon Historical Quarterly,* LVIII (1957), 254.

43. For a good dissertation on the river bar and channels, see Davidson, *United States Coast and Geodetic Survey: Pacific Coast,* 456–58.

44. Howay, *Voyages of the "Columbia" to the Northwest Coast,* 399.

45. Gray reached Canton in December. His "catch was sold to good advantage." Coman, *Economic Beginnings of the Far West,* 216.

46. Frank E. Ross, "American Adventures in the Early Marine Fur Trade with China," *Chinese Social and Political Science Review,* LXXI, 2 (July, 1937), 240.

47. For a listing of vessels on the coast from 1785 to 1794, see Frederick W. Howay, "A List of Trading Vessels in Maritime Fur Trade, 1785–1794," *Proceedings and Transactions of the Royal Society of Canada,* 3d ser. XXIV (1930), 111–34.

48. *Proceedings of the Massachusetts Historical Society, Vol. I, 1791–1835,* 68.

49. Howay, "Early Followers of Captain Gray," 13.

50. Thomas Dunbabin, "Who Discovered the Columbia?" *The Beaver*, Outfit 285, 3 (Winter, 1954), 52–55.

51. Spaulding (ed.), *On the Oregon Trail*, 42.

52. Dunbabin, "Who Discovered the Columbia?" 53.

53. Frederic W. Howay and T. C. Elliott, "Voyages of the 'Jenny' to Oregon, 1792–94," *Oregon Historical Quarterly*, XXX (1929), 202.

54. Jos[ep]h Baker, in "A Log of His Majesty's Ship Discovery from 22nd December 1790 to 27 November 1792," Oregon Historical Society, entry October 20, 1792, writes, "While we were at Nootka we received information that the Columbia had entered the River, & that it was called after that Ship."

55. J. Neilson Barry, "Broughton, Up Columbia River, 1792," *Oregon Historical Quarterly*, XXXII (1931), 301.

56. For a presentation of the various facts in the argument, see Barry, "Who Discovered the Columbia River?" 160.

57. Thomas Manby, "Manby's Journal of H.M.S. Discovery 1791 & 2," Beinecke Library.

58. See Edward Bell's narrative in Barry, "Columbia River Explorations, 1792," 37.

59. *Ibid.*, 39.

60. *Ibid.*

61. Manby, "Manby's Journal of H.M.S. Discovery 1791 & 2."

62. *Ibid.*

63. Barry, "Columbia River Exploration, 1792," 42.

64. The Friendly Old Chief was subsequently seen by Lewis and Clark and by fur men David Thompson and Gabriel Franchère. Barry, "Columbia River Explorations, 1792," 42n.

65. Names given to landmarks may be found in Barry, "Broughton on the Columbia in 1792," *Oregon Historical Quarterly*, XXVII (1926), 410–11.

66. George Vancouver, *Voyage of Discovery to the North Pacific Ocean and Round the World*, II, 61.

67. *Ibid.*

68. Barry, "Columbia River Exploration, 1792," 143.

69. Manby, "Manby's Journal of H.M.S. Discovery 1791 & 2."

70. "Log Book of the Chatham Tender Aug. 1792–Dec. 1793," University Microfilm Services, Ann Arbor, Mi.

71. Vancouver, *Voyage of Discovery to the North Pacific Ocean and Round the World*, II, 62.

72. *Ibid.*, 77.

73. "Log Book of the Chatham Tender Aug. 1792–Dec. 1793."

CHAPTER 4
Clamor and Clamons

1. Henry R. Wagner, "The Last Spanish Exploration of the Northwest

Coast and the Attempt to Colonize Bodega Bay," *California Historical Quarterly*, X, 4 (December, 1931), 326–37.

2. Henry R. Wagner, *Spanish Explorations in the Strait of Juan de Fuca*, 27.

3. Wagner, "Last Spanish Exploration of the Northwest Coast," 327.

4. *Ibid.*, 324–25.

5. *Ibid.*, 327.

6. *Ibid.*

7. The chart which the crew of the *Mexicana* made of the Columbia River mouth is now in the Library of Congress. It is entitled "Plano de la Entrade de Ezeta O Rio de la Columbia." Harry M. Majors, "Science and Exploration on the Northwest Coast of North America 1542–1841," John Carter Brown Library, Brown University, 460.

8. Coman, *Economic Beginnings of the Far West*, 211.

9. The *Jefferson* sailed from Boston on November 28, 1791. Horatio Appleton Lamb, "Notes on Trade With the Northwest Coast, 1790–1810. Made by Horatio Appleton Lamb, from the records of James and Thomas Lamb, Merchant Shippers of Boston, 1781–1813," Houghton Library, Harvard University, 21.

The *Jefferson* had carried parts of the *Resolution* to Resolution Bay, Santa Christina Island of the Marquesas group, where her keel was laid on November 19, 1792, and she was launched on February 8, 1793. She left those islands on February 24, 1793, in company with the *Jefferson*. Howay, "Yankee Trader on the Northwest Coast, 1791–1795," 83–84.

10. Frederic W. Howay, "The Resolution on the Oregon Coast, 1793–94," *Oregon Historical Quarterly*, XXXIV (1937), 207.

11. Howay, *Voyages of the "Columbia" to the Northwest Coast*, 400 and n.

12. Howay, "Resolution on the Oregon Coast, 1793–94," 208.

13. Howay, "Yankee Trader on the Northwest Coast, 1791–1795," 87.

14. Samuel Eliot Morison, *The Maritime History of Massachusetts, 1783–1860*, 56; Charles Greely Loring (ed.), *Memoir of the Hon. William Sturgis*, PNW Reel 17, Microfilm History of the Pacific Northwest, 27.

15. Howay, "Resolution on the Oregon Coast, 1793–94," 212–13.

16. Howay and Elliott, "Voyages of the 'Jenny' to Oregon, 1792–94," 204.

17. *Ibid.*

18. For the whereabouts of the *Jenny* on the coast during this visit, see Howay, "Early Followers of Captain Gray," 13.

19. Bishop, "Commercial Journal . . . of Ship Ruby's voyage to the N.W.T.," 148.

20. Francis Norbert Blanchet, *Historical Sketches of the Catholic Church in Oregon for the Past Forty Years*, PNW Reel 3, Microfilm History of the Pacific Northwest, Sketch VIII, 220–22.

21. Thwaites (ed.), *Original Journals of the Lewis and Clark Expedition*, III, 294.

22. Bishop, "Commercial Journal . . . of Ship Ruby's voyage to the N.W.T.," 148.

23. Gibbs, *Tribes of Western Washington and Northwestern Oregon*, 199; *Hinds*, "Journal." A medication of powdered rattlesnake tail in some places in the Pacific Northwest was used in stimulating uterine contractions to produce abortion. Scott, "Indian Diseases as Aids to Pacific Northwest Settlement," 160.

24. W. P. Strickland, *History of the Missions of the Methodist Episcopal Church, from the Organization of the Missionary Society to the Present Time*, 139–40.

25. *Washington Standard*, November 4, 1871, p. 1.

26. Herbert Beaver, "Further Information Respecting the Aborigines; Containing Reports of the Committee on Indian Affairs at Philadelphia, Extracts from the Proceedings of the Yearly Meetings of Philadelphia, New York, New England, Maryland[,] Virginia, and Ohio," Oregon Historical Society.

27. Samuel Parker, *Journal of an Exploring Tour beyond the Rocky Mountains*, 248.

28. T. W. Davenport, "Recollections of an Indian Agent," *Oregon Historical Quarterly*, VIII (1907), 247.

29. George C. Shaw, *The Chinook Jargon and How to Use It*, ix.

30. White traders, for example, would not permit Indian women to eat at their tables.

31. Elliot C. Cowdin, "The Northwest Fur Trade," *Hunt's Merchant's Magazine*, XIV (1846), 533.

32. T. C. Elliott, "The Journal of the Ship Ruby," *Oregon Historical Quarterly*, XXVIII (1927), 259; Frederic W. Howay, "A List of Trading Vessels in the Maritime Fur Trade, 1795–1804," *Proceedings and Transactions of the Royal Society of Canada*, 3d ser., XXV (1931), 120.

33. John Myers, *The Life, Voyages and Travels of Capt. John Myers, Detailing His Adventures during Four Voyages Round the World*, 62. Judge Frederic W. Howay, who has made a study of maritime trading vessels on the Pacific Northwest Coast, evaluates Myers' book as being "absolutely unreliable." "A List of Trading Vessels in the Maritime Fur Trade, 1795–1804," 120.

34. Myers, *Life, Voyages and Travels of Capt. John Myers*, 61–62.

35. Bishop, "Commercial Journal ... of Ship Ruby's voyage to the N.W.T.," 71.

36. Howay, "Early Followers of Captain Gray," 14.

37. Howay, "William Sturgis," 22.

38. Bishop, "Commercial Journal ... of Ship Ruby's voyage to the N.W.T.," 73.

39. *Ibid.*, 71.

40. Edward S. Curtis, *The North American Indian, Being a Series of Volumes Picturing and Describing the Indians of the United States and Alaska*, VIII, 85.

41. Scott, "Indian Women as Food Providers and Tribal Counselors," 217;

Edmond S. Meany (ed.), "Journal of William Fraser Tolmie—1833," *Washington Historical Quarterly*, III, 3 (July, 1912), 232.

42. These islands are now eroded away. Michael Roe (ed.), *The Journal and Letters of Captain Charles Bishop on the North-West Coast of America, in the Pacific and in New South Wales, 1794–1799*, 58n.

43. Samuel Eliot Morison, "Nova Albion and New England," *Oregon Historical Quarterly*, XXVIII (1927), 9, 10.

44. John Boit, "Journal of a Voyage Round the Globe," Massachusetts Historical Society, entry July 15–25, 1795.

45. Bishop, "Commercial Journal . . . of Ship Ruby's voyage to the N.W.T.," 143.

46. *Ibid.*, 146.

47. *Ibid.*, 148.

48. *Ibid.*, 149.

49. *Ibid.*, 164.

50. *Ibid.*, 152.

51. *Ibid.*, 153.

52. *Ibid.*

53. *Ibid.*, 158.

54. *Ibid.*, 154. T. C. Elliott discusses Bishop's misuse of the name Chinook River for the Columbia River in his journal. "The Journal of the Ship Ruby," 260–61.

55. Bishop, "Commercial Journal . . . of Ship Ruby's voyage to the N.W.T.," 150–51.

56. Howay, "Early Followers of Captain Gray," 17.

57. Bishop, "Commercial Journal . . . of Ship Ruby's voyage to the N.W.T.," 162.

58. Howay, "Early Followers of Captain Gray," 14.

59. Howay, "List of Trading Vessels in the Maritime Fur Trade, 1795–1804," 118.

CHAPTER 5

Ladies in the Trade

1. L. Vernon Briggs, *History and Genealogy of the Cabot Family, 1475–1927*, I, 392.

2. *Ibid.*

3. *Ibid.*

4. The *Hazard* was owned by James Magee, Russel Sturgis, James and Thomas Lamb, and Capt. E. Johnson, who had several vessels on the Northwest coast in the trade. Lamb, "Notes on Trade With the Northwest Coast, 1790–1819," 33.

5. Howay, "List of Trading Vessels in the Maritime Fur Trade, 1795–1804," 127.

6. When the *Hazard* returned home with exotic wares of the Orient she was sold to J. and T. H. Perkins, Magee, and Johnson.

7. Morison, *Maritime History of Massachusetts*, 66.

8. Hunter, *Fan Kwae' at Canton before Treaty Days*, 118.

9. Howard Corning (ed.), "Letters of Sullivan Dorr," *Proceedings of the Massachusetts Historical Society*, LXVII (1941–44), 178; Howard Corning, "Sullivan Dorr, an Early China Merchant," *Essex Institute Historical Collections*, LXXVIII (1942), 158.

10. Elma Loines, "Hoqua, Sometime Chief of the Co-Hong at Canton (1769–1843)," *Essex Institute Historical Collections*, LXXXIX (1953), 100.

11. John Ebbets to John Jacob Astor, Macao, January 11, 1818, "Pacific Fur Company, 1806–1823," Vol. XX, John Jacob Astor Papers, Baker Library, Harvard University Graduate School of Business Administration.

12. Dudley L. Pickman, "Memoranda from Dudley L. Pickman on Doing Business in Canton," Papers of Benjamin Shreve.

13. Hunter, *Fan Kwae' at Canton before Treaty Days*, 21, 34–36, 53–55, 99; Howay, "Captains Gray and Kendrick," 266.

14. See the following: Ralph Haskins, "Journal of a voyage From Boston to the North West Coast of America, Thence to Canton, and Back to Boston—Kept on Board Ship Atahualpa by Ralph Haskins in the Years 1800, 1801, 1802, & 1803," Beinecke Library; "Account book of the ship Eliza, 1805, on voyage from New York to Canton," and "Account book of the ship, *Mary*, on voyage from New York to Canton (April–December, 1799)," Constable-Pierrepont Papers, William Bell Papers.

15. Morison, *Maritime History of Massachusetts*, 66.

16. Cowdin, "Northwest Fur Trade," 537.

17. Frederic W. Howay, "A List of Trading Vessels in the Maritime Fur Trade, 1820–1825," *Transactions of the Royal Society of Canada, Section II*, 3d ser., XXVIII (1934), 12.

18. Arthur Woodward, "Sea Otter Hunting on the Pacific Coast," *Quarterly of the Historical Society of Southern California*, XX, 3 (September, 1938), 119–20.

19. Alaska natives (Aleuts) were even forced to draw Russian plows. Coman, *Economic Beginnings of the Far West*, I, 198–200.

20. For accounts of the capture of the *Boston*, see Samuel Hill, "Autobiography," New York Public Library; Frederic W. Howay, "An Early Account of the Loss of the Boston in 1803," *Washington Historical Quarterly*, XVII, 4 (October, 1926), 280–88. From an account of the massacre of the crew members of the *Atahualpa*, see "Supercargo's log of the brig *Lydia*, Capt. Samuel Hill, on a fur-trading voyage from Boston to the N.W. Coast of North America, Aug. 31, 1804–July 14, 1805," Beinecke Library, entry June 24, 1805.

21. H.W.S. Cleveland, *Voyages of a Merchant Navigator of the Days That Are Past*, 40, 42; Richard Jeffry Cleveland, "Narrative of the fur trading of the brig *Caroline* from China to the Northwest Coast of America, January 10 to Sept. 13, 1799," Beinecke Library.

22. Ebenezer Clinton, "Remarks on board the ship Vancouver, Capt. Brown commanding. Bound from Boston to the N. West Coast of America and China from August 4, 1804 to September 8, 1806," Beinecke Library, entry Sept. 8, 1806.

23. Lamb, "Notes on Trade with the Northwest Coast," 14. Samuel A. Dorr to Ebenezer Dorr, Mear's Bay, August 15, 1801. Ebenezer Dorr, "Collection of letters, ship documents and receipts, 1795–1820," Archives of British Columbia.

24. Swan, *Northwest Coast*, 156; Ross, "American Adventures in the Early Marine Fur Trade with China," 238.

25. Thwaites (ed.), *Original Journals of the Lewis and Clark Expedition*, IV, 51; O. Larsell, "Medical Aspects of the Lewis and Clark Expedition," *Oregon Historical Quarterly*, LVI (1955), 222.

26. Gibbs, *Tribes of Western Washington and Northwestern Oregon*, 207; Scott, "Indian Diseases as Aids to Pacific Northwest Settlement," 160; Scott, "Indian Women as Food Providers and Tribal Counselors," 214.

27. O. Larsell, *The Doctor in Oregon*, 6; Scouler, "Dr. John Scouler's Journal of a Voyage to N.W. America," 176.

28. Dunn, *History of the Oregon Territory*, 118; Merk (ed.), *Fur Trade and Empire*, 100; Hubert Howe Bancroft, *The Native Races* Vol. III, *Myths and Languages*. Vol. III of *The Works of Hubert Howe Bancroft*, 156.

29. Howay, "William Sturgis," 14, 16.

30. *Ibid.*, 11, 12. Owners of the *Caroline* were James and Thomas Lamb, James and Thomas H. Perkins, Ebenezer Preble, Charles Derby, and Russell Sturgis, an uncle of William Sturgis. Lamb, "Notes on Trade with the Northwest Coast, 1790–1810," 40–41.

31. May Fidelia Boudinot, "The Case of the Mercury, as Typical of Contraband Trade on the California Coast, 1790–1820," thesis, University of California, Berkeley, 16; Cowdin, "The Northwest Fur Trade," 536. For a list of American trading vessels on the coast at this time, see William Tufts, "List of American vessels engaged in the trade of the Northern Coast of America for sea-otter skins from 1787–1808," Elwood Evans Papers, Beinecke Library. For a list of ships and their arrival dates in Canton, see Howard Corning, "List of Ships Arriving at the Port of Canton and Other Pacific Ports, 1799–1803," *Essex Institute Historical Collections*, LXXVIII, 331–44.

32. Howay, "William Sturgis," 12 and n., 21, 22.

33. Lamb, "Notes on Trade With the Northwest Coast," 41.

34. B. C. Payette, *The Oregon Country under the Union Jack*, 641.

35. *Ibid.*, 642.

36. Lamb, "Notes on Trade with the Northwest Coast," 41, 43.

37. Loring (ed.), *Memoir of the Hon. William Sturgis*, 25–26.

38. Gibbs, *Tribes of Western Washington and Northwestern Oregon*, 198.

39. Howay, "William Sturgis," 23.

40. In April, 1809, Sturgis again sailed for China commanding the *Atahualpa* in a voyage productive for its owners despite numerous dangers, including unsuccessful pirate attacks on the ship.

41. Clarence Hines, "Adams, Russia and Northwest Trade, 1824," *Oregon Historical Quarterly*, XXXVI (1935), 349.

42. Howay, "William Sturgis," 23.

43. *Ibid.*, 15.

44. Alexander Ross, *Adventures of the First Settlers on the Oregon or Columbia River, Being a Narrative of the Expedition Fitted Out by John Jacob Astor, to Establish the "Pacific Fur Company"; with an Account of Some Indian Tribes on the Coast of the Pacific*, 4. Other successful fur merchants were Josiah Marshall, J. P. Cushing, and the Thorndikes.

45. Thwaites (ed.), *Original Journals of the Lewis and Clark Expedition*, IV, 185.

46. For comparative prices of nankeens in China, see "Invoice of the Ship *Resource* [1803]," Baker Library, Harvard University.

47. Pickman, "Memoranda from Dudley L. Pickman on Doing Business in Canton." Americans also purchased sugar in China. "Account book of the ship, *Mary*, on voyage from New York to Canton."

48. Lewis and Clark, who crossed the Rocky Mountains in 1805 and 1806, saw trade items among the mountain tribes. Thwaites (ed.), *Original Journals of the Lewis and Clark Expedition*, III, 81–82.

49. William Shaler, *Journal of a Voyage Between China and the Northwestern Coast of America, Made in 1804 by William Shaler*, 26.

50. Cleveland, *Voyages of a Merchant Navigator of the Days That Are Past*, 40.

51. "Log-Book of the Brig Lydia on a Fur-Trading voyage from Boston to the Northwest Coast of America 1804–1805 With the Return Voyage by way of The Sandwich Islands and Canton Aboard the Ships Atahualpa and Swift 1805–1807," Beinecke Library.

52. "Supercargo's log of the brig *Lydia*, Aug 31, 1804–July 14, 1805," entry April 8, 1805.

53. *Ibid.*, entry April 10, 1805. Theodore Lyman, owner of the *Lydia*, was also part owner of the *Vancouver*.

54. Briggs, *History and Genealogy of the Cabot Family, 1475–1927*, I, 392.

55. "Supercargo's log of the brig *Lydia*, Aug 31, 1804–July 14, 1805," entry April 11, 1805.

56. Thwaites (ed.), *Original Journals of the Lewis and Clark Expedition*, III, 346.

57. "Supercargo's log of the brig *Lydia*, Aug 31, 1804–July 14, 1805," entry May 24, 1805.

58. *Ibid.*, entry April 22, 1805.

59. Captain Hill estimated his journey took him 140 miles up the Columbia. Hill, "Autobiography," 12.

60. "Supercargo's log of the brig Lydia, Aug 31, 1804–July 14, 1805," entry May 10, 1805.

61. "Log-Book of the Brig *Lydia* on a Fur-Trading voyage from Boston to the Northwest Coast of America 1804–1805."

62. Hill, "Autobiography," 13.

63. John Rodgers Jewitt, *Narrative of the Adventures and Sufferings of John R. Jewitt*, 160.

64. Hill, "Autobiography," 13.

65. *Ibid.*, 13, 14.

CHAPTER 6
Cloth Men Soldiers

1. Frank E. Ross, "The Early Fur Trade of the Great Northwest," *Oregon Historical Quarterly*, XXXIX (1938), 389.

2. Walter O'Meara, *The Savage Country*, 7.

3. The ownership of lands (including the Louisiana country) of what are now the United States, the treaties and agreements and boundaries of those lands are defined in Thomas Falconer, *The Oregon Question; or, a Statement of the British Claims to the Oregon Territory, in Opposition to the Pretensions of the Government of the United States of America*, 5–10.

4. *Journal of Cook's Last Voyage.*

5. Joseph Schafer, *A History of the Pacific Northwest*, 21, 22.

6. Richard W. Van Alstyne, "International Rivalries in Pacific Northwest," *Oregon Historical Quarterly*, XLVI (1945), 188.

7. Thomas Jefferson to a Mr. Dunbar, Monticello, Virginia, Thomas Jefferson Papers 1798–99, Thomas Jefferson Coolidge Collection.

8. Ross, "Early Fur Trade of the Great Northwest," 392.

9. Bulfinch, *Oregon and Eldorado*, 17.

10. Nicholas Biddle (ed.), *The Journals of the Expedition Under the Command of Capts. Lewis and Clark to the Sources of the Missouri, Thence Across the Rocky Mountains and down the River Columbia to the Pacific Ocean, Performed during the Years 1804–5–6 by Order of the Government of the United States*, I, xx, xxi.

11. *Ibid.*, xxii–xxiv.

12. Bulfinch, *Oregon and Eldorado*, 18.

13. Thwaites (ed.), *Original Journals of the Lewis and Clark Expedition*, III, 207.

14. Donald Jackson (ed.), *Letters of the Lewis and Clark Expedition, with Related Documents, 1783–1854*, 499.

15. The camp was probably near Fort Columbia, where the party camped until November 25. Thwaites (ed.), *Original Journals of the Lewis and Clark Expedition*, III, 227n.

16. *Ibid.*, 238.

17. Patrick Gass, *A Journal of the Voyages and Travels of a Corps of Discovery*, 203.

18. Thwaites (ed.), *Original Journals of the Lewis and Clark Expedition*, III, 239.

19. *Ibid.*, 241.

20. Gass, *Journal of the Voyages and Travels of a Corps of Discovery*, 229.

21. Thwaites (ed.), *Original Journals of the Lewis and Clark Expedition*, III, 206–207.

22. For a diagram of the buildings of the fort, see *ibid.*, 298.

23. For a history of the life of the Indian woman who accompanied Lewis and Clark, see Harold F. Howard, *Sacajawea.*

24. Thwaites (ed.), *Original Journals of the Lewis and Clark Expedition*, III, 289.

25. *Ibid.*, 315.

26. Seven years later, fur trading Astorians would meet this same man. *Ibid.*, 301n.

27. *Ibid.*, 302.

28. Bancroft, *History of the Northwest Coast*, Vol. II. Vol. XXVIII of *The Works of Hubert Howe Bancroft*, 56; Jackson (ed.), *Letters of the Lewis and Clark Expedition*, 541.

29. Milo M. Quaife (ed.), *The Journals of Captain Meriwether Lewis and Sergeant John Ordway, Kept on the Expedition of Western Exploration, 1803–1806*, Publications of the State Historical Society of Wisconsin, 319.

30. Thwaites (ed.), *Original Journals of the Lewis and Clark Expedition*, III, 311.

31. Quaife (ed.), *Journals of Captain Meriwether Lewis and Sergeant John Ordway*, 319.

32. Thwaites (ed.), *Original Journals of the Lewis and Clark Expedition*, III, 302.

33. *Ibid.*, 322. The expedition carried medals of various sizes. George T. Watkins of the Washington State University English Department discusses the sizes and makes of the medals in "Washington's Lewis and Clark Medal," typed copy of manuscript in possession of authors.

34. Thwaites (ed.), *Original Journals of the Lewis and Clark Expedition*, III, 328.

35. *Ibid.*, IV, 185.

36. *Ibid.*, 95.

37. *Ibid.*, 24.

38. Gass, *Journal of the Voyages and Travels of a Corps of Discovery*, 229.

39. Thwaites (ed.), *Original Journals of the Lewis and Clark Expedition*, IV, 161.

40. Larsell, "Medical Aspects of the Lewis and Clark Expedition," 221.

41. Jackson (ed.), *Letters of the Lewis and Clark Expedition*, 503.

42. Thwaites (ed.), *Original Journals of the Lewis and Clark Expedition*, IV, 169.

43. *Ibid.*, 180, 181. Eva Emery Dye in her fictionalized story based on fact, *The Conquest: The True Story of Lewis and Clark*, 256, gives a copy of the paper with the date "23d day of March, 1806" inserted.

44. Thwaites (ed.), *Original Journals of the Lewis and Clark Expedition*,

IV, 169; Hosmer (ed.), *History of the Expedition of Captains Lewis and Clark*, II, 71, 153.

45. All winter the explorers had kept a watch for trading ships. Charles G. Clarke, "The Roster of the Expedition of Lewis and Clark," *Oregon Historical Quarterly*, XLV (1944), 302.

CHAPTER 7
Guardians of the River

1. Clinton, "Remarks on board the ship *Vancouver*," entry July 7 and 8, 1806.

2. Nikolai Petrovich Rezanov, *The Rezanov Voyage to Nueva California in 1806: The Report of Count Nikolai Petrovich Rezanov of His Voyage to That Provincia of Nueva España from New Archangel*, 6. Rezanov "had already sketched his plans for removing the [Russian] settlement from Sitka to the Columbia River. . . ." George Henrich Langsdorff, *Voyages and Travels in Various Parts of the World, during the Years 1803, 1804, 1805, 1806, and 1807*, II, 139.

3. Petr Aleksandrovich Tikhmenev, *The Historical Review of the Formation of the Russian-American Company and Its Activity up to the Present Time*, I, 187.

4. Hector Chevigny, *Russian America: The Great Alaskan Venture, 1741–1867*, 116.

5. Hines, "Adams, Russia and Northwest Trade, 1824," 349.

6. William Walker, Jr., "Supercargo's log of the brig Lydia, Capt. Samuel Hill, on a fur-trading voyage on the N.W. Coast of North America, July 10, 1805—Jan. 3, 1807," Beinecke Library, entry, July 12, 1806.

7. Hill would carry the Lewis and Clark paper via China to America, arriving in Boston on May 12, 1807.

8. Walker, "Supercargo's log of the brig Lydia," entry July 19, 1806.

9. Fur trader George Simpson says faces were not tattooed. Merk (ed.), *Fur Trade and Empire*, 96. Bancroft, however, says Chinook faces were tattooed, *Native Races*, Vol. I, *Wild Tribes*, 229.

10. Walker, "Supercargo's log of the brig Lydia," entry August 1, 1806.

11. *Ibid.*, entry August 3, 1806.

12. *Ibid.*, entry August 10, 1806.

13. Morison, *Maritime History of Massachusetts*, 67.

14. James Gilchrist Swan to Professor S. F. Baird, December 28, 1863, James Gilchrist Swan Correspondence, microfilm copies of manuscripts in the Smithsonian Institution, Washington. Suzzallo Library, University of Washington.

15. George Gibbs, *A Dictionary of the Chinook Jargon, or Trade Language of Oregon*. Smithsonian Miscellaneous Collections, No. 161, vi–viii.

16. E. D. Keyes, *Fifty Years' Observation of Men and Events Civil and*

Military, 262; Lord, *The Naturalist in Vancouver Island and British Columbia,* II, 217.

17. Meany, *Vancouver's Discovery of Puget Sound,* 44.

18. Chester Anders Fee, "Oregon's Historical Esperanto—The Chinook Jargon," *Oregon Historical Quarterly,* XLII (1941), 177–78.

19. Meares, *Voyages Made in the Years 1788 and 1789,* 165.

20. Shaw, *Chinook Jargon and How to Use It,* ix.

21. Vancouver, *Voyage of Discovery to the North Pacific Ocean and Round the World,* II, 58.

22. Blanchet, *Historical Sketches of the Catholic Church in Oregon for the Past Forty Years,* Sketch VIII, 220–22.

23. William Fraser Tolmie, "Diary," Clarence Booth Bagley Collection, Suzzallo Library, entry July 28, 1833.

24. Davenport, "Recollections of an Indian Agent," *Oregon Historical Quarterly,* VIII (1907), 247.

25. Modeste Demers, *J.M.J. Chinook Dictionary, Catechism, Prayers, and Hymns, Composed in 1838 & 1839 by Rt. Rev. Modeste Demers; Rev., Cor. and Completed, in 1867 by Most Rev. F. N. Blanchet, with Modifications and Additions by Rev. L. N. St. Onge, Missionary Among the Yakamas and Other Indian Tribes,* 9, 12; Eugene V. Smalley, "From Puget Sound to the Upper Columbia," *Century Magazine,* VII (November, 1884), 834; "The Lost Tribes of the Chinooks and Clatsops," *San Francisco Chronicle,* June 1, 1884, p. 4.

26. Kate Ball Powers, Flora Ball Hopkins, and Lucy Ball (eds.), *Autobiography of John Ball,* 96.

27. Shaw, *Chinook Jargon and How to Use It,* ix; Samuel F. Coombs, *Dictionary of the Chinook Jargon as Spoken on Puget Sound and the Northwest, with Original Indian Names for Prominent Places and Localities with Their Meanings,* 3.

28. John Hussey, *Chinook Point and the Story of Fort Columbia,* 14.

29. Frederic W. Howay, "A List of Trading Vessels in the Maritime Fur Trade, 1805–1814," *Transactions of the Royal Society of Canada, Section II,* 3d ser., XXVI (1932), 44.

30. *Independent Chronicle,* August 10, 1807, p. 1.

31. A copy of the Embargo Act may be read in William MacDonald (ed.), *Documentary Source Book of American History, 1606–1913,* 282–83.

32. Howay, "List of Trading Vessels in the Maritime Fur Trade, 1805–1814," 62.

33. Briggs, *History and Genealogy of the Cabot Family, 1475–1927,* 407.

34. Howay, "List of Trading Vessels in the Maritime Fur Trade, 1805–1814," 57.

35. For a listing of the *Derby* cargo, see Lamb, "Notes on Trade with the Northwest Coast, 1790–1810," 81.

36. Stephen Reynolds, *The Voyage of the New Hazard to the Northwest Coast, Hawaii and China, 1810–1813,* xv.

37. See *ibid.,* 28, 29n., 37 and n.

38. Dennis, "Indian Slavery in Pacific Northwest," 73–74.

39. Drucker, *Cultures of the North Pacific Coast*, 170.

40. Samuel Furgerson, "Journal of a voyage from Boston to the North-West Coast of America, in the Brig Otter, Samuel Hill Commander," entry February 19, 1811.

41. Drucker, *Cultures of the North Pacific Coast*, 170.

42. Thwaites (ed.), *Original Journals of the Lewis and Clark Expedition*, IV, 118.

43. Ephriam W. Tucker, *A History of Oregon*, 73; Wilbur (ed.), *Duflot de Mofras' Travels on the Pacific Coast*, II, 185.

44. Dennis, "Indian Slavery in Pacific Northwest," 185. Dennis reports prices offered for slaves by tribes along the coast.

45. Boudinot, "Case of the Mercury," 28.

46. Gabriel Franchère, *Narrative of a Voyage to the Northwest Coast of America*, 187.

47. Kiril T. Khlebnikof, "Biography of Alexander Andreevich Baranof by Kiril Khlebnikof," undated translation of the 1835 Saint Petersburg edition, Archives of British Columbia, 121.

48. Van Alstyne, "International Rivalries in Pacific Northwest," 196.

49. Director of the Russian American Company to the Spanish Ambassador, August (n.d.), 1817, Microcopy of Records in the National Archives, "Records of the Russian-American Company, 1802–67," *Records of Former Russian Agencies*, RG 261. Translated by Elisabeth Seeger, Seattle, Wash., 1972.

50. Tikhmenev, *Historical Review of Formation of the Russian-American Company*, I, 187.

51. *Ibid.*, 250.

52. Chevigny, *Russian America*, 136. One account says four women were on the voyage. Tikhmenev, *Historical Review of Formation of the Russian-American Company*, I, 251.

53. Khlebnikof, "Biography of Alexander Andreevich Baranof by Kiril Khlebnikof," 125. Andrews, "Wreck of the St. Nicholas," 27.

54. Chevigny, *Russian America*, 136–45.

55. Hines, "Adams, Russia and Northwest Trade, 1824," 351. At one time the Russians would consider an outfitting post in the West Indies for their Alaskan operation. Clarence A. Manning, *Russian Influence on Early America*, 122–26.

56. William Dane Phelps, "Solid Men of Boston in the Northwest," Bancroft Library, 9.

57. Woodward, "Sea Otter Hunting on the Pacific Coast," 125.

58. Furgerson, "Journal of a voyage from Boston to the North-West Coast of America," entry May 24, 1810.

59. Coman, *Economic Beginnings of the Far West*, 221.

60. Alexander Andreievitch Baranov to John Jacob Astor, New Archangel, August 13, 1811; Astor to Ebbets, Philadelphia, November (n.d.), 1809;

"Account Sales of Cargo of Ship Enterprise," Documents 1788–1813, John Jacob Astor Papers; *Annals of the Congress of the United States. The Debates and Proceedings in the Congress of the United States; with an Appendix, Containing Important State Papers and Public Documents,* 17 Cong., 2 sess., Appendix, 1211.

61. Hines, "Adams, Russia and Northwest Trade, 1824," 351.

62. John Jacob Astor to William Bell, New York, April 27, 1799; "Account book of the ship, *Mary,* on voyage from New York to Canton."

63. "Denuncia de José Sevilla, de Comercio clandestino, q. dice hacerse en las Coastas de Californias," in *"Mercury* Case Documents" (containing excerpts from the log of the *Mercury,* letters and correspondence between Spanish officials about the capture of Captain George Washington Eayers, his stay at California ports, the disposition of his goods and ship, and his subsequent removal to Mexico), Cauderno No. 17, Los Angeles Public Library, 11.

64. Howay, *Voyages of the "Columbia" to the Northwest Coast, 1787–1790 and 1790–1793,* 399.

65. Phelps, "Solid Men of Boston in the Northwest," 29, 30.

66. Allen Weir, "William Weir," *Washington Historical Quarterly,* IV, 1 (January, 1913), 33–35.

67. Furgerson, "Journal of a voyage from Boston to the North-West Coast of America," entry May 24, 1810.

68. Bancroft, *History of the Northwest Coast,* Vol. II, XXVIII, 131–32.

69. Those Hawaiians were the first enlisted as colonists on the Pacific Northwest coast since Meares's failure to enlist Hawaiians as colonists. George Verne Blue, "Early Relations between Hawaii and the Northwest Coast," *Thirty-Third Annual Report of the Hawaiian Historical Society,* 17.

70. Furgerson, "Journal of a voyage from Boston to the North-West Coast of America," entry May 26, 1810.

71. Donald C. Davidson, "Relations of the Hudson's Bay Company with the Russian American Company on the Northwest Coast, 1829–1867," *British Columbia Historical Quarterly,* V, I (January, 1941), 34; Hines, "Adams, Russia and Northwest Trade, 1824," 350.

72. Natives told the Winship party the freshets always covered that locality. Clarke, *Pioneer Days of Oregon History,* I, 39. The water rose eighteen inches in the partially erected building. "First Trading Settlement on the Columbia River," *Hunt's Merchant Magazine,* XIV, 2 (February, 1846), 202.

73. Phelps, "Solid Men of Boston in the Northwest," 43. Phelps prepared his account of the settlement from June 4 until they left the area from a journal kept by William A. Gale, Captain Winship's assistant. A microfilm copy of "Journal kept on board the ship Albatross, Nathan Winship, Commander, on a Voyage from Boston to the North West Coast and China in the Years 1809. 10. 11. 12," is in the Washington State Library. The Astorian fur trader, Robert Stuart, traveling up the Columbia in July, 1812, passed the site of the Winship venture. Stuart wrote in his notes that a Mr. Washington

employed by the Winships had disputed with Indians there he called the Chilwits, a tribe living near the post site, after which he had put several of them in irons believing them to have been Chehalis Indians who had previously attacked a schooner belonging to Alaskan Russians whose governor had employed him to capture these Indians. Because the Chilwits had made formidable preparations to release the captives, and because Washington had mistaken them for the Chehalis, they had been released. Spaulding (ed.), *On the Oregon Trail Robert Stuart's Journey of Discovery*, 44–45.

74. Phelps, "Solid Men of Boston in the Northwest," 44, 45.

75. *Ibid.*, 46.

76. *Ibid.*

77. *Ibid.*, 47.

78. *Ibid.*

79. *Ibid.*

80. *Daily Astorian*, October 26, 1884.

81. Phelps, "Solid Men of Boston in the Northwest," 48.

82. *Ibid.*, 49–50.

83. Winston Wutkee, Researcher, Oral History Program, University of California, Los Angeles, to the authors, Thousand Oaks, California, January 17, 1971; *"Mercury* Case Documents," Cauderno No. 16, 31.

84. Phelps, "Solid Men of Boston in the Northwest," 50.

85. Chevigny, *Russian America*, 146.

86. *Ibid.*, 147.

87. Phelps, "Solid Men of Boston in the Northwest," 50–51.

88. *Ibid.*, 51.

89. *Ibid.*, 33; *"Mercury* Case Documents," Cauderno No. 16, 32.

90. Ebbets to Astor, Macao, January 11, 1811, "Pacific Fur Company, 1806–1823," Vol. XX, Folder no. 1, John Jacob Astor Papers.

91. "Americans at Sea," *Niles' Weekly Register*, XVIII, n.s. VI (March–September, 1820), 418.

92. "Records of the Russian-American Company, 1802–67."

93. Rickard, "Sea-Otter in History," 201.

94. Van Alstyne, "International Rivalries in Pacific Northwest," 195.

95. P. H. and Sam G. Perkins and Co. and John Bryant and William Sturgis to Captain Samuel Hill of the ship *Ophelia*, June 30, 1815, John Bryant and William Sturgis, "Letterbook IX," John Bryant and William Sturgis Collection, 1811–1872.

96. John Bryant and William Sturgis to Lambert Dexter, February 19, 1822; John Bryant and William Sturgis to George Newell, June 20, 1822; John Bryant and William Sturgis to John Q. Adams, Secretary of State, April 21, 1823, "Letterbook X," John Bryant and William Sturgis Collection, 1811–1872.

97. It had been the Russians with Bering who had brought firearms to the Northwest coast. Two blunderbusses had been fired when natives apprehended

the party's interpreter, frightening the natives with the multiple reports of the echo reverberating from cliff to cliff. Jefferys, *Voyages from Asia to America,* 47.

98. Hines, "Adams, Russia and Northwest Trade, 1824," 350–51. Bryant and Sturgis maintained a forceful interest in the trade along the north part of the Pacific Northwest coast. See their letters in "Letterbook X," John Bryant and William Sturgis Collection, 1811–1872.

99. Scouler, "Dr. John Scouler's Journal," 180. Coues (ed.), *New Light on the Early History of the Greater Northwest,* II, 755–56.

100. Lee and Frost, *Ten Years in Oregon,* 314.

CHAPTER 8
Emporium in the Wilderness

1. Terms of the agreement may be found in Irving, *Astoria,* 36–38.

2. For an explanation of various Chinook games, see Ray, *Lower Chinook Ethnographic Notes,* 96–97; Ross, *Adventures of the First Settlers,* 93–94.

3. Dunn, *History of the Oregon Territory,* 224.

4. Cox, *Adventures on the Columbia River,* I, 72.

5. Ross, *Adventures of the First Settlers,* 91.

6. *Ibid.,* 92.

7. *Ibid.,* 74.

8. *Ibid.,* 76.

9. *Ibid.*

10. For a listing of Comcomly's numerous family, see Lewis and Murakami (eds.), *Ranald MacDonald, 1824–1894,* 75–78 and n. In such a listing it should be noted that kinship designations such as "son" and "daughter" are used quite loosely in Pacific Northwest Indian culture.

11. Peter Corney, *Early Voyages in the North Pacific, 1813–1818,* 154.

12. Coues (ed.), *New Light on the Early History of the Greater Northwest,* II, 793.

13. Ross, *Adventures of the First Settlers,* 79–80.

14. *Ibid.*

15. Spaulding (ed.), *On the Oregon Trail,* 28.

16. Ross, *Adventures of the First Settlers,* 82.

17. Gabriel Franchère, in his *Adventures at Astoria, 1810–1814,* 117, tells of the natives' limited use of firearms.

18. Ross, *Adventures of the First Settlers,* 87–88.

19. Testimony of Samuel Mallette, "Copy of Testimony . . . in support of a claim of *Chinook Indian Tribe against the United States,*" 147.

20. Ross, *Adventures of the First Settlers,* 95–96.

21. *Ibid.,* 89.

22. Jesse S. Douglas (ed.), "Matthews' Adventures on the Columbia,"

Oregon Historical Quarterly, XL (1939), 120; Ray, *Lower Chinook Ethnographic Notes*, 51.

23. Ross, *Adventures of the First Settlers*, 83–84.

24. Franchère, *Adventure at Astoria, 1810–1824*, 55–56.

25. *Ibid.*, 56–57.

26. Alexander Ross, *The Fur Hunters of the Far West*, 55.

27. Franchère, *Adventure at Astoria, 1810–1824*, 55–56 and n.

28. Whealdon, "On Whealdon Hill (Ilwaco, Wash.) Eve of July 16, 1860"; Ray, *Lower Chinook Ethnographic Notes*, 51–52.

29. Boas, *Chinook Texts*, 273–74.

30. James G. Swan, *The Northwest Coast; or, Three Years' Residence in Washington Territory*, 169–70. Irving covers the overland expedition, like other aspects of the Astorian enterprise, with dramatic emphasis. For a modern account of this phase of the undertaking, see William Brandon, "Two Thousand Miles From the Counting House: Wilson Price Hunt and the Founding of Astoria," *American West*, V, 4 (July, 1968), 24–29, 61–63. See also Philip Ashton Rollins (ed.), *Wilson Price Hunt's Diary of His Overland Journey Westward to Astoria in 1811–12; The Discovery of the Oregon Trail: Robert Stuart's Narratives of His Overland Trip Eastward From Astoria in 1812–13.*

31. The arrival of the *Beaver* is found in "A Copy of the Log Book of the Ship Beaver on a Voyage from New York to the Columbia River 1812 &c," Washington State Library. See Franchère, *Adventure at Astoria, 1810–1814*, 69–73.

32. *Ibid.*

33. Cox, *Adventures on the Columbia River*, 266.

34. Astor to Ebbets, Philadelphia, John Jacob Astor Papers. Letters dealing with Astor's efforts to set up a fur post may be found in "Original Manuscript Letters of John Jacob Astor concerning Fort Astoria on the Columbia River and his Efforts to secure the Protection & Defense of the American Fur Company's Post at Fort Astoria," letters to James Monroe, Secretary of State, February, 1813; to William Jones, Secretary of the Navy, July 6, 1813, and July 30, 1813, Beinecke Library. See also Astor to President Jefferson, October 18, 1813, "Pacific Fur Company, 1806–1823," Vol. XX, Folder no. 2, John Jacob Astor Papers.

35. Alexander Ross to Donald McGillis, May 4, 1812, H.B. [Hudson's Bay Company], Oregon Historical Society.

36. "A General Statement of Inventories, Furs, Men's Accts. of P.F. [Pacific Fur] Co. in 1812 & 1813"; "Recapitulation of the Furs & Skins from April 1811 to 31 May, 1812 viz at Astoria," "Pacific Fur Company, 1806–1823," Vol. XX, Folder no. 2, John Jacob Astor Papers.

37. Rollins (ed.), *Wilson Price Hunt's Diary; Robert Stuart's Narratives*, 32.

38. *Ibid.*

39. *Ibid.*, 28–29.

40. Hines, "Adams, Russia and Northwest Trade, 1824," 351–52.

41. Ross, *Adventures of the First Settlers*, 154. David Thompson in 1811 noted that Chinooks and Clatsops had "been unable to settle any steady rate of barter, either for furrs or provisions, every Sturgeon, or Salmon had to be again valued in barter; a great part of this fault lay in the very low quality of the goods, especially the cotton goods, and all their Tobacco was in leaf and of the lowest price. The Natives were displeased with several of their articles." *Thompson's Narrative*, 362–63.

42. We get a good idea of Astor's mercantile policies in a letter he wrote to C. C. Cambreleng on June 21, 1813. "Copy of Letters J. J. Astor, 1813–15," Letterbook Vol. XVI, 1, John Jacob Astor Papers.

43. As might be expected, there are numerous accounts of the *Tonquin* disaster. Although there are minor discrepancies between the event as recorded by Franchère, *Adventure at Astoria, 1810–1814*, 80–85, and that described by Cox, *Adventures on the Columbia River*, 88–96, they appear to record the event more faithfully than does Ross, *Adventures of the First Settlers*, 156–73, thirty-five years after the event when he was in his sixty-fifth year. For a critical analysis of these and other sources of accounts of the disaster, see Frederic W. Howay, "The Loss of the 'Tonquin,'" *Washington Historical Quarterly*, XIII, 2 (April, 1922), 83–92.

44. Cox, *Adventures on the Columbia River*, I, 314–15.

45. Franchère, *Adventure at Astoria, 1810–1814*, 73–75.

46. *Ibid.*, 115–17.

47. Ross, *Adventures of the First Settlers*, 219.

48. Franchère, *Adventure at Astoria, 1810–1814*, 74.

49. "Abstract of Returns from Columbia River Pacific Fur Company Outfit 1811 & 1812," and "Fort Astoria Returns from 1st June to 28th [20th?] Janry. 1813," "Pacific Fur Company, 1806–1823," Folder no. 1, John Jacob Astor Papers.

50. T. C. Elliott, "Sale of Astoria, 1813," *Oregon Historical Quarterly*, XXXIII (1932), 44.

51. Wayne R. Kime, "Alfred Seton's Journal: A Source for Irving's *Tonquin* Disaster Account," *Oregon Historical Quarterly*, LXXI (1970), 313.

52. *Ibid.*, 45.

53. *Ibid.*, 44–46.

54. Franchère, *Adventure at Astoria, 1810–1814*, 76–77.

55. Elliott, "Sale of Astoria, 1813," 7.

56. Irving, *Astoria*, 461.

57. Lewis and Murakami (eds.), *Ranald MacDonald, 1824–1894*, 75n.; Miller, *Clatsop County, Oregon*, 63; *Sunday Oregonian*, December 17, 1899, p. 28.

58. Cox, *Adventures on the Columbia*, I, 302.

59. For primary source accounts of Chinook marriage customs, see Rollins (ed.), *Wilson Price Hunt's Diary; Robert Stuart's Narratives*, 34–35, and Cox, *Adventures on the Columbia*, I, 318–19. See also Santee, "Comcomly

and the Chinooks," 274–76, and Whealdon, "On Whealdon Hill (Ilwaco, Wash.) Eve of July 16, 1860," 18.

60. McDougall's no longer extant "Journal of Astoria" provided details of the wedding for Irving's *Astoria*, 462–63 and n.; "Historical Notes," *Pacific Monthly*, VI, 6 (November–December, 1901), 265–66.

61. Kane, *Wanderings of an Artist among the Indians of North America*, 120–21.

62. Coues (ed.), *New Light on the Early History of the Greater Northwest*, II, 901.

63. "Astoria Journal, October 9, 1813–March 14, 1814" [account book], Vol. IIb, John Jacob Astor Papers.

64. Coues (ed.), *New Light on the Early History of the Greater Northwest*, II, 901.

65. Lewis and Murakami (eds.), *Ranald MacDonald, 1824–1894*, 78n.

66. Irving, *Astoria*, 463.

67. Franchère, *Adventure at Astoria, 1810–1814*, 119; Cox, *Adventures on the Columbia River*, I, 317.

68. *Ibid.*, 330.

69. Douglas (ed.), "Matthews' Adventures on the Columbia," 106–107 and n.; John Minto to Eva Emery Dye, August 26, 1891, Eva Emery Dye Papers.

70. J. Neilson Barry, "What Became of Benjamin Clapp?" *Washington Historical Quarterly*, XXI, 1 (January, 1930), 13–17.

71. Oswald West, "Oregon's First White Settlers on French Prairie," *Oregon Historical Quarterly*, XLIII (1942), 198–209. See also Barry, "Astorians Who Became Permanent Settlers," 282–301.

72. West, "Oregon's First White Settlers on French Prairie," 205.

73. Merk (ed.), *Fur Trade and Empire*, 101.

CHAPTER 9
King George's Fort and King Comcomly's Canoe

1. Ross, *Adventures of the First Settlers*, 247, 252. For a further account of the journeys and activities of the *Isaac Todd*, see Marion O'Neil, "The Maritime Activities of the North West Company, 1813–1821," *Washington Historical Quarterly*, XXI, 4 (October, 1930), 248–53.

2. For provisions of the sale, see Elliott, "Sale of Astoria, 1813," 48–50, and Payette, "Oregon Country under the Union Jack," xiv–xix.

3. Ross, *Adventures of the First Settlers*, 256.

4. Cox, *Adventures on the Columbia River*, I, 267–68.

5. Frederic W. Howay, "Vessels Trading on the Northwest Coast of America, 1804–1814," *Washington Historical Quarterly*, XIX, 4 (October, 1928), 294–95.

6. Ross, *Adventures of the First Settlers*, 257–58.

7. Franchère, *Adventure at Astoria, 1810–1814*, 90–91; Cox, *Adventures on the Columbia River*, I, 266–67.

8. Franchère, *Adventure at Astoria, 1810–1814*, 91.

9. Irving, *Astoria*, 489.

10. Coues (ed.), *New Light on the Early History of the Greater Northwest*, II, 770–71, 781.

11. Ross, *Adventures of the First Settlers*, 267. For further discussion of the evolving Chinook jargon, see Frederic W. Howay, "Origin of the Chinook Jargon on the North West Coast," *Oregon Historical Quarterly*, XLIV (1943), 50; James Swan, "The Chinook Jargon," *Washington Standard*, July 27, 1861, p. 1.

12. Kane, "Incidents of Travel on the North-West Coast," 274.

13. Swan, *Northwest Coast*, 156.

14. Cox, *Adventures on the Columbia River*, I, 266–70.

15. Coues (ed.), *New Light on the Early History of the Greater Northwest*, II, 772.

16. *Ibid.*, 779.

17. Douglas, "Matthews' Adventures on the Columbia," 113.

18. Coues (ed.), *New Light on the Early History of the Greater Northwest*, II, 753, 789, 901.

19. Swan, *Northwest Coast*, 156.

20. Cox, *Adventures on the Columbia River*, I, 321; John West, *The Substance of a Journal during a Residence at the Red River Colony, British North America; and Frequent Excursions among the North-West American Indians, in the Years 1820, 1821, 1822, 1823 by John West, M.A.*, 145–46.

21. Cox, *Adventures on the Columbia River*, II, 76–77.

22. Coues (ed.), *New Light on the Early History of the Greater Northwest*, II, 783–90.

23. Douglas, "Matthews' Adventures on the Columbia," 136.

24. Ross, *Fur Hunters*, 12–16. For accounts of the expedition, see Douglas, "Matthews' Adventures on the Columbia," 137; Coues (ed.), *New Light on the Early History of the Greater Northwest*, II, 790–808 and n.; Franchère, *Adventure at Astoria, 1810–1814*, 96–99. Quite understandably these accounts of the expedition vary.

25. Douglas, "Matthews' Adventure on the Columbia," 106; Franchère, *Adventure at Astoria, 1810–1814*, 99; Coues (ed.), *New Light on the Early History of the Greater Northwest*, II, 827, 831–35.

26. Ross, *Fur Hunters*, 45.

27. Coues (ed.), *New Light on the Early History of the Greater Northwest*, II, 839.

28. *Ibid.*, 826.

29. *Ibid.*, 890.

30. *Ibid.*, 825–26.

31. *Ibid.*, 835.

32. *Ibid.*, 838.

33. *Ibid.*, 840.

34. *Ibid.*, 837.

35. *Ibid.*, 850.

36. A. C. O. Ermatinger, "The Columbia River under Hudson's Bay Company Rule," *Washington Historical Quarterly*, V, 3 (July, 1914), 204–205.

37. Coues (ed.), *New Light on the Early History of the Greater Northwest*, II, 850.

38. *Ibid.*, 859.

39. Ross, *Fur Hunters*, 20.

40. L. R. Masson, *Les Bourgeois de la Compagnie du Nord-Ouest; Recits de voyages, lettres et rapports inedits relatifs au nord-ouest canadien, publiés avec une esquisse historique et des annotations par L. R. Masson*, II, 52.

41. Coues (ed.), *New Light on the Early History of the Greater Northwest*, II, 836n.

42. *Ibid.*, 855. For a further explanation of the natives' war preparations, weaponry, and generally bloodless confrontations, see Franchère, *Adventure at Astoria, 1810–1814*, 115–17.

43. Douglas, "Matthews' Adventure on the Columbia," 144.

44. Coues (ed.), *New Light on the Early History of the Greater Northwest*, II, 888.

45. *Ibid.*, 890.

46. *Ibid.*, 864–65.

47. *Ibid.*, 912.

48. *Ibid.*, 866.

49. *Ibid.*, 877.

50. *Ibid.*, 890–91.

51. Cox, *Adventures on the Columbia River*, 306–307.

52. Barry, "Astorians Who Became Permanent Settlers," 299.

53. For an account of the North West Company maritime activities, see O'Neil, "Maritime Activities of the North West Company, 1813–1821," 243–67.

54. Cox, *Adventures on the Columbia River*, I, 286–87.

55. *Ibid.*, 287–90; Coues (ed.), *New Light on the Early History of the Greater Northwest*, II, 895–901.

56. *Ibid.*, 895, 901.

57. William J. Pigot to John Ebbets, Esq., March 22, 1814, "Documents, 1788–1813," Folder no. 1, John Jacob Astor Papers.

58. Coues (ed.), *New Light on the Early History of the Greater Northwest*, II, 901.

59. *Ibid.*, 902.

60. *Ibid.*, 906.

61. Lee and Frost, *Ten Years in Oregon*, 64.

62. Coues (ed.), *New Light on the Early History of the Greater Northwest*, II, 867.

63. *Ibid.*, 911.

64. Main sources for an accounting of the events precipitating the trial are Douglas, "Matthews' Adventures on the Columbia," 144; Cox, *Adventures on the Columbia*, 291–97; and Corney, *Early Voyages*, 126.

65. Cox, *Adventures on the Columbia*, 297–99.

66. Coues (ed.), *New Light on the Early History of the Greater Northwest*, II, 915–16.

67. *Ibid.*, 858.

68. Corney, *Early Voyages*, 113.

69. Coues (ed.), *New Light on the Early History of the Greater Northwest*, II, 850.

70. For details of these arrangements, see O'Neil, "The Maritime Activities of the North West Company, 1813–1821," 265–66. For an accounting of contents and values of these cargoes, see Gordon Charles Davidson, *The North West Company*, 167 and n., 222–23 and n. For correspondence relative to company fears of definite assurance of British support, see Katharine B. Judson, "The British Side of the Restoration of Fort Astoria," *Oregon Historical Quarterly*, XX (1919), 257–60.

71. James Keith, company agent on the Columbia, received a letter from the Perkins firm written October 15, 1818, with a statement of returns of these furs. Letter quoted in Payette, *Oregon Country under the Union Jack*, 660.

72. *Ibid.*

73. O'Neil, "Maritime Activities of the North West Company, 1813–1821," 266.

74. For a listing of ships in the service of the company as well as for a listing of ships trading on the Northwest coast in the years 1815–1819, see Frederic W. Howay, "A List of Trading Vessels in the Maritime Fur Trade, 1815–1819," *Transactions of the Royal Society of Canada, Section II*, 3d ser., XXVII (1933), 119–41. For a similar listing for the years 1820–1825, see Howay, "List of Trading Vessels in the Maritime Fur Trade, 1820–1825," 18.

75. Ross, *Fur Hunters*, 60.

76. Hines, "Adams, Russia and Northwest Trade, 1824," 355.

77. "Extract from Log of the U.S.S. Ontario, Capt. James Biddle," *Oregon Historical Quarterly*, III (1902), 310–11; John H. Aulick, "Extracts from a Journal on board the U.S. Ship Ontario on a Cruise to the N.W. Coast. By Lieutenant John H. Aulick of the U.S. Navy," July 1–October 23, 1818, Oregon Historical Society.

78. Davidson, *North West Company*, 164.

79. *Annals of the Congress of the United States*, 17 Cong., 2 sess., 1206–10.

80. Corney, *Early Voyages*, 176.

81. *Ibid.*, 175–76.

82. Daniel Williams Harmon, *A Journal of Voyages and Travels in the Interiour of North America*, 268.

83. Ross, *Fur Hunters*, 72–74.

84. Corney, *Early Voyages*, 172–75.

85. Ross, *Fur Hunters*, 133.

86. *Ibid.*, 130–32.

87. Corney, *Early Voyages*, 151–52.

88. Ross, *Fur Hunters*, 134.

CHAPTER 10
Merchants and Chiefs

1. Merk (ed.), *Fur Trade and Empire*, 65.

2. Like North West Company ships before them, the Perkinses' ships had been primarily carriers rather than coastal traders.

3. Robert C. Clark, "The Archives of the Hudson's Bay Company," *Pacific Northwest Quarterly*, XXIX, 1 (January, 1938), 4–6.

4. Remittance from W. Smith, Secretary, to Messrs. James P. Sturgis & Co., Canton, China, "The China Trade," Appendix X in Rich (ed.), *Simpson's 1828 Journey*, 144.

5. "Governor and Committee to the Chief Factors in Charge of the Columbia Department, July 22, 1824," Appendix A, in Merk (ed.), *Fur Trade and Empire*, 240, 242.

6. *Ibid.*, 102.

7. *Ibid.*, 86–87.

8. Ranald MacDonald to Malcolm McLeod, June 4, 1891, "Correspondence: Outward Letters to Malcolm McLeod, 1880–1894," Archives of British Columbia.

9. William C. McKay to Eva Emery Dye, February 1, 1892, Eva Emery Dye Papers.

10. Merk (ed.), *Fur Trade and Empire*, 104ff.

11. John West, *The Substance of a Journal during a Residence at the Red River Colony*, 146–47.

12. Merk (ed.), *Fur Trade and Empire*, 123.

13. *Ibid.*, 104.

14. Elliott, "Journal of John Work," 205–206.

15. E. E. Rich (ed.), *McLoughlin's Fort Vancouver Letters, First Series, 1825–38*, Publications of the Champlain Society, 1.

16. Merk (ed.), *Fur Trade and Empire*, 98.

17. Rich (ed.), *McLoughlin's Fort Vancouver Letters*, 3.

18. Merk (ed.), *Fur Trade and Empire*, 122.

19. *Ibid.*, 71.

20. Rich (ed.), *McLoughlin's Fort Vancouver Letters*, 4.

21. Merk (ed.), *Fur Trade and Empire*, Appendix a, 257 and n., 258.

22. "Letter from Dr. Tolmie," *Transactions of the Twelfth Annual Re-Union of the Oregon Pioneer Association for 1884*, 31.

23. Simpson describes the Fort George environs in Merk (ed.), *Fur Trade and Empire*, 105–106.

24. Susan Kardas, "The People Bought This and the Clatsop Became Rich:

A View of Nineteenth-Century Fur Trade Relationships on the Lower Columbia between Chinookan Speakers, Whites, and Kanakas," photocopy of typescript thesis, Bryn Mawr College, 1971. University Microfilms, Ann Arbor, Mi., 1973.

25. Merk (ed.), *Fur Trade and Empire*, 95.

26. This was the journey on which John Work was a member of the party. Elliott, "Journal of John Work," 198–228.

27. Rich (ed.), *Simpson's 1828 Journey*, 72.

28. John Work, "Journal, April 15–November 17, 1824," Oregon Historical Society.

29. Merk (ed.), *Fur Trade and Empire*, 109–10.

30. *Ibid.*, 100.

31. *Ibid.*, 103.

32. Scouler, "Observations on the Indigenous Tribes of the N.W. Coast of America," 220.

33. Merk (ed.), *Fur Trade and Empire*, 111.

34. Scouler, "Observations on the Indigenous Tribes of the N.W. Coast of America," 220.

35. David Douglas, *Journal Kept By David Douglas during His Travels in North America in 1832–1837*, 129, 138, 144, 159. See also Merk (ed.), *Fur Trade and Empire*, 173. Douglas to Scouler, April 3, 1826, in David Douglas, "Correspondence Outward," manuscript, Archives of British Columbia.

36. Scouler, "Dr. John Scouler's Journal," 203–204.

37. *Ibid.*, 176. John Work also writes of such sudden deaths. John Work, "Journal March 21–May 14, 1825," Oregon Historical Society.

38. "The Lost Tribes of the Chinooks and Clatsops," *San Francisco Chronicle*, June 1, 1884; *Daily Astorian*, June 10, 1884, p. 3; Merk (ed.), *Fur Trade and Empire*, 102.

39. Rich (ed.), *McLoughlin's Fort Vancouver Letters*, 5–6.

40. *Ibid.*; Merk (ed.), *Fur Trade and Empire*, 123–24.

41. Scouler, "Dr. John Scouler's Journal," 165–66.

42. "Part of Dispatch from George Simpson Esqr[.], Governor of Ruperts Land to the Governor & Committee of the Hudson's Bay Company, London, March 1, 1829," in Rich (ed.), *Simpson's 1828 Journey*, 24 and n.

43. John Work, "Untitled journal," Oregon Historical Society.

44. Scouler, "Dr. John Scouler's Journal," 167.

45. Work, "Journal April 15–November 17, 1824," 55–56.

46. Rich (ed.), *McLoughlin's Fort Vancouver Letters*, lxix.

47. Scouler, "Dr. John Scouler's Journal," 165.

48. Douglas, *Journal*, 58, 137–38, 239–40.

49. Scouler, "Dr. John Scouler's Journal," 276–77.

50. Alexander Kennedy, "Report of Chief Factor Alexander Kennedy 1824–'25," The Hudson's Bay Company Archives, London.

51. Scouler, "Dr. John Scouler's Journal," 276–77. There were cases where people were "purchased" from the dead. For an explanation of Chinook burial

customs and beliefs regarding death, see, Ella E. Clark, "George Gibbs' Account of Indian Mythology in Oregon and Western Washington Territories," *Oregon Historical Quarterly*, LVI (1955), 316–18.

52. Scouler, "Dr. John Scouler's Journal," 224.

53. *Ibid.*, 277.

54. Grace P. Morris, "Development of Astoria, 1811–1850," *Oregon Historical Quarterly*, XXXVIII (1937), 419–20.

55. Kane, "Incidents of Travel on the North-West Coast," 277; "John McLoughlin to the Governor, Chief Factors and Chief Traders, August 10, 1825," Appendix A in Merk (ed.), *Fur Trade and Empire*, 253–54; Rich (ed.), *McLoughlin's Fort Vancouver Letters*, 11n.

56. Rich (ed.), *McLoughlin's Fort Vancouver Letters*, 23 and n.

57. *Ibid.*, 13.

58. *Ibid.*, lxxix and n. For an account of the *Owhyhee*'s activities at the time, see Frederic H. Howay, "Brig Owhyhee in the Columbia, 1827," *Oregon Historical Quarterly*, XXXIV (1933), 324–29.

59. D. W. Thompson to Josiah Marshall, March 26, 1829. In Samuel Eliot Morison, "New England and the Opening of the Columbia River Salmon Trade, 1830," *Oregon Historical Quarterly*, XXVIII (1927), 123; Rich (ed.), *McLoughlin's Fort Vancouver Letters*, 76 and n., 77.

60. William Todd, "William Todd to Edward Ermatinger, July 15, 1829," appears in "Documents," *Washington Historical Quarterly*, I, 4 (July, 1907), 258.

61. *Ibid.*

62. *Memorial of William A. Slacum, Praying Compensation for His Services in Obtaining Information in Relation to the Settlement on the Oregon River*, Senate *Exec. Doc.* No. 24, 25 Cong., 2 sess., 8.

63. Rich (ed.), *McLoughlin's Fort Vancouver Letters*, 5; Morris, "Development of Astoria, 1811–1850," 419–20.

64. McLoughlin to Manson, March 28, 1829, in Burt Brown Barker (ed.), *Letters of Dr. John McLoughlin Written at Fort Vancouver 1829–1832*, 10–11.

65. Frederic W. Howay, "The Brig Owhyhee in the Columbia, 1829–30," *Oregon Historical Quarterly*, XXV (1934), 18–19.

66. *Ibid.*

67. Willard H. Rees, "Donald Manson," *Transactions of the Seventh Annual Re-Union of the Oregon Pioneer Association; for 1879*, 59–60.

68. Frank Ermatinger, "Earliest Expeditions against Puget Sound Indians," *Washington Historical Quarterly*, I, 2 (January, 1907), 16–29.

69. Dorothy O. Johansen, "McLoughlin and the Indians," *The Beaver*, Outfit 277, 1 (June, 1946), 20; Rich (ed.), *McLoughlin's Fort Vancouver Letters*, 71–73; Rich (ed.), *Simpson's 1828 Journey*, 107–108. Among some of the other references in which the event is discussed are Dunn, *History of the Oregon Territory*, 159–60; Barker (ed.), *Letters of Dr. John McLoughlin*, 18–25; Alexander Caulfield Anderson, "History of the Northwest Coast," Suzzallo Library; Evans, *History of the Pacific Northwest*, II, 570–71.

70. "Journal of a voyage in the Brig Owhyhee from Oahu to and from the northwest coast, 1827–1830," California Historical Society.

71. Jonathan S. Green, *Journal of a Tour on the North West Coast of America in the Year 1829*, 90, 100–101n. See also George Verne Blue, "Green's Missionary Report on Oregon, 1829," *Oregon Historical Quarterly*, XXX (1929), 259–71.

72. Howay, "The Brig Owhyhee in the Columbia, 1829–30," 19; D. W. Thompson to Josiah Marshall, November 7, 1829, in Morison, "New England and the Opening of the Columbia River Salmon Trade, 1830," 124–25. The letter states that when Thompson left the river on October 6, 1829, that trader wrote that "our collections" were about 2,900 land furs.

73. Scouler, "Dr. John Scouler's Journal," 163–67, 276–77.

CHAPTER 11
The Cold Sick

1. Evans, *History of the Pacific Northwest*, II, 92.

2. "A Century Ago," *West Shore*, V, 6 (June, 1879), 164–65. This concept of the spirit as a casual factor in disease and other disasters is explained in Domenech, *Seven Years' Residence in the Great Deserts of North America*, I, 398.

3. Jason Lee, "Journal of Jason Lee" [written at Mission House, Willamette, March 15, 1841], Clarence Booth Bagley Miscellaneous Selections of Historical Writing, Suzzallo Library; Lee and Frost, *Ten Years in Oregon*, 108.

4. Ray, *Lower Chinook Ethnographic Notes*, 81–82; Clark, "George Gibbs' Account of Indian Mythology in Oregon and Washington Territories," 137–38.

5. The most complete account of the native tradition explaining the introduction of disease by Captain Dominis and subsequent events is found in the annual report (September 3, 1854) of William H. Tappan, agent for the Southern Indian District of Washington Territory, Microcopy of Records in the National Archives, *Washington Superintendency of Indian Affairs, 1853–1874*, No. 5, Roll 17. Letters From Employees Assigned to the Columbia River, or Southern District, and the Yakima Agency, May 1, 1854–July 20, 1861.

6. Herbert C. Taylor, Jr., and Lester L. Hoaglin, Jr., "The 'Intermittent Fever' Epidemic of the 1830s on the Lower Columbia River," *Ethnohistory*, IX, 2 (Spring, 1962), 170.

7. *Ibid.*, 169. For an account of the extent and magnitude of the outbreak, see S. F. Cook, "The Epidemic of 1830–1833 in California and Oregon," *University of California Publications in American Archeaology and Ethnology*, XLIII, 3 (1955), 303–25.

8. Tappan, Annual Report, September 3, 1854, *Washington Superintendency*, No. 5, Roll 17.

9. Rev. Modeste Demers to Rev. C. F. Cazeau, March 1, 1839, in Francis Norbert Blanchet, "Historical Sketches of the Catholic Church in Oregon

during the Past Forty Years (1838–1878)," *Catholic Sentinel*, March 28, 1878.

10. *Washington Standard*, November 4, 1871, p. 1.

11. Peter Skene Ogden [?], *Traits of American Indian Life & Character, By a Fur Trader*, 67–71, 104.

12. *Ibid.*

13. John K. Townsend, *Townsend's Narrative of Journey across the Rocky Mountains, to the Columbia River*, 232.

14. *Memorial of William A. Slacum*, 8–9.

15. William Fraser Tolmie, "Journal 1833–36," Suzzallo Library.

16. Fred Wilbur Powell, "Hall Jackson Kelley—Prophet of Oregon," *Oregon Historical Quarterly*, XVIII (1917), 287.

17. Dunn, *History of the Oregon Territory*, 116.

18. George B. Roberts, "Recollections," Bancroft Library.

19. Ogden, *Traits of American Indian Life*, 71.

20. Rev. Modest Demers to Rev. C. F. Cazeau, in Blanchet, "Historical Sketches of the Catholic Church in Oregon during the Past Forty Years."

21. Ball, Hopkins, and Ball (eds.), *Autobiography of John Ball*, 97–98; A. N. Armstrong, *Oregon: Comprising a Brief History and Full Description of the Territories of Oregon and Washington*, 104.

22. W. S. Wallace (ed.), *John McLean's Notes of Twenty-Five Years' Service in the Hudson's Bay Territory*, 179.

23. "Oregon Archives, Letters, Reports, Messages, Memorials, and other Papers not published in the Office of the Secretary of State, Salem 1878," Bancroft Library, 15–16.

24. Rich (ed.), *McLoughlin's Fort Vancouver Letters*, 88, 115, 232–33.

25. Townsend, *Narrative*, 241.

26. Edward R. Hodgson, "The Epidemic on the Lower Columbia," *Pacific Northwesterner*, I, 4 (Fall, 1957), 1–8.

27. Taylor and Hoaglin, " 'Intermittent Fever' of the 1830's," 170–73.

28. Larsell, *Doctor in Oregon*, 85.

29. Taylor and Hoaglin, " 'Intermittent Fever' of the 1830's," 171–73.

30. Rich (ed.), *McLoughlin's Fort Vancouver Letters*, 88, 94–95.

31. *Ibid.*, lxxxi, cxv, 276–77.

32. For an account of this expedition, see Alice Bay Maloney (ed.), *Fur Brigade to the Bonaventure: John Work's California Expedition, 1832–1833, for the Hudson's Bay Company*.

33. John Work, "John Work to Edward Ermatinger, February 24, 1834," *Washington Historical Quarterly*, II, 2 (January, 1908), 164.

34. Hall J. Kelley, "A History of the Settlement of Oregon and the Interior of Upper California," in Fred Wilbur Powell, *Hall J. Kelley on Oregon*, 326. Douglas to Ever Esteemed and dear Sir, October 11, 1830, Douglas, "Correspondence Outward."

35. *Territory of Oregon*, ["Mr. Kelley's Memoir," January 31, 1839], *House Rep. No. 101*, 25 Cong., 3 sess., 61.

36. Congressman Floyd's efforts are presented in John H. Schroeder, "Rep.

John Floyd, 1817–1829: Harbinger of Oregon Territory," *Oregon Historical Quarterly,* LXX (1969), 333–46.

37. Hall J. Kelley [general agent of the American Society For Encouraging the Settlement of the Oregon Territory], "A General Circular to All Persons of Good Character, Who Wish to Emigrate to the Oregon Territory," in Powell, *Hall J. Kelley on Oregon,* 85.

38. Judson, "British Side of the Restoration of Fort Astoria," 44.

39. *Territory of Oregon,* 61.

40. Hinds, "Journal."

41. John McLoughlin, "An Account of His Services in Oregon," Bancroft Library.

42. "Missionary Meeting in Lynn," typescript copy from *Oregonian and Indian's Advocate,* I, 10 (October, 1838–July, 1839), Seattle Public Library.

43. Parker, *Journal of an Exploring Tour beyond the Rocky Mountains,* 193–94.

44. *Memorial of William A. Slacum,* 10.

45. Wilbur, (ed.), *Duflot de Mofras' Travels on the Pacific Coast,* II, 185.

46. *Ibid.*

47. *Ibid.*; Dunn, *History of the Oregon Territory,* 120.

48. Ray, *Lower Chinook Ethnographic Notes,* 53–54.

49. *The Oregon Territory, Consisting of a Brief Description of the Country and Its Productions,* 52.

50. Dunn, *History of the Oregon Territory,* 128.

51. James Birnie to Rev. Mrs. [H. K. W.] Perkins, February 27, 1840, quoted in Strickland, *History of the Missions of the Methodist Episcopal Church,* 139–40. See also Blanchet et al., *Notices and Voyages of the Famed Quebec Mission to the Pacific Northwest,* 188.

52. Sylvester, "Voyages of the Pallas and Chenamus, 1843–45," 262–63.

53. Beaver, "Further Information Respecting the Aborigines," 15–22.

54. Dunn, *History of the Oregon Territory,* 71, 73.

55. Rich (ed.), *McLoughlin's Fort Vancouver Letters, 1825–38,* 261.

56. Tucker, *History of Oregon,* 47.

57. Roberts, "Recollections," 15.

58. For an account of Wyeth's activities, see John B. Wyeth, *Oregon; or, a Short History of a Long Journey from the Atlantic Ocean to the Region of the Pacific by Land;* Washington Irving, *The Adventures of Captain Bonneville, U.S.A., in the Rocky Mountains and the Far West,* Appendix A, "Nathaniel J. Wyeth, and the Trade of the Far West," 374–77; Dunn, *History of the Oregon Territory,* 139–40; Townsend, *Narrative.*

59. *Ibid.,* 179.

60. Morison, "New England and the Opening of the Columbia River Salmon Trade, 1830," 130.

61. J. Quinn Thornton, *Oregon and California in 1848,* I, 392–93.

62. J. W. Nesmith, "Annual Address," *Transactions of the Eighth Annual Re-Union of the Oregon Pioneer Association; for 1880,* 25.

63. *Ibid.*, 26.

64. *Ibid.*, 17.

65. William Fraser Tolmie, "Fort Nisqually Journal of Occurences, 1833–39," Vol. I, Suzzallo Library.

66. Trade in these northern quarters, especially at Fort Langley, is discussed in Walter N. Sage, "Life at a Fur Trading Post in British Columbia a Century Ago," *Washington Historical Quarterly*, XXV, 1 (January, 1934), 11–22.

67. Philip L. Edwards, *California in 1837: Diary of Col. Philip L. Edwards Containing An Account of a Trip to the Pacific Coast*, 31.

68. Merk (ed.), *Fur Trade and Empire*, 170.

69. James Birnie to Reverend Perkins, February 27, 1840, quoted in Strickland, *History of the Missions of the Methodist Episcopal Church*, 139.

70. Nellie B. Pipes (ed.), "Journal of John A. Frost, 1840–43," *Oregon Historical Quarterly*, XXXV (1934), 58.

71. Herbert C. Taylor, "Anthropological Investigation of the Chehalis Indians Relative to Tribal Identity and Aboriginal Possession of Lands," Washington State Library.

72. *Territory of Oregon*, 61.

73. Lee and Frost, *Ten Years in Oregon*, 286.

74. Wilkes, *Narrative of the United States Exploring Expedition*, IV, 322–23.

75. For a discussion of this and other Japanese junks wrecked, see Brooks, *Japanese Wrecks Stranded and Picked Up Adrift in the North Pacific Ocean*. Grace P. Morris, in her "Wreck of a Japanese Junk, 1834," *Oregon Historical Quarterly*, XXXVIII (1937), 160–63, presents a bibliography on discussion of Japanese junks wrecked on the Pacific Coast.

76. Joel E. Ferris, "Ranald MacDonald, the Sailor Boy Who Visited Japan," *Pacific Northwest Quarterly*, XLVII, 1 (January, 1957), 13–14.

77. The adventure is chronicled in Lewis and Murakami (eds.), *Ranald MacDonald, 1824–1894*, 120–266.

78. There is interesting correspondence between Ranald's father and Edward Ermatinger regarding his son's education and welfare. Archibald MacDonald, "Letters to Edward Ermatinger 1830–1937," April 1, 1836; January 25, 1837; March 10, 1839; March 15, 1843; March 22, 1844, Oregon Historical Society. Political and cultural repercussions of Ranald's visit are discussed in Ferris, "Ranald MacDonald, the Sailor Boy Who Visited Japan," 14–17.

79. Hodgson, in his "The Epidemic on the Lower Columbia," places the chief's death at 1830. Another source, Silas B. Smith, places the chief's death date at 1829. Silas B. Smith to Eva Emery Dye, October 20, 1891, Eva Emery Dye Papers.

80. Ray, *Lower Chinook Ethnographic Notes*, 58.

81. A. G. Harvey, "Chief Concomly's Skull," *Oregon Historical Quarterly*, XL, (1939), 161–67; T. D. Stewart, "The Chinook Sign of Freedom: A Study

of the Skull of the Famous Chief Comcomly," 563–76; Miller, *Clatsop County, Oregon*, 64.

82. *Memorial of William A. Slacum*, 14–15.

83. Tolmie, "Diary," entry of Friday, July 5, 1833.

84. Parker, *Journal of an Exploring Tour beyond the Rocky Mountains*, 250–51. Lee and Frost, *Ten Years in Oregon*, 233, narrate the incident.

85. Parker, *Journal of an Exploring Tour beyond the Rocky Mountains*, 258–59.

86. Ruby and Brown, *Cayuse Indians*, 166.

87. Wilkes, *Narrative of the United States Exploring Expedition*, V, 120; *Memorial of William A. Slacum*, 4, 14–15.

88. Overton Johnson and William H. Winter, *Route across the Rocky Mountains, with a Description of Oregon and California; Their Geographical Features, Their Resources, Soil, Climate, Production, &c., &c.*, 52. The *Oregonian*, December 17, 1899, p. 28, states that the death date of Chenamus was 1845. Lee and Frost, in their *Ten Years in Oregon*, 97–98, leave the impression that it was about that time or possibly a short time before.

89. *Memorial of William A. Slacum*, 4.

90. Hinds, "Journal."

91. Sturgis, "Extract from the Journal of Josiah Sturgis kept on board the Ship Levant on a Voyage from Boston to the North West Coast and China in the Year 1818," Oregon Historical Society. In his *Lower Chinook Ethnographic Notes*, 36, Ray discusses Chinook-Chehalis relationships.

92. Townsend, *Narrative*, 256–57.

93. Hinds, "Journal."

94. *Ibid.*; Townsend, *Narrative*, 257.

95. Kane, "Incidents of Travel on the North-West Coast," 277.

96. Hinds, "Journal." Activities of the *Sulphur* on the Columbia River are found in Edward Belcher, *Narrative of a Voyage Round the World Performed in Her Majesty's Ship Sulphur, during the Years 1836–1842*, I, 288–310.

97. Cambreleng to Benton, January 12, 1839, *Territory of Oregon*, 20.

98. John Floyd, "Occupation of the Columbia River," *Oregon Historical Quarterly*, VIII (1907), 293–94.

99. *Memorial of William A. Slacum*, 17–18.

100. Townsend, *Narrative*, 182.

101. Hinds, "Journal"; Lee and Frost, *Ten Years in Oregon*, 314.

102. Pipes (ed.), "Journal of John H. Frost," 52.

CHAPTER 12
The Great Reinforcement

1. John M. Canse, "The Diary of Henry Bridgeman Brewer, Being a Log of the Lausanne and the Time-Book of the Dalles Mission," *Oregon Historical Quarterly*, XXIX (1928), 189.

2. Oscar Osburn Winther, *The Great Northwest*, 116. Canse, in "The Diary of Henry Bridgeman Brewer, Being a Log of the Lausanne and the Time-Book of the Dalles Mission," 189, states that there were sixty people in the "Reinforcement." In their *Empire of the Columbia*, 210, Johansen and Gates list the number at fifty persons.

3. Claude E. Schaeffer, "William Brooks, Chinook Publicist," *Oregon Historical Quarterly*, LXIV (1963), 41–54.

4. *Ibid.*, 41–43.

5. *Ibid.*, 41–54.

6. Lee and Frost, *Ten Years in Oregon*, 222.

7. Lee, "Journal of Jason Lee," entry of May 21, 1840.

8. Gustavus Hines, *Life on the Plains of the Pacific: Oregon, Its History, Condition and Prospects*, 88.

9. *Ibid.*, 88–89.

10. Edwin V. O'Hara, *Pioneer Catholic History of Oregon*, 44; Blanchet, "Historical Sketches of the Catholic Church in Oregon during the Past Forty Years (1838–1878)."

11. Blanchet et al., *Notices and Voyages of the Famed Quebec Mission to the Pacific Northwest*, 19–20.

12. *Ibid.*, 163.

13. Pipes (ed.), "Journal of John H. Frost," 52.

14. Canse, "The Diary of Henry Bridgeman Brewer," 356–57.

15. *Ibid.*

16. Lee and Frost, *Ten Years in Oregon*, 223–24.

17. Lee, "Journal of Jason Lee," entry of May 28, 1840; Lee and Frost, *Ten Years in Oregon*, 224–25.

18. Lee and Frost, *Ten Years in Oregon*, 224–25; "Mr. Smith's Address," *Morning Oregonian*, December 11, 1899, p. 9.

19. Canse, "The Diary of Henry Bridgeman Brewer," 359.

20. Lee and Frost, *Ten Years in Oregon*, 233.

21. Pipes (ed.), "Journal of John H. Frost," 57.

22. *Ibid.*

23. Robert Moulton Gathke, "A Document of Mission History, 1833–43," *Oregon Historical Quarterly*, XXXVI (1935), 87.

24. Canse, "The Diary of Henry Bridgeman Brewer," 55; Lee and Frost, *Ten Years in Oregon*, 270.

25. *Ibid.*, 271.

26. Pipes (ed.), "Journal of John H. Frost," 58–60; Lee and Frost, *Ten Years in Oregon*, 271–72; John Minto to Eva Emery Dye, January 31, 1903, Eva Emery Dye Papers.

27. Wilkes, *Narrative of the United States Exploring Expedition*, IV, 322–23. Details of the search and trial may be found in Lee and Frost, *Ten Years in Oregon*, 271–74, and Pipes (ed.), "Journal of John H. Frost," 60–61.

28. *Ibid.*, 61–62.

29. Blanchet, "Historical Sketches of the Catholic Church in Oregon during the Past Forty Years (1838–1878)."

30. Pipes (ed.), "Journal of John H. Frost," 62.

31. *Ibid.*, 71.

32. *Ibid.*, 72–73; Lee and Frost, *Ten Years in Oregon*, 283–85.

33. Pipes (ed.), "Journal of John H. Frost," 366–67.

34. *Ibid.*, 140–41. The belief that Kotata was not a real chief was expressed by Clara Munson, mayor of nearby Warrenton, Oregon. Miller, *Clatsop County, Oregon*, 57.

35. Pipes (ed.), "Journal of John H. Frost," 140–44; Lee and Frost, *Ten Years in Oregon*, 292–94.

36. *Ibid.*, 297.

37. *Ibid.*, 299–300; Boas, *Chinook Texts*, 106.

38. Wilkes, *Narrative of the United States Exploring Expedition*, V, 116; Pipes (ed.), "Journal of John H. Frost," 164–67; Lee and Frost, *Ten Years in Oregon*, 306.

39. Pipes (ed.), "Journal of John H. Frost," 234–55.

40. *Ibid.*, 356.

41. Lee and Frost, *Ten Years in Oregon*, 314.

42. Lee, "Jason Lee, Special Statement to the Board, July 1, 1844," Jason Lee Papers, Oregon Historical Society.

43. P. L. Edwards, *Sketch of the Oregon Territory; or, Emigrants' Guide*, 19.

44. Lee and Frost, *Ten Years in Oregon*, 97.

45. Blanchet et al., *Notices and Voyages of the Famed Quebec Mission to the Pacific Northwest*, 187.

46. Pipes (ed.), "Journal of John H. Frost," 368.

47. "Solomon Howard Smith," *Transactions of the Fifteenth Annual Reunion of the Oregon Pioneer Association for 1887*, 86–88; John Minto to Eva Emery Dye, June 5, 1904, Eva Emery Dye Papers. Frost does not mention the hatchet incident in his journal.

48. Johnson and Winter, *Route across the Rocky Mountains*, 55.

49. Pipes (ed.), "Journal of John H. Frost," 368; Lee and Frost, *Ten Years in Oregon*, 316–17.

50. Schaeffer, "William Brooks, Chinook Publicist," 48.

51. White to Birnie, March 1, 1843, Microcopy of Records in the National Archives, *Oregon Superintendency of Indian Affairs, 1842–1880*, No. 234, Roll 607. Letters Received by the Office of Indian Affairs, 1842–52.

52. George Abernethy to Legislature of Oregon Territory, December 17, 1846, "Oregon Provisional Government," microfilm copy of letters, documents, reports and papers, copy 1613, Oregon Historical Society. A good account of the formation of the Provisional Government may be found in John A. Hussey, *Champoeg: Place of Transition A Disputed History*, 150–72.

53. White to House of Representatives, August 16, 1845, "Oregon Provisional Government," copy 1399.

54. For a discussion of this change in the law, see Marie Merriman Bradley, "Political Beginnings in Oregon," *Oregon Historical Quarterly*, IX (1908), 63.

55. Lee and Frost, *Ten Years in Oregon*, 313.

56. Pipes (ed.), "Journal of John H. Frost," 374.

57. J. L. Parrish, "Anecdotes of Intercourse with the Indians," Bancroft Library.

58. "Jason Lee, Special Statement to the Board, July 1, 1844," Jason Lee Papers.

59. "Letters of the Sisters of Notre Dame Established at St. Paul, Willamette, Oregon," in Clarence Booth Bagley, *Early Catholic Missions in Old Oregon, and Travels over the Rocky Mountains in 1845–46*, II, 82–83; Hiram Martin Chittenden and Alfred Talbot Richardson (eds.), *Life, Letters, and Travels of Father Pierre-Jean de Smet, S.J. 1801–1873*, II, 440–41; Pierre Jean de Smet, *Oregon Missions and Travels over the Rocky Mountains, in 1845–46*, 66–67.

60. Sylvester, "Voyages of the Pallas and Chenamus, 1843–45," 270n., 360–67 and n.

61. *Ibid.*, 369.

62. Minto, "The Number and Condition of the Native Race," 299 and n.

63. "Mr. Smith's Address," *Morning Oregonian*, December 11, 1899, p. 9.

64. Pipes (ed.), "Journal of John H. Frost," 368; "Mr. Smith's Address," *Morning Oregonian*, December 11, 1899, p. 9.

65. "C. F. Seymour, Commander in Chief, to Thomas Baillie, Esq., Commander of H.M. sloop Modeste, 7 April, 1844," manuscript copy of letter from Public Records Office, London, in Kenneth L. Holmes Collection.

66. "Secret Mission of Warre and Vavasour," *Washington Historical Quarterly*, III, 2 (April, 1912), 149–50; Joseph Schafer (ed.), "Documents Relative to Warre and Vavasour's Military Reconnoissance in Oregon, 1845–6," *Oregon Historical Quarterly*, X (1909), 9.

67. James W. Welch "Dictation," Bancroft Library.

68. Samuel Terry, Jr., "Reminiscences," Oregon Historical Society; J. M. Shively to Dr. John McLoughlin, September 15, 1884, John McLoughlin Papers; "Alexander Lattie's Fort George Journal, 1846," *Oregon Historical Quarterly*, LXIV (1963), 202–203n., 222–23.

69. *Ibid.*, 226.

70. *Ibid.*, 245.

71. *Ibid.*, 213.

72. *Oregon Spectator*, July 22 and August 5, 1847.

73. Howison, *Report of Lieut. Neil M. Howison*, 31.

74. *Ibid.*, 24; M. P. Deady, "History & Progress of Oregon after 1845," Bancroft Library.

75. Charles H. Carey (ed.), *The Journals of Theodore Talbot, 1843 and 1849–52, with the Fremont Expedition of 1843 and with the First Military Company in Oregon Territory, 1849–1852*, 86–87.

76. *Before the Indian Claims Commission: The Chinook Tribe and Bands*

of Indians, Plaintiffs, v. *the United States of America, Defendant. Docket No. 234. Decided: November 4, 1970. Additional Findings of Fact,* 70.

77. Fred Lockley, *History of the Columbia River Valley from The Dalles to the Sea,* I, 240.

78. Thornton, *Oregon and California in 1848,* I, 347. *The Oregonian,* January 31, 1852, p. 2, tells of white men at the time bringing gold down to the Columbia River from the Queen Charlotte Islands.

79. William C. McKay to Eva Emery Dye, February 11, 1892, Eva Emery Dye Papers.

80. Samuel C. Damon, "Journal, May, 1849," Oregon Historical Society, 19; "Adventures in the Far West," *The Leisure Hour,* XI (1862), 221–22.

81. Eden Colvile to Sir J. H. Pelly, March 5, 1850, in E. E. Rich (ed.), *The Publications of the Hudson's Bay Record Society: Eden Colvile's Letters, 1849–52,* 19–21.

82. Damon, "Journal, May, 1849."

83. "The Lost Tribes of the Chinooks and Clatsops," *San Francisco Chronicle,* June 1, 1884.

84. *Oregon Spectator,* January 24, 1850, p. 2.

85. Lockley, *History of the Columbia River Valley from The Dalles to the Sea,* I, 109.

86. Wyndham Robertson, Jr., *Oregon, Our Right and Title: Containing an Account of the Condition of the Oregon Territory,* 130.

CHAPTER 13

Tansey Point and Beyond

1. Swan, *Northwest Coast,* 376.

2. P. W. Crawford, "Narrative of the Overland Journey to Oregon," Bancroft Library.

3. George Gibbs identifies this Abernethy as George, former provisional governor. Gibbs to Secretary of the Interior, April, n.d., 1850, *Oregon Superintendency,* No. 2, Roll 12. Letters Received, September 30, 1848–December 25, 1852.

4. Whealdon, "Stories and Sketches from Pacific County," 188.

5. Other information on the Scarboroughs is found in Edward Huggins to Eva Emery Dye, May 23, 1904, Eva Emery Dye Papers; "The Round Hand of George B. Roberts: Letters to Mrs. F. F. Victor, 1878–83," *Oregon Historical Quarterly,* LXIII (1962), 236. Roberts, an acquaintance of many Indians and whites on the lower Columbia at the time, later wrote to Mrs. Victor that Scarborough's wife bore the name Polly and was a sister of Princess Charlotte, Comcomly's daughter. *Ibid.*

6. Walker Allison Tompkins, "Oysterville, 1840–97," *Oregon Historical Quarterly,* XXXIII (1932), 160–63.

7. Carey, *Journals of Theodore Talbot 1843 and 1849–52*, 86.

8. Whealdon, "Stories and Sketches from Pacific County," 189; Whealdon, "On Whealdon Hill (Ilwaco, Wash.) Eve of July 16, 1860," 10.

9. Robert Shortess to Johnson, February 4, 1851, Robert Shortess Papers, Oregon Historical Society.

10. Washington Hall, "Affidavit July 27, 1855," William Lair Hill Papers, Oregon Historical Society.

11. In their *Ranald MacDonald, 1824–1894*, 76n., Lewis and Murakami (eds.) state that the town Ilwaco, Washington, was named for "Elowahka," a Comcomly daughter by a "Willapa" woman.

12. James Swan explains this relationship in his *Northwest Coast*, 55.

13. Hall, "Affidavit July 27, 1855," William Lair Hill Papers.

14. Washington Hall, "Washington Hall (Ogn.) Affidavit Claim," February 24, 1851, photocopy of manuscript, Oregon Historical Society.

15. Hall to Shortess, March 10, 1851, Robert Shortess Papers.

16. Testimonies of Catherine George and Julia Russel, "Copy of Testimony . . . in support of a claim of *Chinook Indian Tribe against the United States*," 173–215.

17. James S. Lawson, "Autobiography," Bancroft Library, 35; Colbert, "Naming and Early Settlement of Ilwaco, Washington," 182–83. See also Marshall Hanft, "The Cape Forts: Guardians of the Columbia," *Oregon Historical Quarterly*, LXV (1964), 352.

18. Nellie B. Pipes, "John Mix Stanley, Indian Painter," *Oregon Historical Quarterly*, XXXIII (1932), 257; Kane, "Incidents of Travel on the North-West Coast," 278.

19. "The Lost Tribes of the Chinooks and Clatsops," *San Francisco Chronicle*, June 1, 1884.

20. Gibbs, *Tribes of Western Washington and Northwestern Oregon*, 189.

21. *Ibid.*, 204.

22. Whealdon, "On Whealdon Hill (Ilwaco, Wash.) Eve of July 16, 1860," 17.

23. Blanchet, "Historical Sketches of the Catholic Church in Oregon during the Past Forty Years (1838–1878)."

24. Lionnet's correspondence from Stella Maris Mission, July 9, 1849, and September 19, 1849, is from "Deceased Clergy, Mesplié, Lionnet Rev. Letters to Archbp. Blanchet," manuscript, The Chancery, Archdiocese of Seattle, Washington.

25. R. G. Large (ed.), *The Journals of William Fraser Tolmie, Physician and Fur Trader*, 210; "Mr. Beaver Objects," *The Beaver*, Outfit 272 (September, 1941), 10.

26. Demers, *J.M.J. Chinook Dictionary, Catechism, Prayers and Hymns*.

27. Wilbur (ed.), *Duflot de Mofras' Travels on the Pacific Coast*, II, 183.

28. Lionnet's July 3, 1850, correspondence is from "Deceased Clergy, Mesplié, Lionnet Rev. Letters to Archbp. Blanchet," The Chancery, Archdiocese of Seattle.

29. M. de Saint-Amant, *Voyages en Californie et dans l'Orégon par M. de Saint-Amant envoye du gouvernement francais en 1851–1852*, 386–89.

30. Damon, "Journal May, 1849," 3.

31. Testimony of Patrick James McGowan, "Copy of Testimony . . . in support of a claim of *Chinook Indian Tribe against the United States*," 17.

32. Swan, *Northwest Coast*, 192–93.

33. Hussey, *Chinook Point and the Story of Fort Columbia*, 11.

34. Gile, "Notes on Columbia River Salmon," 141.

35. Samuel Terry McKean, Jr., "Reminiscences," Oregon Historical Society. In his *Northwest Coast*, 103–109, James Swan describes salmon fishing in the Chinook area at about the same time.

36. Testimony of Mary Kelly, "Copy of Testimony . . . in support of a claim of *Chinook Indian Tribe against the United States*," 65–72.

37. Guy Reed Ramsey to authors, July 8, 1972.

38. *Oregon Spectator*, July 22, 1847, p. 4.

39. Meek to Solicitor of the Treasury, November 10, 1849, "Selections from the United States Department of Justice Archives Regarding Liquor Traffic among the Indians in the Territories of Washington and Oregon, 1849–1860," Joseph P. Donnelly, S.J., Collection, Oregon Historical Society.

40. *Oregon Spectator*, March 21, 1850, p. 2.

41. Shortess to Anson Dart, Oregon Superintendent of Indian Affairs, January 5, 1851, Robert Shortess Papers.

42. *Oregon Spectator*, April 4, 1850, p. 2; April 18, 1850, p. 2. For an account of the establishment and early years as United States Army Fort Vancouver, see Major Osborne Cross, *March of the Regiment of Mounted Riflemen to Oregon in 1849*, 144.

43. C. F. Coan, "The First Stage of the Federal Indian Policy in the Pacific Northwest, 1849–1852," *Oregon Historical Quarterly*, XXII (1921), 49–50.

44. *Ibid.*, 54.

45. Shortess to Dart, February 5, 1851, *Oregon Superintendency*, No. 2, Roll 3, Letter Books, 1848–1872. Letter Book B:10, July, 1850–December, 1853.

46. Shortess to Dart, February 5, 1851, *ibid.*

47. George Gibbs to Secretary of Interior, April (n.d.), 1850, *Oregon Superintendency*, No. 2, Roll 12. Register of Letters Received September 30, 1848–January 14, 1873, Letters Received September 30, 1848–December 25, 1852.

48. Shortess to Dart, February 5, 1851, *Oregon Superintendency*, No. 2, Roll 3.

49. Howison, *Report of Lieut. Neil M. Howison*, 28.

50. Lea to Dart, July 20, 1850, *Oregon Superintendency*, No. 2, Roll 11.

51. Swan, *Northwest Coast*, 383.

52. Dart to Shortess, April 22, 1851, Robert Shortess Papers.

53. Shortess to Dart, March 15, 1851, *Oregon Superintendency*, No. 2, Roll 3.

54. Shortess to Dart, May 5, 1851, *ibid.*

55. Rockwood (ed.), "Letters of Charles Stevens" (Letter of June 6, 1854), 79.

56. Sidney S. Ford to Governor Isaac I. Stevens, November 26, 1856, *Washington Superintendency*, No. 5, Roll 16. Letters from Employees Assigned to the Western, or Coast, District, and the Chehalis Locality, Serving Indians Parties to No Treaty, March 11, 1856–August 31, 1874.

57. Shortess to Dart, November 18, 1850, Robert Shortess Papers.

58. *Ibid.*

59. George Gibbs to Secretary of Interior (n.d.), 1850, *Oregon Superintendency*, No. 2, Roll 12.

60. Shortess to Dart, February 5, 1851, *Oregon Superintendency*, No. 2, Roll 3.

61. Shortess to Dart, November 18, 1850, Robert Shortess Papers.

62. Shortess to Dart, February 5, 1851, *Oregon Superintendency*, No. 2, Roll 3; Lea to Dart, July 20, 1850, *Oregon Superintendency*, No. 2, Roll 11.

63. C. M. Conrad (War Department) to Secretary of Interior, June 4, 1851, *Oregon Superintendency*, No. 2, Roll 3.

64. *Before the Indian Claims Commission of the United States: The Chinook Tribe, the Wauhkiakum Band and the Willapa or Shoalwater Bay Bands of Chinook, the Kathlamet Tribe of Chinook, the Clatsop Tribe of Chinook, and the Nucqueclahwemuck Band of Chinook, Petitioners, vs. The United States of America, Defendant, Docket No. 234. Petitioner's Findings of Fact and Brief*, 26–27.

65. Anson Dart, "Report [to Luke Lea, November 7, 1851] concerning treaties negotiated as Superintendent of Indian Affairs, Oregon Territory, with Chinook and other Indian Tribes," Bancroft Library; L. H. Judson to Dart, December 15, 1857, *Oregon Superintendency*, No. 2, Roll 3.

66. Information on the Clatsop treaty is found in Dart, "Report concerning treaties negotiated as Superintendent of Indian Affairs."

67. Shortess to Dart, February 5, 1851, *Oregon Superintendency*, No. 2, Roll 3.

68. Coan, "First Stage of the Federal Indian Policy in the Pacific Northwest," 61.

69. Dart, "Report concerning treaties negotiated as Superintendent of Indian Affairs."

70. Dart to Commissioner of Indian Affairs, October 22, 1850, *Oregon Superintendency*, No. 2, Roll 11.

71. Swan, *Northwest Coast*, 112–13.

72. Spier, *Tribal Distribution in Washington*, 22.

73. Coan, "First Stage of the Federal Indian Policy in the Pacific Northwest," 81–82.

74. Dart, "Report concerning treaties negotiated as Superintendent of Indian Affairs."

75. Coan, "First Stage of the Federal Indian Policy in the Pacific Northwest," 61.

76. Dart, "Report concerning treaties negotiated as Superintendent of Indian Affairs."

77. Dart to Lea, August 16, 1851, *Oregon Superintendency*, No. 2, Roll 3.

78. Swan, *Northwest Coast*, 166.

79. C. T. Chamberlain to James K. Polk, January 22, 1849; Richard Young, Commissioner, to Chamberlain, February 22, 1849, *Oregon Superintendency*, No. 234, Roll 607.

80. Dart, "Report concerning treaties negotiated as Superintendent of Indian Affairs."

81. *Ibid.*

82. Hall to Dart, September 14, 1851, *Oregon Superintendency*, No. 2, Roll 3.

83. Gibbs to Secretary of Interior, April (n.d.) 1850, *Oregon Superintendency*, No. 2, Roll 12.

84. Coan, "First Stage of the Federal Indian Policy in the Pacific Northwest," 62–64.

85. Gibbs to Secretary of the Interior, April (n.d.) 1850, *Oregon Superintendency*, No. 2, Roll 12.

86. *Oregon Superintendency*, No. 2, Roll 7, Letter Books, 1848–1872. Letter Book F:10, July, 1853–August, 1855; September, 1857–September, 1859.

87. Report of Subagent W. W. Raymond, October 17, 1853, *Oregon Superintendency*, No. 2, Roll 3.

CHAPTER 14
From River Bar to Bar of Justice

1. A report of the devastating effects of the smallpox epidemic appears in *Report on Claims of Chinook and Chehalis Indians. House Exec. Doc.* No. 517, 60 Cong., 1 sess., 1908, 7; Palmer to Commissioner of Indian Affairs, May 2, 1853, *Oregon Superintendency*, No. 2, Roll 3; Tappan, Annual Report, September 3, 1854, *Washington Superintendency*, No. 5, Roll 17; E. A. Starling (agent in charge of the Puget Sound District) to Stevens, December 4, 1853, *Washington Superintendency*, No. 5, Roll 9. Letters from Agents Assigned to the Puget Sound District as a Whole, December 4, 1853–August 16, 1862.

2. Testimonies of Julia Russel and Samuel Mallette, "Copy of Testimony . . . in support of a claim of *Chinook Indian Tribe against the United States*," 123.

3. William Strong to Stevens, January 12, 1854, *Washington Superintendency*, No. 5, Roll 23. Miscellaneous Letters Received August 22, 1853–April 9, 1861.

4. Rockwood (ed.), "Letters of Charles Stevens," letter of June 6, 1854, 79.

5. *Weekly Oregonian*, June 16, 1855, p. 2.

6. Rockwood (ed.), "Letters of Charles Stevens," letter of June 6, 1854, 75.

7. *Ibid.*, letter of September 7, 1854, 87. Mary Kelly testifying in 1902 told of early cranberry sales. "Copy of Testimony . . . in support of a claim of *Chinook Indian Tribe against the United States,*" 71–72.

8. Subagent J. L. Parrish to Dart (no month) 30, 1852, *Oregon Superintendency*, No. 2, Roll 12.

9. *Oregonian*, June 11, 1853, p. 2.

10. *Washington Standard*, February 11, 1854, p. 2.

11. *Report of the Superintendent of the Coast Survey Showing the Progress of the Survey during the Year 1858, Senate Exec. Doc.* No. 14, 35 Cong., 2 sess., 405.

12. Swan tells of numerous Indians coming to Willapa Bay for the oyster harvests. *The Northwest Coast*, 59; "The Oyster Enigma," *The Sou'wester*, II, 1 (Spring, 1967), 5–6.

13. Parrish to Dart (no month), 1852, *Oregon Superintendency*, No. 2, Roll 12.

14. *Oregonian*, February 5, 1853, p. 2.

15. Tappan, Annual Report, September 3, 1854, *Washington Superintendency*, No. 5, Roll 17; Geo. Dawson to Gibbs, January 15, 1854, *Washington Superintendency*, No. 5, Roll 23.

16. Whealdon, "On Whealdon Hill (Ilwaco, Wash.) Eve of July 16, 1860," 23–24.

17. *Report on Claims of Chinook and Chehalis Indians*, 6.

18. "Records of the proceedings of the Commission to hold Treaties with the Indian tribes in Washington territory and the Blackfeet Country" [Olympia, W.T., December 7, 1854], Clarence Booth Bagley Collection, Suzzallo Library. Details of these and subsequent Stevens treaties are found in Edmond S. Meany, *History of the State of Washington*, 167–75.

19. Tappan to Stevens, January 18, 1855, *Washington Superintendency*, No. 5, Roll 17.

20. Tappan to Stevens, February 14, 1855, *ibid.*

21. Meany, *History of the State of Washington*, 169.

22. A. J. Cain to Nesmith, December 9, 1858, *Washington Superintendency*, No. 5, Roll 16.

23. Quoted in Swan, *Northwest Coast*, 345. Hazard Stevens quotes the identical speech in a biography of his father, the governor. *The Life of Isaac Ingalls Stevens*, II, 6.

24. Swan, *Northwest Coast*, 345.

25. It was fortuitous that Swan was invited to the council, for from his pen there is a most complete account of its proceedings and the events surrounding them. *Ibid.*, 327–52.

26. Edward R. Geary to George Washington Manypenny (Commissioner of Indian Affairs), October 3, 1855, *Oregon Superintendency*, Letter Books, 1848–1872. Letter Book D:10, March, 1854–January, 1856.

27. A recommendation would be made in 1869 to transfer the agency at Alsea to the Siletz. By 1876 the Alsea would be abolished, but because of inadequate congressional appropriations sixty-seven Alsea Indians (including Tillamooks and Clatsops) would join some of their fellows in about 1880 on the Siletz. *Report on Claims of Chinook and Chehalis Indians*, 7–8; *Report of the Secretary of the Interior, House Exec. Doc.*, No. 1, pt. 3, 41 Cong., 2 sess., 597; *Annual Report of the Commissioner of Indian Affairs to the Secretary of the Interior for the Year 1874*, 21–22; *Annual Report of the Commissioner of Indian Affairs to the Secretary of the Interior for the Year 1876*, xxiii; *Report of the Secretary of the Interior, House Exec. Doc.*, No. 1, pt. 5, 47 Cong., 2 sess., 202.

28. Edward Geary to S. H. Smith, March 13, 1861, *Oregon Superintendency*, Letter Books, 1848–1872. Letter Book G:10, September, 1859–July, 1861.

29. [Rev. S. J.] Po[a]ndo[s]y to Rev. Toussaint Mesplié, April, 1853, *Oregon Superintendency*, No. 234, Roll 611. Letters Received by the Office of Indian Affairs, 1853–55.

30. Some of the efforts to form alliances among these Indians are cited in Lockley, *History of the Columbia River Valley from The Dalles to the Sea*, I, 98; U. E. Hicks, "Taking the Census in 1853," *Washington Historian*, II, 2 (January, 1901), 77–78; Travis Daniel, Special Indian Agent, to Stevens, April 12, 1856, *Washington Superintendency*, No. 5, Roll 16.

31. Swan, *Northwest Coast*, 385.

32. Rockwood, "Letters of Charles Stevens," Letter of May 27, 1856, 178.

33. *Weekly Oregonian*, July 19, 1856, p. 2.

34. *Pioneer and Democrat*, June 27, 1856, p. 2.

35. Government attempts to contain the Indians living west of the Cascade Mountains and some Indian problems following the war are discussed in A. J. Cain to Nesmith, November 9, 1857, and December 9, 1858; A. C. Smith to Geary, October 2, 1860, *Washington Superintendency*, No. 5, Roll 16.

36. B. Kindred to Nesmith, July 14, 1858, *Oregon Superintendency*, No. 2, Roll 16. Letters Received by the Office of Indian Affairs, January 1–December 30, 1858; Citizens to Geary, December 2, 1859, *Oregon Superintendency*, No. 2, Roll 17. Letters Received by the Office of Indian Affairs, January 3–December 30, 1859; William Johnson to Capt. Miller, February 7, 1860, *Oregon Superintendency*, No. 2, Roll 18. Letters Received by the Office of Indian Affairs, January 1–December 31, 1860; S. H. Smith to Geary, March 4, 1861, *Oregon Superintendency*, No. 2, Roll 19. Letters Received by the Office of Indian Affairs January 3–December 27, 1861.

37. *Report on Claims of Chinook and Chehalis Indians*, 7–8.

38. S. H. Smith to Geary, June 23, 1861, *Oregon Superintendency*, No. 2, Roll 19.

39. Alex Anderson to Nesmith, May 17, 1858, *Oregon Superintendency*, No. 2, Roll 16. Oregon State was formed on February 14, 1859; Washington State was formed on November 11, 1889. Maloney to McGill, February 21,

1861; McGill to Maloney, March 2, 1861. "Documents," *Washington Historical Quarterly*, IV, 4 (October, 1913).

40. *Morning Oregonian*, August 25, 1865, p. 4; *Washington Standard*, August 19, 1865, p. 2; W. B. Gosnell to Geary, December 7, 1860, *Washington Superintendency*, No. 5, Roll 16.

41. Colbert, "Naming and Early Settlement of Ilwaco, Washington," 188, 194.

42. Whealdon, "On Whealdon Hill (Ilwaco, Wash.) Eve of July 16, 1860," 4.

43. C. Aubrey Angelo, *Sketches of Travel in Oregon and Idaho with Map of South Boisie*, 15.

44. *Morning Oregonian*, August 17, 1864.

45. *Ibid.*, June 11, 1864, p. 3.

46. Edward Huggins Writings, Manuscript Folder 2, Suzzallo Library.

47. Swan, *Northwest Coast*, 96–97. Between 1826 and 1852 the company at Fort Vancouver had bought 490 large and 150 pup otter skins and one tail. Victor B. Scheffer, "The Sea Otter on the Washington Coast," *Pacific Northwest Quarterly*, XXXI, 4 (October, 1940), 376.

48. Edward Huggins Writings; Testimony of Silas Smith, "Copy of Testimony . . . in support of a claim of *Chinook Indian Tribe against the United States*," 225–26; Swan, *The Northwest Coast*, 96.

49. *Revised Outline Descriptions of the Posts and Stations of Troops in the Military Division of the Pacific Commanded by Major-General John M. Schofield*, 33. For an account of United States fortifications at the mouth of the Columbia River, see Hanft, "The Cape Forts: Guardians at the Columbia," 325–61.

50. A. J. Cain to Nesmith, December 9, 1858, *Washington Superintendency*, No. 5, Roll 16; R. H. Milroy to Capt. G. H. Burton, U.S.A., March 20, 1878, Robert Huston Milroy Letterbook, Vol. I, February 19, 1877 to November 18, 1878, Agency for the Puyallup, Nisqually and other Indian Tribes, Suzzallo Library; *Report with Respect to the House Resolution Authorizing the Committee on Interior and Insular Affairs to Conduct an Investigation of the Bureau of Indian Affairs, House Report* No. 2503, 82 Cong., 2 sess., 964, 1309–10.

51. William F. Prosser, "An Interesting Collection of Indian Relics," *The Washington Historian* I, 1 (September, 1899), 27.

52. Hazeltine, *Historical and Regional Geography of the Willapa Bay Area*, 56.

53. McKenny to William Billings, March 2, 1868; McKenny to Edwin Harmon, June 6, 1868; McKenny, Annual Report, August, 1868, *Washington Superintendency*, No. 5, Roll 4. Copies and Drafts of Letters Sent June 2, 1857–January 31, 1874.

54. McKenny to Cyril Ward, February 1, 1869, *ibid*.

55. Samuel Ross, Washington Superintendent of Indian Affairs, Annual Report, September 1, 1870, *Washington Superintendency*, No. 5, Roll 6.

Copies of Letters Sent by Superintendents Samuel Ross and Thomas J. Mc-Kenny, August 4, 1869–September 22, 1872.

56. Testimony of Silas Smith, "Copy of Testimony . . . in support of a claim of *Chinook Indian Tribe against the United States,*" 233.

57. Statement of Annie Hallet Strong (Statement No. 69), *Rolls of Certain Indian Tribes in Oregon and Washington, House Exec. Doc.* No. 133, 59 Cong., 2 sess., 56.

58. *Oregonian,* December 17, 1899, 28.

59. Hussey, *Chinook Point and the Story of Fort Columbia,* 23.

60. For the story of Chinook Point Military Reservation and the building of Fort Columbia and nearby Forts Stevens and Canby, see *ibid.*

61. B. F. Alley and J. P. Munro-Fraser, *History of Clarke County, Washington Territory,* 294.

62. J. P. Wagner, "William Cameron McKay," *East Oregonian,* January 2, 1889.

63. Alley and Munro-Fraser, *History of Clarke County,* 292–96.

64. Horace Briggs, *Letters From Alaska and the Pacific Coast,* 19.

65. Crawford, "Narrative of the Overland Journey to Oregon," 128.

66. Davidson, *United States Coast and Geodetic Survey: Pacific Coast,* 459–61.

67. See Glenn Cunningham, "Oregon's First Salmon Cannery, 'Captain' John West," *Oregon Historical Quarterly,* LIV (1953), 240–48.

68. Frances Fuller Victor, *Atlantis Arisen; or, Talks of a Tourist About Oregon and Washington,* 43.

69. Gibbs, *Tribes of Western Washington and Northwestern Oregon,* 196; Swan, *Northwest Coast,* 107–108.

70. Whealdon, "On Whealdon Hill (Ilwaco, Wash.) Eve of July 16, 1860," 16.

71. *Ilwaco Tribune,* March 13, 1953; *Raymond Herald,* March 19, 1953; *Oregonian,* March 23, 1953.

72. Victor, *Atlantis Arisen,* 34.

73. *Washington Standard,* September 30, 1865, p. 1.

74. Hussey, *Chinook Point and the Story of Fort Columbia,* 20.

75. "The Lost Tribes of the Chinooks and Clatsops," *San Francisco Chronicle,* June 1, 1884.

76. Boas, *Chinook Texts,* 5–6.

77. Ray, "Historical Position of the Lower Chinook in the Native Culture of the Northwest," and *Lower Chinook Ethnographic Notes.*

78. J. Murphy, "Summer Ramblings in Washington Territory," *Appletons' Journal: A Monthly Miscellany of Popular Literature,* n.s. III (November, 1877), 388.

79. Edward S. Curtis, *The North American Indian, Being a Series of Volumes Picturing and Describing the Indians of the United States and Alaska,* VIII, 85–154.

80. Act of June 7, 1897, 30 Stat. 62.

81. *Report on Claims of Chinook and Chehalis Indians*, 9.

82. 33 Stat. 1073.

83. 34 Stat. 325, 368.

84. *Report on Claims of Chinook and Chehalis Indians*, 8.

85. *Ibid.*, 11.

86. Western Oregon Indians brought their case before the court of claims under a special jurisdictional act of August 26, 1935 (49 Stat. 801), in the Alcea Band of Tillamooks *et al.* 103 C. Cls. including the Chinook, Clatsop, Nehalem and Siletz Confederated Tribes and Confederated Tribes of the Grand Ronde Community. The case, No. 45230, was given a decision on April 2, 1945, which was against any recovery for the Chinooks, Clatsops, and Nehalems. *Cases Decided in the Court of Claims of the United States, February 1, 1945, to May 7, 1945 (Partial), with Report of Decisions of the Supreme Court in Court of Claims Cases*, Vol. CIII (Washington, 1946), 494.

87. *Code of Federal Regulations, Title 25–Indians*, 70 USCA.

88. E. L. Crawford, attorney for the Chinooks, to the authors, September 29, 1970.

89. *Before the Indian Claims Commission of the United States, The Chinook Tribe and Bands of Indians, Petitioner*, vs. *The United States of America, Defendant, Petition No. 234* (filed August 8, 1951), 8.

90. Anna Koontz, secretary for the Chinook Nation, to the authors, Taholah, Washington, June 3, 1971.

91. Stephen A. Meriwether, Chinook Tribal secretary, to the authors, Ilwaco, Washington, June 2, 1971.

92. Stephen A. Meriwether to the authors, June 2, 1971.

93. *Before the Indian Claims Commission, The Chinook Tribe and Bands of Indians, Plaintiffs*, vs. *The United States of America, Defendant, Docket No. 234. Final Award, November 4, 1970*, 88; Guy Lovell, Chief, Tribal Claims Section, Bureau of Indian Affairs, to the authors, Washington D.C., June 14, 1971. For a presentation of the commission's consideration of land values, see *Before the Indian Claims Commission, The Chinook Tribe and Bands of Indians, Plaintiffs, v. The United States of America, Defendant, Docket No. 234, Decided: November 4, 1970. Opinion of the Commission*, 56–63.

94. "Mr. Smith's Address," *Morning Oregonian*, December 11, 1899, p. 9.

Bibliography

Unpublished Materials and Manuscripts

"Account book of the ship Eliza, 1805, on voyage from New York, to Canton." Manuscript, William Bell Papers, Constable-Pierrepont Papers, New York Public Library.

"Account book of the ship, *Mary*, on voyage from New York to Canton." Manuscript, William Bell Papers, Constable-Pierrepont Papers, New York Public Library.

Anderson, Alexander Caulfield. "History of the Northwest Coast." Manuscript, Microfilm 25, 2 reels, Suzzallo Library, University of Washington, Seattle.

Anonymous. "Missionary Meeting in Lynn." Typescript copy from *Oregonian and Indian's Advocate*, I, 10, (October, 1838–July, 1839). Seattle Public Library, 8.

Ash, Andrew D., Jr., librarian, Massachusetts Historical Society, Boston. Letter to authors, February 8, 1972.

Astor, John Jacob. John Jacob Astor Papers. Manuscript 1–71. Baker Library, Harvard University Graduate School of Business Administration, Cambridge, Mass.

———. "Original Manuscript Letters of John Jacob Astor concerning Fort Astoria on the Columbia River and his Efforts to secure the Protection & Defense of the American Fur Company's Post at Fort Astoria." Manuscript 13, Beinecke Library, Yale University, New Haven, Conn.

Aulick, John H. "Extracts from a Journal on board the U.S. Ship Ontario on a Cruise to N.W. Coast. By Lieutenant John H. Aulick of the U. S. Navy." July 1–October 23, 1818, Microfilm Copy of Manuscript 101, Oregon Historical Society, Portland.

Baker, Jos[ep]h. "A Log of His Majesty's Ship Discovery from 22nd December 1790 to 27 November 1792." Photocopy, Oregon Historical Society, Portland.

Barrell, Joseph. "Miscellany." Manuscript 1124, Oregon Historical Society, Portland.

Beaver, Herbert. "Further Information Respecting the Aborigines; Containing Reports of the Committee on Indian Affairs at Philadelphia, Extracts from the Proceedings of the Yearly Meetings of Philadelphia, New York, New England, Maryland [,] Virginia, and Ohio." Typescript copy of Manuscript 372, Oregon Historical Society, Portland.

Bishop, Charles. "Commercial Journal Copy's of Letters and Accts, of Ship Ruby's voyage to the N.W.T. coast of America and China, 1794, 5, 6." Manuscript A/A/20.5/R.82B, Archives of British Columbia, Victoria.

Boit, John. "Journal of a Voyage Round the Globe." Microfilm copy of Manuscript 62, Massachusetts Historical Society, Boston.

Boudinot, May Fidelia. "The Case of the Mercury, as Typical of Contraband Trade on the California Coast, 1790–1820." Thesis, University of California, Berkeley, 1907.

Bryant, John, and William Sturgis. John Bryant and William Sturgis Collection, 1811–72, Baker Library, Harvard University Graduate School of Business Administration, Cambridge, Mass.

Chapman, Douglas G., Dean, College of Fisheries, University of Washington, Seattle. Letter to authors, April 21, 1972.

Cleveland, Richard Jeffry. "Narrative of the fur trading of the brig *Caroline* from China to the Northwest Coast of America, January 10 to Sept. 13, 1799." Manuscript 90, Beinecke Library, Yale University, New Haven, Conn.

Clinton, Ebenezer. "Remarks on board the ship *Vancouver*, Capt. Brown commanding. Bound from Boston to the N. West Coast of America and China from August 4, 1804, to September 8, 1806." Manuscript 92, Beinecke Library, Yale University, New Haven, Conn.

"Copies of certain treaties made Aug. 8–9, 1851, at Tansey Point." Photocopy of Manuscript P-A 302:1, Bancroft Library, University of California, Berkeley.

"A Copy of the Log Book of the Ship Beaver on a voyage from New York to the Columbia River 1812 &c." Microfilm copy of manuscript, Washington State Library, Olympia.

"Copy of Testimony taken in 1902, at Astoria, in support of a claim of *Chinook Indian Tribe against the United States* for land in the State of Washington, near the mouth of the Columbia River. Containing historical material relating to the Chinook villages and the people, with some reference to the Clatsop Indian Tribe in Oregon." Manuscript 5, Oregon Historical Society, Portland.

Crawford, E. L., attorney for Chinooks. Letters to authors, September 29, 1970, and August 1, 1972.

Crawford, P. W. "Narrative of the Overland Journey to Oregon." Manuscript P-A 20, Bancroft Library, University of California, Berkeley.

Damon, Samuel C. "Journal May, 1849." Manuscript 803, Oregon Historical Society, Portland.

Dart, Anson. "Report [to Luke Lea, November 7, 1851] concerning treaties negotiated as Superintendent of Indian Affairs, Oregon Territory, with Chinook and other Indian Tribes." Photocopy of Manuscript P-A 302:2, Bancroft Library, University of California, Berkeley.

Daugherty, Richard, Professor and Chairman, Department of Anthropology, Washington State University, Pullman, Washington. Letter to authors, April 17, 1972.

Davidov, Gabriel Ivan. "Extracts from Davidov's Diary by Gabriel Ivan Davidov, 1810–1812." Translated from the Russian by Michael E. Affonin, Seattle, Washington, 1832–33. Typescript copy of Manuscript H.G. In7, Archives in British Columbia, Victoria.

Deady, M. P. "History & Progress of Oregon after 1845." Manuscript P-A 24, Bancroft Library, University of California, Berkeley.

"Deceased Clergy, Mesplié, Lionnet Rev. Letters to Archbp. Blanchet." Manuscript, The Chancery, Archdiocese of Seattle.

Dorr, Ebenezer. "Collection of letters ship documents and receipts, 1795–1820." Manuscript AA 40 D73, Archives of British Columbia, Victoria.

———. "Papers of Ebenezer Dorr." Manuscript Box 1, Peabody Museum, Salem, Massachusetts.

Douglas, David. "Correspondence Outward." Manuscript EA D75, Archives of British Columbia, Victoria.

Dye, Eva Emery. Eva Emery Dye Papers. Manuscript 1089, Oregon Historical Society, Portland.

Furgerson, Samuel. "Journal of a voyage from Boston to the North-West Coast of America, in the Brig Otter, Samuel Hill Commander." Manuscript 207, Beinecke Library, Yale University, New Haven, Conn.

Gale, William A. "Journal kept on board the ship Albatross, Nathan Winship, Commander. On a voyage from Boston to the North West Coast and China in the Years 1809. 10. 11. 12." Microfilm copy of manuscript, Washington State Library, Olympia, Wash.

Gormly, Mary. "Early culture contact on the Northwest Coast 1774–95. Analysis of Spanish Source Material." Thesis, University of Washington, Seattle, 1959.

Hall, Washington. "Affidavit July 27, 1855" Manuscript 1112, William Lair Hill Papers, Oregon Historical Society, Portland.

———. "Washington Hall (Ogn.) Affidavit Claim." Photocopy of manuscript, Oregon Historical Society, Portland.

Haskins, Ralph. "Journal of a voyage From Boston to the North West Coast of America, Thence to Canton, and Back to Boston—Kept on Board Ship Atahualpa by Ralph Haskins in the Years 1800, 1801, 1802, & 1803." Manuscript S-126, Beinecke Library, Yale University, New Haven, Conn.

Haswell, Robert. "A voyage on Discoveries in the Ship Columbia Rediviva." Copy of Manuscript AA 20.5 C 72 Ha, Archives of British Columbia, Victoria.

Hezeta, Bruno de. "Diario de la Navegacion écha por el Teniente de Navio de la Real Armada, D. Bruno de Hezeta, a explorar la Costa Septentrional de Californias. Año de 1775." Microfilm of the original, AGN, Historia, CCCXXIV, 3, Reel 209, Bancroft Library, University of California, Berkeley.

Hill, Samuel. "Autobiography." Manuscript, New York Public Library, New York.

Hinds, Richard Brinsley. "Journal." Pen copy, Folder XIII, Kenneth L. Holmes Collection, Oregon Historical Society, Portland.

Huggins, Edward. Manuscript Folder 2 of 2 H873w, Edward Huggins Writings, Suzzallo Library, University of Washington, Seattle.

Ingraham, Joseph. "Journal of a voyage in the Hope, 1790–1792." Photocopy of original manuscript in the Library of Congress, Archives of British Columbia, Victoria.

"Invoice of the Ship *Resource* [1803]." Manuscript 733, Baker Library, Harvard University Graduate School of Business Administration, Cambridge, Mass.

Jefferson, Thomas. Manuscript, Jefferson Papers, 1798–99, Thomas Jefferson Coolidge Collection, Massachusetts Historical Society, Boston.

"Journal of a voyage in the Brig Owhyhee from Oahu to and from the northwest coast, 1827–1830." Manuscript 091 J8, Case 15, California Historical Society, San Francisco.

Kardas, Susan. "The People Bought This and the Clatsop Became Rich: A View of Nineteenth-Century Fur Trade Relationships on the Lower Columbia between Chinookan Speakers, Whites, and Kanakas." Photocopy of typescript thesis, Bryn Mawr College, 1971. University Microfilms, Ann Arbor, Mi., 1973.

Kelley, Hall Jackson. "Correspondence re Oregon Land Claims." Manuscript G Or3 K28, Archives of British Columbia, Victoria.

————. "Quit claim to the heirs of Capt. John Kendrick in the ownership of lands in Oregon, 1838." Manuscript G Or3 K 28q, Archives of British Columbia, Victoria.

"Kendrick, John, ca. 1740–1794." Manuscript 282, Beinecke Library, Yale University, New Haven, Conn.

Kennedy, Alexander. "Report of Chief Factor Alexander Kennedy 1824–'25." Manuscript H.B.C. Arch. B. 76/2/1, fo. 5d, The Hudson's Bay Company Archives, London.

Kenyon, Karl W., Biologist, United States Department of the Interior, Fish and Wildlife Service. Letter to authors, April 21, 1972.

Khlebnikof, Kiril T. "Biography of Alexander Andreevich Baranov by Kiril Khlebnikof." Undated translation of the 1835 St. Petersburg publication. Typescript copy of Manuscript W B 23 K, Archives of British Columbia, Victoria.

————. "Russian America: Excerpts From Life of Baranof by K. T. Khleb-nikof, 1835." Translated from the Russian by Michael E. Affonin, Seattle, Wash., 1832–33. Typescript copy of Manuscript H G In7, Archives of British Columbia, Victoria.

Koontz, Anna, Secretary, Chinook Nation. Letter to authors, June 3, 1971.

Kuykendall, Jerome K., Chairman, Indian Claims Commission. Letter to Warren Magnuson, United States Senator, September 9, 1971.

Lamb, Horatio Appleton. "Notes on Trade With the Northwest Coast, 1790–1810. Made by Horatio Appleton Lamb, from the records of James and Thomas Lamb, Merchant Shippers of Boston, 1781–1813." Manuscript transcript by Thomas P. Martin, Houghton Library, Harvard University, Cambridge, Mass.

Lawson, James S. "Autobiography." Manuscript P-A 44, Bancroft Library, University of California, Berkeley.

Lee, Jason. Jason Lee Papers. Manuscript 936, Oregon Historical Society, Portland.

————. "Journal of Jason Lee." Typescript copy of manuscript, Clarence Booth Bagley Miscellaneous Selections of Historical Writings, AIA 2/6, Box 22, Suzzallo Library, University of Washington, Seattle.

"Log-Book of the Brig Lydia on a Fur-Trading voyage from Boston to the Northwest Coast of America 1804–1805 With the Return Voyage by way of The Sandwich Islands and Canton Aboard the Ships Atahualpa and Swift 1805–1807." Typescript copy of manuscript added to "Super-cargo's log of the brig *Lydia*, Capt. Samuel Hill, on a fur-trading voyage from Boston to the N.W. Coast of North America, Aug 31, 1804–July 14, 1805." Manuscript S-213, Beinecke Library, Yale University, New Haven, Conn.

"Log Book of the Chatham Tender, Aug. 1792–Dec. 1793." Manuscript 17544, British Museum Library, London. Microfilm Copy 51, University Microfilms, Ann Arbor, Mi.

McDonald, Archibald. "Letters to Edward Ermatinger, 1830–1837." Typescript and photo copies of Manuscript 1012, Oregon Historical Society, Portland.

MacDonald, Ranald. "Correspondence: Outward Letters to Malcolm McLeod, 1880–1894." Manuscript AEM 22 M 14 M22, Archives of British Columbia, Victoria.

McKean, Samuel Terry, Jr. "Reminiscences." Manuscript 483, Oregon Historical Society, Portland.

McLoughlin, John. "An Account of His Services in Oregon." Typescript copy of Manuscript P-A 155:5, Bancroft Library, University of California, Berkeley.

————. John McLoughlin Papers. Manuscript 271 G (Part 2), Suzzallo Library, University of Washington, Seattle.

Majors, Harry M., historian. Letter to authors, July 25, 1971.

————. "Science and Exploration on the Northwest Coast of North America

1542–1841." Mimeographed copy of manuscript, John Carter Brown Library, Brown University, Providence, R.I.

Manby, Thomas. "Manby's Journal of H.M.S. Discovery 1791 & 2." Manuscript 325, Beinecke Library, Yale University, New Haven, Conn.

"*Mercury* Case Documents," Cauderno Nos. 16 and 17, manuscript, Los Angeles Public Library.

Meriwether, Stephen A., Secretary, Chinook Indian Tribe, Inc. Letters to authors, June 2, 1971, and January 9 and 20, 1973.

Milroy, Robert Huston, Letterbook, Vol. I, February 19, 1877, to November 18, 1878. Agency for the Puyallup, Nisqually, and other Indian Tribes. Manuscript 164, Suzzallo Library, University of Washington, Seattle.

"Oregon Archives, Letters, Reports, Messages, Memorials, and other Papers not published in the Office of the Secretary of State, Salem 1878." Manuscript P-A 55, Bancroft Library, University of California, Berkeley.

"Oregon Provisional Government." Microfilm copies of letters, documents, reports and papers, Manuscripts 1399 and 1613, Oregon Historical Society, Portland.

Parrish, J. L. "Anecdotes of Intercourse With the Indians." Manuscript P-A 59, Bancroft Library, University of California, Berkeley.

Phelps, William Dane. "Solid Men of Boston in the Northwest." Manuscript, Bancroft Library, University of California, Berkeley.

Pickman, Dudley L. "Memoranda from Dudley L. Pickman on Doing Business in Canton." Manuscript Box 4, Benjamin Shreve Papers, Peabody Museum, Salem, Mass.

Post, Frederick W., attorney for Chinooks. Letter to authors, July 19, 1972.

Ramsey, Guy Reed, historian. Letter to authors, July 8, 1972, and August 8, 1972.

"Records of the proceedings of the Commission to hold Treaties with the Indian tribes in Washington Territory and the Blackfeet Country." (Olympia, W.T., December 7, 1854.) Typescript manuscript, Miscellaneous Selections IX, Clarence Booth Bagley Collection, Suzzallo Library, University of Washington, Seattle.

Roberts, George B. "Recollections." Manuscript P-A 83, Bancroft Library, University of California, Berkeley.

Rogers, Robert. "Petition of Major Robert Rogers." Xerofax copy of manuscript from the Public Record Office, London. Kenneth L. Holmes Collection, Oregon Historical Society, Portland.

Ross, Alexander, to Donald McGillis, May 4, 1812, H.B. [Hudson's Bay Company]. Photocopy of Manuscript 6, Oregon Historical Society, Portland.

"Selections From the United States Department of Justice Archives Regarding Liquor Traffic Among the Indians in the Territories of Washington and Oregon 1849–1860." Manuscript 765, Joseph P. Donnelly, S.J., Collection, Oregon Historical Society, Portland.

Seymour, G. F. "G. F. Seymour, Commander in Chief, to Thomas Baillie,

Esq., Commander of H. M. sloop Modeste, 7 April, 1844." Copy of manuscript from Public Record Office, London. Kenneth L. Holmes Collection, Oregon Historical Society, Portland.

"Ship Hancock Logbook." Manuscript, Houghton Library, Harvard University, Cambridge, Mass.

Shischkov, Vice Admiral. "Russian America: Preliminary Information Regarding the Life of Khvostov and Davidov by Vice Admiral Shischkov, 1810–
1812." Translated from the Russian by Michael E. Affonin, Seattle, 1932–
33. Typescript copy of Manuscript HG In7, Archives of British Columbia,
Victoria.

Shortess, Robert. Robert Shortess Papers, 1855–1877. Manuscript 762, Oregon
Historical Society, Portland.

Stuart, John. "Oregon or River of the West." Typescript copy. Folder XVI-2,
Kenneth L. Holmes Collection, Oregon Historical Society, Portland.

Sturgis, Josiah. "Extract from the Journal of Josiah Sturgis kept on board the
Ship Levant on a Voyage from Boston to the North West Coast and China
in the Year 1818." Typescript copy of Manuscript 153, Oregon Historical
Society, Portland.

"Supercargo's log of the brig *Lydia*, Capt. Samuel Hill, on a fur-trading voyage
from Boston to the N.W. Coast of North America, Aug. 31, 1804–July
14, 1805." Manuscript S-213, Beinecke Library, Yale University, New
Haven, Conn.

Swan, James Gilchrist. Correspondence, Microfilm copies of manuscripts in
the Smithsonian Institution. Suzzallo Library, University of Washington,
Seattle.

Taylor, Herbert C. "Anthropological Investigation of the Chehalis Indians
Relative to Tribal Identity and Aboriginal Possession of Lands." Mimeographed copy of manuscript, Washington State Library, Olympia, Wash.

———. "John Work on the Chehalis." Mimeographed copy of manuscript,
Washington State Library, Olympia, Wash.

Terry, Samuel, Jr. "Reminiscences." Manuscript 483, Oregon Historical Society, Portland.

Timko, Norman E., Deputy Clerk, Indian Claims Commission. Letter to
authors, January 11, 1971.

Tolmie, William Fraser. "Diary." Typescript copy manuscript, Clarence Booth
Bagley Collection, Miscellaneous selections of Historical Writings, Carton
2 of 2 AIA 2/6, Box 22, Clarence Booth Bagley Collection, Suzzallo Library, University of Washington, Seattle.

———. "Fort Nisqually Journal of Occurrences 1833–39." Photocopy of Manuscript H 867nj, Vol. I, Suzzallo Library, University of Washington,
Seattle.

———. "Journal 1833–36." Manuscript AIA 8-3, Box 1, Suzzallo Library.
University of Washington, Seattle.

Tufts, William. "List of American vessels engaged in the trade of the Northern coast of America for sea-otter skins from 1787–1808." Manuscript

173, Elwood Evans Papers, Beinecke Library, Yale University, New Haven, Conn.

"Voyage Aug.–Nov. 1790 Ship Columbia." Microfilm copy of Manuscript 0-312, Massachusetts Historical Society, Boston.

Walbran, John Thomas. "Miscellaneous papers." Manuscript EDB 72.4, Archives of British Columbia, Victoria.

Walker, William, Jr. "Supercargo's log of the brig Lydia, Capt. Samuel Hill, on a fur-trading voyage on the N.W. Coast of North America, July 10, 1805–Jan. 3, 1807." Manuscript S-214, Beinecke Library, Yale University, New Haven, Conn.

Watkins, George T. "Washington's Lewis and Clark Medal." Typescript copy of manuscript in possession of authors.

Welch, James W. "Dictation." Manuscript P-A 160, Bancroft Library, University of California, Berkeley.

Whealdon, Bon I. "On Whealdon Hill (Ilwaco, Wash.) Eve of July 16, 1860." Manuscript 50, Oregon Historical Society, Portland.

Work, John. "Journal April 15–November 17, 1824." Typescript copy of Manuscript 319, Oregon Historical Society, Portland.

———. "Journal March 21–May 14, 1825." Typescript copy of manuscript, Oregon Historical Society, Portland.

———. "Untitled journal." Typescript copy of manuscript, Oregon Historical Society, Portland.

Wutkee, Winston, Researcher, Oral History Program, University of California, Los Angeles. Letter to authors, January 17, 1971.

Wyeth, Nathaniel J., and Joseph Thing. "Articles of Agreement." Manuscript S-934, Beinecke Library, Yale University, New Haven, Conn.

Personal Interviews

Peterson, Helen. Neah Bay, Wash., August 7, 1970.
Stanton, Nellie Lynch. Chesaw, Wash., July 29, 1970.

Government Documents

Acts of the Legislative Assembly of the Territory of Washington, Passed at the Second Regular Session, Begun and Held at Olympia, December 4, 1854. Olympia, Wash., 1855.

Annals of the Congress of the United States. The Debates and Proceedings in the Congress of the United States; with an Appendix, Containing Important State Papers and Public Documents. 17 Cong., 2 sess.

Annual Reports of the Commissioner of Indian Affairs to the Secretary of the Interior, 1874, 1876.

Annual Reports of the Secretary of the Interior, 1869, 1882.

Before the Indian Claims Commission of the United States: The Chinook Tribe and Bands of Indians, Petitioner, vs. *The United States of America, Defendant*. Petition No. 234 (Filed August 8, 1951); Docket No. 234. Defendant's Requested Findings of Fact, Objections to Petitioner's Proposed Findings of Fact, and Brief; Decided: November 4, 1970. Additional Findings of Fact; Opinion of the Commission; Final Award. November 4, 1970.

Before the Indian Claims Commission of the United States: The Chinook Tribe, the Wauhkiakum Band and the Willapa or Shoalwater Bay Bands of Chinook, the Kathlamet Tribe of Chinook, the Clatsop Tribe of Chinook, and the Nucqueclahwemuck Band of Chinook, Petitioners, vs. *The United States of America, Defendant*, Docket No. 234. Petitioner's Findings of Fact and Brief.

Before the Indian Claims Commission of the United States: Upper Chehalis, et al, Plaintiffs, vs. *The United States, Defendant*, Docket No. 237. Defendant Motion to File Amended Petition.

Boas, Franz. *Chinook Texts*. Bureau of American Ethnology *Bulletin 20*. Washington, 1894.

———. *Kathlamet Texts*. Bureau of American Ethnology *Bulletin 26*. Washington, 1901.

———. *The Social Organization and the Secret Societies of the Kwakiutl Indians*. U.S. National Museum Annual Report for 1895. Washington, 1897.

Cases Decided in the Court of Claims of the United States February 1, 1945, to May 7, 1945 (Partial), with Report of Decisions of the Supreme Court in Court of Claims Cases, Vol. CIII. Washington, 1946.

Code of Federal Regulations, Title 25—Indians, 70 USCA.

Creation of an Indian Village. House Report No. 1098, 73 Cong., 2 sess. Washington, 1934. Serial 9775.

Davidson, George. *United States Coast and Geodetic Survey, Pacific Coast: Coast Pilot of California, Oregon, and Washington*. Washington, 1889.

Gibbs, George. *A Dictionary of the Chinook Jargon, or Trade Language of Oregon*. Smithsonian Miscellaneous Collections, No. 161. Washington, 1863.

———. *Tribes of Western Washington and Northwestern Oregon*. Contributions to North American Ethnology, Vol. I. Washington, 1877.

Hodge, Frederick Webb (ed.). *Handbook of American Indians North of Mexico*. Bureau of American Ethnology *Bulletin 30*. 2 vols. Washington, 1907.

Howison, Neil M. *Report of Lieut. Neil M. Howison, United States Navy, to the Commander of the Pacific Squadron; Being the Result of an Examination in the Year 1846 of the Coast, Harbors, Rivers, Soil, Productions, Climate, and Population of the Territory of Oregon*. House Exec. Doc., *Miscellaneous* No. 29, 30 Cong., 1 sess. Washington, 1848, Serial 523.

Memorial of William A. Slacum, Praying Compensation for His Services in Obtaining Information in Relation to the Settlements on the Oregon River. Senate Exec. Doc. No. 24, 25 Cong., 2 sess. Washington, 1937.

Message from the President of the United States, Communicating the Letter of Mr. Prevost, and other Documents, Relating to an Establishment Made at the Mouth of the Columbia River. January 25, 1823. House Doc. No. 45, 17 Cong., 2 sess. Washington, 1823. Serial 78.

Microcopy of Records in the National Archives. *Oregon Superintendency of Indian Affairs, 1842–1880.* Microfilm No. 2, Rolls 3, 5, 7, 8, 11, 12, 16–19; Microfilm No. 234, Rolls 607, 611.

———. *Washington Superintendency of Indian Affairs, 1853–1874.* Microfilm No. 5, Rolls 4, 6, 9, 16, 17, 23.

Mooney, James. *The Aboriginal Population of America North of Mexico.* Publication 2955, Smithsonian Miscellaneous Collections, LXXX, 7 (1928).

"Records of the Russian-American Company, 1802–67," Microfilm Reel 1, *Records of Former Russian Agencies,* RG 261.

Report of the Superintendent of the Coast Survey Showing the Progress of the Survey during the Year 1858. Senate Exec. Doc. No. 14, 35 Cong., 2 sess. Washington, 1859. Serial 990.

Report on Claims of Chinook and Chehalis Indians. House Exec. Doc. No. 517, 60 Cong., 1 sess. Washington, 1908. Serial 5377.

Report with Respect to the House Resolution Authorizing the Committee on Interior and Insular Affairs to Conduct an Investigation of the Bureau of Indian Affairs. House Report No. 2503, 82 Cong., 2 sess. Washington, 1953. Serial 11582.

Revised Outline Descriptions of the Posts and Stations of Troops in the Military Division of the Pacific Commanded by Major-General John M. Schofield. Washington, 1872.

Rolls of Certain Indian Tribes in Oregon and Washington. House Exec. Doc. No. 133, 59 Cong., 2 sess. Washington, 1907. Serial 5151.

Stewart, T. D. "The Chinook Sign of Freedom: A Study of the Skull of the Famous Chief Comcomly," *Annual Report of the Board of Regents of the Smithsonian Institution Showing the Operations, Expenditures, and Condition of the Institution for the Year Ended June 30, 1959,* Publication 4392. Washington, 1960.

Swan, James G. "The Indians of Cape Flattery at the Entrance to the Strait of Fuca, Washington Territory." *Smithsonian Contributions to Knowledge,* XVI, 8 (1870).

Territory of Oregon ["Mr. Kelley's Memoir," January 31, 1839]. *Rep.* No. 101, 25 Cong., 3 sess. Washington. Serial 351.

Yarrow, H. A. "A Further Contribution to the Study of the Mortuary Customs of the North American Indians," *First Annual Report of the Bureau of Ethnology to the Secretary of the Smithsonian Institution 1879–80.* Washington, 1881.

Newspapers

Catholic Sentinel. Portland, Oregon, 1870, 1878.

Daily Astorian. Astoria, Oregon, 1884.

East Oregonian. Pendleton, Oregon, 1889.

Ilwaco Tribune. Ilwaco, Washington, 1953.

Independent Chronicle. Boston, Massachusetts, 1801.

Morning Oregonian. Portland, Oregon, 1864, 1865, 1867, 1899.

Oregonian. Portland, Oregon Territory, 1852, 1853: Portland, Oregon, 1899, 1953.

Oregon Spectator. Oregon City, Oregon Territory, 1847, 1850.

Oregon Sunday Journal. Portland, Oregon, 1928, 1929.

Pioneer and Democrat. Olympia, Washington Territory, 1856.

Raymond Herald. Raymond, Washington, 1953.

San Francisco Chronicle. San Francisco, California, 1884.

Sunday Oregonian. Portland, Oregon, 1899, 1937, 1970.

Washington Standard. Olympia, Washington Territory, 1854, 1861, 1865, 1871.

Weekly Oregonian. Portland, Oregon Territory, 1855; Portland, Oregon, 1893.

Wenatchee Daily World. Wenatchee, Washington, 1966.

Books and Pamphlets

Alley, B. F., and J. P. Munro-Fraser. *History of Clarke County, Washington Territory.* Portland, 1885.

Angelo, C. Aubrey. *Sketches of Travel in Oregon and Idaho with Map of South Boisie.* New York, 1866.

Armstrong, A. N. *Oregon: Comprising a Brief History and Full Description of the Territories of Oregon and Washington.* Chicago, 1857.

Atcheson, Nathaniel. *On the Origin and Progress of the North-West Company of Canada, with a History of the Fur Trade As Connected with That Concern.* London, 1811.

Bagley, Clarence B. *Early Catholic Missions in Old Oregon, and Travels over the Rocky Mountains, in 1845–46.* 2 vols. Seattle, 1932.

Bancroft, Hubert Howe. *The Works of Hubert Howe Bancroft.* Vol. 1. *The Native Races,* Vol. I, *Wild Tribes;* Vol. III. *The Native Races,* Vol. III, *Myths and Languages;* Vol. XXVII. *History of the Northwest Coast,* Vol. I; Vol. XXVIII. *History of the Northwest Coast,* Vol. II.

Barker, Burt Brown (ed.). *Letters of Dr. John McLoughlin Written at Fort Vancouver, 1829–1832.* Portland, 1948.

Barrett-Lennard, C. E. *Travels in British Columbia.* London, 1862.

Belcher, Edward. *Narrative of a Voyage Round the World Performed in Her Majesty's Ship Sulphur, during the Years 1836–1842.* 2 vols. London, 1843.

Biddle, Nicholas (ed.). *The Journals of the Expedition Under the Command of Capts. Lewis and Clark to the Sources of the Missouri, thence Across the Rocky Mountains and down the River Columbia to the Pacific Ocean, Performed during the Years 1804–5–6. By Order of the Government of the United States.* 2 vols. New York, 1962.

Blanchet, Francis Norbert. *Historical Sketches of the Catholic Church in Oregon for the Past Forty Years.* Portland, 1878. PNW Reel 3, Microfilm History of the Pacific Northwest, New Haven, Conn., 1966.

———, et al. *Notices and Voyages of the Famed Quebec Mission to the Pacific Northwest; Being the Correspondence, Notices, etc., of Fathers Blanchet and Demers, Together with Those of Fathers Bolduc and Langlois.* Portland, 1956.

Blue, George Verne. "Early Relations between Hawaii and the Northwest Coast." In *Thirty-Third Annual Report of the Hawaiian Historical Society.* Honolulu, 1925.

Briggs, Horace. *Letters From Alaska and the Pacific Coast.* Buffalo, 1889.

Briggs, L. Vernon. *History and Genealogy of the Cabot Family, 1475–1927.* 2 vols. Boston, 1927.

Brooks, Wolcott. *Japanese Wrecks Stranded and Picked Up Adrift in the Pacific Ocean.* Fairfield, Wash., 1964.

Brownell, Charles De Wolf. *The Indian Races of North and South America.* Boston, 1853.

Bulfinch, Thomas. *Oregon and Eldorado; or, Romance of the Rivers.* Boston, 1866.

Carey, Charles H. (ed.). *The Journals of Theodore Talbot, 1843 and 1849–59, with the Fremont Expedition of 1843 and with the First Military Company in Oregon Territory, 1849–1852.* Portland, 1931.

Carstensen, Vernon (ed.). *Pacific Northwest Letters of George Gibbs.* Portland, 1954.

Carver, Jonathan. *Travels through the Interior Parts of North America, in the Years 1766, 1767, and 1768,* 3d ed. Minneapolis, 1956.

Chapman, Charles Edward. *A History of California: The Spanish Period.* New York, 1921.

Chevigny, Hector. *Russian America: The Great Alaskan Venture, 1741–1867.* New York, 1965.

Chittenden, Hiram Martin, and Alfred Talbot Richardson (eds.). *Life, Letters and Travels of Father Pierre-Jean de Smet, S.J., 1810–1873.* 2 vols. New York, 1905.

Clark, Ella E. *Indian Legends from the Northern Rockies.* Norman, Okla., 1966.

———. *Indian Legends of the Pacific Northwest.* Berkeley, Calif., 1960.

Clarke, Charles G. *The Men of the Lewis and Clark Expedition.* Glendale, Calif., 1970.

Clarke, S. A. *Pioneer Days of Oregon History.* 2 vols. Portland, 1905.

Cleveland, H. W. S. *Voyages of a Merchant Navigator of the Days That Are Past.* New York, 1886.

Colbert, Mildred. *Kutkos Chinook Tyee.* Boston, 1942.

Coman, Katharine. *Economic Beginnings of the Far West.* 2 vols. New York, 1925.

Coombs, Samuel F. *Dictionary of the Chinook Jargon as Spoken on Puget Sound and the Northwest, with Original Indian Names for Prominent Places and Localities with Their Meanings.* Seattle, 1891.

Corney, Peter. *Early Voyages in the North Pacific, 1813–1818.* Fairfield, Wash., 1965.

Cotton, S. J. *Stories of Nehalem.* Chicago, n.d.

Coues, Elliott (ed.). *New Light on the Early History of the Greater Northwest: The Manuscript Journals of Alexander Henry, Fur Trader of the Northwest Company, and of David Thompson, Official Geographer and Explorer of the Same Company, 1799–1814.* 3 vols. Minneapolis, 1965.

Cox, Ross. *Adventures on the Columbia River, Including the Narrative of a Residence of Six Years on the Western Side of the Rocky Mountains, among Various Tribes of Indians Hitherto Unknown; Together with a Journey across the American Continent.* 2 vols. London, 1831.

Coxe, William. *Account of the Russian Discoveries between Asia and America, to Which are Added, the Conquest of Siberia, and the History of the Transactions and Commerce between Russia and China.* London, 1803.

Cross, Osborne. *March of the Regiment of Mounted Riflemen to Oregon in 1849.* Fairfield, Wash., 1967.

Curtis, Edward S. *The North American Indian, Being a Series of Volumes Picturing and Describing the Indians of the United States and Alaska.* 20 vols. Norwood, Mass., 1907–30.

Davidson, Gordon Charles. *The North West Company.* University of California Publications in History, Vol. VII. Berkeley, Calif., 1918.

Demers, Modeste. *J.M.J. Chinook Dictionary, Catechism, Prayers and Hymns, Composed in 1838 & 1839 by Rt. Rev. Modeste Demers; Rev., Cor. and Completed, in 1867 by Most Rev. F. N. Blanchet, with Modifications and Additions by Rev. L. N. St. Onge, Missionary among the Yakamas and Other Indian Tribes.* Montreal, 1871.

Domenech, Abbé EM. *Seven Years' Residence in the Great Deserts of North America.* 2 vols. London, 1860.

Douglas, David. *Journal Kept by David Douglas during His Travels in North America in 1823–1827.* New York, 1959.

Drucker, Phillip. *Cultures of the North Pacific Coast.* San Francisco, 1965.

———. *Indians of the Northwest Coast.* New York, 1955.

Dunn, John. *History of the Oregon Territory and British North-American Fur Trade, with an Account of the Habits and Customs of the Principal Native Tribes on the Northern Continent.* London, 1846.

Dye, Eva Emery. *The Conquest: The True Story of Lewis and Clark.* New York, 1922.

Edwards, Philip L. *California in 1837: Diary of Col. Philip L. Edwards, Containing An Account of a Trip to the Pacific Coast.* Sacramento, 1890.

———. *A Sketch of the Oregon Territory; or, Emigrants' Guide.* Liberty, Mo., 1842.

Evans, Elwood. *History of the Pacific Northwest: Oregon and Washington.* 2 vols. Portland, 1889.

Ewers, John C. *The Blackfeet: Raiders on the Northwestern Plains*. Norman, Okla., 1958.

Falconer, Thomas. *The Oregon Question; or, a Statement of the British Claims to the Oregon Territory, in Opposition to the Pretensions of the Government of the United States of America*. New York, 1845.

Fiske, John. "Oration." In *Transactions of the Twentieth Annual Reunion of the Oregon Pioneer Association for 1892*. Portland, 1912.

Franchère, Gabriel. *Adventure at Astoria, 1810–1814*. Norman, Okla., 1967.

————. *Narrative of a Voyage to the Northwest Coast of America in the Years 1811, 1812, 1813, and 1814; or, the First American Settlement on the Pacific*. Ed. by J. V. Huntington. New York, 1854.

Galvin John (ed.). *A Journal of Explorations Northward along the Coast from Monterey in the Year 1775*. San Francisco, 1964.

Gass, Patrick. *A Journal of the Voyages and Travels of a Corps of Discovery, under the Command of Capt. Lewis and Capt. Clarke of the Army of the United States*. Ed. by David McKeehan. Minneapolis, 1958.

Gill, John Kaye. *Dictionary of the Chinook Jargon with Examples of Its Use in Conversation*. Portland, 1884.

Glover, Richard (ed.). *David Thompson's Narrative 1784–1812*. Toronto, 1962.

Green, John. *Remarks in Support of the New Chart of North and South America*. London, 1753.

Green, Jonathan S. *Journal of a Tour on the North West Coast of America in the Year 1829*. New York, 1915.

Greenhow, Robert. *The History of Oregon and California, and the Other Territories on the North-West Coast of North America*. London, 1844.

Gunther, Erna. *Northwest Coast Indian Art*. Seattle, 1962.

Harmon, Daniel Williams. *A Journal of Voyages and Travels in the Interiour of North America*. Andover, Maine, 1820.

Hazeltine, Jean. *The Historical and Regional Geography of The Willapa Bay Area, Washington*. N.p., n.d.

Hines, Gustavus. *Life on the Plains of the Pacific: Oregon, Its History, Condition and Prospects*. Buffalo, 1851.

History of the Pacific Northwest: Oregon and Washington. Portland, 1889.

Hosmer, James K. *History of the Expedition of Captains Lewis and Clark 1804–5–6*. 2 vols. Chicago, 1902.

Howard, Harold F. *Sacajawea*. Norman, Okla., 1971.

Howay, Frederic W. "The Ship Margaret: Her History and Historian." In *Thirty-Eighth Annual Report of the Hawaiian Historical Society*. Honolulu, 1930.

————. *Voyages of the "Columbia" to the Northwest Coast, 1787–1790 and 1790 and 1793*. Boston, 1941.

Hunter, William C. *The Fan Kwae' at Canton before Treaty Days, 1825–1844*, 2d ed. Shanghai, 1911.

Hurd, D. William (ed.). *History of Essex County, Massachusetts, with Bio-*

graphical Sketches of Many of Its Pioneers and Prominent Men. 2 vols. Philadelphia, 1888.

Hussey, John. *Chinook Point and the Story of Fort Columbia.* Olympia, Wash., 1957.

———. *Champoeg: Place of Transition A Disputed History.* Portland, 1967.

Irving, Washington. *The Adventures of Captain Bonneville, U.S.A., in the Rocky Mountains and the Far West.* Norman, Okla., 1961.

———. *Astoria; or, Anecdotes of an Enterprise Beyond the Rocky Mountains.* Norman, Okla., 1964.

Jackson, Donald (ed.). *Letters of the Lewis and Clark Expedition, with Related Documents, 1783–1854.* Urbana, Ill., 1962.

Jefferys, Thomas. *Voyages from Asia to America, for Completing the Discoveries of the North West Coast of America.* London, 1761.

Jewitt, John Rodgers. *Narrative of the Adventures and Sufferings of John R. Jewitt.* Fairfield, Wash., 1967.

Johansen, Dorothy O. *Voyage of the Columbia around the World with John Boit, 1790–1793.* Portland, 1960.

———, and Charles M. Gates. *Empire of the Columbia: A History of the Pacific Northwest.* New York, 1957.

Johnson, Overton, and William H. Winter. *Route across the Rocky Mountains, with a Description of Oregon and California; Their Geographical Features, Their Resources, Soil, Climate, Productions, &c., &c.* Lafayette, Ind., 1846.

Jones, Roy Franklin. *Wappato Indians of the Lower Columbia River Valley.* N.p., 1972.

Kane, Paul. *Wanderings of an Artist among the Indians of North America from Canada to Vancouver's Island and Oregon through the Hudson's Bay Company's Territory and Back Again, by Paul Kane.* Toronto, 1925.

Keyes, E. D. *Fifty Years' Observation of Men and Events Civil and Military.* New York, 1884.

Kroeber, A. L. "The Tribes of the Pacific Coast of North America," in *XIX International Congress of Americanists.* Washington, 1915.

Lamb, W. Kaye. *The Letters and Journal of Simon Fraser, 1806–1808.* New York, 1959.

Langsdorff, George Henrich. *Voyages and Travels in Various Parts of the World, during the Years 1803, 1804, 1805, 1806, and 1807.* 2 vols. London, 1813–1814.

La Pérouse, Jean Francois de Galaup, comte de. *A Voyage Round the World Performed in the Years 1785, 1786, 1787 and 1788.* 2 vols. London, 1789–1799.

Large, R. G. (ed.). *The Journals of William Fraser Tolmie, Physician and Fur Trader.* Vancouver, B.C., 1963.

Larsell, O. *The Doctor in Oregon: A Medical History.* Portland, 1947.

Lee, D., and J. H. Frost. *Ten Years in Oregon.* New York, 1844.

Ledyard, John. *Journal of Cook's Last Voyage.* Hartford, Conn., 1783.

Lewis, Albert Buell. *Tribes of the Columbia Valley and the Coast of Washington and Oregon.* Memoirs of the American Anthropological Association, Vol. I, pt. 2. Lancaster, Pa., 1906.

Lewis, William S., and Naojiro Murakami (eds.). *Ranald MacDonald: The Narrative of His Early Life on the Columbia under the Hudson's Bay Company's Regime; of His Experiences in the Pacific Whale Fishery; and of His Great Adventure to Japan; with a Sketch of His Later Life on the Western Frontier, 1824–1894.* Spokane, 1923.

Lockley, Fred. *History of the Columbia River Valley from The Dalles to the Sea.* 2 vols. Chicago, 1928.

Lord, John Keast. *The Naturalist in Vancouver Island and British Columbia.* 2 vols. London, 1866.

Loring, Charles Greely (ed.). *Memoir of the Hon. William Sturgis.* Boston, 1864. PNW Reel 17, Microfilm History of the Pacific Northwest. New Haven, Conn., 1966.

McChesney, Charles E., et al. *Rolls of Certain Indian Tribes in Oregon and Washington.* Fairfield, Wash., 1969.

McDonald, T. H. (ed.). *Exploring the Northwest Territory.* Norman, Okla., 1966.

MacDonald, William (ed.). *Documentary Source Book of American History, 1606–1913.* New York, 1921.

MacInnes, Tom. *Chinook Days.* N.p., British Columbia, 1926.

Maloney, Alice Bay (ed.). *Fur Brigade to the Bonaventura: John Work's California Expedition, 1832–1833, for the Hudson's Bay Company.* San Francisco, 1945.

Manning, Clarence A. *Russian Influence on Early America.* New York, 1953.

Marshall, James Stirrat, and Carrie Marshall. *Pacific Voyages.* Portland, 1960.

Masson, L. R. *Les Bourgeois de la Compagnie du Nord-Ouest; Recits de voyages, lettres et rapports inedits relatifs au nord-ouest canadien, publiés avec une esquisse historique et des annotations par L. R. Masson.* 2 vols. New York, 1960.

Meany, Edmond S. *History of the State of Washington.* New York, 1941.

———. *A New Log of the Columbia by John Boit on the Discovery of the Columbia River and Grays Harbor.* Seattle, 1921.

———. *Vancouver's Discovery of Puget Sound.* Portland, 1957.

Meares, John. *Voyages Made in the Years 1788 and 1789, from China to the North West Coast of America.* London, 1790.

Merk, Frederick (ed.). *Fur Trade and Empire: George Simpson's Journal.* Cambridge, Mass., 1931.

Miller, Emma Gene. *Clatsop County, Oregon: A History.* Portland, 1958.

Morison, Samuel Eliot. *The Maritime History of Massachusetts, 1783–1860.* Boston, 1921.

Mourelle, Francisco Antonio. *Voyage of the Sonora in the Second Bucareli Expedition to Explore the Northwest Coast Survey, the Port of San Francisco and Found Franciscan Missions and a Presidio and Pueblo at That Port.* San Francisco, 1920.

Mudge, Zechariah Atwell. *Sketches of Mission Life among the Indians of Oregon.* New York, 1854.

Myers, John. *The Life, Voyages and Travels of Capt. John Myers, Detailing His Adventures during Four Voyages Round the World.* London, 1817.

Nichols, M. Leona. *The Mantle of Elias: The Story of Fathers Blanchet and Demers in Early Oregon.* Portland, 1941.

Ogden, Adele. *The California Sea Otter Trade, 1784–1848.* Berkeley, Calif., 1941.

Ogden, Peter Skene [?]. *Traits of American Indian Life & Character, by a Fur Trader.* San Francisco, 1933.

O'Hara, Edwin V. *Pioneer Catholic History of Oregon.* Paterson, N.J., 1939.

Olson, Ronald L. *The Quinault Indians and Adze, Canoe, and House Types of the Northwest Coast.* Seattle, 1967.

O'Meara, Walter. *The Savage Country.* Boston, 1960.

The Oregon Territory, Consisting of a Brief Description of the Country and Its Productions; and of the Habits and Manners of the Native Indian Tribes. London, 1846.

Parker, Samuel. *Journal of an Exploring Tour beyond the Rocky Mountains, Under the Direction of the A.B.C.F.M.* Ithaca, N.Y., 1844.

Payette, B. C. *The Oregon Country under the Union Jack.* Montreal, 1962.

Porter, Kenneth Wiggins. *John Jacob Astor, Business Man.* 2 vols. Cambridge, Mass., 1931.

Powell, Fred Wilbur. *Hall J. Kelley on Oregon.* Princeton, N.J., 1932.

Powers, Kate Ball, Flora Ball Hopkins, and Lucy Ball (eds.). *Autobiography of John Ball.* Grand Rapids, Mi., 1925.

Proceedings of the Massachusetts Historical Society, 1791–1835. Boston, 1879.

Proceedings of the Massachusetts Historical Society, Vol. II (1835–1855). Boston, 1880.

Quaife, Milo M. (ed.). *The Journals of Captain Meriwether Lewis and Sergeant John Ordway Kept on the Expedition of Western Exploration, 1803–1806* Publications of the State Historical Society of Wisconsin, Vol. XXII. Madison, 1916.

Ray, Verne F. *Lower Chinook Ethnographic Notes.* University of Washington Publications in Anthropology, Vol. VII, No. 2. Seattle, 1938.

Reynolds, Stephen. *The Voyage of the New Hazard to the Northwest Coast, Hawaii and China, 1810–1813.* Salem, Mass., 1938.

Rezanov, Nikolai Petrovich. *The Rezanov Voyage to Nueva California in 1806: The Report of Count Nikolai Petrovich Rezanov of His Voyage to That Provincia of Nueva España from New Archangel.* San Francisco, 1926.

Rich, E. E. (ed.). *Eden Colvile's Letters 1849–52.* Publications of the Hudson's Bay Record Society. London, 1956.

———. *McLoughlin's Fort Vancouver Letters: First Series, 1825–38.* Publications of the Champlain Society. Toronto, 1941.

————. *Simpson's 1828 Journey to the Columbia.* Publications of the Champlain Society. Toronto, 1947.

Robertson, Wyndham, Jr. *Oregon, Our Right and Title; Containing an Account of the Condition of the Oregon Territory.* Washington, 1846.

Roe, Michael. *The Journal and Letters of Captain Charles Bishop on the North-West Coast of America, in the Pacific and in New South Wales, 1794–1799.* London, 1967.

Rollins, Philip Ashton (ed.). *Wilson Price Hunt's Diary on His Overland Journey Westward to Astoria in 1811–12; The Discovery of the Oregon Trail: Robert Stuart's Narratives of His Overland Trip Eastward From Astoria in 1812–13.* New York, 1935.

Ross, Alexander. *Adventures of the First Settlers on the Oregon or Columbia River, Being a Narrative of the Expedition Fitted Out by John Jacob Astor, to Establish the "Pacific Fur Company"; with an Account of Some Indian Tribes on the Coast of the Pacific.* London, 1849.

————. *The Fur Hunters of the Far West.* Norman, Okla., 1956.

Ruby, Robert H., and John A. Brown. *The Cayuse Indians: Imperial Tribesmen of Old Oregon.* Norman, Okla., 1972.

Saint-Amant, M. de. *Voyages en Californie et dans l'Orégon par M. de Saint-Amant, envoyé du gouvernement francais en 1851–1852.* Paris, 1854.

Schafer, Joseph. *A History of the Pacific Northwest.* New York, 1921.

Schurz, William L. *Manila Galleon.* New York, 1959.

Shaler, William. *Journal of a Voyage between China and the Northwestern Coast of America, Made in 1804 by William Shaler.* Claremont, Calif., 1935.

Shaw, George C. *The Chinook Jargon and How to Use it.* Seattle, 1909.

Sheppe, Walter (ed.). *First Man West: Alexander Mackenzie's Journal of His Voyage to the Pacific Coast of Canada in 1793.* Berkeley, Calif., 1962.

Smet, Pierre Jean de. *Oregon Missions and Travels over the Rocky Mountains, in 1845–46.* New York, 1847.

Snowden, Clinton A. *History of Washington: The Rise and Progress of an American State.* 4 vols. New York, 1909.

Spaulding, Kenneth (ed.). *On the Oregon Trail: Robert Stuart's Journey of Discovery, 1812–1813.* Norman, Okla., 1953.

Speck, Gordon. *Northwest Explorations.* Portland, 1954.

————. *Samuel Hearne and the Northwest Passage.* Caldwell, Idaho, 1963.

Spier, Leslie. *Tribal Distribution in Washington.* General Series in Anthropology, No. 3. Menasha, Wis., 1936.

————, and Edward Sapir. *Wishram Ethnography.* University of Washington Publications in Anthropology, Vol. III, No. 3. Seattle, 1930.

Stevens, Hazard. *The Life of Isaac Ingalls Stevens.* 2 vols. Boston and New York, 1901.

Strange, James. *James Strange's Journal and Narrative of the Commercial Expedition from Bombay to the North-West Coast of America.* Madras, India, 1928.

Strickland, W. P. *History of the Missions of the Methodist Episcopal Church, from the Organization of the Missionary Society to the Present Time.* Cincinnati, 1850.

Strong, James C. *Wah-Kee-Nah and Her People: The Curious Customs, Traditions, and Legends of the North American Indians.* New York, 1893.

Swan, James G. *The Northwest Coast; or, Three Years' Residence in Washington Territory.* Fairfield, Wash., 1966.

Thornton, J. Quinn. *Oregon and California in 1848.* 2 vols. New York, 1864.

Thwaites, Reuben Gold (ed.). *The Jesuit Relations and Allied Documents: Travels and Explorations of the Jesuit Missionaries in New France, 1610–1791.* 73 vols. Cleveland, 1896–1901.

———. *Original Journals of the Lewis and Clark Expedition, 1804–1806.* 8 vols. New York, 1959.

Tikhmenev, Petr Aleksandrovich. *The Historical Review of the Formation of the Russian-American Company and Its Activity up to the Present Time.* 2 pts. Seattle, 1939–40.

Townsend, John K. *Narrative of Journey across the Rocky Mountains, to the Columbia River.* Vol. II in Reuben Gold Thwaites (ed.), *Early Western Travels.* Cleveland, 1905.

Transactions of the Seventh Annual Re-Union of the Oregon Pioneer Association; for 1879. Salem, Ore., 1880.

Transactions of the Eighth Annual Re-Union of the Oregon Pioneer Association; for 1880. Salem, Ore., 1881.

Transactions of the Twelfth Annual Re-Union of the Oregon Pioneer Association for 1884. Portland, 1885.

Transactions of the Fifteenth Annual Reunion of the Oregon Pioneer Association for 1887. Portland, 1887.

Tucker, Ephriam W. *A History of Oregon.* Fairfield, Wash., 1970.

Vancouver, George. *Voyage of Discovery to the North Pacific Ocean and Round the World.* 3 vols. New York, 1967.

Victor, Frances Fuller. *Atlantis Arisen; or, Talks of a Tourist about Oregon and Washington.* Philadelphia, 1891.

Vining, Edward P. *An Inglorious Columbus.* New York, 1885.

Wagner, Henry R. *The Cartography of the Northwest Coast of America to the Year 1800.* 2 vols. Berkeley, Calif., 1937.

———. *Spanish Explorations in the Strait of Juan de Fuca.* Santa Ana, Calif., 1933.

Wallace, W. S. (ed.). *John McLean's Notes of a Twenty-five Years' Service in the Hudson's Bay Territory.* Toronto, 1932.

Wauchope, Robert. *Lost Tribes & Sunken Continents.* Chicago, 1962.

West, John. *The Substance of a Journal during a Residence at the Red River Colony, British North America; and Frequent Excursions among the North-West American Indians, in the Years 1820, 1821, 1822, 1823 by John West, M.A.* London, 1824.

Wike, Joyce Anabel. *The Effect of the Maritime Fur Trade on Northwest*

Coast Indian Society. Ann Arbor, Mi., University Microfilms, 1972.
Wilbur, Marguerite Eyer (ed.). Duflot de Mofras' Travels on the Pacific Coast. 2 vols. Santa Ana, Calif., 1937.
Wilkes, Charles. Narrative of the United States Exploring Expedition during the Years 1838, 1839, 1840, 1841, 1842. 5 vols. Philadelphia, 1845.
Williams, Lewis R. Chinook by the Sea. Portland, 1924.
———. Our Pacific County. Raymond, Wash., 1930.
Winter, Oscar Osburn. The Great Northwest. New York, 1955.
Wright, E. W. (ed.). Lewis & Dryden's Marine History of the Pacific Northwest. New York, 1961.
Wyeth, John B. Oregon; or, a Short History of a Long Journey from the Atlantic Ocean to the Region of the Pacific, by Land. In Vol. XXI, Reuben Gold Thwaites (ed.), Early Western Travels. Cleveland, 1905.

Articles

"Adventures in the Far West," The Leisure Hour [London], XI (1862).
"Alexander Lattie's Fort George Journal, 1846," Oregon Historical Quarterly, LXIV (1963).
"Americans at Sea," Niles' Weekly Register, XVIII (n.s. VI) (March–September, 1820).
Andrews, C. L. "The Wreck of the St. Nicholas," Washington Historical Quarterly, XIII, 1 (January, 1922).
"Artificial Deformities," Chambers's Edinburgh Journal, X (1840).
Avery, Mary. "An Additional Chapter on Jane Barnes," Pacific Northwest Quarterly, XLII, 4 (October, 1951).
Bagley, Clarence B. "Journal of Occurences at Nisqually House, 1833," Washington Historical Quarterly, VII 1 (January, 1916).
"Bancroft's Native Races of the Pacific States," Atlantic Monthly, XXXV, 208 (February, 1875).
Barnett, H. G. "The Southern Extent of Totem Pole Carving," Pacific Northwest Quarterly, XXXIII, 4 (October, 1942).
Barry, J. Neilson. "Astorians Who Became Permanent Settlers," Washington Historical Quarterly, XXIV, 4 (October, 1933).
———. "Broughton, up Columbia River, 1792," Oregon Historical Quarterly, XXXII (1931).
———. "Broughton on the Columbia in 1792," Oregon Historical Quarterly, XXVII (1926).
———. "Columbia River Exploration, 1792," Oregon Historical Quarterly, XXXIII (1932).
———. "The Indians of Oregon—Geographic Distribution of Lingustic Families," Oregon Historical Quarterly, XXVIII (1927).
———. "Spaniards in Early Oregon," Washington Historical Quarterly, XXIII, 1 (January, 1932).

————. "What Became of Benjamin Clapp?" *Washington Historical Quarterly*, XXI, 1 (January, 1930).

————. "Who Discovered the Columbia River?" *Oregon Historical Quarterly*, XXXIX (1938).

Blue, George Verne. "Green's Missionary Report on Oregon, 1829," *Oregon Historical Quarterly*, XXX (1929).

Boas, Franz. "The Doctrine of Souls and of Disease among the Chinook Indians," *Journal of American Folk-Lore*, VI, 20 (January, 1893).

Bolkhovitinov, N[ikolai]. N. "Russia and the Declaration of the Non-Colonization Principle: New Archival Evidence," *Oregon Historical Quarterly*, LXXII, 2 (June, 1971).

"Book Reviews," *Washington Historical Quarterly*, XI, 4 (October, 1920).

Bradley, Marie Merriman. "Political Beginnings in Oregon," *Oregon Historical Quarterly*, IX (1908).

Brandon, William. "Two Thousand Miles from the Counting House: Wilson Price Hunt and the Founding of Astoria," *American West*, V, 4 (July, 1968).

Canse, John M. "The Diary of Henry Bridgeman Brewer, Being a Log of the Lausanne and the Time-Book of the Dalles Mission," *Oregon Historical Quarterly*, XXIX (1928).

Carstensen, Vernon (ed.). "Pacific Northwest Letters of George Gibbs," *Oregon Historical Quarterly*, LIV (1953).

Caywood, Louis R. "The Exploratory Excavation of Fort Clatsop," *Oregon Historical Quarterly*, XLIX (1948).

"A Century Ago," *The West Shore*, V, 6 (June, 1879).

"The Chinook Wind," *Oregon Historical Quarterly*, XLI (1940).

Clark, Ella E. "George Gibbs' Account of Indian Mythology in Oregon and Washington Territories," *Oregon Historical Quarterly*, LVI (1955).

————. "The Mythology of the Indians in the Pacific Northwest," *Oregon Historical Quarterly*, LIV (1953).

Clark, Robert C. "The Archives of the Hudson's Bay Company," *Pacific Northwest Quarterly*, XXIX, 1 (January, 1938).

Clarke, Charles G. "The Roster of the Expedition of Lewis and Clark," *Oregon Historical Quarterly*, XLV (1944).

Coan, C. F. "The First Stage of the Federal Indian Policy in the Pacific Northwest, 1849–1852," *Oregon Historical Quarterly*, XXII (1921).

Colbert, Mildred. "Naming and Early Settlement of Ilwaco, Washington," *Oregon Historical Quarterly*, XLVII (1946).

Conn, Richard T. "The Iroquois in the West," *The Pacific Northwesterner*, IV, 4 (Fall, 1960).

Cook, S. F. "The Epidemic of 1830–1833 in California and Oregon," *University of California Publications in American Archaeology and Ethnology*, XLIII, 3 (1955).

Corning, Howard. "Augustine Heard and the China Trade in the 1830's," *Essex Institute Historical Collections*, LXXX (1944).

————. "List of Ships Arriving at the Port of Canton and Other Pacific Ports, 1799–1803," *Essex Institute Historical Collections*, LXXVIII (1942).

————. "Sullivan Dorr, an Early China Merchant," *Essex Institute Historical Collections*, LXXVIII (1942).

————. (ed.). "Letters of Sullivan Dorr," *Proceedings of the Massachusetts Historical Society*, LXVII (1941–44).

Cowdin, Elliott C. "The Northwest Fur Trade," *Hunt's Merchant Magazine*, XIV, (1846), Microfilm Reel 341, University Microfilms, Ann Arbor, Michigan.

Cunningham, Glenn. "Oregon's First Salmon Cannery, 'Captain' John West," *Oregon Historical Quarterly*, LIV (1953).

Davenport, T. W. "Recollections of an Indian Agent," *Oregon Historical Quarterly*, VIII (1907).

Davidson, Donald C. "Relations of the Hudson's Bay Company with the Russian American Company on the Northwest Coast, 1829–1867," *British Columbia Historical Quarterly*, V, 1 (January, 1941).

Dennis, Elsie Frances. "Indian Slavery in Pacific Northwest," *Oregon Historical Quarterly*, XXXI (1930).

"Documents. Captain M. Maloney to Acting Governor Henry M. McGill," *Washington Historical Quarterly*, IV, 4 (October, 1913).

Donovan, John. "Chinook Victory," *Cowlitz Country Historical Quarterly*, II, 4 (February, 1961).

Douglas, Jesse E. (ed.). "Matthews' Adventures on the Columbia," *Oregon Historical Quarterly*, XL (1939).

Drucker, Philip. "Rank, Wealth, and Kinship in Northwest Coast Society," *American Anthropologist*, n.s., XXXXI, 1 (January, 1939).

Dunbabin, Thomas. "Who Discovered the Columbia?" *The Beaver*, Outfit 285, 3 (Winter, 1954).

Eells, Myron. "The Worship and Traditions of the Aborigines of America; or, Their Testimony to the Religion of the Bible," Victoria Institute, London, *Journal of Transactions*, XIX (1885).

Elliott, Barbara Coit. "Cape Disappointment in History," *Washington Historical Quarterly*, XIV, 4 (October, 1923).

Elliott, T. C. "The Chinook Wind," *Oregon Historical Quarterly*, XXXIII (1932).

————. "Jonathan Carver's Source for the Name Oregon," *Oregon Historical Quarterly*, XXIII (1922).

————. "Journal of John Work, November and December, 1824," *Washington Historical Quarterly*, III, 3 (July, 1912).

————. "The Journal of the Ship Ruby," *Oregon Historical Quarterly*, XXVIII (1927).

———— (ed.). "The Log of H.M.S. 'Chatham,'" *Oregon Historical Quarterly*, XVIII (1917).

————. "The Origin of the Name Oregon," *Oregon Historical Quarterly*, XXII (1921).

————. "Sale of Astoria, 1813," *Oregon Historical Quarterly*, XXXIII (1932).

————. "The Strange Case of Jonathan Carver and the Name Oregon," *Oregon Historical Quarterly*, XXI (1920).

Ermatinger, A. C. O. "The Columbia River under Hudson's Bay Company Rule," *Washington Historical Quarterly*, V, 3 (July, 1914).

Ermatinger, Frank. "Earliest Expeditions against Puget Sound Indians," *Washington Historical Quarterly*, I, 2 (January, 1907).

"Extract from Log of the U.S.S. Ontario, Capt. James Biddle," *Oregon Historical Quarterly*, III (1902).

Fee, Chester Anders. "Oregon's Historical Esperanto—The Chinook Jargon," *Oregon Historical Quarterly*, XLII (1941).

Ferris, Joel E. "Ranald MacDonald, the Sailor Boy Who Visited Japan," *Pacific Northwest Quarterly*, XLVIII, 1 (January, 1957).

"First Trading Settlement on the Columbia River," *Hunt's Merchant Magazine*, XIV, 2 (February, 1846).

Fisher, Edna M. "Prices of Sea Otter Pelts," *California Fish and Game*, XXVII, 4 (October, 1941).

Floyd, John. "Occupation of the Columbia River," *Oregon Historical Quarterly*, VIII (1907).

Galvani, William H. "The Early Explorations and the Origin of the Name of the Oregon Country," *Oregon Historical Quarterly*, XXI (1920).

Gathke, Robert Moulton. "A Document of Mission History, 1833–43," *Oregon Historical Quarterly*, XXXVI (1935).

Gile, Albion. "Notes on Columbia River Salmon," *Oregon Historical Quarterly*, LVI (1955).

Gillette, P. W. "Early Pilotage on the Columbia River," *Pacific Monthly*, VI, 1 (June, 1901).

————. "The Site of Fort Clatsop," *Pacific Monthly*, XII, 2 (August, 1904).

Hanft, Marshall. "The Cape Forts: Guardians of the Columbia," *Oregon Historical Quarterly*, LXV (1964).

Harvey, A. G. "Chief Concomly's Skull," *Oregon Historical Quarterly*, XL (1939).

Hazeltine, Jean. "The Discovery and Cartographical Recognition of Shoalwater Bay," *Oregon Historical Quarterly*, LVIII (1957).

Hicks, U. E. "Taking the Census in 1853," *Washington Historian*, II, 2 (January, 1901).

Hines, Clarence. "Adams, Russia and Northwest Trade," *Oregon Historical Quarterly*, XXXVI (1935).

"Historical Notes," *Pacific Monthly*, VI, 6 (November–December, 1901).

Hobucket, Harry. "Quillayute Indian Tradition," *Washington Historical Quarterly*, XXV, 1 (January, 1934).

Hodgson, Edward R. "The Epidemic on the Lower Columbia," *Pacific Northwesterner*, I, 4 (Fall, 1957).

Howay, Frederic W. "The Ballad of the Bold Northwestman: An Incident in the Life of Captain John Kendrick," *Washington Historical Quarterly*, XX, 2 (April, 1929).

———. "Brig Owhyhee in the Columbia, 1827," *Oregon Historical Quarterly*, XXXIV (1933).

———. "The Brig Owhyhee in the Columbia, 1829–30," *Oregon Historical Quarterly*, XXV (1934).

———. "Captains Gray and Kendrick: The Barrell Letters," *Washington Historical Quarterly*, XII, 4 (October, 1921).

———. "An Early Account of the Loss of the Boston in 1803," *Washington Historical Quarterly*, XVII, 4 (October, 1926).

———. "Early Followers of Captain Gray," *Washington Historical Quarterly*, XVIII, 1 (January, 1927).

———. "Indian Attacks upon Maritime Traders of the North-West Coast, 1785–1805," *Canadian Historical Review*, VI, 4 (December, 1925).

———. "A List of Trading Vessels in the Maritime Fur Trade, 1785–1804," *Proceedings and Transactions of the Royal Society of Canada*, 3d ser. XXIV (1930).

———. "A List of Trading Vessels in the Maritime Fur Trade, 1795–1804," *Proceedings and Transactions of the Royal Society of Canada*, 3d ser. XXV (1931).

———. "A List of Trading Vessels in the Maritime Fur Trade, 1805–1814," *Transactions of the Royal Society of Canada, Section II*, 3d ser. XXVI (1932).

———. "A List of Trading Vessels in the Maritime Fur Trade, 1815–1819," *Transactions of the Royal Society of Canada, Section II*, 3d ser. XXVII (1933).

———. "A List of Trading Vessels in the Maritime Fur Trade, 1820–1825," *Transactions of the Royal Society of Canada, Section II*, 3d ser. XXVIII (1934).

———. "The Loss of the 'Tonquin,' " *Washington Historical Quarterly*, XIII, 2 (April, 1922).

———. "Origin of the Chinook Jargon on the North West Coast," *Oregon Historical Quarterly*, XLIV (1943).

———. "The Resolution on the Oregon Coast, 1793–94," *Oregon Historical Quarterly*, XXXIV (1933).

———. "Vessels Trading on the Northwest Coast of America, 1804–1814," *Washington Historical Quarterly*, XIX, 4 (October, 1928).

———. "William Sturgis: The Northwest Fur Trade," *British Columbia Historical Quarterly*, VIII, 1 (January, 1944).

———, and T. C. Elliott (eds.). "John Boit's Log of the Columbia—1790–1793," *Oregon Historical Quarterly*, XXII (1921).

———, and ——— (eds.). "Vancouver's Brig Chatham in the Columbia," *Oregon Historical Quarterly*, XLIII (1942).

———. "Voyages of the 'Jenny' to Oregon, 1792–94," *Oregon Historical Quarterly*, XXX (1929).

Jacobs, Melville. "Historic Perspectives in Indian Languages of Oregon and Washington," *Pacific Northwest Quarterly*, XXVIII, I (January, 1937).
――――. "Indications of Mental Illness among Pre-Contact Indians of the Northwest States," *Pacific Northwest Quarterly*, L, 2 (April, 1964).
Johansen, Dorothy O. "McLoughlin and the Indians," *The Beaver*, Outfit 277, 1 (June, 1946).
Judson, Katharine B. "The British Side of the Restoration of Fort Astoria," *Oregon Historical Quarterly*, XX (1919).
Kane, Paul. "Incidents of Travel on the North-West Coast, Vancouver's Island, Oregon, Etc.," *Canadian Journal*, III, 12 (July, 1855).
Kelley, Don Greame. "Trees of the Totem Culture," *American West*, VIII, 3 (May, 1971).
Kime, Wayne R. "Alfred Seton's Journal: A Source for Irving's Tonquin Disaster Account," *Oregon Historical Quarterly*, LXXI (1970).
Kroeber, A. L. "American Culture and the Northwest Coast," *American Anthropologist*, n.s., XXV, 1 (January, 1923).
――――. "The Tribes of the Pacific Coast of North America," *XIX International Congress of Americanists*.
Krogman, Wilton Marion. "Medical Practices and Diseases of the Aboriginal American Indians," *Ciba Symposia*, I, 15 (1939).
Larsell, O. "Medical Aspects of the Lewis and Clark Expedition," *Oregon Historical Quarterly*, LVI (1955).
Lee, Henry. "The Magee Family and the Origins of the China Trade," *Proceedings of the Massachusetts Historical Society*, LXXXI (1970).
Lewis, William S. (ed.). "Narrative of Benjamin MacDonald," *Washington Historical Quarterly*, XVI, 3 (July, 1925).
Loines, Elma. "Hoqua, Sometime Chief of the Co-Hong at Canton (1769–1843)," *Essex Institute Historical Collections*, LXXXIX (1953).
Lyman, H. S. "Reminiscences of Louis Labonte," *Oregon Historical Quarterly*, I (1900).
McGuire, Hollister D. "Columbia River Salmon," *Pacific Monthly*, I, 2 (November, 1898).
Mackey, Harold. "Siuslaw Head Flattening," *Oregon Historical Quarterly*, LXIX (1968).
Meany, Edmond S. (ed.). "Journal of William Fraser Tolmie—1833," *Washington Historical Quarterly*, III, 3 (July, 1912).
――――. "The Widow of Captain Robert Gray," *Washington Historical Quarterly*, XX, 3 (July, 1929).
Minto, John. "The Number and Condition of the Native Race in Oregon When First Seen by White Men," *Oregon Historical Quarterly*, I (1900).
Morison, Samuel Eliot. "New England and the Opening of the Columbia River Salmon Trade, 1830," *Oregon Historical Quarterly*, XXVIII (1927).
――――. "Nova Albion and New England," *Oregon Historical Quarterly*, XXVIII (1927).

Morris, Grace P. "Development of Astoria, 1811–1850," *Oregon Historical Quarterly*, XXXVIII (1937).

———. "Wreck of a Japanese Junk, 1834," *Oregon Historical Quarterly*, XXXVIII (1937).

"Mr. Beaver Objects," *The Beaver*, Outfit 272 (September, 1941).

Murphy, J. "Summer Ramblings in Washington Territory," *Appletons' Journal: A Monthly Miscellany of Popular Literature*, n.s., III (November, 1877).

O'Neil, Marion. "The Maritime Activities of the North West Company, 1813–1821," *Washington Historical Quarterly*, XXI, 4 (October, 1930).

"The Oregon Beeswax Mystery," *Shell News*, XXIX, 12 (1961).

"The Oyster Enigma," *The Sou'wester*, II, 1 (Spring, 1867).

Pipes, Nellie B. "John Mix Stanley, Indian Painter," *Oregon Historical Quarterly*, XXXIII (1932).

——— (ed.). "Journal of John H. Frost, 1840–43," *Oregon Historical Quarterly*, XXXV (1934).

Porter, Edward G. "The Ship Columbia and the Discovery of Oregon," *The New England Magazine*, n.s., VI, 4 (June, 1892).

Powell, Fred Wilbur. "Hall Jackson Kelley—Prophet of Oregon," *Oregon Historical Quarterly*, XVIII (1917).

Prosser, William F. "An Interesting Collection of Indian Relics," *Washington Historian*, I, 1 (September, 1899).

Ray, Verne F. "The Historical Position of the Lower Chinook in the Native Culture of the Northwest," *Pacific Northwest Quarterly*, XXVIII, 4 (October, 1937).

Rees, John E. "Oregon—Its Meaning, Origin and Application," *Oregon Historical Quarterly*, XXI (1920).

Rickard, T. A. "Drift Iron, a Fortuitous Factor in Primitive Culture," *Geographical Review*, XXIV, 4 (October, 1934).

———. "The Sea-Otter in History," *British Columbia Historical Quarterly*, XI, 1 (January, 1947).

Rockwood, E. Ruth (ed.). "Letters of Charles Stevens," *Oregon Historical Quarterly*, XXXVII (1936).

Ross, Frank E. "American Adventures in the Early Marine Fur Trade with China," *Chinese Social & Political Science Review*, LXXI, 2 (July, 1937).

———. "The Early Fur Trade of the Great Northwest," *Oregon Historical Quarterly*, XXXIX (1938).

"The Round Hand of George B. Roberts: Letters to Mrs. F. F. Victor, 1878–83," *Oregon Historical Quarterly*, LXIII (1962).

Sage, Walter N. "Life at a Fur Trading Post in British Columbia a Century Ago," *Washington Historical Quarterly*, XXV, 1 (January, 1934).

"Samoan and Chinook Head-Flattening," *Frank Leslie's Popular Monthly*, II, 4 (October, 1876).

Santee, J. F. "Comcomly and the Chinooks," *Oregon Historical Quarterly*, XXXIII (1932).

Sapir, E. "The Social Organization of the West Coast Tribes," *Transactions of the Royal Society of Canada, Section II*, 2d ser., IX (1915).

Schaeffer, Claude E. "William Brooks, Chinook Publicist," *Oregon Historical Quarterly*, LXIV (1963).

Schafer, Joseph (ed.). "Documents Relative to Warre and Vavasour's Military Reconnoissance in Oregon, 1845–6," *Oregon Historical Quarterly*, X (1909).

Scheffer, Victor B. "The Sea Otter on the Washington Coast," *Pacific Northwest Quarterly*, XXXI, 4 (October, 1940).

Schroeder, John H. "Rep. John Floyd, 1817–1829: Harbinger of Oregon Territory," *Oregon Historical Quarterly*, LXX (1969).

Scott, Leslie M. "Indian Diseases as Aids to Pacific Northwest Settlement," *Oregon Historical Quarterly*, XXIX (1928).

———. "Indian Women as Food Providers and Tribal Counselors," *Oregon Historical Quarterly*, XLII (1941).

Scouler, John. "Dr. John Scouler's Journal of a Voyage to N.W. America," *Oregon Historical Quarterly*, VI (1905).

Scouler, John. "Observations on the Indigenous Tribes of the N.W. Coast of America," *Journal of the Royal Geographical Society of London*, XI (1841).

"Secret Mission of Warre and Vavasour," *Washington Historical Quarterly*, III, 2 (April, 1912).

"Shoalwater Reservation Centennial from Carowan through the Charleys— 100 Years," *The Sou'wester*, I, 3 (Autumn, 1966).

Smalley, Eugene V. "From Puget Sound to the Upper Columbia," *Century Magazine*, VII (November, 1884).

Smith, Silas B. "Primitive Customs and Religious Beliefs of the Indians of the Pacific Northwest Coast," *Oregon Historical Quarterly*, II (1901).

Snow, Vernon F. "From Ouragon to Oregon," *Oregon Historical Quarterly*, LX (1959).

Speck, Gordon. "The Journey of Hwui Shan," *Pacific Search*, V, 1 (October, 1970).

Stafford, O. F. "The Wax of Nehalem Beach," *Oregon Historical Quarterly*, IX (1908).

Strong, William Duncan. "The Occurence and Wider Implications of a 'Ghost Cult' on the Columbia River Suggested by Carvings in Wood, Bone and Stone," *American Anthropologist*, n.s., XLVII, 2 (April, 1945).

Sylvester, Avery. "Voyages of the Pallas and Chenamus, 1843–45," *Oregon Historical Quarterly*, XXXIV (1933).

Taylor, Herbert C., Jr. "Aboriginal Populations of the Lower Northwest Coast," *Washington Historical Quarterly*, LIV, 4 (October, 1963).

———, and Lester L. Hoaglin, Jr. "The 'Intermittent Fever' Epidemic of the 1830s on the Lower Columbia River," *Ethnohistory*, IX, 2 (Spring, 1962).

Taylor, Ralph G. "Historic Abernethy Cemetery," *Cowlitz County Historical Quarterly*, VI, 2 (September, 1964).

Tompkins, Walker Allison. "Oysterville, 1840–97," *Oregon Historical Quarterly*, XXXIII (1932).

Van Alstyne, Richard W. "International Rivalries in Pacific Northwest," *Oregon Historical Quarterly*, XLVI (1945).

Wagner, Henry R. "Fray Benito de la Sierra's Account of the Hezeta Expedition to the Northwest Coast in 1775," *California Historical Quarterly*, IX, 3 (September, 1930).

———. "The Last Spanish Exploration of the Northwest Coast and the Attempt to Colonize Bodega Bay," *California Historical Quarterly*, X, 4 (December, 1931).

Waterman, T. T. "Some Conundrums in Northwest Coast Art," *American Anthropologist*, XXV, 4 (October, 1923).

Weir, Allen. "William Weir," *Washington Historical Quarterly*, IV, 1 (January, 1913).

West, Oswald. "Oregon's First White Settlers on French Prairie," *Oregon Historical Quarterly*, XLIII (1942).

Whealdon, Isaac H. "Stories and Sketches from Pacific County," *Washington Historical Quarterly*, IV, 3 (July, 1913).

Woodward, Arthur. "Sea Otter Hunting on the Pacific Coast," *Quarterly of the Historical Society of Southern California*, XX, 3 (September, 1938).

Work, John. "John Work to Edward Ermatinger, February 24, 1834," *Washington Historical Quarterly*, II, 2 (January, 1908).

Index

Abernethy, Alexander S.: 215
Abernethy, George: 299
Abernethy Point: 56
Aboriginal Protection Society: 65; *see also* Rev. Herbert Beaver
Abortion: 64, 69, 81, 200, 269
Acapulco, Mexico: 27n.
Achomawi Indians: 22
Adams, John Quincy (minister): 120, 126–27, 129
Adams, Thomas (Kalapuya Indian): 201
Adamson, Capt. John William: 63
Adventure Cove: 41
Aguilar, Martin de: 25, 26 & n.
Aguilar's River: 26
Ahwahpinpin Point: 227–28
Ainu: *see* Japanese
Alaska: 3, 8, 22, 24, 33, 37, 61, 65, 117, 161, 189
Albatross (ship): 113, 119n., 120–24, 142, 161n.
Aleutian Islands: 33 & n., 162
Aleut Indians: 116, 118, 124, 126
Alexander (brig): 162
Alexander, Capt. W. D.: 161n.
Alsea Reservation: 239; *see* Reservations for Chinooks
Alta California: 26, 27
American Board of Commissioners for Foreign Missions (A.B.C.F.M.): 83, 213
American Fur Company: *see* Pacific Fur Company

Americans: 118–20, 125, 205, 213, 238
Anderson, Mr. (settler): 215
Annuities and services: 223, 234–35, 242
Arabian trade: 42n.
Arctic Ocean: 35n.
Armstrong, A. N.: 48n.
Armstrong, B. C.: 238
Arrastras: 28; *see also* gold
Astor, John Jacob: 50n., 119, 128, 130, 137–38, 142, 147n., 190
Astoria (Oregon country, Territory, State): 98n., 196, 202–203n., 212–13, 217, 222, 227, 233–34, 244
Astorians: 128ff., 160n., 166
Atahualpa: (ship): 79, 84, 88, 90, 107n., 272
Athabaskan-speaking Indians: 5, 255
Atsugewi Indians: 22

Baffin Island: 35n.
Bagot, Sir Charles: 190
Baidarkas: 118–19 & n.
Baillie, Capt. Thomas: 212
Baja California: 26
Baker, Dennis: 243n.
Bakers Bay: 6, 17, 18, 40, 41, 53, 54, 58, 59, 63, 65, 67, 68, 88, 96, 97, 102, 123, 128–29, 134, 143, 148, 160, 163, 179, 180, 196, 201, 204, 217
Baranov, Alexander Andreievitch: 109, 116, 119 & n., 120
Barkley, Capt. Charles W.: 70
Barkley Sound: 62

337